THE COMPLETE
WORKS OF
JOHN M.
SYNGE

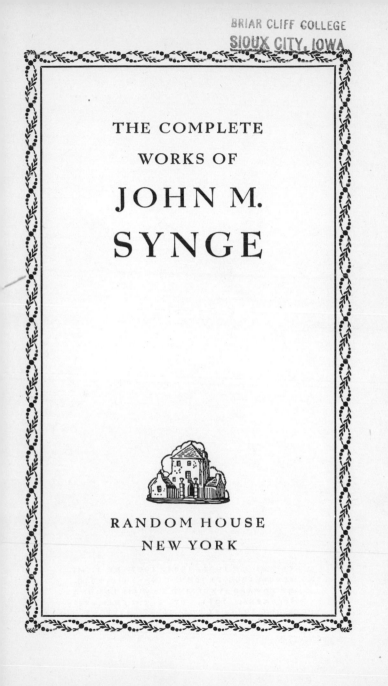

RANDOM HOUSE
NEW YORK

PR
5530
.A2
1936

7215

CONTENTS

Newman 350

Speech 11 Sept 42

IN THE CONGESTED DISTRICTS

THE PLAYBOY OF THE
WESTERN WORLD

PREFACE

IN WRITING *The Playboy of the Western World,* as in my other plays, I have used one or two words only that I have not heard among the country people of Ireland, or spoken in my own nursery before I could read the newspapers. A certain number of the phrases I employ I have heard also from herds and fishermen along the coast from Kerry to Mayo, or from beggar-women and ballad-singers nearer Dublin; and I am glad to acknowledge how much I owe to the folk-imagination of these fine people. Anyone who has lived in real intimacy with the Irish peasantry will know that the wildest sayings and ideas in this play are tame indeed, compared with the fancies one may hear in any little hillside cabin in Geesala, or Carraroe, or Dingle Bay. All art is a collaboration; and there is little doubt that in the happy ages of literature, striking and beautiful phrases were as ready to the story-teller's or the playwright's hand, as the rich cloaks and dresses of his time. It is probable that when the Elizabethan dramatist took his ink-horn and sat down to his work he used many phrases that he had just heard, as he sat at dinner, from his mother or his children. In Ireland, those of us who know the people have the same privilege. When I was writing "The Shadow of the Glen," some years ago, I got more aid than any learning could have given me from a chink in the floor of the old Wicklow house where I was staying, that let me hear what was being said by the servant girls in the kitchen. This matter, I think, is of importance, for in countries where the imagination of the people, and the language they use, is rich and living, it is possible for a writer to be rich and copious in his words, and at the same time to give the reality, which is the root of all poetry, in a comprehensive and natural form. In the modern literature of towns, however, richness is found only in sonnets, or prose poems, or in one or two elaborate books that are far away from the profound and common interests of life. One has, on one side, Mallarmé and Huysmans producing this literature; and on the other, Ibsen and Zola dealing with the reality of life in joyless and pallid words. On the stage one must have reality, and one must have joy; and that is why the intellectual modern drama has failed, and people have grown sick of the false joy of the musical comedy, that has been given them in place of the rich joy found only in what is superb and wild in reality. In a good play every speech should be as fully flavoured as a nut or apple, and such speeches cannot be written by anyone who works among people who have shut their lips on poetry. In Ireland, for a few years more, we have a popular imagination that is fiery and magnificent, and tender; so that those of us who wish to write start with a chance that is not given to writers in places where the springtime of the local life has been forgotten, and the harvest is a memory only, and the straw has been turned into bricks.

J. M. S.

January 21, 1907

THE PLAYBOY OF THE
WESTERN WORLD

A PLAY IN THREE ACTS

PERSONS IN THE PLAY

CHRISTOPHER MAHON

OLD MAHON (*his father, a squatter*)

MICHAEL JAMES FLAHERTY, called MICHAEL JAMES
   (*a publican*)

MARGARET FLAHERTY, called PEGEEN MIKE
   (*his daughter*)

WIDOW QUIN (*a woman of about thirty*)

SHAWN KEOGH (*her cousin, a young farmer*)

PHILLY CULLEN and JIMMY FARRELL
   (*small farmers*)

SARA TANSEY, SUSAN BRADY, and HONOR BLAKE
   (*village girls*)

A BELLMAN

SOME PEASANTS

*The action takes place near a village, on a wild coast of
Mayo. The first Act passes on an evening of autumn,
the other two Acts on the following day.*

THE PLAYBOY OF THE
WESTERN WORLD

ACT I

SCENE. *Country public-house or shebeen, very rough and untidy. There is a sort of counter on the right with shelves, holding many bottles and jugs, just seen above it. Empty barrels stand near the counter. At back, a little to left of counter, there is a door into the open air, then, more to the left, there is a settle with shelves above it, with more jugs, and a table beneath a window. At the left there is a large open fire-place, with turf fire, and a small door into inner room. Pegeen, a wild-looking but fine girl, of about twenty, is writing at table. She is dressed in the usual peasant dress.*

PEGEEN (*slowly as she writes*). Six yards of stuff for to make a yellow gown. A pair of lace boots with lengthy heels on them and brassy eyes. A hat is suited for a wedding-day. A fine tooth comb. To be sent with three barrels of porter in Jimmy Farrell's creel cart on the evening of the coming Fair to Mister Michael James Flaherty. With the best compliments of this season. Margaret Flaherty.

SHAWN KEOGH (*a fat and fair young man comes in as she signs, looks round awkwardly, when he sees she is alone*). Where's himself?

PEGEEN (*without looking at him*). He's coming. (*She directs the letter.*) To Mister Sheamus Mulroy, Wine and Spirit Dealer, Castlebar.

SHAWN (*uneasily*). I didn't see him on the road.

7

PEGEEN. How would you see him (*licks stamp and puts it on letter*) and it dark night this half hour gone by?

SHAWN (*turning towards the door again*). I stood a while outside wondering would I have a right to pass on or to walk in and see you, Pegeen Mike (*comes to fire*), and I could hear the cows breathing, and sighing in the stillness of the air, and not a step moving any place from this gate to the bridge.

PEGEEN (*putting letter in envelope*). It's above at the cross-roads he is, meeting Philly Cullen; and a couple more are going along with him to Kate Cassidy's wake.

SHAWN (*looking at her blankly*). And he's going that length in the dark night?

PEGEEN (*impatiently*). He is surely, and leaving me lonesome on the scruff of the hill. (*She gets up and puts envelope on dresser, then winds clock.*) Isn't it long the nights are now, Shawn Keogh, to be leaving a poor girl with her own self counting the hours to the dawn of day?

SHAWN (*with awkward humour*). If it is, when we're wedded in a short while you'll have no call to complain, for I've little will to be walking off to wakes or weddings in the darkness of the night.

PEGEEN (*with rather scornful good humour*). You're making mighty certain, Shaneen, that I'll wed you now.

SHAWN. Aren't we after making a good bargain, the way we're only waiting these days on Father Reilly's dispensation from the bishops, or the Court of Rome.

PEGEEN (*looking at him teasingly, washing up at dresser*). It's a wonder, Shaneen, the Holy Father'd be taking notice of the likes of you; for if I was him I wouldn't bother with this place where you'll meet none but Red Linahan, has a squint in his eye, and Patcheen is lame in his heel, or the mad Mulrannies were driven from California and they lost in their wits. We're a queer lot these times to go troubling the Holy Father on his sacred seat.

SHAWN (*scandalized*). If we are, we're as good this place as another, maybe, and as good these times as we were for ever.

PEGEEN (*with scorn*). As good, is it? Where now will you meet the like of Daneen Sullivan knocked the eye from a peeler, or Marcus Quin, God rest him, got six months for maiming ewes, and he a great warrant to tell stories of holy Ireland till he'd have the old women shedding down tears about their feet. Where will you find the like of them, I'm saying?

SHAWN (*timidly*). If you don't, it's a good job, maybe; for (*with peculiar emphasis on the words*) Father Reilly has small conceit to have that kind walking around and talking to the girls.

PEGEEN (*impatiently, throwing water from basin out of the door*). Stop tormenting me with Father Reilly (*imitating his voice*) when I'm asking only what way I'll pass these twelve hours of dark, and not take my death with the fear.

[*Looking out of door.*]

SHAWN (*timidly*). Would I fetch you the Widow Quin, maybe?

PEGEEN. Is it the like of that murderer? You'll not, surely.

SHAWN (*going to her, soothingly*). Then I'm thinking himself will stop along with you when he sees you taking on, for it'll be a long night-time with great darkness, and I'm after feeling a kind of fellow above in the furzy ditch, groaning wicked like a maddening dog, the way it's good cause you have, maybe, to be fearing now.

PEGEEN (*turning on him sharply*). What's that? Is it a man you seen?

SHAWN (*retreating*). I couldn't see him at all; but I heard him groaning out, and breaking his heart. It should have been a young man from his words speaking.

PEGEEN (*going after him*). And you never went near to see was he hurted or what ailed him at all?

SHAWN. I did not, Pegeen Mike. It was a dark, lonesome place to be hearing the like of him.

PEGEEN. Well, you're a daring fellow, and if they find his corpse stretched above in the dews of dawn, what'll you say then to the peelers, or the Justice of the Peace?

SHAWN (*thunderstruck*). I wasn't thinking of that. For the love of God, Pegeen Mike, don't let on I was speaking of him. Don't tell your father and the men is coming above; for if they heard that story, they'd have great blabbing this night at the wake.

PEGEEN. I'll maybe tell them, and I'll maybe not.

SHAWN. They are coming at the door. Will you whisht, I'm saying?

PEGEEN. Whisht yourself.

[*She goes behind counter. Michael James, fat jovial publican, comes in followed by Philly Cullen, who is thin and mistrusting, and Jimmy Farrell, who is fat and amorous, about forty-five.*]

MEN (*together*). God bless you. The blessing of God on this place.

PEGEEN. God bless you kindly.

MICHAEL (*to men who go to the counter*). Sit down now, and take your rest. (*Crosses to Shawn at the fire.*) And how is it you are, Shawn Keogh? Are you coming over the sands to Kate Cassidy's wake?

SHAWN. I am not, Michael James. I'm going home the short cut to my bed.

PEGEEN (*speaking across the counter*). He's right too, and have you no shame, Michael James, to be quitting off for the whole night, and leaving myself lonesome in the shop?

MICHAEL (*good-humouredly*). Isn't it the same whether I go for the whole night or a part only? and I'm thinking it's a queer daughter you are if you'd have me crossing backward through the Stooks of the Dead Women, with a drop taken.

PEGEEN. If I am a queer daughter, it's a queer father'd be leaving me lonesome these twelve hours of dark, and I piling the turf with the dogs barking, and the calves mooing, and my own teeth rattling with the fear.

JIMMY (*flatteringly*). What is there to hurt you, and you a fine, hardy girl would knock the head of any two men in the place?

PEGEEN (*working herself up*). Isn't there the harvest boys with their tongues red for drink, and the ten tinkers is camped in the east glen, and the thousand militia—bad cess to them!—walking idle through the land. There's lots surely to hurt me, and I won't stop alone in it, let himself do what he will.

MICHAEL. If you're that afeard, let Shawn Keogh stop along with you. It's the will of God, I'm thinking, himself should be seeing to you now.

[*They all turn on Shawn.*]

SHAWN (*in horrified confusion*). I would and welcome, Michael James, but I'm afeard of Father Reilly; and what at all would the Holy Father and the Cardinals of Rome be saying if they heard I did the like of that?

MICHAEL (*with contempt*). God help you! Can't you sit in by the hearth with the light lit and herself beyond in the room? You'll do that surely, for I've heard tell there's a queer fellow above, going mad or getting his death, maybe, in the gripe of the ditch, so she'd be safer this night with a person here.

SHAWN (*with plaintive despair*). I'm afeard of Father Reilly, I'm saying. Let you not be tempting me, and we near married itself.

PHILLY (*with cold contempt*). Lock him in the west room. He'll stay then and have no sin to be telling to the priest.

MICHAEL (*to Shawn, getting between him and the door*). Go up now.

SHAWN (*at the top of his voice*). Don't stop me, Michael James. Let me out of the door, I'm saying, for the love of the Almighty God. Let me out (*trying to dodge past him*). Let me out of it, and may God grant you His indulgence in the hour of need.

MICHAEL (*loudly*). Stop your noising, and sit down by the hearth.

[*Gives him a push and goes to counter laughing.*]

SHAWN (*turning back, wringing his hands*). Oh, Father Reilly and the saints of God, where will I hide myself to-day? Oh, St. Joseph and St. Patrick and St. Brigid, and St. James, have mercy on me now!

[*Shawn turns round, sees door clear, and makes a rush for it.*]

MICHAEL (*catching him by the coat-tail*). You'd be going, is it?

SHAWN (*screaming*). Leave me go, Michael James, leave me go, you old Pagan, leave me go, or I'll get the curse of the priests on you, and of the scarlet-coated bishops of the courts of Rome.

[*With a sudden movement he pulls himself out of his coat, and disappears out of the door, leaving his coat in Michael's hands.*]

MICHAEL (*turning round, and holding up coat*). Well, there's the coat of a Christian man. Oh, there's sainted glory this day in the lonesome west; and by the will of God I've got you a decent man, Pegeen, you'll have no call to be spying after if you've a score of young girls, maybe, weeding in your fields.

PEGEEN (*taking up the defence of her property*). What right have you to be making game of a poor fellow for minding the priest, when it's your own the fault is, not paying a penny pot-boy to stand along with me and give me courage in the doing of my work?

[*She snaps the coat away from him, and goes behind counter with it.*]

MICHAEL (*taken aback*). Where would I get a pot-boy? Would you have me send the bellman screaming in the streets of Castlebar?

SHAWN (*opening the door a chink and putting in his head, in a small voice*). Michael James!

MICHAEL (*imitating him*). What ails you?

SHAWN. The queer dying fellow's beyond looking over the ditch. He's come up, I'm thinking, stealing your hens. (*Looks over his shoulder.*) God help me, he's following me now (*he runs into room*), and if he's heard what I said, he'll be having my life, and I going home lonesome in the darkness of the night.

[*For a perceptible moment they watch the door with curiosity. Some one coughs outside. Then Christy Mahon, a slight young man, comes in very tired and frightened and dirty.*]

CHRISTY (*in a small voice*). God save all here!

MEN. God save you kindly.

CHRISTY (*going to the counter*). I'd trouble you for a glass of porter, woman of the house.

[*He puts down coin.*]

PEGEEN (*serving him*). You're one of the tinkers, young fellow, is beyond camped in the glen?

CHRISTY. I am not; but I'm destroyed walking.

MICHAEL (*patronizingly*). Let you come up then to the fire. You're looking famished with the cold.

CHRISTY. God reward you. (*He takes up his glass and goes a little way across to the left, then stops and looks about him.*) Is it often the police do be coming into this place, master of the house?

MICHAEL. If you'd come in better hours, you'd have seen "Licensed for the sale of Beer and Spirits, to be consumed on the premises," written in white letters above the door, and what would the polis want spying on me, and not a decent house within four miles, the way every living Christian is a bona fide, saving one widow alone?

CHRISTY (*with relief*). It's a safe house, so.

[*He goes over to the fire, sighing and moaning. Then he sits down, putting his glass beside him and begins gnawing a turnip, too miserable to feel the others staring at him with curiosity.*]

MICHAEL (*going after him*). Is it yourself is fearing the polis? You're wanting, maybe?

CHRISTY. There's many wanting.

MICHAEL. Many surely, with the broken harvest and the ended wars. (*He picks up some stockings, etc., that are near the fire, and carries them away furtively.*) It should be larceny, I'm thinking?

CHRISTY (*dolefully*). I had it in my mind it was a different word and a bigger.

PEGEEN. There's a queer lad. Were you never slapped in school, young fellow, that you don't know the name of your deed?

CHRISTY (*bashfully*). I'm slow at learning, a middling scholar only.

MICHAEL. If you're a dunce itself, you'd have a right to know that larceny's robbing and stealing. Is it for the like of that you're wanting?

CHRISTY (*with a flash of family pride*). And I the son of a strong farmer (*with a sudden qualm*), God rest his soul, could have bought up the whole of your old house a while since, from the butt of his tailpocket, and not have missed the weight of it gone.

MICHAEL (*impressed*). If it's not stealing, it's maybe something big.

CHRISTY (*flattered*). Aye; it's maybe something big.

JIMMY. He's a wicked-looking young fellow. Maybe he followed after a young woman on a lonesome night.

CHRISTY (*shocked*). Oh, the saints forbid, mister; I was all times a decent lad.

PHILLY (*turning on Jimmy*). You're a silly man, Jimmy Farrell. He said his father was a farmer a while since, and there's himself now in a poor state. Maybe the land was grabbed from him, and he did what any decent man would do.

MICHAEL (*to Christy, mysteriously*). Was it bailiffs?

CHRISTY. The divil a one.

MICHAEL. Agents?

CHRISTY. The divil a one.

MICHAEL. Landlords?

CHRISTY (*peevishly*). Ah, not at all, I'm saying. You'd see the like of them stories on any little paper of a Munster town. But I'm not calling to mind any person, gentle, simple, judge or jury, did the like of me.

[*They all draw nearer with delighted curiosity.*]

PHILLY. Well, that lad's a puzzle-the-world.

JIMMY. He'd beat Dan Davies' circus, or the holy missioners making sermons on the villainy of man. Try him again, Philly.

PHILLY. Did you strike golden guineas out of solder, young fellow, or shilling coins itself?

CHRISTY. I did not, mister, not sixpence nor a farthing coin.

JIMMY. Did you marry three wives maybe? I'm told there's a sprinkling have done that among the holy Luthers of the preaching north.

CHRISTY (*shyly*). I never married with one, let alone with a couple or three.

PHILLY. Maybe he went fighting for the Boers, the like of the man beyond, was judged to be hanged, quartered and drawn. Were you off east, young fellow, fighting bloody wars for Kruger and the freedom of the Boers?

CHRISTY. I never left my own parish till Tuesday was a week.

PEGEEN (*coming from counter*). He's done nothing, so. (*To Christy.*) If you didn't commit murder or a bad, nasty thing, or false coining, or robbery, or butchery, or the like of them, there isn't anything that would be worth your troubling for to run from now. You did nothing at all.

CHRISTY (*his feelings hurt*). That's an unkindly thing to be saying to a poor orphaned traveller, has a prison behind him, and hanging before, and hell's gap gaping below.

PEGEEN (*with a sign to the men to be quiet*). You're only saying it. You did nothing at all. A soft lad the like of you wouldn't slit the windpipe of a screeching sow.

CHRISTY (*offended*). You're not speaking the truth.

PEGEEN (*in mock rage*). Not speaking the truth, is it? Would you have me knock the head of you with the butt of the broom?

CHRISTY (*twisting round on her with a sharp cry of horror*). Don't strike me. I killed my poor father, Tuesday was a week, for doing the like of that.

PEGEEN (*with blank amazement*). Is it killed your father?

CHRISTY (*subsiding*). With the help of God I did surely, and that the Holy Immaculate Mother may intercede for his soul.

PHILLY (*retreating with Jimmy*). There's a daring fellow.

JIMMY. Oh, glory be to God!

MICHAEL (*with great respect*). That was a hanging crime, mister honey. You should have had good reason for doing the like of that.

CHRISTY (*in a very reasonable tone*). He was a dirty man, God forgive him, and he getting old and crusty, the way I couldn't put up with him at all.

PEGEEN. And you shot him dead?

CHRISTY (*shaking his head*). I never used weapons. I've no license, and I'm a law-fearing man.

MICHAEL. It was with a hilted knife maybe? I'm told, in the big world it's bloody knives they use.

CHRISTY (*loudly, scandalized*). Do you take me for a slaughter-boy?

PEGEEN. You never hanged him, the way Jimmy Farrell hanged his dog from the license, and had it screeching and wriggling three hours at the butt of a string, and himself swearing it was a dead dog, and the peelers swearing it had life?

CHRISTY. I did not then. I just riz the loy and let fall the edge of it on the ridge of his skull, and he went down at my feet like an empty sack, and never let a grunt or groan from him at all.

MICHAEL (*making a sign to Pegeen to fill Christy's glass*). And what way weren't you hanged, mister? Did you bury him then?

CHRISTY (*considering*). Aye. I buried him then. Wasn't I digging spuds in the field?

MICHAEL. And the peelers never followed after you the eleven days that you're out?

CHRISTY (*shaking his head*). Never a one of them, and I walking forward facing hog, dog, or divil on the highway of the road.

PHILLY (*nodding wisely*). It's only with a common week-day kind of a murderer them lads would be trusting their carcase, and that man should be a great terror when his temper's roused.

MICHAEL. He should then. (*To Christy.*) And where was it, mister honey, that you did the deed?

CHRISTY (*looking at him with suspicion*). Oh, a distant place, master of the house, a windy corner of high, distant hills.

PHILLY (*nodding with approval*). He's a close man, and he's right, surely.

PEGEEN. That'd be a lad with the sense of Solomon to have for a pot-boy, Michael James, if it's the truth you're seeking one at all.

PHILLY. The peelers is fearing him, and if you'd that lad in the house there isn't one of them would come smelling around if the dogs itself were lapping poteen from the dung-pit of the yard.

JIMMY. Bravery's a treasure in a lonesome place, and a lad would kill his father, I'm thinking, would face a foxy divil with a pitchpike on the flags of hell.

PEGEEN. It's the truth they're saying, and if I'd that lad in the house, I wouldn't be fearing the looséd kharki cut-throats, or the walking dead.

CHRISTY (*swelling with surprise and triumph*). Well, glory be to God!

MICHAEL (*with deference*). Would you think well to stop here and be pot-boy, mister honey, if we gave you good wages, and didn't destroy you with the weight of work?

SHAWN (*coming forward uneasily*). That'd be a queer kind to bring into a decent quiet household with the like of Pegeen Mike.

PEGEEN (*very sharply*). Will you whisht? Who's speaking to you?

SHAWN (*retreating*). A bloody-handed murderer the like of . . .

PEGEEN (*snapping at him*). Whisht I am saying; we'll take no fooling from your like at all. (*To Christy with a honeyed voice.*) And you, young fellow, you'd have a right to stop, I'm thinking, for we'd do our all and utmost to content your needs.

CHRISTY (*overcome with wonder*). And I'd be safe in this place from the searching law?

MICHAEL. You would, surely. If they're not fearing you, itself, the peelers in this place is decent droughty poor fellows, wouldn't touch a cur dog and not give warning in the dead of night.

PEGEEN (*very kindly and persuasively*). Let you stop a short while anyhow. Aren't you destroyed walking with your feet in bleeding blisters, and your whole skin needing washing like a Wicklow sheep.

CHRISTY (*looking round with satisfaction*). It's a nice room, and if it's not humbugging me you are, I'm thinking that I'll surely stay.

JIMMY (*jumps up*). Now, by the grace of God, herself will be safe this night, with a man killed his father holding danger from the door, and let you come on, Michael James, or they'll have the best stuff drunk at the wake.

MICHAEL (*going to the door with men*). And begging your pardon, mister, what name will we call you, for we'd like to know?

CHRISTY. Christopher Mahon.

MICHAEL. Well, God bless you, Christy, and a good rest till we meet again when the sun'll be rising to the noon of day.

CHRISTY. God bless you all.

MEN. God bless you.

[*They go out except Shawn, who lingers at door.*]

SHAWN (*to Pegeen*). Are you wanting me to stop along with you and keep you from harm?

PEGEEN (*gruffly*). Didn't you say you were fearing Father Reilly?

SHAWN. There'd be no harm staying now, I'm thinking, and himself in it too.

PEGEEN. You wouldn't stay when there was need for you, and let you step off nimble this time when there's none.

SHAWN. Didn't I say it was Father Reilly . . .

PEGEEN. Go on, then, to Father Reilly (*in a jeering tone*), and let him put you in the holy brotherhoods, and leave that lad to me.

SHAWN. If I meet the Widow Quin . . .

PEGEEN. Go on, I'm saying, and don't be waking this place with your noise. (*She hustles him out and bolts the door.*) That lad would wear the spirits from the saints of peace. (*Bustles about, then takes off her apron and pins it up in the window as a blind. Christy watching her timidly. Then she comes to him and speaks with bland good-humour.*) Let you stretch out now by the fire, young fellow. You should be destroyed travelling.

CHRISTY (*shyly again, drawing off his boots*). I'm tired, surely, walking wild eleven days, and waking fearful in the night.

[*He holds up one of his feet, feeling his blisters, and looking at them with compassion.*]

PEGEEN (*standing beside him, watching him with delight*). You should have had great people in your family, I'm thinking, with the little, small feet you have, and you with a kind of a quality name, the like of what you'd find on the great powers and potentates of France and Spain.

CHRISTY (*with pride*). We were great surely, with wide and windy acres of rich Munster land.

PEGEEN. Wasn't I telling you, and you a fine, handsome young fellow with a noble brow?

CHRISTY (*with a flash of delighted surprise*). Is it me?

PEGEEN. Aye. Did you never hear that from the young girls where you come from in the west or south?

CHRISTY (*with venom*). I did not then. Oh, they're bloody liars in the naked parish where I grew a man.

PEGEEN. If they are itself, you've heard it these days, I'm thinking, and you walking the world telling out your story to young girls or old.

CHRISTY. I've told my story no place till this night, Pegeen Mike, and it's foolish I was here, maybe, to be talking free, but you're decent people, I'm thinking, and yourself a kindly woman, the way I wasn't fearing you at all.

PEGEEN (*filling a sack with straw*). You've said the like of that, maybe, in every cot and cabin where you've met a young girl on your way.

CHRISTY (*going over to her, gradually raising his voice*). I've said it nowhere till this night, I'm telling you, for I've seen none the like of you the eleven long days I am walking the world, looking over a low ditch or a high ditch on my north or my south, into stony scattered fields, or scribes of bog, where you'd see young, limber girls, and fine prancing women making laughter with the men.

PEGEEN. If you weren't destroyed travelling, you'd have as much talk and streeleen, I'm thinking, as Owen Roe O'Sullivan or the poets of the Dingle Bay, and I've heard all times it's the poets are your like, fine fiery fellows with great rages when their temper's roused.

CHRISTY (*drawing a little nearer to her*). You've a power of rings, God bless you, and would there be any offence if I was asking are you single now?

PEGEEN. What would I want wedding so young?

CHRISTY (*with relief*). We're alike, so.

PEGEEN (*she puts sack on settle and beats it up*). I never killed my father. I'd be afeard to do that, except I was the like of yourself with blind rages tearing me within, for I'm thinking you should have had great tussling when the end was come.

CHRISTY (*expanding with delight at the first confidential talk he has ever had with a woman*). We had not then. It was a hard woman was come over the hill, and if he was always a crusty kind when he'd a hard woman setting him on, not the divil himself or his four fathers could put up with him at all.

PEGEEN (*with curiosity*). And isn't it a great wonder that one wasn't fearing you?

CHRISTY (*very confidentially*). Up to the day I killed my father, there wasn't a person in Ireland knew the kind I was, and I there drinking, waking, eating, sleeping, a quiet, simple poor fellow with no man giving me heed.

PEGEEN (*getting a quilt out of the cupboard and putting it on the sack*). It was the girls were giving you heed maybe, and I'm thinking it's most conceit you'd have to be gaming with their like.

CHRISTY (*shaking his head, with simplicity*). Not the girls itself, and I won't tell you a lie. There wasn't anyone heeding me in that place saving only the dumb beasts of the field.

[*He sits down at fire.*]

PEGEEN (*with disappointment*). And I thinking you should have been living the like of a king of Norway or the Eastern world.

[*She comes and sits beside him after placing bread and mug of milk on the table.*]

CHRISTY (*laughing piteously*). The like of a king, is it? And I after toiling, moiling, digging, dodging from the dawn till dusk with never a sight of joy or sport saving only when I'd be abroad in the dark night poaching rabbits on hills, for I was a devil to poach, God forgive me, (*very naïvely*) and I near got six months for going with a dung fork and stabbing a fish.

PEGEEN. And it's that you'd call sport, is it, to be abroad in the darkness with yourself alone?

CHRISTY. I did, God help me, and there I'd be as happy as the sunshine of St. Martin's Day, watching the light passing the north or the patches of fog, till I'd hear a rabbit starting to screech and I'd go running in the furze. Then when I'd my full share I'd come walking down where you'd see the ducks and geese stretched sleeping on the highway of the road, and before I'd pass the dunghill, I'd hear himself snoring out, a loud lonesome snore he'd be making all times, the while he was sleeping, and he a man 'd be raging all times, the while he was waking, like a gaudy officer you'd hear cursing and damning and swearing oaths.

PEGEEN. Providence and Mercy, spare us all!

CHRISTY. It's that you'd say surely if you seen him and he after drinking for weeks, rising up in the red dawn, or before it maybe, and going out into the yard as naked as an ash tree in the moon of May, and shying clods against the visage of the stars till he'd put the fear of death into the banbhs and the screeching sows.

PEGEEN. I'd be well-nigh afeard of that lad myself, I'm thinking. And there was no one in it but the two of you alone?

CHRISTY. The divil a one, though he'd sons and daughters walking all great states and territories of the world, and not a one of them, to this day, but would say their seven curses on him, and they rousing up to let a cough or sneeze, maybe, in the deadness of the night.

PEGEEN (nodding her head). Well, you should have been a queer lot. I never cursed my father the like of that, though I'm twenty and more years of age.

CHRISTY. Then you'd have cursed mine, I'm telling you, and he a man never gave peace to any, saving when he'd get two months or three, or be locked in the asylums for battering peelers or assaulting men (with *depression*) the way it was a bitter life he led me till I did up a Tuesday and halve his skull.

PEGEEN (*putting her hand on his shoulder*). Well, you'll have peace in this place, Christy Mahon, and none to trouble you, and it's near time a fine lad like you should have your good share of the earth.

CHRISTY. It's time surely, and I a seemly fellow with great strength in me and bravery of . . .

[*Someone knocks.*]

CHRISTY (*clinging to Pegeen*). Oh, glory! it's late for knocking, and this last while I'm in terror of the peelers, and the walking dead.

[*Knocking again.*]

PEGEEN. Who's there?

VOICE (*outside*). Me.

PEGEEN. Who's me?

VOICE. The Widow Quin.

PEGEEN (*jumping up and giving him the bread and milk*). Go on now with your supper, and let on to be sleepy, for if she found you were such a warrant to talk, she'd be stringing gabble till the dawn of day. (*He takes bread and sits shyly with his back to the door.*)

PEGEEN (*opening door, with temper*). What ails you, or what is it you're wanting at this hour of the night?

WIDOW QUIN (*coming in a step and peering at Christy*). I'm after meeting Shawn Keogh and Father Reilly below, who told me of your curiosity man, and they fearing by this time he was maybe roaring, romping on your hands with drink.

PEGEEN (*pointing to Christy*). Look now is he roaring, and he stretched away drowsy with his supper and his mug of milk. Walk down and tell that to Father Reilly and to Shaneen Keogh.

WIDOW QUIN (*coming forward*). I'll not see them again, for I've their word to lead that lad forward for to lodge with me.

PEGEEN (*in blank amazement*). This night, is it?

WIDOW QUIN (*going over*). This night. "It isn't fitting," says the priesteen, "to have his likeness lodging with an orphaned girl." (*To Christy.*) God save you, mister!

CHRISTY (*shyly*). God save you kindly.

WIDOW QUIN (*looking at him with half-amazed curiosity*). Well, aren't you a little smiling fellow? It should have been great and bitter torments did rouse your spirits to a deed of blood.

CHRISTY (*doubtfully*). It should, maybe.

WIDOW QUIN. It's more than "maybe" I'm saying, and it'd soften my heart to see you sitting so simple with your cup and cake, and you fitter to be saying your catechism than slaying your da.

PEGEEN (*at counter, washing glasses*). There's talking when any'd see he's fit to be holding his head high with the wonders of the world. Walk on from this, for I'll not have him tormented and he destroyed travelling since Tuesday was a week.

WIDOW QUIN (*peaceably*). We'll be walking surely when his supper's done, and you'll find we're great company, young fellow, when it's of the like of you and me you'd hear the penny poets singing in an August Fair.

CHRISTY (*innocently*). Did you kill your father?

PEGEEN (*contemptuously*). She did not. She hit himself with a worn pick, and the rusted poison did corrode his blood the way he never overed it, and died after. That was a sneaky kind of murder did win small glory with the boys itself.

[*She crosses to Christy's left.*]

WIDOW QUIN (*with good-humour*). If it didn't, maybe all knows a widow woman has buried her children and destroyed her man is a wiser comrade for a young lad than a girl, the like of you, who'd go helter-skeltering after any man would let you a wink upon the road.

PEGEEN (*breaking out into wild rage*). And you'll say that, Widow Quin, and you gasping with the rage you had racing the hill beyond to look on his face.

WIDOW QUIN (*laughing derisively*). Me, is it? Well, Father Reilly has cuteness to divide you now. (*She pulls Christy up.*) There's great temptation in a man did slay his da, and we'd best be going, young fellow; so rise up and come with me.

PEGEEN (*seizing his arm*). He'll not stir. He's pot-boy in this place, and I'll not have him stolen off and kidnabbed while himself's abroad.

WIDOW QUIN. It'd be a crazy pot-boy'd lodge him in the shebeen where he works by day, so you'd have a right to come on, young fellow, till you see my little houseen, a perch off on the rising hill.

PEGEEN. Wait till morning, Christy Mahon. Wait till you lay eyes on her leaky thatch is growing more pasture for her buck goat than her square of fields, and she without a tramp itself to keep in order her place at all.

WIDOW QUIN. When you see me contriving in my little gardens, Christy Mahon, you'll swear the Lord God

formed me to be living lone, and that there isn't my
match in Mayo for thatching, or mowing, or shearing
a sheep.

PEGEEN (*with noisy scorn*). It's true the Lord God
formed you to contrive indeed. Doesn't the world know
you reared a black lamb at your own breast, so that the
Lord Bishop of Connaught felt the elements of a
Christian, and he eating it after in a kidney stew?
Doesn't the world know you've been seen shaving the
foxy skipper from France for a threepenny bit and a
sop of grass tobacco would wring the liver from a
mountain goat you'd meet leaping the hills?

WIDOW QUIN (*with amusement*). Do you hear her now,
young fellow? Do you hear the way she'll be rating at
your own self when a week is by?

PEGEEN (*to Christy*). Don't heed her. Tell her to go
into her pigsty and not plague us here.

WIDOW QUIN. I'm going; but he'll come with me.

PEGEEN (*shaking him*). Are you dumb, young fellow?

CHRISTY (*timidly, to Widow Quin*). God increase you;
but I'm pot-boy in this place, and it's here I'd liefer stay.

PEGEEN (*triumphantly*). Now you have heard him,
and go on from this.

WIDOW QUIN (*looking round the room*). It's lonesome
this hour crossing the hill, and if he won't come along
with me, I'd have a right maybe to stop this night with
yourselves. Let me stretch out on the settle, Pegeen
Mike; and himself can lie by the hearth.

PEGEEN (*short and fiercely*). Faith, I won't. Quit off
or I will send you now.

WIDOW QUIN (*gathering her shawl up*). Well, it's a
terror to be aged a score. (*To Christy.*) God bless you

now, young fellow, and let you be wary, or there's right torment will await you here if you go romancing with her like, and she waiting only, as they bade me say, on a sheepskin parchment to be wed with Shawn Keogh of Killakeen.

CHRISTY (*going to Pegeen as she bolts the door*). What's that she's after saying?

PEGEEN. Lies and blather, you've no call to mind. Well, isn't Shawn Keogh an impudent fellow to send up spying on me? Wait till I lay hands on him. Let him wait, I'm saying.

CHRISTY. And you're not wedding him at all?

PEGEEN. I wouldn't wed him if a bishop came walking for to join us here.

CHRISTY. That God in glory may be thanked for that.

PEGEEN. There's your bed now. I've put a quilt upon you I'm after quilting a while since with my own two hands, and you'd best stretch out now for your sleep, and may God give you a good rest till I call you in the morning when the cocks will crow.

CHRISTY (*as she goes to inner room*). May God and Mary and St. Patrick bless you and reward you, for your kindly talk. (*She shuts the door behind her. He settles his bed slowly, feeling the quilt with immense satisfaction.*) Well, it's a clean bed and soft with it, and it's great luck and company I've won me in the end of time —two fine women fighting for the likes of me—till I'm thinking this night wasn't I a foolish fellow not to kill my father in the years gone by.

CURTAIN

ACT II

SCENE, *as before. Brilliant morning light. Christy, looking bright and cheerful, is cleaning a girl's boots.*

CHRISTY (*to himself, counting jugs on dresser*). Half a hundred beyond. Ten there. A score that's above. Eighty jugs. Six cups and a broken one. Two plates. A power of glasses. Bottles, a school-master'd be hard set to count, and enough in them, I'm thinking, to drunken all the wealth and wisdom of the County Clare. (*He puts down the boot carefully.*) There's her boots now, nice and decent for her evening use, and isn't it grand brushes she has? (*He puts them down and goes by degrees to the looking-glass.*) Well, this'd be a fine place to be my whole life talking out with swearing Christians, in place of my old dogs and cat, and I stalking around, smoking my pipe and drinking my fill, and never a day's work but drawing a cork an odd time, or wiping a glass, or rinsing out a shiny tumbler for a decent man. (*He takes the looking-glass from the wall and puts it on the back of a chair; then sits down in front of it and begins washing his face.*) Didn't I know rightly I was handsome, though it was the divil's own mirror we had beyond, would twist a squint across an angel's brow; and I'll be growing fine from this day, the way I'll have a soft lovely skin on me and won't be the like of the clumsy young fellows do be ploughing all times in the earth and dung. (*He starts.*) Is she coming again? (*He looks out.*) Stranger girls. God help me, where'll I hide myself away and my long neck naked to the world? (*He looks out.*) I'd best go to the room maybe till I'm dressed again.

[*He gathers up his coat and the looking-glass, and runs into the inner room. The door is pushed open, and Susan Brady looks in, and knocks on door.*]

SUSAN. There's nobody in it.

[*Knocks again.*]

NELLY (*pushing her in and following her, with Honor Blake and Sara Tansey*). It'd be early for them both to be out walking the hill.

SUSAN. I'm thinking Shawn Keogh was making game of us and there's no such man in it at all.

HONOR (*pointing to straw and quilt*). Look at that. He's been sleeping there in the night. Well, it'll be a hard case if he's gone off now, the way we'll never set our eyes on a man killed his father, and we after rising early and destroying ourselves running fast on the hill.

NELLY. Are you thinking them's his boots?

SARA (*taking them up*). If they are, there should be his father's track on them. Did you never read in the papers the way murdered men do bleed and drip?

SUSAN. Is that blood there, Sara Tansey?

SARA (*smelling it*). That's bog water, I'm thinking, but it's his own they are surely, for I never seen the like of them for whity mud, and red mud, and turf on them, and the fine sands of the sea. That man's been walking, I'm telling you.

[*She goes down right, putting on one of his boots.*]

SUSAN (*going to window*). Maybe he's stolen off to Belmullet with the boots of Michael James, and you'd have a right so to follow after him, Sara Tansey, and you the one yoked the ass cart and drove ten miles to set your eyes on the man bit the yellow lady's nostril on the northern shore.

[*She looks out.*]

SARA (*running to window with one boot on*). Don't be talking, and we fooled to-day. (*Putting on other boot.*) There's a pair do fit me well, and I'll be keeping them for walking to the priest, when you'd be ashamed this place, going up winter and summer with nothing worth while to confess at all.

HONOR (*who has been listening at the door*). Whisht! there's someone inside the room. (*She pushes door a chink open.*) It's a man.

[*Sara kicks off boots and puts them where they were. They all stand in a line looking through chink.*]

SARA. I'll call him. Mister! Mister! (*He puts in his head.*) Is Pegeen within?

CHRISTY (*coming in as meek as a mouse, with the looking-glass held behind his back*). She's above on the cnuceen, seeking the nanny goats, the way she'd have a sup of goat's milk for to colour my tea.

SARA. And asking your pardon, is it you's the man killed his father?

CHRISTY (*sidling toward the nail where the glass was hanging*). I am, God help me!

SARA (*taking eggs she has brought*). Then my thousand welcomes to you, and I've run up with a brace of duck's eggs for your food to-day. Pegeen's ducks is no use, but these are the real rich sort. Hold out your hand and you'll see it's no lie I'm telling you.

CHRISTY (*coming forward shyly, and holding out his left hand*). They're a great and weighty size.

SUSAN. And I run up with a pat of butter, for it'd be a poor thing to have you eating your spuds dry, and you after running a great way since you did destroy your da.

CHRISTY. Thank you kindly.

HONOR. And I brought you a little cut of cake, for you should have a thin stomach on you, and you that length walking the world.

NELLY. And I brought you a little laying pullet—boiled and all she is—was crushed at the fall of night by the curate's car. Feel the fat of that breast, mister.

CHRISTY. It's bursting, surely.

[*He feels it with the back of his hand, in which he holds the presents.*]

SARA. Will you pinch it? Is your right hand too sacred for to use at all? (*She slips round behind him.*) It's a glass he has. Well, I never seen to this day a man with a looking-glass held to his back. Them that kills their fathers is a vain lot surely.

[*Girls giggle.*]

CHRISTY (*smiling innocently and piling presents on glass*). I'm very thankful to you all to-day . . .

WIDOW QUIN (*coming in quickly, at door*). Sara Tansey, Susan Brady, Honor Blake! What in glory has you here at this hour of day?

GIRLS (*giggling*). That's the man killed his father.

WIDOW QUIN (*coming to them*). I know well it's the man; and I'm after putting him down in the sports below for racing, leaping, pitching, and the Lord knows what.

SARA (*exuberantly*). That's right, Widow Quin. I'll bet my dowry that he'll lick the world.

WIDOW QUIN. If you will, you'd have a right to have him fresh and nourished in place of nursing a feast. (*Taking presents.*) Are you fasting or fed, young fellow?

CHRISTY. Fasting, if you please.

WIDOW QUIN (*loudly*). Well, you're the lot. Stir up now and give him his breakfast. (*To Christy.*) Come here to me (*she puts him on bench beside her while the girls make tea and get his breakfast*) and let you tell us your story before Pegeen will come, in place of grinning your ears off like the moon of May.

CHRISTY (*beginning to be pleased*). It's a long story; you'd be destroyed listening.

WIDOW QUIN. Don't be letting on to be shy, a fine, gamey, treacherous lad the like of you. Was it in your house beyond you cracked his skull?

CHRISTY (*shy but flattered*). It was not. We were digging spuds in his cold, sloping, stony, divil's patch of a field.

WIDOW QUIN. And you went asking money of him, or making talk of getting a wife would drive him from his farm?

CHRISTY. I did not, then; but there I was, digging and digging, and "You squinting idiot," says he, "let you walk down now and tell the priest you'll wed the Widow Casey in a score of days."

WIDOW QUIN. And what kind was she?

CHRISTY (*with horror*). A walking terror from beyond the hills, and she two score and five years, and two hundredweights and five pounds in the weighing scales, with a limping leg on her, and a blinded eye, and she a woman of noted misbehaviour with the old and young.

GIRLS (*clustering round him, serving him*). Glory be.

WIDOW QUIN. And what did he want driving you to wed with her?

[*She takes a bit of the chicken.*]

CHRISTY (*eating with growing satisfaction*). He was letting on I was wanting a protector from the harshness of the world, and he without a thought the whole while but how he'd have her hut to live in and her gold to drink.

WIDOW QUIN. There's maybe worse than a dry hearth and a widow woman and your glass at night. So you hit him then?

CHRISTY (*getting almost excited*). I did not. "I won't wed her," says I, "when all know she did suckle me for six weeks when I came into the world, and she a hag this day with a tongue on her has the crows and seabirds scattered, the way they wouldn't cast a shadow on her garden with the dread of her curse."

WIDOW QUIN (*teasingly*). That one should be right company.

SARA (*eagerly*). Don't mind her. Did you kill him then?

CHRISTY. "She's too good for the like of you," says he, "and go on now or I'll flatten you out like a crawling beast has passed under a dray." "You will not if I can help it," says I. "Go on," says he, "or I'll have the divil making garters of your limbs to-night." "You will not if I can help it," says I.

[*He sits up, brandishing his mug.*]

SARA. You were right surely.

CHRISTY (*impressively*). With that the sun came out between the cloud and the hill, and it shining green in my face. "God have mercy on your soul," says he, lifting a scythe; "or on your own," says I, raising the loy.

SUSAN. That's a grand story.

HONOR. He tells it lovely.

CHRISTY (*flattered and confident, waving bone*). He gave a drive with the scythe, and I gave a lep to the east. Then I turned around with my back to the north, and I hit a blow on the ridge of his skull, laid him stretched out, and he split to the knob of his gullet.

[*He raises the chicken bone to his Adam's apple.*]

GIRLS (*together*). Well, you're a marvel! Oh, God bless you! You're the lad surely!

SUSAN. I'm thinking the Lord God sent him this road to make a second husband to the Widow Quin, and she with a great yearning to be wedded, though all dread her here. Lift him on her knee, Sara Tansey.

WIDOW QUIN. Don't tease him.

SARA (*going over to dresser and counter very quickly, and getting two glasses and porter*). You're heroes surely, and let you drink a supeen with your arms linked like the outlandish lovers in the sailor's song. (*She links their arms and gives them the glasses.*) There now. Drink a health to the wonders of the western world, the pirates, preachers, poteen-makers, with the jobbing jockies; parching peelers, and the juries fill their stomachs selling judgments of the English law.

[*Brandishing the bottle.*]

WIDOW QUIN. That's a right toast, Sara Tansey. Now Christy.

[*They drink with their arms linked, he drinking with his left hand, she with her right. As they are drinking,*

Pegeen Mike comes in with a milk can and stands aghast. They all spring away from Christy. He goes down left. Widow Quin remains seated.]

PEGEEN (*angrily, to Sara*). What is it you're wanting?

SARA (*twisting her apron*). An ounce of tobacco.

PEGEEN. Have you tuppence?

SARA. I've forgotten my purse.

PEGEEN. Then you'd best be getting it and not fooling us here. (*To the Widow Quin, with more elaborate scorn.*) And what is it you're wanting, Widow Quin?

WIDOW QUIN (*insolently*). A penn'orth of starch.

PEGEEN (*breaking out*). And you without a white shift or a shirt in your whole family since the drying of the flood. I've no starch for the like of you, and let you walk on now to Killamuck.

WIDOW QUIN (*turning to Christy, as she goes out with the girls*). Well, you're mighty huffy this day, Pegeen Mike, and, you young fellow, let you not forget the sports and racing when the noon is by.

[*They go out.*]

PEGEEN (*imperiously*). Fling out that rubbish and put them cups away. (*Christy tidies away in great haste.*) Shove in the bench by the wall. (*He does so.*) And hang that glass on the nail. What disturbed it at all?

CHRISTY (*very meekly*). I was making myself decent only, and this a fine country for young lovely girls.

PEGEEN (*sharply*). Whisht your talking of girls.

[*Goes to counter—right.*]

CHRISTY. Wouldn't any wish to be decent in a place . . .

PEGEEN. Whisht I'm saying.

CHRISTY (*looks at her face for a moment with great misgivings, then as a last effort, takes up a loy, and goes towards her, with feigned assurance*). It was with a loy the like of that I killed my father.

PEGEEN (*still sharply*). You've told me that story six times since the dawn of day.

CHRISTY (*reproachfully*). It's a queer thing you wouldn't care to be hearing it and them girls after walking four miles to be listening to me now.

PEGEEN (*turning round astonished*). Four miles.

CHRISTY (*apologetically*). Didn't himself say there were only four bona fides living in the place?

PEGEEN. It's bona fides by the road they are, but that lot came over the river lepping the stones. It's not three perches when you go like that, and I was down this morning looking on the papers the post-boy does have in his bag. (*With meaning and emphasis.*) For there was great news this day, Christopher Mahon.

[*She goes into room left.*]

CHRISTY (*suspiciously*). Is it news of my murder?

PEGEEN (*inside*). Murder, indeed.

CHRISTY (*loudly*). A murdered da?

PEGEEN (*coming in again and crossing right*). There was not, but a story filled half a page of the hanging of a man. Ah, that should be a fearful end, young fellow, and it worst of all for a man who destroyed his da, for the like of him would get small mercies, and when it's dead he is, they'd put him in a narrow grave, with cheap sacking wrapping him round, and pour down quicklime on his head, the way you'd see a woman pouring any frish-frash from a cup.

CHRISTY (*very miserably*). Oh, God help me. Are you thinking I'm safe? You were saying at the fall of night, I was shut of jeopardy and I here with yourselves.

PEGEEN (*severely*). You'll be shut of jeopardy no place if you go talking with a pack of wild girls the like of them do be walking abroad with the peelers, talking whispers at the fall of night.

CHRISTY (*with terror*). And you're thinking they'd tell?

PEGEEN (*with mock sympathy*). Who knows, God help you.

CHRISTY (*loudly*). What joy would they have to bring hanging to the likes of me?

PEGEEN. It's queer joys they have, and who knows the thing they'd do, if it'd make the green stones cry itself to think of you swaying and swiggling at the butt of a rope, and you with a fine, stout neck, God bless you! the way you'd be a half an hour, in great anguish, getting your death.

CHRISTY (*getting his boots and putting them on*). If there's that terror of them, it'd be best, maybe, I went on wandering like Esau or Cain and Abel on the sides of Neifin or the Erris plain.

PEGEEN (*beginning to play with him*). It would, maybe, for I've heard the Circuit Judges this place is a heartless crew.

CHRISTY (*bitterly*). It's more than Judges this place is a heartless crew. (*Looking up at her.*) And isn't it a poor thing to be starting again and I a lonesome fellow will be looking out on women and girls the way the needy fallen spirits do be looking on the Lord?

PEGEEN. What call have you to be that lonesome when there's poor girls walking Mayo in their thousands now?

CHRISTY (*grimly*). It's well you know what call I have. It's well you know it's a lonesome thing to be passing small towns with the lights shining sideways when the night is down, or going in strange places with a dog noising before you and a dog noising behind, or drawn to the cities where you'd hear a voice kissing and talking deep love in every shadow of the ditch, and you passing on with an empty, hungry stomach failing from your heart.

PEGEEN. I'm thinking you're an odd man, Christy Mahon. The oddest walking fellow I ever set my eyes on to this hour to-day.

CHRISTY. What would any be but odd men and they living lonesome in the world?

PEGEEN. I'm not odd, and I'm my whole life with my father only.

CHRISTY (*with infinite admiration*). How would a lovely handsome woman the like of you be lonesome when all men should be thronging around to hear the sweetness of your voice, and the little infant children should be pestering your steps I'm thinking, and you walking the roads.

PEGEEN. I'm hard set to know what way a coaxing fellow the like of yourself should be lonesome either.

CHRISTY. Coaxing?

PEGEEN. Would you have me think a man never talked with the girls would have the words you've spoken to-day? It's only letting on you are to be lonesome, the way you'd get around me now.

CHRISTY. I wish to God I was letting on; but I was lonesome all times, and born lonesome, I'm thinking, as the moon of dawn.

[*Going to door.*]

PEGEEN (*puzzled by his talk*). Well, it's a story I'm not understanding at all why you'd be worse than another, Christy Mahon, and you a fine lad with the great savagery to destroy your da.

CHRISTY. It's little I'm understanding myself, saving only that my heart's scalded this day, and I going off stretching out the earth between us, the way I'll not be waking near you another dawn of the year till the two of us do arise to hope or judgment with the saints of God, and now I'd best be going with my wattle in my hand, for hanging is a poor thing (*turning to go*), and it's little welcome only is left me in this house to-day.

PEGEEN (*sharply*). Christy! (*He turns round.*) Come here to me. (*He goes towards her.*) Lay down that switch and throw some sods on the fire. You're pot-boy in this place, and I'll not have you mitch off from us now.

CHRISTY. You were saying I'd be hanged if I stay.

PEGEEN (*quite kindly at last*). I'm after going down and reading the fearful crimes of Ireland for two weeks or three, and there wasn't a word of your murder. (*Getting up and going over to the counter.*) They've likely not found the body. You're safe so with ourselves.

CHRISTY (*astonished, slowly*). It's making game of me you were (*following her with fearful joy*), and I can stay so, working at your side, and I not lonesome from this mortal day.

PEGEEN. What's to hinder you from staying, except the widow woman or the young girls would inveigle you off?

CHRISTY (*with rapture*). And I'll have your words from this day filling my ears, and that look is come upon you meeting my two eyes, and I watching you loafing around in the warm sun, or rinsing your ankles when the night is come.

PEGEEN (*kindly, but a little embarrassed*). I'm thinking you'll be a loyal young lad to have working around, and if you vexed me a while since with your leaguing with the girls, I wouldn't give a thraneen for a lad hadn't a mighty spirit in him and a gamey heart.

[*Shawn Keogh runs in carrying a cleeve on his back, followed by the Widow Quin.*]

SHAWN (*to Pegeen*). I was passing below, and I seen your mountainy sheep eating cabbages in Jimmy's field. Run up or they'll be bursting surely.

PEGEEN. Oh, God mend them!

[*She puts a shawl over her head and runs out.*]

CHRISTY (*looking from one to the other. Still in high spirits*). I'd best go to her aid maybe. I'm handy with ewes.

WIDOW QUIN (*closing the door*). She can do that much, and there is Shaneen has long speeches for to tell you now.

[*She sits down with an amused smile.*]

SHAWN (*taking something from his pocket and offering it to Christy*). Do you see that, mister?

CHRISTY (*looking at it*). The half of a ticket to the Western States!

SHAWN (*trembling with anxiety*). I'll give it to you and my new hat (*pulling it out of hamper*); and my breeches with the double seat (*pulling it off*); and my new coat is woven from the blackest shearings for three miles around (*giving him the coat*); I'll give you the whole of them, and my blessing, and the blessing of Father Reilly itself, maybe, if you'll quit from this and leave us in the peace we had till last night at the fall of dark.

CHRISTY (*with a new arrogance*). And for what is it you're wanting to get shut of me?

SHAWN (*looking to the Widow for help*). I'm a poor scholar with middling faculties to coin a lie, so I'll tell you the truth, Christy Mahon. I'm wedding with Pegeen beyond, and I don't think well of having a clever fearless man the like of you dwelling in her house.

CHRISTY (*almost pugnaciously*). And you'd be using bribery for to banish me?

SHAWN (*in an imploring voice*). Let you not take it badly, mister honey, isn't beyond the best place for you where you'll have golden chains and shiny coats and you riding upon hunters with the ladies of the land.

[*He makes an eager sign to the Widow Quin to come to help him.*]

WIDOW QUIN (*coming over*). It's true for him, and you'd best quit off and not have that poor girl setting her mind on you, for there's Shaneen thinks she wouldn't suit you though all is saying that she'll wed you now.

[*Christy beams with delight.*]

SHAWN (*in terrified earnest*). She wouldn't suit you, and she with the divil's own temper the way you'd be strangling one another in a score of days. (*He makes the movement of strangling with his hands.*) It's the like of me only that she's fit for, a quiet simple fellow wouldn't raise a hand upon her if she scratched itself.

WIDOW QUIN (*putting Shawn's hat on Christy*). Fit them clothes on you anyhow, young fellow, and he'd maybe loan them to you for the sports. (*Pushing him towards inner door.*) Fit them on and you can give your answer when you have them tried.

CHRISTY (*beaming, delighted with the clothes*). I will then. I'd like herself to see me in them tweeds and hat.

[*He goes into room and shuts the door.*]

SHAWN (*in great anxiety*). He'd like herself to see them. He'll not leave us, Widow Quin. He's a score of divils in him the way it's well nigh certain he will wed Pegeen.

WIDOW QUIN (*jeeringly*). It's true all girls are fond of courage and do hate the like of you.

SHAWN (*walking about in desperation*). Oh, Widow Quin, what'll I be doing now? I'd inform again him, but he'd burst from Kilmainham and he'd be sure and certain to destroy me. If I wasn't so God-fearing, I'd near have courage to come behind him and run a pike into his side. Oh, it's a hard case to be an orphan and not to have your father that you're used to, and you'd easy kill and make yourself a hero in the sight of all. (*Coming up to her.*) Oh, Widow Quin, will you find me some contrivance when I've promised you a ewe?

WIDOW QUIN. A ewe's a small thing, but what would you give me if I did wed him and did save you so?

SHAWN (*with astonishment*). You?

WIDOW QUIN. Aye. Would you give me the red cow you have and the mountainy ram, and the right of way across your rye path, and a load of dung at Michaelmas, and turbary upon the western hill?

SHAWN (*radiant with hope*). I would surely, and I'd give you the wedding-ring I have, and the loan of a new suit, the way you'd have him decent on the wedding-day. I'd give you two kids for your dinner, and a gallon of poteen, and I'd call the piper on the long car to your wedding from Crossmolina or from Ballina. I'd give you . . .

WIDOW QUIN. That'll do so, and let you whisht, for he's coming now again.

[*Christy comes in very natty in the new clothes. Widow Quin goes to him admiringly.*]

WIDOW QUIN. If you seen yourself now, I'm thinking you'd be too proud to speak to us at all, and it'd be a pity surely to have your like sailing from Mayo to the Western World.

CHRISTY (*as proud as a peacock*). I'm not going. If this is a poor place itself, I'll make myself contented to be lodging here.

[*Widow Quin makes a sign to Shawn to leave them.*]

SHAWN. Well, I'm going measuring the race-course while the tide is low, so I'll leave you the garments and my blessing for the sports to-day. God bless you!

[*He wriggles out.*]

WIDOW QUIN (*admiring Christy*). Well, you're mighty spruce, young fellow. Sit down now while you're quiet till you talk with me.

CHRISTY (*swaggering*). I'm going abroad on the hill-side for to seek Pegeen.

WIDOW QUIN. You'll have time and plenty for to seek Pegeen, and you heard me saying at the fall of night the two of us should be great company.

CHRISTY. From this out I'll have no want of company when all sorts is bringing me their food and clothing (*he swaggers to the door, tightening his belt*), the way they'd set their eyes upon a gallant orphan cleft his father with one blow to the breeches belt. (*He opens door, then staggers back.*) Saints of glory! Holy angels from the throne of light!

WIDOW QUIN (*going over*). What ails you?

CHRISTY. It's the walking spirit of my murdered da?

WIDOW QUIN (*looking out*). Is it that tramper?

CHRISTY (*wildly*). Where'll I hide my poor body from that ghost of hell?

[*The door is pushed open, and old Mahon appears on threshold. Christy darts in behind door.*]

WIDOW QUIN (*in great amusement*). God save you, my poor man.

MAHON (*gruffly*). Did you see a young lad passing this way in the early morning or the fall of night?

WIDOW QUIN. You're a queer kind to walk in not saluting at all.

MAHON. Did you see the young lad?

WIDOW QUIN (*stiffly*). What kind was he?

MAHON. An ugly young streeler with a murderous gob on him, and a little switch in his hand. I met a tramper seen him coming this way at the fall of night.

WIDOW QUIN. There's harvest hundreds do be passing these days for the Sligo boat. For what is it you're wanting him, my poor man?

MAHON. I want to destroy him for breaking the head on me with the clout of a loy. (*He takes off a big hat, and shows his head in a mass of bandages and plaster, with some pride.*) It was he did that, and amn't I a great wonder to think I've traced him ten days with that rent in my crown?

WIDOW QUIN (*taking his head in both hands and examining it with extreme delight*). That was a great blow. And who hit you? A robber maybe?

MAHON. It was my own son hit me, and he the divil a robber, or anything else, but a dirty, stuttering lout.

WIDOW QUIN (*letting go his skull and wiping her hands in her apron*). You'd best be wary of a mortified scalp, I think they call it, lepping around with that wound in the splendour of the sun. It was a bad blow surely, and you should have vexed him fearful to make him strike that gash in his da.

MAHON. Is it me?

WIDOW QUIN (*amusing herself*). Aye. And isn't it a great shame when the old and hardened do torment the young?

MAHON (*raging*). Torment him is it? And I after holding out with the patience of a martyred saint till there's nothing but destruction on, and I'm driven out in my old age with none to aid me.

WIDOW QUIN (*greatly amused*). It's a sacred wonder the way that wickedness will spoil a man.

MAHON. My wickedness, is it? Amn't I after saying it is himself has me destroyed, and he a liar on walls, a talker of folly, a man you'd see stretched the half of the day in the brown ferns with his belly to the sun.

WIDOW QUIN. Not working at all?

MAHON. The divil a work, or if he did itself, you'd see him raising up a haystack like the stalk of a rush, or driving our last cow till he broke her leg at the hip, and when he wasn't at that he'd be fooling over little birds he had —finches and felts—or making mugs at his own self in the bit of a glass we had hung on the wall.

WIDOW QUIN (*looking at Christy*). What way was he so foolish? It was running wild after the girls may be?

MAHON (*with a shout of derision*). Running wild, is it? If he seen a red petticoat coming swinging over the hill, he'd be off to hide in the sticks, and you'd see him shooting out his sheep's eyes between the little twigs and the leaves, and his two ears rising like a hare looking out through a gap. Girls, indeed!

WIDOW QUIN. It was drink maybe?

MAHON. And he a poor fellow would get drunk on the smell of a pint. He'd a queer rotten stomach, I'm telling you, and when I gave him three pulls from my pipe a while since, he was taken with contortions till I had to send him in the ass cart to the females' nurse.

WIDOW QUIN (*clasping her hands*). Well, I never till this day heard tell of a man the like of that!

MAHON. I'd take a mighty oath you didn't surely, and wasn't he the laughing joke of every female woman where four baronies meet, the way the girls would stop their weeding if they seen him coming the road to let a roar at him, and call him the looney of Mahon's.

WIDOW QUIN. I'd give the world and all to see the like of him. What kind was he?

MAHON. A small low fellow.

WIDOW QUIN. And dark?

MAHON. Dark and dirty.

WIDOW QUIN (*considering*). I'm thinking I seen him.

MAHON (*eagerly*). An ugly young blackguard.

WIDOW QUIN. A hideous, fearful villain, and the spit of you.

MAHON. What way is he fled?

WIDOW QUIN. Gone over the hills to catch a coasting steamer to the north or south.

MAHON. Could I pull up on him now?

WIDOW QUIN. If you'll cross the sands below where the .tide is out, you'll be in it as soon as himself, for he had to go round ten miles by the top of the bay. (*She points to the door.*) Strike down by the head beyond and then follow on the roadway to the north and east.

[*Mahon goes abruptly.*]

WIDOW QUIN (*shouting after him*). Let you give him a good vengeance when you come up with him, but don't put yourself in the power of the law, for it'd be a poor thing to see a judge in his black cap reading out his sentence on a civil warrior the like of you.

[*She swings the door to and looks at Christy, who is cowering in terror, for a moment, then she bursts into a laugh.*]

WIDOW QUIN. Well, you're the walking Playboy of the Western World, and that's the poor man you had divided to his breeches belt.

CHRISTY (*looking out: then, to her*). What'll Pegeen say when she hears that story? What'll she be saying to me now?

WIDOW QUIN. She'll knock the head of you, I'm thinking, and drive you from the door. God help her to be taking you for a wonder, and you a little schemer making up the story you destroyed your da.

CHRISTY (*turning to the door, nearly speechless with rage, half to himself*). To be letting on he was dead, and coming back to his life, and following after me like an old weazel tracing a rat, and coming in here laying desolation between my own self and the fine women of Ireland, and he a kind of carcase that you'd fling upon the sea . . .

WIDOW QUIN (*more soberly*). There's talking for a man's one only son.

CHRISTY (*breaking out*). His one son, is it? May I meet him with one tooth and it aching, and one eye to be seeing seven and seventy divils in the twists of the road, and one old timber leg on him to limp into the scalding grave. (*Looking out.*) There he is now crossing the strands, and that the Lord God would send a high wave to wash him from the world.

WIDOW QUIN (*scandalized*). Have you no shame? (*Putting her hand on his shoulder and turning him round.*) What ails you? Near crying, is it?

CHRISTY (*in despair and grief*). Amn't I after seeing the love-light of the star of knowledge shining from her brow, and hearing words would put you thinking on the holy Brigid speaking to the infant saints, and now she'll be turning again, and speaking hard words to me, like an old woman with a spavindy ass she'd have, urging on a hill.

WIDOW QUIN. There's poetry talk for a girl you'd see itching and scratching, and she with a stale stink of poteen on her from selling in the shop.

CHRISTY (*impatiently*). It's her like is fitted to be handling merchandise in the heavens above, and what'll I be doing now, I ask you, and I a kind of wonder was jilted by the heavens when a day was by.

[*There is a distant noise of girls' voices. Widow Quin looks from window and comes to him, hurriedly.*]

WIDOW QUIN. You'll be doing like myself, I'm thinking, when I did destroy my man, for I'm above many's the day, odd times in great spirits, abroad in the sunshine, darning a stocking or stitching a shift; and odd times again looking out on the schooners, hookers, trawlers is sailing the sea, and I thinking on the gallant hairy fellows are drifting beyond, and myself long years living alone.

CHRISTY (*interested*). You're like me, so.

WIDOW QUIN. I am your like, and it's for that I'm taking a fancy to you, and I with my little houseen above where there'd be myself to tend you, and none to ask were you a murderer or what at all.

CHRISTY. And what would I be doing if I left Pegeen?

WIDOW QUIN. I've nice jobs you could be doing, gathering shells to make a whitewash for our hut within, building up a little goose-house, or stretching a new skin on an old curragh I have, and if my hut is far from all sides, it's there you'll meet the wisest old men, I tell you, at the corner of my wheel, and it's there yourself and me will have great times whispering and hugging. . . .

VOICES (*outside, calling far away*). Christy! Christy Mahon! Christy!

CHRISTY. Is it Pegeen Mike?

WIDOW QUIN. It's the young girls, I'm thinking, coming

to bring you to the sports below, and what is it you'll have me to tell them now?

CHRISTY. Aid me for to win Pegeen. It's herself only that I'm seeking now. (*Widow Quin gets up and goes to window.*) Aid me for to win her, and I'll be asking God to stretch a hand to you in the hour of death, and lead you short cuts through the Meadows of Ease, and up the floor of Heaven to the Footstool of the Virgin's Son.

WIDOW QUIN. There's praying.

VOICES (*nearer*). Christy! Christy Mahon!

CHRISTY (*with agitation*). They're coming. Will you swear to aid and save me for the love of Christ?

WIDOW QUIN (*looks at him for a moment*). If I aid you, will you swear to give me a right of way I want, and a mountainy ram, and a load of dung at Michaelmas, the time that you'll be master here?

CHRISTY. I will, by the elements and stars of night.

WIDOW QUIN. Then we'll not say a word of the old fellow, the way Pegeen won't know your story till the end of time.

CHRISTY. And if he chances to return again?

WIDOW QUIN. We'll swear he's a maniac and not your da. I could take an oath I seen him raving on the sands to-day.

[*Girls run in.*]

SUSAN. Come on to the sports below. Pegeen says you're to come.

SARA TANSEY. The lepping's beginning, and we've a jockey's suit to fit upon you for the mule race on the sands below.

HONOR. Come on, will you?

CHRISTY. I will then if Pegeen's beyond.

SARA TANSEY. She's in the boreen making game of Shaneen Keogh.

CHRISTY. Then I'll be going to her now.

[*He runs out followed by the girls.*]

WIDOW QUIN. Well, if the worst comes in the end of all, it'll be great game to see there's none to pity him but a widow woman, the like of me, has buried her children and destroyed her man.

[*She goes out.*]

CURTAIN

ACT III

SCENE, *as before. Later in the day. Jimmy comes in, slightly drunk.*

JIMMY (*calls*). Pegeen! (*Crosses to inner door.*) Pegeen Mike! (*Comes back again into the room.*) Pegeen! (*Philly comes in in the same state.*) (*To Philly.*) Did you see herself?

PHILLY. I did not; but I sent Shawn Keogh with the ass cart for to bear him home. (*Trying cupboards which are locked.*) Well, isn't he a nasty man to get into such staggers at a morning wake? and isn't herself the divil's daughter for locking, and she so fussy after that young gaffer, you might take your death with drought and none to heed you?

JIMMY. It's little wonder she'd be fussy, and he after bringing bankrupt ruin on the roulette man, and the trick-o'-the-loop man, and breaking the nose of the cockshot-man, and winning all in the sports below, racing, lepping, dancing, and the Lord knows what! He's right luck, I'm telling you.

PHILLY. If he has, he'll be rightly hobbled yet, and he not able to say ten words without making a brag of the way he killed his father, and the great blow he hit with the loy.

JIMMY. A man can't hang by his own informing, and his father should be rotten by now.

[Old Mahon passes window slowly.]

PHILLY. Supposing a man's digging spuds in that field with a long spade, and supposing he flings up the two halves of that skull, what'll be said then in the papers and the courts of law?

JIMMY. They'd say it was an old Dane, maybe, was drowned in the flood. (Old Mahon comes in and sits down near door listening.) Did you never hear tell of the skulls they have in the city of Dublin, ranged out like blue jugs in a cabin of Connaught?

PHILLY. And you believe that?

JIMMY (pugnaciously). Didn't a lad see them and he after coming from harvesting in the Liverpool boat? "They have them there," says he, "making a show of the great people there was one time walking the world. White skulls and black skulls and yellow skulls, and some with full teeth, and some haven't only but one."

PHILLY. It was no lie, maybe, for when I was a young lad there was a graveyard beyond the house with the remnants of a man who had thighs as long as your arm. He was a horrid man, I'm telling you, and there was many a fine Sunday I'd put him together for fun, and he with shiny bones, you wouldn't meet the like of these days in the cities of the world.

MAHON (*getting up*). You wouldn't, is it? Lay your eyes on that skull, and tell me where and when there was another the like of it, is splintered only from the blow of a loy.

PHILLY. Glory be to God! And who hit you at all?

MAHON (*triumphantly*). It was my own son hit me. Would you believe that?

JIMMY. Well, there's wonders hidden in the heart of man!

PHILLY (*suspiciously*). And what way was it done?

MAHON (*wandering about the room*). I'm after walking hundreds and long scores of miles, winning clean beds and the fill of my belly four times in the day, and I doing nothing but telling stories of that naked truth. (*He comes to them a little aggressively.*) Give me a supeen and I'll tell you now.

[*Widow Quin comes in and stands aghast behind him. He is facing Jimmy and Philly, who are on the left.*]

JIMMY. Ask herself beyond. She's the stuff hidden in her shawl.

WIDOW QUIN (*coming to Mahon quickly*). You here, is it? You didn't go far at all?

MAHON. I seen the coasting steamer passing, and I got a drought upon me and a cramping leg, so I said, "The divil go along with him," and turned again. (*Looking under her shawl.*) And let you give me a supeen, for I'm destroyed travelling since Tuesday was a week.

WIDOW QUIN (*getting a glass, in a cajoling tone*). Sit down then by the fire and take your ease for a space. You've a right to be destroyed indeed, with your walking, and fighting, and facing the sun (*giving him poteen from a stone jar she has brought in*). There now is a drink for you, and may it be to your happiness and length of life.

MAHON (*taking glass greedily and sitting down by fire*). God increase you!

WIDOW QUIN (*taking men to the right stealthily*). Do you know what? That man's raving from his wound to-day, for I met him a while since telling a rambling tale of a tinker had him destroyed. Then he heard of Christy's deed, and he up and says it was his son had cracked his skull. O isn't madness a fright, for he'll go killing someone yet, and he thinking it's the man has struck him so?

JIMMY (*entirely convinced*). It's a fright, surely. I knew a party was kicked in the head by a red mare, and he went killing horses a great while, till he eat the insides of a clock and died after.

PHILLY (*with suspicion*). Did he see Christy?

WIDOW QUIN. He didn't. (*With a warning gesture.*) Let you not be putting him in mind of him, or you'll be likely summoned if there's murder done. (*Looking round at Mahon.*) Whisht! He's listening. Wait now till you hear me taking him easy and unravelling all. (*She goes to Mahon.*) And what way are you feeling, mister? Are you in contentment now?

MAHON (*slightly emotional from his drink*). I'm poorly only, for it's a hard story the way I'm left to-day, when it was I did tend him from his hour of birth, and he a dunce never reached his second book, the way he'd come from school, many's the day, with his legs lamed under him, and he blackened with his beatings like a tinker's ass. It's a hard story, I'm saying, the way some do have their next and nighest raising up a hand of murder on them, and some is lonesome getting their death with lamentation in the dead of night.

WIDOW QUIN (*not knowing what to say*). To hear you talking so quiet, who'd know you were the same fellow we seen pass to-day?

MAHON. I'm the same surely. The wrack and ruin of three score years; and it's a terror to live that length, I tell you, and to have your sons going to the dogs against you, and you wore out scolding them, and skelping them, and God knows what.

PHILLY (*to Jimmy*). He's not raving. (*To Widow Quin.*) Will you ask him what kind was his son?

WIDOW QUIN (*to Mahon, with a peculiar look*). Was your son that hit you a lad of one year and a score maybe, a great hand at racing and lepping and licking the world?

MAHON (*turning on her with a roar of rage*). Didn't you hear me say he was the fool of men, the way from this out he'll know the orphan's lot with old and young making game of him and they swearing, raging, kicking at him like a mangy cur.

[*A great burst of cheering outside, some way off.*]

MAHON (*putting his hands to his ears*). What in the name of God do they want roaring below?

WIDOW QUIN (*with the shade of a smile*). They're cheering a young lad, the champion Playboy of the Western World.

[*More cheering.*]

MAHON (*going to window*). It'd split my heart to hear them, and I with pulses in my brain-pan for a week gone by. Is it racing they are?

JIMMY (*looking from door*). It is then. They are mounting him for the mule race will be run upon the sands. That's the playboy on the winkered mule.

MAHON (*puzzled*). That lad, is it? If you said it was a fool he was, I'd have laid a mighty oath he was the likeness of my wandering son (*uneasily, putting his hand to his head*). Faith, I'm thinking I'll go walking for to view the race.

WIDOW QUIN (*stopping him, sharply*). You will not. You'd best take the road to Belmullet, and not be dilly-dallying in this place where there isn't a spot you could sleep.

PHILLY (*coming forward*). Don't mind her. Mount there on the bench and you'll have a view of the whole. They're hurrying before the tide will rise, and it'd be near over if you went down the pathway through the crags below.

MAHON (*mounts on bench, Widow Quin beside him*). That's a right view again the edge of the sea. They're coming now from the point. He's leading. Who is he at all?

WIDOW QUIN. He's the champion of the world, I tell you, and there isn't a hop'orth isn't falling lucky to his hands to-day.

PHILLY (*looking out, interested in the race*). Look at that. They're pressing him now.

JIMMY. He'll win it yet.

PHILLY. Take your time, Jimmy Farrell. It's too soon to say.

WIDOW QUIN (*shouting*). Watch him taking the gate. There's riding.

JIMMY (*cheering*). More power to the young lad!

MAHON. He's passing the third.

JIMMY. He'll lick them yet!

WIDOW QUIN. He'd lick them if he was running races with a score itself.

MAHON. Look at the mule he has, kicking the stars.

WIDOW QUIN. There was a lep! (*Catching hold of Mahon in her excitement.*) He's fallen! He's mounted again! Faith, he's passing them all!

JIMMY. Look at him skelping her!

PHILLY. And the mountain girls hooshing him on!

JIMMY. It's the last turn! The post's cleared for them now!

MAHON. Look at the narrow place. He'll be into the bogs! (*With a yell.*) Good rider! He's through it again!

JIMMY. He neck and neck!

MAHON. Good boy to him! Flames, but he's in!

[*Great cheering, in which all join.*]

MAHON (*with hesitation*). What's that? They're raising him up. They're coming this way. (*With a roar of rage and astonishment.*) It's Christy! by the stars of God! I'd know his way of spitting and he astride the moon.

[*He jumps down and makes for the door, but Widow Quin catches him and pulls him back.*]

WIDOW QUIN. Stay quiet, will you. That's not your son.

(*To Jimmy.*) Stop him, or you'll get a month for the abetting of manslaughter and be fined as well.

JIMMY. I'll hold him.

MAHON (*struggling*). Let me out! Let me out, the lot of you! till I have my vengeance on his head to-day.

WIDOW QUIN (*shaking him, vehemently*). That's not your son. That's a man is going to make a marriage with the daughter of this house, a place with fine trade, with a license, and with poteen too.

MAHON (*amazed*). That man marrying a decent and a moneyed girl! Is it mad yous are? Is it in a crazy-house for females that I'm landed now?

WIDOW QUIN. It's mad yourself is with the blow upon your head. That lad is the wonder of the Western World.

MAHON. I seen it's my son.

WIDOW QUIN. You seen that you're mad. (*Cheering outside.*) Do you hear them cheering him in the zig-zags of the road? Aren't you after saying that your son's a fool, and how would they be cheering a true idiot born?

MAHON (*getting distressed*). It's maybe out of reason that that man's himself. (*Cheering again.*) There's none surely will go cheering him. Oh, I'm raving with a madness that would fright the world! (*He sits down with his hand to his head.*) There was one time I seen ten scarlet divils letting on they'd cork my spirit in a gallon can; and one time I seen rats as big as badgers sucking the life blood from the butt of my lug; but I never till this day confused that dribbling idiot with a likely man. I'm destroyed surely.

WIDOW QUIN. And who'd wonder when it's your brain-pan that is gaping now?

MAHON. Then the blight of the sacred drought upon myself and him, for I never went mad to this day, and I not three weeks with the Limerick girls drinking myself silly, and parlatic from the dusk to dawn. (*To Widow Quin, suddenly.*) Is my visage astray?

WIDOW QUIN. It is then. You're a sniggering maniac, a child could see.

MAHON (*getting up more cheerfully*). Then I'd best be going to the union beyond, and there'll be a welcome before me, I tell you (*with great pride*), and I a terrible and fearful case, the way that there I was one time, screeching in a straitened waistcoat, with seven doctors writing out my sayings in a printed book. Would you believe that?

WIDOW QUIN. If you're a wonder itself, you'd best be hasty, for them lads caught a maniac one time and pelted the poor creature till he ran out, raving and foaming, and was drowned in the sea.

MAHON (*with philosophy*). It's true mankind is the divil when your head's astray. Let me out now and I'll slip down the boreen, and not see them so.

WIDOW QUIN (*showing him out*). That's it. Run to the right, and not a one will see.

[*He runs off.*]

PHILLY (*wisely*). You're at some gaming, Widow Quin; but I'll walk after him and give him his dinner and a time to rest, and I'll see then if he's raving or as sane as you.

WIDOW QUIN (*annoyed*). If you go near that lad, let you be wary of your head, I'm saying. Didn't you hear him telling he was crazed at times?

PHILLY. I heard him telling a power; and I'm thinking we'll have right sport, before night will fall.

[*He goes out.*]

JIMMY. Well, Philly's a conceited and foolish man. How could that madman have his senses and his brain-pan slit? I'll go after them and see him turn on Philly now.

[*He goes; Widow Quin hides poteen behind counter. Then hubbub outside.*]

VOICES. There you are! Good jumper! Grand lepper! Darlint boy! He's the racer! Bear him on, will you!

[*Christy comes in, in Jockey's dress, with Pegeen Mike, Sara, and other girls, and men.*]

PEGEEN (*to crowd*). Go on now and don't destroy him and he drenching with sweat. Go along, I'm saying, and have your tug-of-warring till he's dried his skin.

CROWD. Here's his prizes! A bagpipes! A fiddle was played by a poet in the years gone by! A flat and three-thorned blackthorn would lick the scholars out of Dublin town!

CHRISTY (*taking prizes from the men*). Thank you kindly, the lot of you. But you'd say it was little only I did this day if you'd seen me a while since striking my one single blow.

TOWN CRIER (*outside, ringing a bell*). Take notice, last event of this day! Tug-of-warring on the green below! Come on, the lot of you! Great achievements for all Mayo men!

PEGEEN. Go on, and leave him for to rest and dry. Go on, I tell you, for he'll do no more. (*She hustles crowd out; Widow Quin following them.*)

MEN (*going*). Come on then. Good luck for the while!

PEGEEN (*radiantly, wiping his face with her shawl*). Well, you're the lad, and you'll have great times from this out when you could win that wealth of prizes, and you sweating in the heat of noon!

CHRISTY (*looking at her with delight*). I'll have great times if I win the crowning prize I'm seeking now, and that's your promise that you'll wed me in a fortnight, when our banns is called.

PEGEEN (*backing away from him*). You've right daring to go ask me that, when all knows you'll be starting to some girl in your own townland, when your father's rotten in four months, or five.

CHRISTY (*indignantly*). Starting from you, is it? (*He follows her.*) I will not, then, and when the airs is warming in four months, or five, it's then yourself and me should be pacing Neifin in the dews of night, the times sweet smells do be rising, and you'd see a little shiny new moon, maybe, sinking on the hills.

PEGEEN (*looking at him playfully*). And it's that kind of a poacher's love you'd make, Christy Mahon, on the sides of Neifin, when the night is down?

CHRISTY. It's little you'll think if my love's a poacher's, or an earl's itself, when you'll feel my two hands stretched around you, and I squeezing kisses on your puckered lips, till I'd feel a kind of pity for the Lord God is all ages sitting lonesome in his golden chair.

PEGEEN. That'll be right fun, Christy Mahon, and any girl would walk her heart out before she'd meet a young man was your like for eloquence, or talk, at all.

CHRISTY (*encouraged*). Let you wait, to hear me talking, till we're astray in Erris, when Good Friday's by, drinking a sup from a well, and making mighty kisses with our wetted mouths, or gaming in a gap or sunshine, with yourself stretched back unto your necklace, in the flowers of the earth.

PEGEEN (*in a lower voice, moved by his tone*). I'd be nice so, is it?

CHRISTY (*with rapture*). If the mitred bishops seen you that time, they'd be the like of the holy prophets, I'm thinking, do be straining the bars of Paradise to lay eyes on the Lady Helen of Troy, and she abroad, pacing back and forward, with a nosegay in her golden shawl.

PEGEEN (*with real tenderness*). And what is it I have, Christy Mahon, to make me fitting entertainment for the like of you, that has such poet's talking, and such bravery of heart?

CHRISTY (*in a low voice*). Isn't there the light of seven heavens in your heart alone, the way you'll be an angel's lamp to me from this out, and I abroad in the darkness, spearing salmons in the Owen, or the Carrowmore?

PEGEEN. If I was your wife, I'd be along with you those nights, Christy Mahon, the way you'd see I was a great hand at coaxing bailiffs, or coining funny nick-names for the stars of night.

CHRISTY. You, is it? Taking your death in the hailstones, or in the fogs of dawn.

PEGEEN. Yourself and me would shelter easy in a narrow bush, (*with a qualm of dread*) but we're only talking, maybe, for this would be a poor, thatched place to hold a fine lad is the like of you.

CHRISTY (*putting his arm round her*). If I wasn't a good Christian, it's on my naked knees I'd be saying my prayers and paters to every jackstraw you have roofing your head, and every stony pebble is paving the laneway to your door.

PEGEEN (*radiantly*). If that's the truth, I'll be burning candles from this out to the miracles of God that have brought you from the south to-day, and I, with my gowns bought ready, the way that I can wed you, and not wait at all.

CHRISTY. It's miracles, and that's the truth. Me there toiling a long while, and walking a long while, not knowing at all I was drawing all times nearer to this holy day.

PEGEEN. And myself, a girl, was tempted often to go sailing the seas till I'd marry a Jew-man, with ten kegs of gold, and I not knowing at all there was the like of you drawing nearer, like the stars of God.

CHRISTY. And to think I'm long years hearing women talking that talk, to all bloody fools, and this the first time I've heard the like of your voice talking sweetly for my own delight.

PEGEEN. And to think it's me is talking sweetly, Christy Mahon, and I the fright of seven townlands for my biting tongue. Well, the heart's a wonder; and, I'm thinking, there won't be our like in Mayo, for gallant lovers, from this hour, to-day. (*Drunken singing is heard outside.*) There's my father coming from the wake, and when he's had his sleep we'll tell him, for he's peaceful then.

[*They separate.*]

MICHAEL (*singing outside*).
          The jailor and the turnkey
              They quickly ran us down,

And brought us back as prisoners
Once more to Cavan town.

[*He comes in supported by Shawn.*]

There we lay bewailing
All in a prison bound. . . .

[*He sees Christy. Goes and shakes him drunkenly by
the hand, while Pegeen and Shawn talk on the left.*]

MICHAEL (*to Christy*). The blessing of God and the
holy angels on your head, young fellow. I hear tell
you're after winning all in the sports below; and wasn't
it a shame I didn't bear you along with me to Kate Cassidy's wake, a fine, stout lad, the like of you, for you'd
never see the match of it for flows of drink, the way
when we sunk her bones at noonday in her narrow
grave, there were five men, aye, and six men, stretched
out retching speechless on the holy stones.

CHRISTY (*uneasily, watching Pegeen*). Is that the
truth?

MICHAEL. It is then, and aren't you a louty schemer to
go burying your poor father unbeknownst when you'd
a right to throw him on the crupper of a Kerry mule and
drive him westwards, like holy Joseph in the days gone
by, the way we could have given him a decent burial,
and not have him rotting beyond, and not a Christian
drinking a smart drop to the glory of his soul?

CHRISTY (*gruffly*). It's well enough he's lying, for the
likes of him.

MICHAEL (*slapping him on the back*). Well, aren't you
a hardened slayer? It'll be a poor thing for the household man where you go sniffing for a female wife; and
(*pointing to Shawn*) look beyond at that shy and decent
Christian I have chosen for my daughter's hand, and I

after getting the gilded dispensation this day for to wed them now.

CHRISTY. And you'll be wedding them this day, is it?

MICHAEL (*drawing himself up*). Aye. Are you thinking, if I'm drunk itself, I'd leave my daughter living single with a little frisky rascal is the like of you?

PEGEEN (*breaking away from Shawn*). Is it the truth the dispensation's come?

MICHAEL (*triumphantly*). Father Reilly's after reading it in gallous Latin, and "It's come in the nick of time," says he; "so I'll wed them in a hurry, dreading that young gaffer who'd capsize the stars."

PEGEEN (*fiercely*). He's missed his nick of time, for it's that lad, Christy Mahon, that I'm wedding now.

MICHAEL (*loudly with horror*). You'd be making him a son to me, and he wet and crusted with his father's blood?

PEGEEN. Aye. Wouldn't it be a bitter thing for a girl to go marrying the like of Shaneen, and he a middling kind of a scarecrow, with no savagery or fine words in him at all?

MICHAEL (*gasping and sinking on a chair*). Oh, aren't you a heathen daughter to go shaking the fat of my heart, and I swamped and drownded with the weight of drink? Would you have them turning on me the way that I'd be roaring to the dawn of day with the wind upon my heart? Have you not a word to aid me, Shaneen? Are you not jealous at all?

SHANEEN (*in great misery*). I'd be afeard to be jealous of a man did slay his da.

PEGEEN. Well, it'd be a poor thing to go marrying your like. I'm seeing there's a world of peril for an orphan girl, and isn't it a great blessing I didn't wed you, before himself came walking from the west or south?

SHAWN. It's a queer story you'd go picking a dirty tramp up from the highways of the world.

PEGEEN (*playfully*). And you think you're a likely beau to go straying along with, the shiny Sundays of the opening year, when it's sooner on a bullock's liver you'd put a poor girl thinking than on the lily or the rose?

SHAWN. And have you no mind of my weight of passion, and the holy dispensation, and the drift of heifers I am giving, and the golden ring?

PEGEEN. I'm thinking you're too fine for the like of me, Shawn Keogh of Killakeen, and let you go off till you'd find a radiant lady with droves of bullocks on the plains of Meath, and herself bedizened in the diamond jewelleries of Pharaoh's ma. That'd be your match, Shaneen. So God save you now!

[*She retreats behind Christy.*]

SHAWN. Won't you hear me telling you . . . ?

CHRISTY (*with ferocity*). Take yourself from this, young fellow, or I'll maybe add a murder to my deeds to-day.

MICHAEL (*springing up with a shriek*). Murder is it? Is it mad yous are? Would you go making murder in this place, and it piled with poteen for our drink to-night? Go on to the foreshore if it's fighting you want, where the rising tide will wash all traces from the memory of man.

[*Pushing Shawn towards Christy.*]

SHAWN (*shaking himself free, and getting behind Michael*). I'll not fight him, Michael James. I'd liefer live a bachelor, simmering in passions to the end of time, than face a lepping savage the like of him has descended from the Lord knows where. Strike him yourself, Michael James, or you'll lose my drift of heifers and my blue bull from Sneem.

MICHAEL. Is it me fight him, when it's father-slaying he's bred to now? (*Pushing Shawn.*) Go on you fool and fight him now.

SHAWN (*coming forward a little*). Will I strike him with my hand?

MICHAEL. Take the loy is on your western side.

SHAWN. I'd be afeard of the gallows if I struck him with that.

CHRISTY (*taking up the loy*). Then I'll make you face the gallows or quit off from this.

[*Shawn flies out of the door.*]

CHRISTY. Well, fine weather be after him, (*going to Michael, coaxingly*) and I'm thinking you wouldn't wish to have that quaking blackguard in your house at all. Let you give us your blessing and hear her swear her faith to me, for I'm mounted on the springtide of the stars of luck, the way it'll be good for any to have me in the house.

PEGEEN (*at the other side of Michael*). Bless us now, for I swear to God I'll wed him, and I'll not renege.

MICHAEL (*standing up in the centre, holding on to both of them*). It's the will of God, I'm thinking, that all should win an easy or a cruel end, and it's the will of God that all should rear up lengthy families for the nurture of the earth. What's a single man, I ask you, eating a bit in one house and drinking a sup in another, and he with no place of his own, like an old braying jackass strayed upon the rocks? (*To Christy.*) It's many would be in dread to bring your like into their house for to end them, maybe, with a sudden end; but I'm a decent man of Ireland, and I liefer face the grave untimely and I seeing a score of grandsons growing up little gallant swearers by the name of God, than go peopling my bedside with puny weeds the like of what you'd breed, I'm thinking, out of Shaneen Keogh. (*He joins their hands.*) A daring fellow is the jewel of the world, and a man did split his father's middle with a single clout, should have the bravery of ten, so may God and Mary and St. Patrick bless you, and increase you from this mortal day.

CHRISTY AND PEGEEN. Amen, O Lord!

[*Hubbub outside.*]

[*Old Mahon rushes in, followed by all the crowd, and Widow Quin. He makes a rush at Christy, knocks him down, and begins to beat him.*]

PEGEEN (*dragging back his arm*). Stop that, will you. Who are you at all?

MAHON. His father, God forgive me!

PEGEEN (*drawing back*). Is it rose from the dead?

MAHON. Do you think I look so easy quenched with the tap of a loy?

[*Beats Christy again.*]

PEGEEN (*glaring at Christy*). And it's lies you told, letting on you had him slitted, and you nothing at all.

CHRISTY (*catching Mahon's stick*). He's not my father. He's a raving maniac would scare the world. (*Pointing to Widow Quin.*) Herself knows it is true.

CROWD. You're fooling Pegeen! The Widow Quin seen him this day, and you likely knew! You're a liar!

CHRISTY (*dumbfounded*). It's himself was a liar, lying stretched out with an open head on him, letting on he was dead.

MAHON. Weren't you off racing the hills before I got my breath with the start I had seeing you turn on me at all?

PEGEEN. And to think of the coaxing glory we had given him, and he after doing nothing but hitting a soft blow and chasing northward in a sweat of fear. Quit off from this.

CHRISTY (*piteously*). You've seen my doings this day, and let you save me from the old man; for why would you be in such a scorch of haste to spur me to destruction now?

PEGEEN. It's there your treachery is spurring me, till I'm hard set to think you're the one I'm after lacing in my heart-strings half-an-hour gone by. (*To Mahon.*) Take him on from this, for I think bad the world should see me raging for a Munster liar, and the fool of men.

MAHON. Rise up now to retribution, and come on with me.

CROWD (*jeeringly*). There's the playboy! There's the lad thought he'd rule the roost in Mayo. Slate him now, mister.

CHRISTY (*getting up in shy terror*). What is it drives you to torment me here, when I'd asked the thunders of the might of God to blast me if I ever did hurt to any saving only that one single blow.

MAHON (*loudly*). If you didn't, you're a poor good-for-nothing, and isn't it by the like of you the sins of the whole world are committed?

CHRISTY (*raising his hands*). In the name of the Almighty God. . . .

MAHON. Leave troubling the Lord God. Would you have him sending down droughts, and fevers, and the old hen and the cholera morbus?

CHRISTY (*to Widow Quin*). Will you come between us and protect me now?

WIDOW QUIN. I've tried a lot, God help me, and my share is done.

CHRISTY (*looking round in desperation*). And I must go back into my torment is it, or run off like a vagabond straying through the Unions with the dusts of August making mudstains in the gullet of my throat, or the winds of March blowing on me till I'd take an oath I felt them making whistles of my ribs within?

SARA. Ask Pegeen to aid you. Her like does often change.

CHRISTY. I will not then, for there's torment in the splendour of her like, and she a girl any moon of midnight would take pride to meet, facing southwards on the heaths of Keel. But what did I want crawling forward to scorch my understanding at her flaming brow?

PEGEEN (*to Mahon, vehemently, fearing she will break into tears*). Take him on from this or I'll set the young lads to destroy him here.

MAHON (*going to him, shaking his stick*). Come on now if you wouldn't have the company to see you skelped.

PEGEEN (*half laughing, through her tears*). That's it, now the world will see him pandied, and he an ugly liar was playing off the hero, and the fright of men.

CHRISTY (*to Mahon, very sharply*). Leave me go!

CROWD. That's it. Now Christy. If them two set fighting, it will lick the world.

MAHON (*making a grab at Christy*). Come here to me.

CHRISTY (*more threateningly*). Leave me go, I'm saying.

MAHON. I will maybe, when your legs is limping, and your back is blue.

CROWD. Keep it up, the two of you. I'll back the old one. Now the playboy.

CHRISTY (*in low and intense voice*). Shut your yelling, for if you're after making a mighty man of me this day by the power of a lie, you're setting me now to think if it's a poor thing to be lonesome, it's worse maybe to go mixing with the fools of earth.

[*Mahon makes a movement towards him.*]

CHRISTY (*almost shouting*). Keep off . . . lest I do show a blow unto the lot of you would set the guardian angels winking in the clouds above.

[*He swings round with a sudden rapid movement and picks up a loy.*]

CROWD (*half frightened, half amused*). He's going mad! Mind yourselves! Run from the idiot!

CHRISTY. If I am an idiot, I'm after hearing my voice this day saying words would raise the topknot on a poet in a merchant's town. I've won your racing, and your lepping, and . . .

MAHON. Shut your gullet and come on with me.

CHRISTY. I'm going, but I'll stretch you first.

[*He runs at old Mahon with the loy, chases him out of the door, followed by crowd and Widow Quin. There is a great noise outside, then a yell, and dead silence for a moment. Christy comes in, half dazed, and goes to fire.*]

WIDOW QUIN (*coming in, hurriedly, and going to him*). They're turning again you. Come on, or you'll be hanged, indeed.

CHRISTY. I'm thinking, from this out, Pegeen'll be giving me praises the same as in the hours gone by.

WIDOW QUIN (*impatiently*). Come by the back-door. I'd think bad to have you stifled on the gallows tree.

CHRISTY (*indignantly*). I will not, then. What good'd be my life-time, if I left Pegeen?

WIDOW QUIN. Come on, and you'll be no worse than you were last night; and you with a double murder this time to be telling to the girls.

CHRISTY. I'll not leave Pegeen Mike.

WIDOW QUIN (*impatiently*). Isn't there the match of her in every parish public, from Binghamstown unto the plain of Meath? Come on, I tell you, and I'll find you finer sweethearts at each waning moon.

CHRISTY. It's Pegeen I'm seeking only, and what'd I care if you brought me a drift of chosen females, standing in their shifts itself, maybe, from this place to the Eastern World?

SARA (*runs in, pulling off one of her petticoats*). They're going to hang him. (*Holding out petticoat and shawl.*) Fit these upon him, and let him run off to the east.

WIDOW QUIN. He's raving now; but we'll fit them on him, and I'll take him, in the ferry, to the Achill boat.

CHRISTY (*struggling feebly*). Leave me go, will you? when I'm thinking of my luck to-day, for she will wed me surely, and I a proven hero in the end of all.

[*They try to fasten petticoat round him.*]

WIDOW QUIN. Take his left hand, and we'll pull him now. Come on, young fellow.

CHRISTY (*suddenly starting up*).You'll be taking me from her? You're jealous, is it, of her wedding me? Go on from this.

[*He snatches up a stool, and threatens them with it.*]

WIDOW QUIN (*going*). It's in the mad-house they should put him, not in jail, at all. We'll go by the back-door, to call the doctor, and we'll save him so.

[*She goes out, with Sara, through inner room. Men crowd in the doorway. Christy sits down again by the fire.*]

MICHAEL (*in a terrified whisper*). Is the old lad killed surely?

PHILLY. I'm after feeling the last gasps quitting his heart.

[*They peer in at Christy.*]

MICHAEL (*with a rope*). Look at the way he is. Twist a hangman's knot on it, and slip it over his head, while he's not minding at all.

PHILLY. Let you take it, Shaneen. You're the soberest of all that's here.

SHAWN. Is it me to go near him, and he the wickedest and worst with me? Let you take it, Pegeen Mike.

PEGEEN. Come on, so.

[*She goes forward with the others, and they drop the double hitch over his head.*]

CHRISTY. What ails you?

SHAWN (*triumphantly, as they pull the rope tight on his arms*). Come on to the peelers, till they stretch you now.

CHRISTY. Me!

MICHAEL. If we took pity on you, the Lord God would, maybe, bring us ruin from the law to-day, so you'd best come easy, for hanging is an easy and a speedy end.

CHRISTY. I'll not stir. (*To Pegeen.*) And what is it you'll say to me, and I after doing it this time in the face of all?

PEGEEN. I'll say, a strange man is a marvel, with his mighty talk; but what's a squabble in your back-yard, and the blow of a loy, have taught me that there's a great gap between a gallous story and a dirty deed. (*To Men.*) Take him on from this, or the lot of us will be likely put on trial for his deed to-day.

CHRISTY (*with horror in his voice*). And it's yourself will send me off, to have a horny-fingered hangman hitching his bloody slip-knots at the butt of my ear.

MEN (*pulling rope*). Come on, will you?

[*He is pulled down on the floor.*]

CHRISTY (*twisting his legs round the table*). Cut the rope, Pegeen, and I'll quit the lot of you, and live from this out, like the madmen of Keel, eating muck and green weeds, on the faces of the cliffs.

PEGEEN. And leave us to hang, is it, for a saucy liar, the like of you? (*To Men.*) Take him on, out from this.

SHAWN. Pull a twist on his neck, and squeeze him so.

PHILLY. Twist yourself. Sure he cannot hurt you, if you keep your distance from his teeth alone.

SHAWN. I'm afeard of him. (*To Pegeen.*) Lift a lighted sod, will you, and scorch his leg.

PEGEEN (*blowing the fire, with a bellows*). Leave go now, young fellow, or I'll scorch your shins.

CHRISTY. You're blowing for to torture me. (*His voice rising and growing stronger.*) That's your kind, is it? Then let the lot of you be wary, for, if I've to face the gallows, I'll have a gay march down, I tell you, and shed the blood of some of you before I die.

SHAWN (*in terror*). Keep a good hold, Philly. Be wary, for the love of God. For I'm thinking he would liefest wreak his pains on me.

CHRISTY (*almost gaily*). If I do lay my hands on you, it's the way you'll be at the fall of night, hanging as a scarecrow for the fowls of hell. Ah, you'll have a gallous jaunt I'm saying, coaching out through Limbo with my father's ghost.

SHAWN (*to Pegeen*). Make haste, will you? Oh, isn't he a holy terror, and isn't it true for Father Reilly, that all drink's a curse that has the lot of you so shaky and uncertain now?

CHRISTY. If I can wring a neck among you, I'll have a royal judgment looking on the trembling jury in the courts of law. And won't there be crying out in Mayo the day I'm stretched upon the rope with ladies in their silks and satins snivelling in their lacy kerchiefs, and they rhyming songs and ballads on the terror of my fate?

[*He squirms round on the floor and bites Shawn's leg.*]

SHAWN (*shrieking*). My leg's bit on me. He's the like

of a mad dog, I'm thinking, the way that I will surely die.

CHRISTY (*delighted with himself*). You will then, the way you can shake out hell's flags of welcome for my coming in two weeks or three, for I'm thinking Satan hasn't many have killed their da in Kerry, and in Mayo too.

[*Old Mahon comes in behind on all fours and looks on unnoticed.*]

MEN (*to Pegeen*). Bring the sod, will you?

PEGEEN (*coming over*). God help him so. (*Burns his leg.*)

CHRISTY (*kicking and screaming*). O, glory be to God!

[*He kicks loose from the table, and they all drag him towards the door.*]

JIMMY (*seeing old Mahon*). Will you look what's come in?

[*They all drop Christy and run left.*]

CHRISTY (*scrambling on his knees face to face with old Mahon*). Are you coming to be killed a third time, or what ails you now?

MAHON. For what is it they have you tied?

CHRISTY. They're taking me to the peelers to have me hanged for slaying you.

MICHAEL (*apologetically*). It is the will of God that all should guard their little cabins from the treachery of law, and what would my daughter be doing if I was ruined or was hanged itself?

MAHON (*grimly, loosening Christy*). It's little I care if you put a bag on her back, and went picking cockles till the hour of death; but my son and myself will be going our own way, and we'll have great times from this out telling stories of the villainy of Mayo, and the fools is here. (*To Christy, who is freed.*) Come on now.

CHRISTY. Go with you, is it? I will then, like a gallant captain with his heathen slave. Go on now and I'll see you from this day stewing my oatmeal and washing my spuds, for I'm master of all fights from now. (*Pushing Mahon.*) Go on, I'm saying.

MAHON. Is it me?

CHRISTY. Not a word out of you. Go on from this.

MAHON (*walking out and looking back at Christy over his shoulder*). Glory be to God! (*With a broad smile.*) I am crazy again!

[*Goes.*]

CHRISTY. Ten thousand blessings upon all that's here, for you've turned me a likely gaffer in the end of all, the way I'll go romancing through a romping lifetime from this hour to the dawning of the judgment day.

[*He goes out.*]

MICHAEL. By the will of God, we'll have peace now for our drinks. Will you draw the porter, Pegeen?

SHAWN (*going up to her*). It's a miracle Father Reilly can wed us in the end of all, and we'll have none to trouble us when his vicious bite is healed.

PEGEEN (*hitting him a box on the ear*). Quit my sight. (*Putting her shawl over her head and breaking out into wild lamentations.*) Oh my grief, I've lost him surely. I've lost the only Playboy of the Western World.

CURTAIN

RIDERS TO THE SEA

A PLAY IN ONE ACT

PERSONS IN THE PLAY

First performed at the Molesworth Hall, Dublin,
February 25, 1904.

MAURYA (*an old woman*)	Honor Lavelle
BARTLEY (*her son*)	W. G. Fay
CATHLEEN (*her daughter*)	Sarah Allgood
NORA (*a younger daughter*)	Emma Vernon
MEN and WOMEN	

RIDERS TO THE SEA

SCENE. *An Island off the West of Ireland.*

(*Cottage kitchen, with nets, oil-skins, spinning wheel, some new boards standing by the wall, etc. Cathleen, a girl of about twenty, finishes kneading cake, and puts it down in the pot-oven by the fire; then wipes her hands, and begins to spin at the wheel. Nora, a young girl, puts her head in at the door.*)

NORA (*in a low voice*). Where is she?

CATHLEEN. She's lying down, God help her, and may be sleeping, if she's able.

[*Nora comes in softly, and takes a bundle from under her shawl.*]

CATHLEEN (*spinning the wheel rapidly*). What is it you have?

NORA. The young priest is after bringing them. It's a shirt and a plain stocking were got off a drowned man in Donegal.

[*Cathleen stops her wheel with a sudden movement, and leans out to listen.*]

NORA. We're to find out if it's Michael's they are, some time herself will be down looking by the sea.

CATHLEEN. How would they be Michael's, Nora. How would he go the length of that way to the far north?

NORA. The young priest says he's known the like of it. "If it's Michael's they are," says he, "you can tell herself he's got a clean burial by the grace of God, and if they're not his, let no one say a word about them, for she'll be getting her death," says he, "with crying and lamenting."

[*The door which Nora half closed is blown open by a gust of wind.*]

CATHLEEN (*looking out anxiously*). Did you ask him would he stop Bartley going this day with the horses to the Galway fair?

NORA. "I won't stop him," says he, "but let you not be afraid. Herself does be saying prayers half through the night, and the Almighty God won't leave her destitute," says he, "with no son living."

CATHLEEN. Is the sea bad by the white rocks, Nora?

NORA. Middling bad, God help us. There's a great roaring in the west, and it's worse it'll be getting when the tide's turned to the wind.

[*She goes over to the table with the bundle.*]

Shall I open it now?

CATHLEEN. Maybe she'd wake up on us, and come in before we'd done. (*Coming to the table.*) It's a long time we'll be, and the two of us crying.

NORA (*goes to the inner door and listens*). She's moving about on the bed. She'll be coming in a minute.

CATHLEEN. Give me the ladder, and I'll put them up in the turf-loft, the way she won't know of them at all, and maybe when the tide turns she'll be going down to see would he be floating from the east.

[*They put the ladder against the gable of the chimney; Cathleen goes up a few steps and hides the bundle in the turf-loft. Maurya comes from the inner room.*]

MAURYA (*looking up at Cathleen and speaking querulously*). Isn't it turf enough you have for this day and evening?

CATHLEEN. There's a cake baking at the fire for a short

space (*throwing down the turf*) and Bartley will want it when the tide turns if he goes to Connemara.

[*Nora picks up the turf and puts it round the pot-oven.*]

MAURYA (*sitting down on a stool at the fire*). He won't go this day with the wind rising from the south and west. He won't go this day, for the young priest will stop him surely.

NORA. He'll not stop him, mother, and I heard Eamon Simon and Stephen Pheety and Colum Shawn saying he would go.

MAURYA. Where is he itself?

NORA. He went down to see would there be another boat sailing in the week, and I'm thinking it won't be long till he's here now, for the tide's turning at the green head, and the hooker's tacking from the east.

CATHLEEN. I hear some one passing the big stones.

NORA (*looking out*). He's coming now, and he in a hurry.

BARTLEY (*comes in and looks round the room. Speaking sadly and quietly*). Where is the bit of new rope, Cathleen, was bought in Connemara?

CATHLEEN (*coming down*). Give it to him, Nora; it's on a nail by the white boards. I hung it up this morning, for the pig with the black feet was eating it.

NORA (*giving him a rope*). Is that it, Bartley?

MAURYA. You'd do right to leave that rope, Bartley, hanging by the boards. (*Bartley takes the rope.*) It will be wanting in this place, I'm telling you, if Michael is washed up to-morrow morning, or the next morning, or any morning in the week, for it's a deep grave we'll make him by the grace of God.

BARTLEY (*beginning to work with the rope*). I've no halter the way I can ride down on the mare, and I must go now quickly. This is the one boat going for two weeks or beyond it, and the fair will be a good fair for horses I heard them saying below.

MAURYA. It's a hard thing they'll be saying below if the body is washed up and there's no man in it to make the coffin, and I after giving a big price for the finest white boards you'd find in Connemara.

[*She looks round at the boards.*]

BARTLEY. How would it be washed up, and we after looking each day for nine days, and a strong wind blowing a while back from the west and south?

MAURYA. If it wasn't found itself, that wind is raising the sea, and there was a star up against the moon, and it rising in the night. If it was a hundred horses, or a thousand horses you had itself, what is the price of a thousand horses against a son where there is one son only?

BARTLEY (*working at the halter, to Cathleen*). Let you go down each day, and see the sheep aren't jumping in on the rye, and if the jobber comes you can sell the pig with the black feet if there is a good price going.

MAURYA. How would the like of her get a good price for a pig?

BARTLEY (*to Cathleen*). If the west wind holds with the last bit of the moon let you and Nora get up weed enough for another cock for the kelp. It's hard set we'll be from this day with no one in it but one man to work.

MAURYA. It's hard set we'll be surely the day you're drownd'd with the rest. What way will I live and the girls with me, and I an old woman looking for the grave?

[*Bartley lays down the halter, takes off his old coat, and puts on a newer one of the same flannel.*]

BARTLEY (*to Nora*). Is she coming to the pier?

NORA (*looking out*). She's passing the green head and letting fall her sails.

BARTLEY (*getting his purse and tobacco*). I'll have half an hour to go down, and you'll see me coming again in two days, or in three days, or maybe in four days if the wind is bad.

MAURYA (*turning round to the fire, and putting her shawl over her head*). Isn't it a hard and cruel man won't hear a word from an old woman, and she holding him from the sea?

CATHLEEN. It's the life of a young man to be going on the sea, and who would listen to an old woman with one thing and she saying it over?

BARTLEY (*taking the halter*). I must go now quickly. I'll ride down on the red mare, and the gray pony 'll run behind me. . . . The blessing of God on you.

[*He goes out.*]

MAURYA (*crying out as he is in the door*). He's gone now, God spare us, and we'll not see him again. He's gone now, and when the black night is falling I'll have no son left me in the world.

CATHLEEN. Why wouldn't you give him your blessing and he looking round in the door? Isn't it sorrow enough is on every one in this house without your sending him out with an unlucky word behind him, and a hard word in his ear?

[*Maurya takes up the tongs and begins raking the fire aimlessly without looking round.*]

NORA (*turning towards her*). You're taking away the turf from the cake.

CATHLEEN (*crying out*). The Son of God forgive us, Nora, we're after forgetting his bit of bread.

[*She comes over to the fire.*]

NORA. And it's destroyed he'll be going till dark night, and he after eating nothing since the sun went up.

CATHLEEN (*turning the cake out of the oven*). It's destroyed he'll be, surely. There's no sense left on any person in a house where an old woman will be talking for ever.

[*Maurya sways herself on her stool.*]

CATHLEEN (*cutting off some of the bread and rolling it in a cloth; to Maurya*). Let you go down now to the spring well and give him this and he passing. You'll see him then and the dark word will be broken, and you can say "God speed you," the way he'll be easy in his mind.

MAURYA (*taking the bread*). Will I be in it as soon as himself?

CATHLEEN. If you go now quickly.

MAURYA (*standing up unsteadily*). It's hard set I am to walk.

CATHLEEN (*looking at her anxiously*). Give her the stick, Nora, or maybe she'll slip on the big stones.

NORA. What stick?

CATHLEEN. The stick Michael brought from Connemara.

MAURYA (*taking a stick Nora gives her*). In the big world the old people do be leaving things after them for their sons and children, but in this place it is the young men do be leaving things behind for them that do be old.

[*She goes out slowly. Nora goes over to the ladder.*]

CATHLEEN. Wait, Nora, maybe she'd turn back quickly. She's that sorry, God help her, you wouldn't know the thing she'd do.

NORA. Is she gone round by the bush?

CATHLEEN (*looking out*). She's gone now. Throw it down quickly, for the Lord knows when she'll be out of it again.

NORA (*getting the bundle from the loft*). The young priest said he'd be passing to-morrow, and we might go down and speak to him below if it's Michael's they are surely.

CATHLEEN (*taking the bundle*). Did he say what way they were found?

NORA (*coming down*). "There were two men," says he, "and they rowing round with poteen before the cocks crowed, and the oar of one of them caught the body, and they passing the black cliffs of the north."

CATHLEEN (*trying to open the bundle*). Give me a knife, Nora, the string's perished with the salt water, and there's a black knot on it you wouldn't loosen in a week.

NORA (*giving her a knife*). I've heard tell it was a long way to Donegal.

CATHLEEN (*cutting the string*). It is surely. There was a man in here a while ago—the man sold us that knife—and he said if you set off walking from the rocks beyond, it would be seven days you'd be in Donegal.

NORA. And what time would a man take, and he floating?

[*Cathleen opens the bundle and takes out a bit of a stocking. They look at them eagerly.*]

CATHLEEN (*in a low voice*). The Lord spare us, Nora! isn't it a queer hard thing to say if it's his they are surely?

NORA. I'll get his shirt off the hook the way we can put the one flannel on the other. (*She looks through some clothes hanging in the corner.*) It's not with them, Cathleen, and where will it be?

CATHLEEN. I'm thinking Bartley put it on him in the morning, for his own shirt was heavy with the salt in it (*pointing to the corner*). There's a bit of a sleeve was of the same stuff. Give me that and it will do.

[*Nora brings it to her and they compare the flannel.*]

CATHLEEN. It's the same stuff, Nora; but if it is itself aren't there great rolls of it in the shops of Galway, and isn't it many another man may have a shirt of it as well as Michael himself?

NORA (*who has taken up the stocking and counted the stitches, crying out*). It's Michael, Cathleen, it's Michael; God spare his soul, and what will herself say when she hears this story, and Bartley on the sea?

CATHLEEN (*taking the stocking*). It's a plain stocking.

NORA. It's the second one of the third pair I knitted, and I put up three score stitches, and I dropped four of them.

CATHLEEN (*counts the stitches*). It's that number is in it (*crying out*). Ah, Nora, isn't it a bitter thing to think of him floating that way to the far north, and no one to keen him but the black hags that do be flying on the sea?

NORA (*swinging herself round, and throwing out her arms on the clothes*). And isn't it a pitiful thing when there is nothing left of a man who was a great rower and fisher, but a bit of an old shirt and a plain stocking?

CATHLEEN (*after an instant*). Tell me is herself coming, Nora? I hear a little sound on the path.

NORA (*looking out*). She is, Cathleen. She's coming up to the door.

CATHLEEN. Put these things away before she'll come in. Maybe it's easier she'll be after giving her blessing to Bartley, and we won't let on we've heard anything the time he's on the sea.

NORA (*helping Cathleen to close the bundle*). We'll put them here in the corner.

[*They put them into a hole in the chimney corner. Cathleen goes back to the spinning-wheel.*]

NORA. Will she see it was crying I was?

CATHLEEN. Keep your back to the door the way the light'll not be on you.

[*Nora sits down at the chimney corner, with her back to the door. Maurya comes in very slowly, without looking at the girls, and goes over to her stool at the other side of the fire. The cloth with the bread is still in her hand. The girls look at each other, and Nora points to the bundle of bread.*]

CATHLEEN (*after spinning for a moment*). You didn't give him his bit of bread?

[*Maurya begins to keen softly, without turning round.*]

CATHLEEN. Did you see him riding down?

[*Maurya goes on keening.*]

CATHLEEN (*a little impatiently*). God forgive you; isn't it a better thing to raise your voice and tell what you seen, than to be making lamentation for a thing that's done? Did you see Bartley, I'm saying to you.

MAURYA (*with a weak voice*). My heart's broken from this day.

CATHLEEN (*as before*). Did you see Bartley?

MAURYA. I seen the fearfulest thing.

CATHLEEN (*leaves her wheel and looks out*). God forgive you; he's riding the mare now over the green head, and the gray pony behind him.

MAURYA (*starts, so that her shawl falls back from her head and shows her white tossed hair. With a frightened voice*). The gray pony behind him.

CATHLEEN (*coming to the fire*). What is it ails you, at all?

MAURYA (*speaking very slowly*). I've seen the fearfulest thing any person has seen, since the day Bride Dara seen the dead man with the child in his arms.

CATHLEEN AND NORA. Uah.

[*They crouch down in front of the old woman at the fire.*]

NORA. Tell us what it is you seen.

MAURYA. I went down to the spring well, and I stood there saying a prayer to myself. Then Bartley came along, and he riding on the red mare with the gray pony behind him. (*She puts up her hands, as if to hide something from her eyes.*) The Son of God spare us, Nora!

CATHLEEN. What is it you seen.

MAURYA. I seen Michael himself.

CATHLEEN (*speaking softly*). You did not, mother; It wasn't Michael you seen, for his body is after being found in the far north, and he's got a clean burial by the grace of God.

MAURYA (*a little defiantly*). I'm after seeing him this day, and he riding and galloping. Bartley came first on the red mare; and I tried to say "God speed you," but something choked the words in my throat. He went by quickly; and "the blessing of God on you," says he, and I could say nothing. I looked up then, and I crying, at the gray pony, and there was Michael upon it—with fine clothes on him, and new shoes on his feet.

CATHLEEN (*begins to keen*). It's destroyed we are from this day. It's destroyed, surely.

NORA. Didn't the young priest say the Almighty God wouldn't leave her destitute with no son living?

MAURYA (*in a low voice, but clearly*). It's little the like of him knows of the sea. . . . Bartley will be lost now, and let you call in Eamon and make me a good coffin out of the white boards, for I won't live after them. I've had a husband, and a husband's father, and six sons in this house—six fine men, though it was a hard birth I had with every one of them and they coming to the world—and some of them were found and some of them were not found, but they're gone now the lot of them. . . . There were Stephen, and Shawn, were lost in the great wind, and found after in the Bay of Gregory of the Golden Mouth, and carried up the two of them on the one plank, and in by that door.

[*She pauses for a moment, the girls start as if they heard something through the door that is half open behind them.*]

NORA (*in a whisper*). Did you hear that, Cathleen? Did you hear a noise in the north-east?

CATHLEEN (*in a whisper*). There's some one after crying out by the seashore.

MAURYA (*continues without hearing anything*). There was Sheamus and his father, and his own father again, were lost in a dark night, and not a stick or sign was seen of them when the sun went up. There was Patch after was drowned out of a curagh that turned over. I was sitting here with Bartley, and he a baby, lying on my two knees, and I seen two women, and three women, and four women coming in, and they crossing themselves, and not saying a word. I looked out then, and there were men coming after them, and they holding a thing in the half of a red sail, and water dripping out of it—it was a dry day, Nora—and leaving a track to the door.

[*She pauses again with her hand stretched out towards the door. It opens softly and old women begin to come in, crossing themselves on the threshold, and kneeling down in front of the stage with red petticoats over their heads.*]

MAURYA (*half in a dream, to Cathleen*). Is it Patch, or Michael, or what is it at all?

CATHLEEN. Michael is after being found in the far north, and when he is found there how could he be here in this place?

MAURYA. There does be a power of young men floating round in the sea, and what way would they know if it was Michael they had, or another man like him, for when a man is nine days in the sea, and the wind blowing, it's hard set his own mother would be to say what man was it.

CATHLEEN. It's Michael, God spare him, for they're after sending us a bit of his clothes from the far north.

[*She reaches out and hands Maurya the clothes that belonged to Michael. Maurya stands up slowly and takes them in her hands. Nora looks out.*]

NORA. They're carrying a thing among them and there's water dripping out of it and leaving a track by the big stones.

CATHLEEN (*in a whisper to the women who have come in*). Is it Bartley it is?

ONE OF THE WOMEN. It is surely, God rest his soul.

[*Two younger women come in and pull out the table. Then men carry in the body of Bartley, laid on a plank, with a bit of a sail over it, and lay it on the table.*]

CATHLEEN (*to the women, as they are doing so*). What way was he drowned?

ONE OF THE WOMEN. The gray pony knocked him into the sea, and he was washed out where there is a great surf on the white rocks.

[*Maurya has gone over and knelt down at the head of the table. The women are keening softly and swaying themselves with a slow movement. Cathleen and Nora kneel at the other end of the table. The men kneel near the door.*]

MAURYA (*raising her head and speaking as if she did not see the people around her*). They're all gone now, and there isn't anything more the sea can do to me. . . . I'll have no call now to be up crying and praying when the wind breaks from the south, and you can hear the surf is in the east, and the surf is in the west, making a great stir with the two noises, and they hitting one on the other. I'll have no call now to be going down and getting Holy Water in the dark nights after Samhain, and I won't care what way the sea is when the other women will be keening. (*To Nora.*) Give me the Holy Water, Nora, there's a small sup still on the dresser.

[*Nora gives it to her.*]

MAURYA (*drops Michael's clothes across Bartley's feet, and sprinkles the Holy Water over him*). It isn't that I haven't prayed for you, Bartley, to the Almighty God. It isn't that I haven't said prayers in the dark night till you wouldn't know what I'ld be saying; but it's a great rest I'll have now, and it's time surely. It's a great rest I'll have now, and great sleeping in the long nights after Samhain, if it's only a bit of wet flour we do have to eat, and maybe a fish that would be stinking.

[*She kneels down again, crossing herself, and saying prayers under her breath.*]

CATHLEEN (*to an old man*). Maybe yourself and Eamon would make a coffin when the sun rises. We have fine white boards herself bought, God help her, thinking Michael would be found, and I have a new cake you can eat while you'll be working.

THE OLD MAN (*looking at the boards*). Are there nails with them?

CATHLEEN. There are not, Colum; we didn't think of the nails.

ANOTHER MAN. It's a great wonder she wouldn't think of the nails, and all the coffins she's seen made already.

CATHLEEN. It's getting old she is, and broken.

[*Maurya stands up again very slowly and spreads out the pieces of Michael's clothes beside the body, sprinkling them with the last of the Holy Water.*]

NORA (*in a whisper to Cathleen*). She's quiet now and easy; but the day Michael was drowned you could hear her crying out from this to the spring well. It's fonder she was of Michael, and would any one have thought that?

CATHLEEN (*slowly and clearly*). An old woman will be soon tired with anything she will do, and isn't it nine days herself is after crying and keening, and making great sorrow in the house?

MAURYA (*puts the empty cup mouth downwards on the table, and lays her hands together on Bartley's feet*). They're all together this time, and the end is come. May the Almighty God have mercy on Bartley's soul, and on Michael's soul, and on the souls of Sheamus and Patch, and Stephen and Shawn (*bending her head*); and may He have mercy on my soul, Nora, and on the soul of every one is left living in the world.

[*She pauses, and the keen rises a little more loudly from the women, then sinks away.*]

MAURYA (*continuing*). Michael has a clean burial in the far north, by the grace of the Almighty God. Bartley will have a fine coffin out of the white boards, and a deep grave surely. What more can we want than that? No man at all can be living for ever, and we must be satisfied.

[*She kneels down again and the curtain falls slowly.*]

IN THE SHADOW OF THE GLEN

A PLAY IN ONE ACT

PERSONS IN THE PLAY

First performed at the Molesworth Hall, Dublin, October 8, 1903.

DAN BURKE (*farmer and herd*)   George Roberts

NORA BURKE (*his wife*)   Maire Nic Shiubhlaigh

MICHEAL DARA (*a young herd*)   P. J. Kelly

A TRAMP   W. G. Fay

IN THE SHADOW OF THE GLEN

SCENE. *The last cottage at the head of a long glen in County Wicklow.*

(*Cottage kitchen; turf fire on the right; a bed near it against the wall with a body lying on it covered with a sheet. A door is at the other end of the room, with a low table near it, and stools, or wooden chairs. There are a couple of glasses on the table, and a bottle of whisky, as if for a wake, with two cups, a teapot, and a home-made cake. There is another small door near the bed. Nora Burke is moving about the room, settling a few things, and lighting candles on the table, looking now and then at the bed with an uneasy look. Some one knocks softly at the door. She takes up a stocking with money from the table and puts it in her pocket. Then she opens the door.*)

TRAMP (*outside*). Good evening to you, lady of the house.

NORA. Good evening, kindly stranger, it's a wild night, God help you, to be out in the rain falling.

TRAMP. It is, surely, and I walking to Brittas from the Aughrim fair.

NORA. Is it walking on your feet, stranger?

TRAMP. On my two feet, lady of the house, and when I saw the light below I thought maybe if you'd a sup of new milk and a quiet decent corner where a man could sleep. (*He looks in past her and sees the dead man.*) The Lord have mercy on us all!

NORA. It doesn't matter anyway, stranger, come in out of the rain.

TRAMP (*coming in slowly and going towards the bed*). Is it departed he is?

NORA. It is, stranger. He's after dying on me, God forgive him, and there I am now with a hundred sheep beyond on the hills, and no turf drawn for the winter.

TRAMP (*looking closely at the dead man*). It's a queer look is on him for a man that's dead.

NORA (*half-humorously*). He was always queer, stranger, and I suppose them that's queer and they living men will be queer bodies after.

TRAMP. Isn't it a great wonder you're letting him lie there, and he is not tidied, or laid out itself?

NORA (*coming to the bed*). I was afeard, stranger, for he put a black curse on me this morning if I'ld touch his body the time he'ld die sudden, or let any one touch it except his sister only, and it's ten miles away she lives in the big glen over the hill.

TRAMP (*looking at her and nodding slowly*). It's a queer story he wouldn't let his own wife touch him, and he dying quiet in his bed.

NORA. He was an old man, and an odd man, stranger, and it's always up on the hills he was thinking thoughts in the dark mist. (*She pulls back a bit of the sheet.*) Lay your hand on him now, and tell me if it's cold he is surely.

TRAMP. Is it getting the curse on me you'ld be, woman of the house? I wouldn't lay my hand on him for the Lough Nahanagan and it filled with gold.

NORA (*looking uneasily at the body*). Maybe cold would be no sign of death with the like of him, for he was always cold, every day since I knew him,—and every night, stranger,—(*she covers up his face and comes away from the bed*); but I'm thinking it's dead he is surely, for he's complaining a while back of a pain in his heart, and this morning, the time he was going off to Brittas for three days or four, he was taken with a sharp turn. Then he went into his bed and he was saying it was destroyed he was, the time the shadow was going up through the glen, and when the sun set on the bog beyond he made a great lep, and let a great cry out of him, and stiffened himself out the like of a dead sheep.

TRAMP (*crosses himself*). God rest his soul.

NORA (*pouring him out a glass of whisky*). Maybe that would do you better than the milk of the sweetest cow in County Wicklow.

TRAMP. The Almighty God reward you, and may it be to your good health.

[*He drinks.*]

NORA (*giving him a pipe and tobacco*). I've no pipes saving his own, stranger, but they're sweet pipes to smoke.

TRAMP. Thank you kindly, lady of the house.

NORA. Sit down now, stranger, and be taking your rest.

TRAMP (*filling a pipe and looking about the room*). I've walked a great way through the world, lady of the house, and seen great wonders, but I never seen a wake till this day with fine spirits, and good tobacco, and the best of pipes, and no one to taste them but a woman only.

NORA. Didn't you hear me say it was only after dying on me he was when the sun went down, and how would I go out into the glen and tell the neighbours, and I a lone woman with no house near me?

TRAMP (*drinking*). There's no offence, lady of the house?

NORA. No offence in life, stranger. How would the like of you, passing in the dark night, know the lonesome way I was with no house near me at all?

TRAMP (*sitting down*). I knew rightly. (*He lights his pipe so that there is a sharp light beneath his haggard face.*) And I was thinking, and I coming in through the door, that it's many a lone woman would be afeard of the like of me in the dark night, in a place wouldn't be as lonesome as this place, where there aren't two living souls would see the little light you have shining from the glass.

NORA (*slowly*). I'm thinking many would be afeard, but I never knew what way I'd be afeard of beggar or bishop or any man of you at all. (*She looks towards the window and lowers her voice.*) It's other things than the like of you, stranger, would make a person afeard.

TRAMP (*looking round with a half-shudder*). It is surely, God help us all!

NORA (*looking at him for a moment with curiosity*). You're saying that, stranger, as if you were easy afeard.

TRAMP (*speaking mournfully*). Is it myself, lady of the house, that does be walking round in the long nights, and crossing the hills when the fog is on them, the time a little stick would seem as big as your arm, and a rabbit as big as a bay horse, and a stack of turf as big as a towering church in the city of Dublin? If myself was easily afeard, I'm telling you, it's long ago I'ld have been locked into the Richmond Asylum, or maybe have run up into the back hills with nothing on me but an old shirt, and been eaten with crows the like of Patch

Darcy—the Lord have mercy on him—in the year that's gone.

NORA (*with interest*). You knew Darcy?

TRAMP. Wasn't I the last one heard his living voice in the whole world?

NORA. There were great stories of what was heard at that time, but would any one believe the things they do be saying in the glen?

TRAMP. It was no lie, lady of the house. . . . I was passing below on a dark night the like of this night, and the sheep were lying under the ditch and every one of them coughing, and choking, like an old man, with the great rain and the fog. Then I heard a thing talking—queer talk, you wouldn't believe at all, and you out of your dreams,—and "Merciful God," says I, "if I begin hearing the like of that voice out of the thick mist, I'm destroyed surely." Then I run, and I run, and I run, till I was below in Rathvanna. I got drunk that night, I got drunk in the morning, and drunk the day after, —I was coming from the races beyond—and the third day they found Darcy. . . . Then I knew it was himself I was after hearing, and I wasn't afeard any more.

NORA (*speaking sorrowfully and slowly*). God spare Darcy, he'ld always look in here and he passing up or passing down, and it's very lonesome I was after him a long while (*she looks over at the bed and lowers her voice, speaking very clearly*), and then I got happy again —if it's ever happy we are, stranger,—for I got used to being lonesome.

[*A short pause; then she stands up.*]

NORA. Was there any one on the last bit of the road, stranger, and you coming from Aughrim?

TRAMP. There was a young man with a drift of mountain ewes, and he running after them this way and that.

NORA (*with a half-smile*). Far down, stranger?

TRAMP. A piece only.

[*She fills the kettle and puts it on the fire.*]

NORA. Maybe, if you're not easy afeard, you'ld stay here a short while alone with himself.

TRAMP. I would surely. A man that's dead can do no hurt.

NORA (*speaking with a sort of constraint*). I'm going a little back to the west, stranger, for himself would go there one night and another and whistle at that place, and then the young man you're after seeing—a kind of a farmer has come up from the sea to live in a cottage beyond—would walk round to see if there was a thing we'ld have to be done, and I'm wanting him this night, the way he can go down into the glen when the sun goes up and tell the people that himself is dead.

TRAMP (*looking at the body in the sheet*). It's myself will go for him, lady of the house, and let you not be destroying yourself with the great rain.

NORA. You wouldn't find your way, stranger, for there's a small path only, and it running up between two sluigs where an ass and cart would be drowned. (*She puts a shawl over her head.*) Let you be making yourself easy, and saying a prayer for his soul, and it's not long I'll be coming again.

TRAMP (*moving uneasily*). Maybe if you'd a piece of a grey thread and a sharp needle—there's great safety in a needle, lady of the house—I'ld be putting a little stitch here and there in my old coat, the time I'll be praying for his soul, and it going up naked to the saints of God.

NORA (*takes a needle and thread from the front of her dress and gives it to him*). There's the needle, stranger, and I'm thinking you won't be lonesome, and you used to the back hills, for isn't a dead man itself more company than to be sitting alone, and hearing the winds crying, and you not knowing on what thing your mind would stay?

TRAMP (*slowly*). It's true, surely, and the Lord have mercy on us all!

[*Nora goes out. The Tramp begins stitching one of the tags in his coat, saying the "De Profundis" under his breath. In an instant the sheet is drawn slowly down, and Dan Burke looks out. The Tramp moves uneasily, then looks up, and springs to his feet with a movement of terror.*]

DAN (*with a hoarse voice*). Don't be afeard, stranger; a man that's dead can do no hurt.

TRAMP (*trembling*). I meant no harm, your honour; and won't you leave me easy to be saying a little prayer for your soul?

[*A long whistle is heard outside.*]

DAN (*sitting up in his bed and speaking fiercely*). Ah, the devil mend her. . . . Do you hear that, stranger? Did ever you hear another woman could whistle the like of that with two fingers in her mouth? (*He looks at the table hurriedly.*) I'm destroyed with the drouth, and let you bring me a drop quickly before herself will come back.

TRAMP (*doubtfully*). Is it not dead you are?

DAN. How would I be dead, and I as dry as a baked bone, stranger?

TRAMP (*pouring out the whisky*). What will herself say if she smells the stuff on you, for I'm thinking it's not for nothing you're letting on to be dead?

DAN. It is not, stranger, but she won't be coming near me at all, and it's not long now I'll be letting on, for I've a cramp in my back, and my hip's asleep on me, and there's been the devil's own fly itching my nose. It's near dead I was wanting to sneeze, and you blathering about the rain, and Darcy (*bitterly*)—the devil choke him—and the towering church. (*Crying out impatiently.*) Give me that whisky. Would you have herself come back before I taste a drop at all?

[*Tramp gives him the glass.*]

DAN (*after drinking*). Go over now to that cupboard, and bring me a black stick you'll see in the west corner by the wall.

TRAMP (*taking a stick from the cupboard*). Is it that?

DAN. It is, stranger; it's a long time I'm keeping that stick for I've a bad wife in the house.

TRAMP (*with a queer look*). Is it herself, master of the house, and she a grand woman to talk?

DAN. It's herself, surely, it's a bad wife she is—a bad wife for an old man, and I'm getting old, God help me, though I've an arm to me still. (*He takes the stick in his hand.*) Let you wait now a short while, and it's a great sight you'll see in this room in two hours or three. (*He stops to listen.*) Is that somebody above?

TRAMP (*listening*). There's a voice speaking on the path.

DAN. Put that stick here in the bed and smooth the sheet the way it was lying. (*He covers himself up hastily.*) Be falling to sleep now and don't let on you know anything, or I'll be having your life. I wouldn't have told you at all but it's destroyed with the drouth I was.

TRAMP (*covering his head*). Have no fear, master of the house. What is it I know of the like of you that I'ld be saying a word or putting out my hand to stay you at all?

[*He goes back to the fire, sits down on a stool with his back to the bed and goes on stitching his coat.*]

DAN (*under the sheet, querulously*). Stranger.

TRAMP (*quickly*). Whisht, whisht. Be quiet I'm telling you, they're coming now at the door.

[*Nora comes in with Micheal Dara, a tall, innocent young man behind her.*]

NORA. I wasn't long at all, stranger, for I met himself on the path.

TRAMP. You were middling long, lady of the house.

NORA. There was no sign from himself?

TRAMP. No sign at all, lady of the house.

NORA (*to Micheal*). Go over now and pull down the sheet, and look on himself, Micheal Dara, and you'll see it's the truth I'm telling you.

MICHEAL. I will not, Nora, I do be afeard of the dead.

[*He sits down on a stool next the table facing the Tramp. Nora puts the kettle on a lower hook of the pot-hooks, and piles turf under it.*]

NORA (*turning to Tramp*). Will you drink a sup of tea with myself and the young man, stranger, or (*speaking more persuasively*) will you go into the little room and stretch yourself a short while on the bed, I'm thinking it's destroyed you are walking the length of that way in the great rain.

TRAMP. Is it to go away and leave you, and you having a wake, lady of the house? I will not surely. (*He takes a drink from his glass which he has beside him.*) And it's none of your tea I'm asking either.

[*He goes on stitching. Nora makes the tea.*]

MICHEAL (*after looking at the Tramp rather scornfully for a moment*). That's a poor coat you have, God help you, and I'm thinking it's a poor tailor you are with it.

TRAMP. If it's a poor tailor I am, I'm thinking it's a poor herd does be running back and forward after a little handful of ewes the way I seen yourself running this day, young fellow, and you coming from the fair.

[*Nora comes back to the table.*]

NORA (*to Micheal in a low voice*). Let you not mind him at all, Micheal Dara, he has a drop taken and it's soon he'll be falling asleep.

MICHEAL. It's no lie he's telling, I was destroyed surely. They were that wilful they were running off into one man's bit of oats, and another man's bit of hay, and tumbling into the red bogs till it's more like a pack of old goats than sheep they were. Mountain ewes is a queer breed, Nora Burke, and I'm not used to them at all.

NORA (*settling the tea things*). There's no one can drive a mountain ewe but the men do be reared in the Glen Malure, I've heard them say, and above by Rathvanna, and the Glen Imaal, men the like of Patch Darcy, God spare his soul, who would walk through five hundred sheep and miss one of them, and he not reckoning them at all.

MICHEAL (*uneasily*). Is it the man went queer in his head the year that's gone?

NORA. It is surely.

TRAMP (*plaintively*). That was a great man, young fellow, a great man I'm telling you. There was never a lamb from his own ewes he wouldn't know before it was marked, and he'ld run from this to the city of Dublin and never catch for his breath.

NORA (*turning round quickly*). He was a great man surely, stranger, and isn't it a grand thing when you hear a living man saying a good word of a dead man, and he mad dying?

TRAMP. It's the truth I'm saying, God spare his soul.

[*He puts the needle under the collar of his coat, and settles himself to sleep in the chimney-corner. Nora sits down at the table; their backs are turned to the bed.*]

MICHEAL (*looking at her with a queer look*). I heard tell this day, Nora Burke, that it was on the path below Patch Darcy would be passing up and passing down, and I heard them say he'ld never pass it night or morning without speaking with yourself.

NORA (*in a low voice*). It was no lie you heard, Micheal Dara.

MICHEAL. I'm thinking it's a power of men you're after knowing if it's in a lonesome place you live itself.

NORA (*giving him his tea*). It's in a lonesome place you do have to be talking with some one, and looking for some one, in the evening of the day, and if it's a power of men I'm after knowing they were fine men, for I was a hard child to please, and a hard girl to please (*she looks at him a little sternly*), and it's a hard woman I am to please this day, Micheal Dara, and it's no lie I'm telling you.

MICHEAL (*looking over to see that the Tramp is asleep, and then pointing to the dead man*). Was it a hard woman to please you were when you took himself for your man?

NORA. What way would I live and I an old woman if I didn't marry a man with a bit of a farm, and cows on it, and sheep on the back hills?

MICHEAL (*considering*). That's true, Nora, and maybe it's no fool you were, for there's good grazing on it, if it is a lonesome place, and I'm thinking it's a good sum he's left behind.

NORA (*taking the stocking with money from her pocket, and putting it on the table*). I do be thinking in the long nights it was a big fool I was that time, Micheal Dara, for what good is a bit of a farm with cows on it, and sheep on the back hills, when you do be sitting looking out from a door the like of that door, and seeing nothing but the mists rolling down the bog, and the mists again, and they rolling up the bog, and hearing nothing but the wind crying out in the bits of broken trees were left from the great storm, and the streams roaring with the rain.

MICHEAL (*looking at her uneasily*). What is it ails you, this night, Nora Burke? I've heard tell it's the like of that talk you do hear from men, and they after being a great while on the back hills.

NORA (*putting out the money on the table*). It's a bad night, and a wild night, Micheal Dara, and isn't it a great while I am at the foot of the back hills, sitting up here boiling food for himself, and food for the brood sow, and baking a cake when the night falls? (*She puts up the money, listlessly, in little piles on the table.*) Isn't it a long while I am sitting here in the winter and the summer, and the fine spring, with the young growing behind me and the old passing, saying to myself one time, to look on Mary Brien who wasn't that height (*holding out her hand*), and I a fine girl growing up, and there she is now with two children, and another coming on her in three months or four.

[*She pauses.*]

MICHEAL (*moving over three of the piles*). That's three pounds we have now, Nora Burke.

NORA (*continuing in the same voice*). And saying to myself another time, to look on Peggy Cavanagh, who had the lightest hand at milking a cow that wouldn't be easy, or turning a cake, and there she is now walking round on the roads, or sitting in a dirty old house, with no teeth in her mouth, and no sense and no more hair than you'ld see on a bit of a hill and they after burning the furze from it.

MICHEAL. That's five pounds and ten notes, a good sum, surely! . . . It's not that way you'll be talking when you marry a young man, Nora Burke, and they were saying in the fair my lambs were the best lambs, and I got a grand price, for I'm no fool now at making a bargain when my lambs are good.

NORA. What was it you got?

MICHEAL. Twenty pound for the lot, Nora Burke. . . . We'ld do right to wait now till himself will be quiet awhile in the Seven Churches, and then you'll marry me in the chapel of Rathvanna, and I'll bring the sheep up on the bit of a hill you have on the back mountain, and we won't have anything we'ld be afeard to let our minds on when the mist is down.

NORA (*pouring him out some whisky*). Why would I marry you, Mike Dara? You'll be getting old and I'll be getting old, and in a little while I'm telling you, you'll be sitting up in your bed—the way himself was sitting—with a shake in your face, and your teeth falling, and the white hair sticking out round you like an old bush where sheep do be leaping a gap.

[*Dan Burke sits up noiselessly from under the sheet, with his hand to his face. His white hair is sticking out round his head.*]

NORA (*goes on slowly without hearing him*). It's a pitiful thing to be getting old, but it's a queer thing surely. It's a queer thing to see an old man sitting up there in his bed with no teeth in him, and a rough word in his mouth, and his chin the way it would take the bark from the edge of an oak board you'ld have building a door. ... God forgive me, Micheal Dara, we'll all be getting old, but it's a queer thing surely.

MICHEAL. It's too lonesome you are from living a long time with an old man, Nora, and you're talking again like a herd that would be coming down from the thick mist (*he puts his arm round her*), but it's a fine life you'll have now with a young man, a fine life surely. . . .

[*Dan sneezes violently. Micheal tries to get to the door, but before he can do so, Dan jumps out of the bed in queer white clothes, with his stick in his hand, and goes over and puts his back against it.*]

MICHEAL. Son of God deliver us.

[*Crosses himself, and goes backward across the room.*]

DAN (*holding up his hand at him*). Now you'll not marry her the time I'm rotting below in the Seven Churches, and you'll see the thing I'll give you will follow you on the back mountains when the wind is high.

MICHEAL (*to Nora*). Get me out of it, Nora, for the love of God. He always did what you bid him, and I'm thinking he would do it now.

NORA (*looking at the Tramp*). Is it dead he is or living?

DAN (*turning towards her*). It's little you care if it's dead or living I am, but there'll be an end now of your fine times, and all the talk you have of young men and old men, and of the mist coming up or going down. (*He opens the door.*) You'll walk out now from that door, Nora Burke, and it's not to-morrow, or the next day, or any day of your life, that you'll put in your foot through it again.

TRAMP (*standing up*). It's a hard thing you're saying for an old man, master of the house, and what would the like of her do if you put her out on the roads?

DAN. Let her walk round the like of Peggy Cavanagh below, and be begging money at the cross-road, or selling songs to the men. (*To Nora.*) Walk out now, Nora Burke, and it's soon you'll be getting old with that life, I'm telling you; it's soon your teeth'll be falling and your head'll be the like of a bush where sheep do be leaping a gap.

[*He pauses: she looks round at Micheal.*]

MICHEAL (*timidly*). There's a fine Union below in Rathdrum.

DAN. The like of her would never go there. . . . It's lonesome roads she'll be going and hiding herself away till the end will come, and they find her stretched like a dead sheep with the frost on her, or the big spiders, maybe, and they putting their webs on her, in the butt of a ditch.

NORA (*angrily*). What way will yourself be that day, Daniel Burke? What way will you be that day and you lying down a long while in your grave? For it's bad you are living, and it's bad you'll be when you're dead. (*She looks at him a moment fiercely, then half turns away and speaks plaintively again.*) Yet, if it is itself, Daniel Burke, who can help it at all, and let you be getting up into your bed, and not be taking your death with the wind blowing on you, and the rain with it, and you half in your skin.

DAN. It's proud and happy you'ld be if I was getting my death the day I was shut of yourself. (*Pointing to the door.*) Let you walk out through that door, I'm telling you, and let you not be passing this way if it's hungry you are, or wanting a bed.

TRAMP (*pointing to Micheal*). Maybe himself would take her.

NORA. What would he do with me now?

TRAMP. Give you the half of a dry bed, and good food in your mouth.

DAN. Is it a fool you think him, stranger, or is it a fool you were born yourself? Let her walk out of that door, and let you go along with her, stranger—if it's raining itself—for it's too much talk you have surely.

TRAMP (*going over to Nora*). We'll be going now, lady of the house—the rain is falling, but the air is kind and maybe it'll be a grand morning by the grace of God.

NORA. What good is a grand morning when I'm destroyed surely, and I going out to get my death walking the roads?

TRAMP. You'll not be getting your death with myself, lady of the house, and I knowing all the ways a man can put food in his mouth. . . . We'll be going now, I'm telling you, and the time you'll be feeling the cold, and the frost, and the great rain, and the sun again, and the south wind blowing in the glens, you'll not be sitting up on a wet ditch, the way you're after sitting in the place, making yourself old with looking on each day, and it passing you by. You'll be saying one time, "It's a grand evening, by the grace of God," and another time, "It's a wild night, God help us, but it'll pass surely." You'll be saying—

DAN (*goes over to them crying out impatiently*). Go out of that door, I'm telling you, and do your blathering below in the glen.

[*Nora gathers a few things into her shawl.*]

TRAMP (*at the door*). Come along with me now, lady of the house, and it's not my blather you'll be hearing only, but you'll be hearing the herons crying out over the black lakes, and you'll be hearing the grouse and the owls with them, and the larks and the big thrushes when the days are warm, and it's not from the like of them you'll be hearing a talk of getting old like Peggy Cavanagh, and losing the hair off you, and the light of your eyes, but it's fine songs you'll be hearing when the sun goes up, and there'll be no old fellow wheezing, the like of a sick sheep, close to your ear.

NORA. I'm thinking it's myself will be wheezing that

time with lying down under the Heavens when the night is cold; but you've a fine bit of talk, stranger, and it's with yourself I'll go. (*She goes towards the door, then turns to Dan.*) You think it's a grand thing you're after doing with your letting on to be dead, but what is it at all? What way would a woman live in a lonesome place the like of this place, and she not making a talk with the men passing? And what way will yourself live from this day, with none to care for you? What is it you'll have now but a black life, Daniel Burke, and it's not long I'm telling you, till you'll be lying again under that sheet, and you dead surely.

[*She goes out with the Tramp. Micheal is slinking after them, but Dan stops him.*]

DAN. Sit down now and take a little taste of the stuff, Micheal Dara. There's a great drouth on me, and the night is young.

MICHEAL (*coming back to the table*). And it's very dry I am, surely, with the fear of death you put on me, and I after driving mountain ewes since the turn of the day.

DAN (*throwing away his stick*). I was thinking to strike you, Micheal Dara, but you're a quiet man, God help you, and I don't mind you at all.

[*He pours out two glasses of whisky, and gives one to Micheal.*]

DAN. Your good health, Micheal Dara.

MICHEAL. God reward you, Daniel Burke, and may you have a long life, and a quiet life, and good health with it.

[*They drink.*]

CURTAIN

THE WELL OF THE SAINTS

A PLAY IN THREE ACTS

PERSONS IN THE PLAY

First performed at the Abbey Theatre in February, 1905, by the Irish National Theatre Society, under the direction of W. G. Fay.

MARTIN DOUL (*weather-beaten, blind beggar*)
W. G. Fay

MARY DOUL (*his Wife, weather-beaten, ugly woman, blind also, nearly fifty*)   Emma Vernon

TIMMY (*a middle-aged, almost elderly, but vigorous smith*)   George Roberts

MOLLY BYRNE (*fine-looking girl with fair hair*)
Sara Allgood

BRIDE (*another handsome girl*)
Maire Nic Shiubhlaigh

MAT SIMON   P. Mac Shiubhlaigh

THE SAINT (*a wandering Friar*)   F. J. Fay

OTHER GIRLS and MEN

THE WELL OF THE SAINTS

SCENE. *Some lonely mountainous district in the east of Ireland one or more centuries ago.*

ACT I

Roadside with big stones, etc., on the right; low loose wall at back with gap near centre; at left, ruined doorway of church with bushes beside it. Martin Doul and Mary Doul grope in on left and pass over to stones on right, where they sit.

MARY DOUL. What place are we now, Martin Doul?

MARTIN DOUL. Passing the gap.

MARY DOUL (*raising her head*). The length of that! Well, the sun's getting warm this day if it's late autumn itself.

MARTIN DOUL (*putting out his hands in sun*). What way wouldn't it be warm and it getting high up in the south? You were that length plaiting your yellow hair you have the morning lost on us, and the people are after passing to the fair of Clash.

MARY DOUL. It isn't going to the fair, the time they do be driving their cattle and they with a litter of pigs maybe squealing in their carts, they'd give us a thing at all. (*She sits down.*) It's well you know that, but you must be talking.

MARTIN DOUL (*sitting down beside her and beginning to shred rushes she gives him*). If I didn't talk I'd be destroyed in a short while listening to the clack you do be making, for you've a queer cracked voice, the Lord have mercy on you, if it's fine to look on you are itself.

MARY DOUL. Who wouldn't have a cracked voice sitting out all the year in the rain falling? It's a bad life for the voice, Martin Doul, though I've heard tell there isn't anything like the wet south wind does be blowing upon us for keeping a white beautiful skin—the like of my skin—on your neck and on your brows, and there isn't anything at all like a fine skin for putting splendour on a woman.

MARTIN DOUL (*teasingly, but with good humour*). I do be thinking odd times we don't know rightly what way you have your splendour, or asking myself, maybe, if you have it at all, for the time I was a young lad, and had fine sight, it was the ones with sweet voices were the best in face.

MARY DOUL. Let you not be making the like of that talk when you've heard Timmy the smith, and Mat Simon, and Patch Ruadh, and a power besides saying fine things of my face, and you know rightly it was "the beautiful dark woman" they did call me in Ballinatone.

MARTIN DOUL (*as before*). If it was itself I heard Molly Byrne saying at the fall of night it was little more than a fright you were.

MARY DOUL (*sharply*). She was jealous, God forgive her, because Timmy the smith was after praising my hair—

MARTIN DOUL (*with mock irony*). Jealous!

MARY DOUL. Ay, jealous, Martin Doul; and if she wasn't itself, the young and silly do be always making game of them that's dark, and they'd think it a fine thing if they had us deceived, the way we wouldn't know we were so fine-looking at all.

[*She puts her hand to her face with a complacent gesture.*]

MARTIN DOUL (*a little plaintively*). I do be thinking in the long nights it'd be a grand thing if we could see ourselves for one hour, or a minute itself, the way we'd know surely we were the finest man and the finest woman of the seven counties of the east—(*bitterly*) and then the seeing rabble below might be destroying their souls telling bad lies, and we'd never heed a thing they'd say.

MARY DOUL. If you weren't a big fool you wouldn't heed them this hour, Martin Doul, for they're a bad lot those that have their sight, and they do have great joy, the time they do be seeing a grand thing, to let on they don't see it at all, and to be telling fool's lies, the like of what Molly Byrne was telling to yourself.

MARTIN DOUL. If it's lies she does be telling she's a sweet, beautiful voice you'd never tire to be hearing, if it was only the pig she'd be calling, or crying out in the long grass, maybe, after her hens. (*Speaking pensively.*) It should be a fine, soft, rounded woman, I'm thinking, would have a voice the like of that.

MARY DOUL (*sharply again, scandalized*). Let you not be minding if it's flat or rounded she is; for she's a flighty, foolish woman, you'll hear when you're off a long way, and she making a great noise and laughing at the well.

MARTIN DOUL. Isn't laughing a nice thing the time a woman's young?

MARY DOUL (*bitterly*). A nice thing, is it? A nice thing to hear a woman making a loud braying laugh the like of that? Ah, she's a great one for drawing the men, and you'll hear Timmy himself, the time he does be sitting in his forge, getting mighty fussy if she'll come walking from Grianan, the way you'll hear his breath going, and he wringing his hands.

MARTIN DOUL (*slightly piqued*). I've heard him say a power of times it's nothing at all she is when you see her at the side of you, and yet I never heard any man's breath getting uneasy the time he'd be looking on yourself.

MARY DOUL. I'm not the like of the girls do be running round on the roads, swinging their legs, and they with their necks out looking on the men. . . . Ah, there's a power of villainy walking the world, Martin Doul, among them that do be gadding around with their gaping eyes, and their sweet words, and they with no sense in them at all.

MARTIN DOUL (*sadly*). It's the truth, maybe, and yet I'm told it's a grand thing to see a young girl walking the road.

MARY DOUL. You'd be as bad as the rest of them if you had your sight, and I did well, surely, not to marry a seeing man—it's scores would have had me and welcome—for the seeing is a queer lot, and you'd never know the thing they'd do.

[*A moment's pause.*]

MARTIN DOUL (*listening*). There's some one coming on the road.

MARY DOUL. Let you put the pith away out of their sight, or they'll be picking it out with the spying eyes they have, and saying it's rich we are, and not sparing us a thing at all.

[*They bundle away the rushes. Timmy the smith comes in on left.*]

MARTIN DOUL (*with a begging voice*). Leave a bit of silver for blind Martin, your honour. Leave a bit of silver, or a penny copper itself, and we'll be praying the Lord to bless you and you going the way.

TIMMY (*stopping before them*). And you letting on a while back you knew my step!

[*He sits down.*]

MARTIN (*with his natural voice*). I know it when Molly Byrne's walking in front, or when she's two perches, maybe, lagging behind; but it's few times I've heard you walking up the like of that, as if you'd met a thing wasn't right and you coming on the road.

TIMMY (*hot and breathless, wiping his face*). You've good ears, God bless you, if you're a liar itself; for I'm after walking up in great haste from hearing wonders in the fair.

MARTIN DOUL (*rather contemptuously*). You're always hearing queer wonderful things, and the lot of them nothing at all; but I'm thinking, this time, it's a strange thing surely you'd be walking up before the turn of day, and not waiting below to look on them lepping, or dancing, or playing shows on the green of Clash.

TIMMY (*huffed*). I was coming to tell you it's in this place there'd be a bigger wonder done in a short while (*Martin Doul stops working*) than was ever done on the green of Clash, or the width of Leinster itself; but you're thinking, maybe, you're too cute a little fellow to be minding me at all.

MARTIN DOUL (*amused, but incredulous*). There'll be wonders in this place, is it?

TIMMY. Here at the crossing of the roads.

MARTIN DOUL. I never heard tell of anything to happen in this place since the night they killed the old fellow going home with his gold, the Lord have mercy on him, and threw down his corpse into the bog. Let them not be doing the like of that this night, for it's ourselves have a right to the crossing roads, and we don't want any of your bad tricks, or your wonders either, for it's wonder enough we are ourselves.

TIMMY. If I'd a mind I'd be telling you of a real wonder this day, and the way you'll be having a great joy, maybe, you're not thinking on at all.

MARTIN DOUL (*interested*). Are they putting up a still behind in the rocks? It'd be a grand thing if I'd sup handy the way I wouldn't be destroying myself groping up across the bogs in the rain falling.

TIMMY (*still moodily*). It's not a still they're bringing, or the like of it either.

MARY DOUL (*persuasively, to Timmy*). Maybe they're hanging a thief, above at the bit of a tree. I'm told it's a great sight to see a man hanging by his neck; but what joy would that be to ourselves, and we not seeing it at all?

TIMMY (*more pleasantly*). They're hanging no one this day, Mary Doul, and yet, with the help of God, you'll see a power hanged before you die.

MARY DOUL. Well, you've queer humbugging talk. . . . What way would I see a power hanged, and I a dark woman since the seventh year of my age?

TIMMY. Did ever you hear tell of a place across a bit of the sea, where there is an island, and the grave of the four beautiful saints?

MARY DOUL. I've heard people have walked round from the west and they speaking of that.

TIMMY (*impressively*). There's a green ferny well, I'm told, behind of that place, and if you put a drop of the water out of it on the eyes of a blind man, you'll make him see as well as any person is walking the world.

MARTIN DOUL (*with excitement*). Is that the truth, Timmy? I'm thinking you're telling a lie.

TIMMY (*gruffly*). That's the truth, Martin Doul, and you may believe it now, for you're after believing a power of things weren't as likely at all.

MARY DOUL. Maybe we could send us a young lad to bring us the water. I could wash a naggin bottle in the morning, and I'm thinking Patch Ruadh would go for it, if we gave him a good drink, and the bit of money we have hid in the thatch.

TIMMY. It'd be no good to be sending a sinful man the like of ourselves, for I'm told the holiness of the water does be getting soiled with the villainy of your heart, the time you'd be carrying it, and you looking round on the girls, maybe, or drinking a small sup at a still.

MARTIN DOUL (*with disappointment*). It'd be a long terrible way to be walking ourselves, and I'm thinking that's a wonder will bring small joy to us at all.

TIMMY (*turning on him impatiently*). What is it you want with your walking? It's as deaf as blind you're growing if you're not after hearing me say it's in this place the wonder would be done.

MARTIN DOUL (*with a flash of anger*). If it is, can't you open the big slobbering mouth you have and say what way it'll be done, and not be making blather till the fall of night.

TIMMY (*jumping up*). I'll be going on now (*Mary Doul rises*), and not wasting time talking civil talk with the like of you.

MARY DOUL (*standing up, disguising her impatience*).

Let you come here to me, Timmy, and not be minding him at all. (*Timmy stops, and she gropes up to him and takes him by the coat.*) You're not huffy with myself, and let you tell me the whole story and don't be fooling me more. . . . Is it yourself has brought us the water?

TIMMY. It is not, surely.

MARY DOUL. Then tell us your wonder, Timmy. . . . What person'll bring it at all?

TIMMY (*relenting*). It's a fine holy man will bring it, a saint of the Almighty God.

MARY DOUL (*overawed*). A saint is it?

TIMMY. Ay, a fine saint, who's going round through the churches of Ireland, with a long cloak on him, and naked feet, for he's brought a sup of the water slung at his side, and, with the like of him, any little drop is enough to cure the dying, or to make the blind see as clear as the gray hawks do be high up, on a still day, sailing the sky.

MARTIN DOUL (*feeling for his stick*). What place is he, Timmy? I'll be walking to him now.

TIMMY. Let you stay quiet, Martin. He's straying around saying prayers at the churches and high crosses, between this place and the hills, and he with a great crowd going behind—for it's fine prayers he does be saying, and fasting with it, till he's as thin as one of the empty rushes you have there on your knee; then he'll be coming after to this place to cure the two of you—we're after telling him the way you are—and to say his prayers in the church.

MARTIN DOUL (*turning suddenly to Mary Doul*). And we'll be seeing ourselves this day. Oh, glory be to God, is it true surely?

MARY DOUL (*very pleased, to Timmy*). Maybe I'd have time to walk down and get the big shawl I have below, for I do look my best, I've heard them say, when I'm dressed up with that thing on my head.

TIMMY. You'd have time surely—

MARTIN DOUL (*listening*). Whisht now . . . I hear people again coming by the stream.

TIMMY (*looking out left, puzzled*). It's the young girls I left walking after the Saint. . . . They're coming now (*goes up to entrance*) carrying things in their hands, and they walking as easy as you'd see a child walk who'd have a dozen eggs hid in her bib.

MARTIN DOUL (*listening*). That's Molly Byrne, I'm thinking.

[*Molly Byrne and Bride come on left and cross to Martin Doul, carrying water-can, Saint's bell, and cloak.*]

MOLLY BYRNE (*volubly*). God bless you, Martin. I've Holy Water here, from the grave of the four saints of the west, will have you cured in a short while and seeing like ourselves—

TIMMY (*crosses to Molly, interrupting her*). He's heard that. God help you. But where at all is the Saint, and what way is he after trusting the Holy Water with the likes of you?

MOLLY BYRNE. He was afeard to go a far way with the clouds is coming beyond, so he's gone up now through the thick woods to say a prayer at the crosses of Grianan, and he's coming on this road to the church.

TIMMY (*still astonished*). And he's after leaving the Holy Water with the two of you? It's a wonder, surely.

[*Comes down left a little.*]

MOLLY BYRNE. The lads told him no person could carry
them things through the briars, and steep, slippy-feeling
rocks he'll be climbing above, so he looked round then,
and gave the water, and his big cloak, and his bell to the
two of us, for young girls, says he, are the cleanest holy
people you'd see walking the world.

[*Mary Doul goes near seat.*]

MARY DOUL (*sits down, laughing to herself*). Well, the
Saint's a simple fellow, and it's no lie.

MARTIN DOUL (*leaning forward, holding out his
hands*). Let you give me the water in my hand, Molly
Byrne, the way I'll know you have it surely.

MOLLY BYRNE (*giving it to him*). Wonders is queer
things, and maybe it'd cure you, and you holding it alone.

MARTIN DOUL (*looking round*). It does not, Molly. I'm
not seeing at all. (*He shakes the can.*) There's a small
sup only. Well, isn't it a great wonder the little trifling
thing would bring seeing to the blind, and be showing
us the big women and the young girls, and all the fine
things is walking the world.

[*He feels for Mary Doul and gives her the can.*]

MARY DOUL (*shaking it*). Well, glory be to God—

MARTIN DOUL (*pointing to Bride*). And what is it herself has, making sounds in her hand?

BRIDE (*crossing to Martin Doul*). It's the Saint's bell;
you'll hear him ringing out the time he'll be going up
some place, to be saying his prayers.

[*Martin Doul holds out his hand; she gives it to
him.*]

MARTIN DOUL (*ringing it*). It's a sweet, beautiful sound.

MARY DOUL. You'd know, I'm thinking, by the little

silvery voice of it, a fasting holy man was after carrying it a great way at his side.

[*Bride crosses a little right behind Martin Doul.*]

MOLLY BYRNE (*unfolding Saint's cloak*). Let you stand up now, Martin Doul, till I put his big cloak on you. (*Martin Doul rises, comes forward, centre a little.*) The way we'd see how you'd look, and you a saint of the Almighty God.

MARTIN DOUL (*standing up, a little diffidently*). I've heard the priests a power of times making great talk and praises of the beauty of the saints.

[*Molly Byrne slips cloak round him.*]

TIMMY (*uneasily*). You'd have a right to be leaving him alone, Molly. What would the Saint say if he seen you making game with his cloak?

MOLLY BYRNE (*recklessly*). How would he see us, and he saying prayers in the wood? (*She turns Martin Doul round.*) Isn't that a fine, holy-looking saint, Timmy the smith? (*Laughing foolishly.*) There's a grand, handsome fellow, Mary Doul; and if you seen him now you'd be as proud, I'm thinking, as the archangels below, fell out with the Almighty God.

MARY DOUL (*with quiet confidence going to Martin Doul and feeling his cloak*). It's proud we'll be this day, surely.

[*Martin Doul is still ringing.*]

MOLLY BYRNE (*to Martin Doul*). Would you think well to be all your life walking round the like of that, Martin Doul, and you bell-ringing with the saints of God?

MARY DOUL (*turning on her, fiercely*). How would he

be bell-ringing with the saints of God and he wedded with myself?

MARTIN DOUL. It's the truth she's saying, and if bell-ringing is a fine life, yet I'm thinking, maybe, it's better I am wedded with the beautiful dark woman of Ballinatone.

MOLLY BYRNE (*scornfully*). You're thinking that, God help you; but it's little you know of her at all.

MARTIN DOUL. It's little surely, and I'm destroyed this day waiting to look upon her face.

TIMMY (*awkwardly*). It's well you know the way she is; for the like of you do have great knowledge in the feeling of your hands.

MARTIN DOUL (*still feeling the cloak*). We do, maybe. Yet it's little I know of faces, or of fine beautiful cloaks, for it's few cloaks I've had my hand to, and few faces (*plaintively*); for the young girls is mighty shy, Timmy the smith, and it isn't much they heed me, though they do be saying I'm a handsome man.

MARY DOUL (*mockingly, with good humour*). Isn't it a queer thing the voice he puts on him, when you hear him talking of the skinny-looking girls, and he married with a woman he's heard called the wonder of the western world?

TIMMY (*pityingly*). The two of you will see a great wonder this day, and it's no lie.

MARTIN DOUL. I've heard tell her yellow hair, and her white skin, and her big eyes are a wonder, surely—

BRIDE (*who has looked out left*). Here's the Saint coming from the selvage of the wood. . . . Strip the cloak from him, Molly, or he'll be seeing it now.

MOLLY BYRNE (*hastily to Bride*). Take the bell and put yourself by the stones. (*To Martin Doul.*) Will you hold your head up till I loosen the cloak? (*She pulls off the cloak and throws it over her arm. Then she pushes Martin Doul over and stands him beside Mary Doul.*) Stand there now, quiet, and let you not be saying a word.

[*She and Bride stand a little on their left, demurely, with bell, etc., in their hands.*]

MARTIN DOUL (*nervously arranging his clothes*). Will he mind the way we are, and not tidied or washed cleanly at all?

MOLLY BYRNE. He'll not see what way you are. . . . He'd walk by the finest woman in Ireland, I'm thinking, and not trouble to raise his two eyes to look upon her face. . . . Whisht!

[*The Saint comes left, with crowd.*]

SAINT. Are these the two poor people?

TIMMY (*officiously*). They are, holy father; they do be always sitting here at the crossing of the roads, asking a bit of copper from them that do pass, or stripping rushes for lights, and they not mournful at all, but talking out straight with a full voice, and making game with them that likes it.

SAINT (*to Martin Doul and Mary Doul*). It's a hard life you've had not seeing sun or moon, or the holy priests itself praying to the Lord, but it's the like of you who are brave in a bad time will make a fine use of the gift of sight the Almighty God will bring to you today. (*He takes his cloak and puts it about him.*) It's on a bare starving rock that there's the grave of the four beauties of God, the way it's little wonder, I'm thinking, if it's with bare starving people the water should be used. (*He takes the water and bell and slings them round his shoulders.*) So it's to the like of yourselves I do be going, who are wrinkled and poor, a thing rich men would hardly look at at all, but would throw a coin to or a crust of bread.

MARTIN DOUL (*moving uneasily*). When they look on herself, who is a fine woman—

TIMMY (*shaking him*). Whisht now, and be listening to the Saint.

SAINT (*looks at them a moment, continues*). If it's raggy and dirty you are itself, I'm saying, the Almighty God isn't at all like the rich men of Ireland; and, with the power of the water I'm after bringing in a little curagh into Cashla Bay, He'll have pity on you, and put sight into your eyes.

MARTIN DOUL (*taking off his hat*). I'm ready now, holy father—

SAINT (*taking him by the hand*). I'll cure you first, and then I'll come for your wife. We'll go up now into the church, for I must say a prayer to the Lord. (*To Mary Doul, as he moves off.*) And let you be making your mind still and saying praises in your heart, for it's a great wonderful thing when the power of the Lord of the world is brought down upon your like.

PEOPLE (*pressing after him*). Come now till we watch.

BRIDE. Come, Timmy.

SAINT (*waving them back*). Stay back where you are, for I'm not wanting a big crowd making whispers in the church. Stay back there, I'm saying, and you'd do well to be thinking on the way sin has brought blindness to the world, and to be saying a prayer for your own sakes against false prophets and heathens, and the words of women and smiths, and all knowledge that would soil the soul or the body of a man.

[*People shrink back. He goes into church. Mary Doul gropes half-way towards the door and kneels near path. People form a group at right.*]

TIMMY. Isn't it a fine, beautiful voice he has, and he a fine, brave man if it wasn't for the fasting?

BRIDE. Did you watch him moving his hands?

MOLLY BYRNE. It'd be a fine thing if some one in this place could pray the like of him, for I'm thinking the water from our own blessed well would do rightly if a man knew the way to be saying prayers, and then there'd be no call to be bringing water from that wild place, where, I'm told, there are no decent houses, or fine-looking people at all.

BRIDE (*who is looking in at door from right*). Look at the great trembling Martin has shaking him, and he on his knees.

TIMMY (*anxiously*). God help him. . . . What will he be doing when he sees his wife this day? I'm thinking it was bad work we did when we let on she was fine-looking, and not a wrinkled, wizened hag the way she is.

MAT SIMON. Why would he be vexed, and we after giving him great joy and pride, the time he was dark?

MOLLY BYRNE (*sitting down in Mary Doul's seat and tidying her hair*). If it's vexed he is itself, he'll have other things now to think on as well as his wife; and what does any man care for a wife, when it's two weeks or three, he is looking on her face?

MAT SIMON. That's the truth now, Molly, and it's more joy dark Martin got from the lies we told of that hag is kneeling by the path than your own man will get from you, day or night, and he living at your side.

MOLLY BYRNE (*defiantly*). Let you not be talking, Mat Simon, for it's not yourself will be my man, though you'd be crowing and singing fine songs if you'd that hope in you at all.

TIMMY (*shocked, to Molly Byrne*). Let you not be raising your voice when the Saint's above at his prayers.

BRIDE (*crying out*). Whisht. . . . Whisht. . . . I'm thinking he's cured.

MARTIN DOUL (*crying out in the church*). Oh, glory be to God. . . .

SAINT (*solemnly*). Laus Patri sit et Filio cum Spiritu Paraclito
Qui Suae dono gratiae misertus est Hiberniae. . . .

MARTIN DOUL (*ecstatically*). Oh, glory be to God, I see now surely. . . . I see the walls of the church, and the green bits of ferns in them, and yourself, holy father, and the great width of the sky.

[*He runs out half-foolish with joy, and comes past Mary Doul as she scrambles to her feet, drawing a little away from her as he goes by.*]

TIMMY (*to the others*). He doesn't know her at all.

[*The Saint comes out behind Martin Doul, and leads Mary Doul into the church. Martin Doul comes on to the People. The men are between him and the Girls; he verifies his position with his stick.*]

MARTIN DOUL (*crying out joyfully*). That's Timmy, I know Timmy by the black of his head. . . . That's Mat Simon, I know Mat by the length of his legs. . . . That should be Patch Ruadh, with the gamey eyes in him, and the fiery hair. (*He sees Molly Byrne on Mary Doul's seat, and his voice changes completely.*) Oh, it was no lie they told me, Mary Doul. Oh, glory to God and the seven saints I didn't die and not see you at all. The blessing of God on the water, and the feet carried it round through the land. The blessing of God on this day, and them that brought me the Saint, for it's grand hair you have (*she lowers her head a little confused*), and soft skin, and eyes would make the saints, if they were dark awhile and seeing again, fall down out of the sky. (*He goes nearer to her.*) Hold up your head, Mary, the way I'll see it's richer I am than the great kings of the east. Hold up your head, I'm saying, for it's soon you'll be seeing me, and I not a bad one at all.

[*He touches her and she starts up.*]

MOLLY BYRNE. Let you keep away from me, and not be soiling my chin.

[*People laugh heartily.*]

MARTIN DOUL (*bewildered*). It's Molly's voice you have.

MOLLY BYRNE. Why wouldn't I have my own voice? Do you think I'm a ghost?

MARTIN DOUL. Which of you all is herself? (*He goes up to Bride.*) Is it you is Mary Doul? I'm thinking you're more the like of what they said (*peering at her*). For you've yellow hair, and white skin, and it's the smell of my own turf is rising from your shawl.

[*He catches her shawl.*]

BRIDE (*pulling away her shawl*). I'm not your wife, and let you get out of my way.

[*The People laugh again.*]

MARTIN DOUL (*with misgiving, to another Girl*). Is it yourself it is? You're not so fine-looking, but I'm thinking you'd do, with the grand nose you have, and your nice hands and your feet.

GIRL (*scornfully*). I never seen any person that took me for blind, and a seeing woman, I'm thinking, would never wed the like of you.

[*She turns away, and the People laugh once more, drawing back a little and leaving him on their left.*]

PEOPLE (*jeeringly*). Try again, Martin, try again, and you'll be finding her yet.

MARTIN DOUL (*passionately*). Where is it you have her hidden away? Isn't it a black shame for a drove of pitiful beasts the like of you to be making game of me, and putting a fool's head on me the grand day of my life? Ah, you're thinking you're a fine lot, with your giggling, weeping eyes, a fine lot to be making game of myself and the woman I've heard called the great wonder of the west.

[*During this speech, which he gives with his back towards the church, Mary Doul has come out with her sight cured, and come down towards the right with a silly simpering smile, till she is a little behind Martin Doul.*]

MARY DOUL (*when he pauses*). Which of you is Martin Doul?

MARTIN DOUL (*wheeling round*). It's her voice surely.

[*They stare at each other blankly.*]

MOLLY BYRNE (*to Martin Doul*). Go up now and take her under the chin and be speaking the way you spoke to myself.

MARTIN DOUL (*in a low voice, with intensity*). If I speak now, I'll speak hard to the two of you—

MOLLY BYRNE (*to Mary Doul*). You're not saying a word, Mary. What is it you think of himself, with the fat legs on him, and the little neck like a ram?

MARY DOUL. I'm thinking it's a poor thing when the Lord God gives you sight and puts the like of that man in your way.

MARTIN DOUL. It's on your two knees you should be thanking the Lord God you're not looking on yourself, for if it was yourself you seen you'd be running round in a short while like the old screeching mad-woman is running round in the glen.

MARY DOUL (*beginning to realize herself*). If I'm not so fine as some of them said, I have my hair, and big eyes, and my white skin—

MARTIN DOUL (*breaking out into a passionate cry*). Your hair, and your big eyes, is it? . . . I'm telling you there isn't a wisp on any gray mare on the ridge of the world isn't finer than the dirty twist on your head. There isn't two eyes in any starving sow isn't finer than the eyes you were calling blue like the sea.

MARY DOUL (*interrupting him*). It's the devil cured you this day with your talking of sows; it's the devil cured you this day, I'm saying, and drove you crazy with lies.

MARTIN DOUL. Isn't it yourself is after playing lies on me, ten years, in the day and in the night; but what is that to you now the Lord God has given eyes to me, the way I see you an old wizendy hag, was never fit to rear a child to me itself.

MARY DOUL. I wouldn't rear a crumpled whelp the like of you. It's many a woman is married with finer than yourself should be praising God if she's no child, and isn't loading the earth with things would make the heavens lonesome above, and they scaring the larks, and the crows, and the angels passing in the sky.

MARTIN DOUL. Go on now to be seeking a lonesome place where the earth can hide you away; go on now, I'm saying, or you'll be having men and women with their knees bled, and they screaming to God for a holy water would darken their sight, for there's no man but would liefer be blind a hundred years, or a thousand itself, than to be looking on your like.

MARY DOUL (*raising her stick*). Maybe if I hit you a strong blow you'd be blind again, and having what you want—

[*The Saint is seen in the church door with his head bent in prayer.*]

MARTIN DOUL (*raising his stick and driving Mary Doul back towards left*). Let you keep off from me now if you wouldn't have me strike out the little handful of brains you have about on the road.

[*He is going to strike her, but Timmy catches him by the arm.*]

TIMMY. Have you no shame to be making a great row, and the Saint above saying his prayers?

MARTIN DOUL. What is it I care for the like of him? (*Struggling to free himself.*) Let me hit her one good one, for the love of the Almighty God, and I'll be quiet after till I die.

TIMMY (*shaking him*). Will you whisht, I'm saying.

SAINT (*coming forward, centre*). Are their minds troubled with joy, or is their sight uncertain, the way it does often be the day a person is restored?

TIMMY. It's too certain their sight is, holy father; and they're after making a great fight, because they're a pair of pitiful shows.

SAINT (*coming between them*). May the Lord who has given you sight send a little sense into your heads, the way it won't be on your two selves you'll be looking—on two pitiful sinners of the earth—but on the splendour of the Spirit of God, you'll see an odd time shining out through the big hills, and steep streams falling to the sea. For if it's on the like of that you do be thinking, you'll not be minding the faces of men, but you'll be saying prayers and great praises, till you'll be living the way the great saints do be living, with little but old sacks, and skin covering their bones. (*To Timmy.*) Leave him go now, you're seeing he's quiet again. (*He frees Martin Doul.*) And let you (*he turns to Mary Doul*) not be raising your voice, a bad thing in a woman; but let the lot of you, who have seen the power of the Lord, be thinking on it in the dark night, and be saying to yourselves it's great pity and love He has for the poor, starving people of Ireland. (*He gathers his cloak about him.*) And now the Lord send blessing to you all, for I am going on to Annagolan, where there is a deaf woman, and to Laragh, where there are two men without sense, and to Glenassil, where there are children blind from their birth; and then I'm going to sleep this night in the bed of the holy Kevin, and to be praising God, and asking great blessing on you all.

[*He bends his head.*]

CURTAIN

ACT II

Village roadside, on left the door of a forge, with broken wheels, etc., lying about. A well near centre, with board above it, and room to pass behind it. Martin Doul is sitting near forge, cutting sticks.

TIMMY (*heard hammering inside forge, then calls*). Let you make haste out there. . . . I'll be putting up new fires at the turn of day, and you haven't the half of them cut yet.

MARTIN DOUL (*gloomily*). It's destroyed I'll be whacking your old thorns till the turn of day, and I with no food in my stomach would keep the life in a pig. (*He turns towards the door.*) Let you come out here and cut them yourself if you want them cut, for there's an hour every day when a man has a right to his rest.

TIMMY (*coming out, with a hammer, impatiently*). Do you want me to be driving you off again to be walking the roads? There you are now, and I giving you your food, and a corner to sleep, and money with it; and, to hear the talk of you, you'd think I was after beating you, or stealing your gold.

MARTIN DOUL. You'd do it handy, maybe, if I'd gold to steal.

TIMMY (*throws down hammer; picks up some of the sticks already cut, and throws them into door*). There's no fear of your having gold—a lazy, basking fool the like of you.

MARTIN DOUL. No fear, maybe, and I here with yourself, for it's more I got a while since and I sitting blinded in Grianan, than I get in this place working hard, and destroying myself, the length of the day.

TIMMY (*stopping with amazement*). Working hard? (*He goes over to him.*) I'll teach you to work hard, Martin Doul. Strip off your coat now, and put a tuck in your sleeves, and cut the lot of them, while I'd rake the ashes from the forge, or I'll not put up with you another hour itself.

MARTIN DOUL (*horrified*). Would you have me getting my death sitting out in the black wintry air with no coat on me at all?

TIMMY (*with authority*). Strip it off now, or walk down upon the road.

MARTIN DOUL (*bitterly*). Oh, God help me! (*He begins taking off his coat.*) I've heard tell you stripped the sheet from your wife and you putting her down into the grave, and that there isn't the like of you for plucking your living ducks, the short days, and leaving them running round in their skins, in the great rains and the cold. (*He tucks up his sleeves.*) Ah, I've heard a power of queer things of yourself, and there isn't one of them I'll not believe from this day, and be telling to the boys.

TIMMY (*pulling over a big stick*). Let you cut that now, and give me rest from your talk, for I'm not heeding you at all.

MARTIN DOUL (*taking stick*). That's a hard, terrible stick, Timmy; and isn't it a poor thing to be cutting strong timber the like of that, when it's cold the bark is, and slippy with the frost of the air?

TIMMY (*gathering up another armful of sticks*). What way wouldn't it be cold, and it freezing since the moon was changed?

[*He goes into forge.*]

MARTIN DOUL (*querulously, as he cuts slowly*). What way, indeed, Timmy? For it's a raw, beastly day we do have each day, till I do be thinking it's well for the blind don't be seeing them gray clouds driving on the hill, and don't be looking on people with their noses red, the like of your nose, and their eyes weeping and watering, the like of your eyes, God help you, Timmy the smith.

TIMMY (*seen blinking in doorway*). Is it turning now you are against your sight?

MARTIN DOUL (*very miserably*). It's a hard thing for a man to have his sight, and he living near to the like of you (*he cuts a stick and throws it away*), or wed with a wife (*cuts a stick*); and I do be thinking it should be a hard thing for the Almighty God to be looking on the world, bad days, and on men the like of yourself walking around on it, and they slipping each way in the muck.

TIMMY (*with pot-hooks which he taps on anvil*). You'd have a right to be minding, Martin Doul, for it's a power the Saint cured lose their sight after a while. Mary Doul's dimming again, I've heard them say; and I'm thinking the Lord, if he hears you making that talk, will have little pity left for you at all.

MARTIN DOUL. There's not a bit of fear of me losing my sight, and if it's a dark day itself it's too well I see every wicked wrinkle you have round by your eye.

TIMMY (*looking at him sharply*). The day's not dark since the clouds broke in the east.

MARTIN DOUL. Let you not be tormenting yourself trying to make me afeard. You told me a power of bad lies the time I was blind, and it's right now for you to stop, and be taking your rest (*Mary Doul comes in unnoticed on right with a sack filled with green stuff on her arm*), for it's little ease or quiet any person would get if the big fools of Ireland weren't weary at times. (*He looks up and sees Mary Doul.*) Oh, glory be to God, she's coming again.

[*He begins to work busily with his back to her.*]

TIMMY (*amused, to Mary Doul, as she is going by without looking at them*). Look on him now, Mary Doul. You'd be a great one for keeping him steady at his work, for he's after idling and blathering to this hour from the dawn of day.

MARY DOUL (*stiffly*). Of what is it you're speaking, Timmy the smith?

TIMMY (*laughing*). Of himself, surely. Look on him there, and he with the shirt on him ripping from his back. You'd have a right to come round this night, I'm thinking, and put a stitch into his clothes, for it's long enough you are not speaking one to the other.

MARY DOUL. Let the two of you not torment me at all.

[*She goes out left, with her head in the air.*]

MARTIN DOUL (*stops work and looks after her*). Well, isn't it a queer thing she can't keep herself two days without looking on my face?

TIMMY (*jeeringly*). Looking on your face, is it? And she after going by with her head turned the way you'd see a priest going where there'd be a drunken man in the side ditch talking with a girl. (*Martin Doul gets up and goes to corner of forge, and looks out left.*) Come back here and don't mind her at all. Come back here, I'm saying, you've no call to be spying behind her since she went off, and left you, in place of breaking her heart, trying to keep you in the decency of clothes and food.

MARTIN DOUL (*crying out indignantly*). You know rightly, Timmy, it was myself drove her away.

TIMMY. That's a lie you're telling, yet it's little I care which one of you was driving the other, and let you walk back here, I'm saying, to your work.

MARTIN DOUL (*turning round*). I'm coming, surely.

[*He stops and looks out right, going a step or two towards centre.*]

TIMMY. On what is it you're gaping, Martin Doul?

MARTIN DOUL. There's a person walking above. . . . It's Molly Byrne, I'm thinking, coming down with her can.

TIMMY. If she is itself let you not be idling this day, or minding her at all, and let you hurry with them sticks, for I'll want you in a short while to be blowing in the forge.

[*He throws down pot-hooks.*]

MARTIN DOUL (*crying out*). Is it roasting me now you'd be? (*Turns back and sees pot-hooks; he takes them up.*) Pot-hooks? Is it over them you've been inside sneezing and sweating since the dawn of day?

TIMMY (*resting himself on anvil, with satisfaction*). I'm making a power of things you do have when you're settling with a wife, Martin Doul; for I heard tell last night the Saint'll be passing again in a short while, and I'd have him wed Molly with myself. . . . He'd do it, I've heard them say, for not a penny at all.

MARTIN DOUL (*lays down hooks and looks at him steadily*). Molly'll be saying great praises now to the Almighty God and He giving her a fine, stout, hardy man the like of you.

TIMMY (*uneasily*). And why wouldn't she, if she's a fine woman itself?

MARTIN DOUL (*looking up, right*). Why wouldn't she, indeed, Timmy? ... The Almighty God's made a fine match in the two of you, for if you went marrying a woman was the like of yourself you'd be having the fearfulest little children, I'm thinking, was ever seen in the world.

TIMMY (*seriously offended*). God forgive you! if you're an ugly man to be looking at, I'm thinking your tongue's worse than your view.

MARTIN DOUL (*hurt also*). Isn't it destroyed with the cold I am, and if I'm ugly itself I never seen anyone the like of you for dreepiness this day, Timmy the smith, and I'm thinking now herself's coming above you'd have a right to step up into your old shanty, and give a rub to your face, and not be sitting there with your bleary eyes, and your big nose, the like of an old scarecrow stuck down upon the road.

TIMMY (*looking up the road uneasily*). She's no call to mind what way I look, and I after building a house with four rooms in it above on the hill. (*He stands up.*) But it's a queer thing the way yourself and Mary Doul are after setting every person in this place, and up beyond to Rathvanna, talking of nothing, and thinking of nothing, but the way they do be looking in the face. (*Going towards forge.*) It's the devil's work you're after doing with your talk of fine looks, and I'd do right, maybe, to step in and wash the blackness from my eyes.

[*He goes into forge. Martin Doul rubs his face furtively with the tail of his coat. Molly Byrne comes on right with a water-can, and begins to fill it at the well.*]

MARTIN DOUL. God save you, Molly Byrne.

MOLLY BYRNE (*indifferently*). God save you.

MARTIN DOUL. That's a dark, gloomy day, and the Lord have mercy on us all.

MOLLY BYRNE. Middling dark.

MARTIN DOUL. It's a power of dirty days, and dark mornings, and shabby-looking fellows (*he makes a gesture over his shoulder*) we do have to be looking on when we have our sight, God help us, but there's one fine thing we have, to be looking on a grand, white, handsome girl, the like of you . . . and every time I set my eyes on you I do be blessing the saints, and the holy water, and the power of the Lord Almighty in the heavens above.

MOLLY BYRNE. I've heard the priests say it isn't looking on a young girl would teach many to be saying their prayers.

[*Bailing water into her can with a cup.*]

MARTIN DOUL. It isn't many have been the way I was, hearing your voice speaking, and not seeing you at all.

MOLLY BYRNE. That should have been a queer time for an old, wicked, coaxing fool to be sitting there with your eyes shut, and not seeing a sight of girl or woman passing the road.

MARTIN DOUL. If it was a queer time itself it was great joy and pride I had the time I'd hear your voice speaking and you passing to Grianan (*beginning to speak with plaintive intensity*), for it's of many a fine thing your voice would put a poor dark fellow in mind, and the day I'd hear it it's of little else at all I would be thinking.

MOLLY BYRNE. I'll tell your wife if you talk to me the

like of that. . . . You've heard, maybe, she's below picking nettles for the widow O'Flinn, who took great pity
on her when she seen the two of you fighting, and yourself putting shame on her at the crossing of the roads.

MARTIN DOUL (*impatiently*). Is there no living person
can speak a score of words to me, or say "God speed
you," itself, without putting me in mind of the old
woman, or that day either at Grianan?

MOLLY BYRNE (*maliciously*). I was thinking it should
be a fine thing to put you in mind of the day you called
the grand day of your life.

MARTIN DOUL. Grand day, is it? (*Plaintively again,
throwing aside his work, and leaning towards her.*) Or
a bad black day when I was roused up and found I was
the like of the little children do be listening to the stories
of an old woman, and do be dreaming after in the dark
night that it's in grand houses of gold they are, with
speckled horses to ride, and do be waking again, in a
short while, and they destroyed with the cold, and the
thatch dripping, maybe, and the starved ass braying in
the yard?

MOLLY BYRNE (*working indifferently*). You've great
romancing this day, Martin Doul. Was it up at the still
you were at the fall of night?

MARTIN DOUL (*stands up, comes towards her, but
stands at far [right] side of well*). It was not, Molly
Byrne, but lying down in a little rickety shed. . . . Lying
down across a sop of straw, and I thinking I was seeing
you walk, and hearing the sound of your step on a dry
road, and hearing you again, and you laughing and
making great talk in a high room with dry timber lining
the roof. For it's a fine sound your voice has that time,
and it's better I am, I'm thinking, lying down, the way

a blind man does be lying, than to be sitting here in the gray light taking hard words of Timmy the smith.

MOLLY BYRNE (*looking at him with interest*). It's queer talk you have if it's a little, old, shabby stump of a man you are itself.

MARTIN DOUL. I'm not so old as you do hear them say.

MOLLY BYRNE. You're old, I'm thinking, to be talking that talk with a girl.

MARTIN DOUL (*despondingly*). It's not a lie you're telling, maybe, for it's long years I'm after losing from the world, feeling love and talking love, with the old woman, and I fooled the whole while with the lies of Timmy the smith.

MOLLY BYRNE (*half invitingly*). It's a fine way you're wanting to pay Timmy the smith. . . . And it's not his *lies* you're making love to this day, Martin Doul.

MARTIN DOUL. It is not, Molly, and the Lord forgive us all. (*He passes behind her and comes near her left.*) For I've heard tell there are lands beyond in Cahir Iveragh and the Reeks of Cork with warm sun in them, and fine light in the sky. (*Bending towards her.*) And light's a grand thing for a man ever was blind, or a woman, with a fine neck, and a skin on her the like of you, the way we'd have a right to go off this day till we'd have a fine life passing abroad through them towns of the south, and we telling stories, maybe, or singing songs at the fairs.

MOLLY BYRNE (*turning round half amused, and looking him over from head to foot*). Well, isn't it a queer thing when your own wife's after leaving you because you're a pitiful show, you'd talk the like of that to me?

MARTIN DOUL (*drawing back a little, hurt, but indig-*

nant). It's a queer thing, maybe, for all things is queer in the world. (*In a low voice with peculiar emphasis.*) But there's one thing I'm telling you, if she walked off away from me, it wasn't because of seeing me, and I no more than I am, but because I was looking on her with my two eyes, and she getting up, and eating her food, and combing her hair, and lying down for her sleep.

MOLLY BYRNE (*interested, off her guard*). Wouldn't any married man you'd have be doing the like of that?

MARTIN DOUL (*seizing the moment that he has her attention*). I'm thinking by the mercy of God it's few sees anything but them is blind for a space (*with excitement*). It's a few sees the old woman rotting for the grave, and it's few sees the like of yourself. (*He bends over her.*) Though it's shining you are, like a high lamp would drag in the ships out of the sea.

MOLLY BYRNE (*shrinking away from him*). Keep off from me, Martin Doul.

MARTIN DOUL (*quickly, with low, furious intensity*). It's the truth I'm telling you. (*He puts his hand on her shoulder and shakes her.*) And you'd do right not to marry a man is after looking out a long while on the bad days of the world; for what way would the like of him have fit eyes to look on yourself, when you rise up in the morning and come out of the little door you have above in the lane, the time it'd be a fine thing if a man would be seeing, and losing his sight, the way he'd have your two eyes facing him, and he going the roads, and shining above him, and he looking in the sky, and springing up from the earth, the time he'd lower his head, in place of the muck that seeing men do meet all roads spread on the world.

MOLLY BYRNE (*who has listened half mesmerized, starting away*). It's the like of that talk you'd hear from a man would be losing his mind.

MARTIN DOUL (*going after her, passing to her right*). It'd be little wonder if a man near the like of you would be losing his mind. Put down your can now, and come along with myself, for I'm seeing you this day, seeing you, maybe, the way no man has seen you in the world. (*He takes her by the arm and tries to pull her away softly to the right.*) Let you come on now, I'm saying, to the lands of Iveragh and the Reeks of Cork, where you won't set down the width of your two feet and not be crushing fine flowers, and making sweet smells in the air.

MOLLY BYRNE (*laying down the can; trying to free herself*). Leave me go, Martin Doul! Leave me go, I'm saying!

MARTIN DOUL. Let you not be fooling. Come along now the little path through the trees.

MOLLY BYRNE (*crying out towards forge*). Timmy— Timmy the smith. (*Timmy comes out of forge, and Martin Doul lets her go. Molly Byrne, excited and breathless, pointing to Martin Doul.*) Did ever you hear that them that loses their sight loses their senses along with it, Timmy the smith!

TIMMY (*suspicious, but uncertain*). He's no sense, surely, and he'll be having himself driven off this day from where he's good sleeping, and feeding, and wages for his work.

MOLLY BYRNE (*as before*). He's a bigger fool than that, Timmy. Look on him now, and tell me if that isn't a grand fellow to think he's only to open his mouth to have a fine woman, the like of me, running along by his heels.

[*Martin Doul recoils towards centre, with his hand to his eyes; Mary Doul is seen on left coming forward softly.*]

TIMMY (*with blank amazement*). Oh, the blind is wicked people, and it's no lie. But he'll walk off this day and not be troubling us more.

[*Turns back left and picks up Martin Doul's coat and stick; some things fall out of coat pocket, which he gathers up again.*]

MARTIN DOUL (*turns around, sees Mary Doul, whispers to Molly Byrne with imploring agony*). Let you not put shame on me, Molly, before herself and the smith. Let you not put shame on me and I after saying fine words to you, and dreaming . . . dreams . . . in the night. (*He hesitates, and looks round the sky.*) Is it a storm of thunder is coming, or the last end of the world? (*He staggers towards Mary Doul, tripping slightly over tin can.*) The heavens is closing, I'm thinking, with darkness and great trouble passing in the sky. (*He reaches Mary Doul, and seizes her left arm with both his hands—with a frantic cry.*) Is it darkness of thunder is coming, Mary Doul! Do you see me clearly with your eyes?

MARY DOUL (*snatches her arm away, and hits him with empty sack across the face*). I see you a sight too clearly, and let you keep off from me now.

MOLLY BYRNE (*clapping her hands*). That's right, Mary. That's the way to treat the like of him is after standing there at my feet and asking me to go off with him, till I'd grow an old wretched road-woman the like of yourself.

MARY DOUL (*defiantly*). When the skin shrinks on your chin, Molly Byrne, there won't be the like of you for a

shrunk hag in the four quarters of Ireland. . . . It's a
fine pair you'd be, surely!

[*Martin Doul is standing at back right centre, with
his back to the audience.*]

TIMMY (*coming over to Mary Doul*). Is it no shame
you have to let on she'd ever be the like of you?

MARY DOUL. It's them that's fat and flabby do be
wrinkled young, and that whitish yellowy hair she has
does be soon turning the like of a handful of thin grass
you'd see rotting, where the wet lies, at the north of a
sty. (*Turning to go out on right.*) Ah, it's a better thing
to have a simple, seemly face, the like of my face, for
two-score years, or fifty itself, than to be setting fools
mad a short while, and then to be turning a thing would
drive off the little children from your feet.

[*She goes out; Martin Doul has come forward again,
mastering himself, but uncertain.*]

TIMMY. Oh, God protect us, Molly, from the words of
the blind. (*He throws down Martin Doul's coat and
stick.*) There's your old rubbish now, Martin Doul, and
let you take it up, for it's all you have, and walk off
through the world, for if ever I meet you coming again,
if it's seeing or blind you are itself, I'll bring out the big
hammer and hit you a welt with it will leave you easy
till the judgment day.

MARTIN DOUL (*rousing himself with an effort*). What
call have you to talk the like of that with myself?

TIMMY (*pointing to Molly Byrne*). It's well you know
what call I have. It's well you know a decent girl, I'm
thinking to wed, has no right to have her heart scalded
with hearing talk—and queer, bad talk, I'm thinking—
from a raggy-looking fool the like of you.

MARTIN DOUL (*raising his voice*). It's making game of you she is, for what seeing girl would marry with yourself? Look on him, Molly, look on him, I'm saying, for I'm seeing him still, and let you raise your voice, for the time is come, and bid him go up into his forge, and be sitting there by himself, sneezing and sweating, and he beating pot-hooks till the judgment day.

[*He seizes her arm again.*]

MOLLY BYRNE. Keep him off from me, Timmy!

TIMMY (*pushing Martin Doul aside*). Would you have me strike you, Martin Doul? Go along now after your wife, who's a fit match for you, and leave Molly with myself.

MARTIN DOUL (*despairingly*). Won't you raise your voice, Molly, and lay hell's long curse on his tongue?

MOLLY BYRNE (*on Timmy's left*). I'll be telling him it's destroyed I am with the sight of you and the sound of your voice. Go off now after you wife, and if she beats you again, let you go after the tinker girls is above running the hills, or down among the sluts of the town, and you'll learn one day, maybe, the way a man should speak with a well-reared, civil girl the like of me. (*She takes Timmy by the arm.*) Come up now into the forge till he'll be gone down a bit on the road, for it's near afeard I am of the wild look he has come in his eyes.

[*She goes into the forge. Timmy stops in the door-way.*]

TIMMY. Let me not find you out here again, Martin Doul. (*He bares his arm.*) It's well you know Timmy the smith has great strength in his arm, and it's a power of things it has broken a sight harder than the old bone of your skull.

[*He goes into the forge and pulls the door after him.*]

MARTIN DOUL (*stands a moment with his hand to his eyes*). And that's the last thing I'm to set my sight on in the life of the world—the villainy of a woman and the bloody strength of a man. Oh, God, pity a poor, blind fellow, the way I am this day with no strength in me to do hurt to them at all. (*He begins groping about for a moment, then stops.*) Yet if I've no strength in me I've a voice left for my prayers, and may God blight them this day, and my own soul the same hour with them, the way I'll see them after, Molly Byrne and Timmy the smith, the two of them on a high bed, and they screeching in hell.... It'll be a grand thing that time to look on the two of them; and they twisting and roaring out, and twisting and roaring again, one day and the next day, and each day always and ever. It's not blind I'll be that time, and it won't be hell to me, I'm thinking, but the like of heaven itself; and it's fine care I'll be taking the Lord Almighty doesn't know.

[*He turns to grope out.*]

CURTAIN

ACT III

The same Scene as in first Act, but gap in centre has been filled with briars, or branches of some sort. Mary Doul, blind again, gropes her way in on left, and sits as before. She has a few rushes with her. It is an early spring day.

MARY DOUL (*mournfully*). Ah, God help me ... God help me; the blackness wasn't so black at all the other time as it is this time, and it's destroyed I'll be now, and hard set to get my living working alone, when it's few are passing and the winds are cold. (*She begins shredding rushes.*) I'm thinking short days will be long days to me from this time, and I sitting here, not seeing a blink, or hearing a word, and no thought in my mind but long prayers that Martin Doul'll get his reward in a short while for the villainy of his heart. It's great jokes the people'll be making now, I'm thinking, and they pass me by, pointing their fingers maybe, and asking what place is himself, the way it's no quiet or decency I'll have from this day till I'm an old woman with long white hair and it twisting from my brow. (*She fumbles with her hair, and then seems to hear something. Listens for a moment.*) There's a queer, slouching step coming on the road. . . . God help me, he's coming surely.

[*She stays perfectly quiet. Martin Doul gropes in on right, blind also.*]

MARTIN DOUL (*gloomily*). The devil mend Mary Doul for putting lies on me, and letting on she was grand. The devil mend the old Saint for letting me see it was lies. (*He sits down near her.*) The devil mend Timmy the smith for killing me with hard work, and keeping me with an empty, windy stomach in me, in the day and in the night. Ten thousand devils mend the soul of Molly Byrne—(*Mary Doul nods her head with approval*)—and the bad, wicked souls is hidden in all the women of the world. (*He rocks himself, with his hand over his face.*) It's lonesome I'll be from this day, and if living people is a bad lot, yet Mary Doul, herself, and she a dirty, wrinkled-looking hag, was better maybe to be sitting along with than no one at all. I'll be getting my death now, I'm thinking, sitting alone in the cold air, hearing the night coming, and the blackbirds flying round in the briars crying to themselves, the time you'll hear one cart getting off a long way in the east, and another cart getting off a long way in the west, and a dog barking maybe, and a little wind turning the sticks. (*He listens and sighs heavily.*) I'll be destroyed sitting alone and losing my senses this time the way I'm after losing my sight, for it'd make any person afeard to be sitting up hearing the sound of his breath—(*he moves his feet on the stones*)—and the noise of his feet, when it's a power of queer things do be stirring, little sticks breaking, and the grass moving—(*Mary Doul half sighs, and he turns on her in horror*)—till you'd take your dying oath on sun and moon a thing was breathing on the stones. (*He listens towards her for a moment, then starts up nervously, and gropes about for his stick.*) I'll be going now, I'm thinking, but I'm not sure what place my stick's in, and I'm destroyed with terror and dread. (*He touches her face as he is groping about and cries out.*) There's a thing with a cold, living face on it sitting up at my side. (*He turns to run away, but misses his path and stumbles in against the wall.*) My road is lost on me now! Oh, merciful God, set my foot on the path this day, and I'll be saying prayers morning and night, and not straining my ear after young girls, or doing any bad thing till I die—

MARY DOUL (*indignantly*). Let you not be telling lies to the Almighty God.

MARTIN DOUL. Mary Doul, is it? (*Recovering himself with immense relief.*) Is it Mary Doul, I'm saying.

MARY DOUL. There's a sweet tone in your voice I've not heard for a space. You're taking me for Molly Byrne, I'm thinking.

MARTIN DOUL (*coming towards her, wiping sweat from his face*). Well, sight's a queer thing for upsetting a man. It's a queer thing to think I'd live to this day to be fearing the like of you; but if it's shaken I am for a short while, I'll soon be coming to myself.

MARY DOUL. You'll be grand then, and it's no lie.

MARTIN DOUL (*sitting down shyly, some way off*). You've no call to be talking, for I've heard tell you're as blind as myself.

MARY DOUL. If I am I'm bearing in mind I'm married to a little dark stump of a fellow looks the fool of the world, and I'll be bearing in mind from this day the great hullabuloo he's after making from hearing a poor woman breathing quiet in her place.

MARTIN DOUL. And you'll be bearing in mind, I'm thinking, what you seen a while back when you looked down into a well, or a clear pool, maybe, when there was no wind stirring and a good light in the sky.

MARY DOUL. I'm minding that surely, for if I'm not the way the liars were saying below I seen a thing in them pools put joy and blessing in my heart.

[*She puts her hand to her hair again.*]

MARTIN DOUL (*laughing ironically*). Well, they were saying below I was losing my senses, but I never went any day the length of that. . . . God help you, Mary Doul, if you're not a wonder for looks, you're the maddest female woman is walking the counties of the east.

MARY DOUL (*scornfully*). You were saying all times you'd a great ear for hearing the lies of the world. A great ear, God help you, and you think you're using it now.

MARTIN DOUL. If it's not lies you're telling would you

have me think you're not a wrinkled poor woman is looking like three scores, or two scores and a half!

MARY DOUL. I would not, Martin. (*She leans forward earnestly.*) For when I seen myself in them pools, I seen my hair would be gray or white, maybe, in a short while, and I seen with it that I'd a face would be a great wonder when it'll have soft white hair falling around it, the way when I'm an old woman there won't be the like of me surely in the seven counties of the east.

MARTIN DOUL (*with real admiration*). You're a cute thinking woman, Mary Doul, and it's no lie.

MARY DOUL (*triumphantly*). I am, surely, and I'm telling you a beautiful white-haired woman is a grand thing to see, for I'm told when Kitty Bawn was selling poteen below, the young men itself would never tire to be looking in her face.

MARTIN DOUL (*taking off his hat and feeling his head, speaking with hesitation*). Did you think to look, Mary Doul, would there be a whiteness the like of that coming upon me?

MARY DOUL (*with extreme contempt*). On you, God help you! . . . In a short while you'll have a head on you as bald as an old turnip you'd see rolling round in the muck. You need never talk again of your fine looks, Martin Doul, for the day of that talk's gone for ever.

MARTIN DOUL. That's a hard word to be saying, for I was thinking if I'd a bit of comfort, the like of yourself, it's not far off we'd be from the good days went before, and that'd be a wonder surely. But I'll never rest easy, thinking you're a gray, beautiful woman, and myself a pitiful show.

MARY DOUL. I can't help your looks, Martin Doul. It

wasn't myself made you with your rat's eyes, and your big ears, and your grizzldy chin.

MARTIN DOUL (*rubs his chin ruefully, then beams with delight*). There's one thing you've forgot, if you're a cute thinking woman itself.

MARY DOUL. Your slouching feet, is it? Or your hooky neck, or your two knees is black with knocking one on the other?

MARTIN DOUL (*with delighted scorn*). There's talking for a cute woman. There's talking, surely!

MARY DOUL (*puzzled at joy of his voice*). If you'd anything but lies to say you'd be talking to yourself.

MARTIN DOUL (*bursting with excitement*). I've this to say, Mary Doul. I'll be letting my beard grow in a short while, a beautiful, long, white, silken, streamy beard, you wouldn't see the like of in the eastern world. . . . Ah, a white beard's a grand thing on an old man, a grand thing for making the quality stop and be stretching out their hands with good silver or gold, and a beard's a thing you'll never have, so you may be holding your tongue.

MARY DOUL (*laughing cheerfully*). Well, we're a great pair, surely, and it's great times we'll have yet, maybe, and great talking before we die.

MARTIN DOUL. Great times from this day, with the help of the Almighty God, for a priest itself would believe the lies of an old man would have a fine white beard growing on his chin.

MARY DOUL. There's the sound of one of them twittering yellow birds do be coming in the spring-time from beyond the sea, and there'll be a fine warmth now in the sun, and a sweetness in the air, the way it'll be a grand thing to be sitting here quiet and easy smelling the things growing up, and budding from the earth.

MARTIN DOUL. I'm smelling the furze a while back sprouting on the hill, and if you'd hold your tongue you'd hear the lambs of Grianan, though it's near drowned their crying is with the full river making noises in the glen.

MARY DOUL (*listens*). The lambs is bleating, surely, and there's cocks and laying hens making a fine stir a mile off on the face of the hill. (*She starts.*)

MARTIN DOUL. What's that is sounding in the west?

[*A faint sound of a bell is heard.*]

MARY DOUL. It's not the churches, for the wind's blowing from the sea.

MARTIN DOUL (*with dismay*). It's the old Saint, I'm thinking, ringing his bell.

MARY DOUL. The Lord protect us from the saints of God! (*They listen.*) He's coming this road, surely.

MARTIN DOUL (*tentatively*). Will we be running off, Mary Doul?

MARY DOUL. What place would we run?

MARTIN DOUL. There's the little path going up through the sloughs. . . . If we reached the bank above, where the elders do be growing, no person would see a sight of us, if it was a hundred yeomen were passing itself; but I'm afeard after the time we were with our sight we'll not find our way to it at all.

MARY DOUL (*standing up*). You'd find the way, surely. You're a grand man the world knows at finding your way winter or summer, if there was deep snow in it itself, or thick grass and leaves, maybe, growing from the earth.

MARTIN DOUL (*taking her hand*). Come a bit this way; it's here it begins. (*They grope about gap.*) There's a tree pulled into the gap, or a strange thing happened, since I was passing it before.

MARY DOUL. Would we have a right to be crawling in below under the sticks?

MARTIN DOUL. It's hard set I am to know what would be right. And isn't it a poor thing to be blind when you can't run off itself, and you fearing to see?

MARY DOUL (*nearly in tears*). It's a poor thing, God help us, and what good'll our gray hairs be itself, if we have our sight, the way we'll see them falling each day, and turning dirty in the rain?

[*The bell sounds nearby.*]

MARTIN DOUL (*in despair*). He's coming now, and we won't get off from him at all.

MARY DOUL. Could we hide in the bit of a briar is growing at the west butt of the church?

MARTIN DOUL. We'll try that, surely. (*He listens a moment.*) Let you make haste; I hear them trampling in the wood.

[*They grope over to church.*]

MARY DOUL. It's the words of the young girls making a great stir in the trees. (*They find the bush.*) Here's the briar on my left, Martin; I'll go in first, I'm the big one, and I'm easy to see.

MARTIN DOUL (*turning his head anxiously*). It's easy heard you are; and will you be holding your tongue?

MARY DOUL (*partly behind bush*). Come in now beside of me. (*They kneel down, still clearly visible.*) Do you think they can see us now, Martin Doul?

MARTIN DOUL. I'm thinking they can't, but I'm hard set to know; for the lot of them young girls, the devil save them, have sharp, terrible eyes, would pick out a poor man, I'm thinking, and he lying below hid in his grave.

MARY DOUL. Let you not be whispering sin, Martin Doul, or maybe it's the finger of God they'd see pointing to ourselves.

MARTIN DOUL. It's yourself is speaking madness, Mary Doul; haven't you heard the Saint say it's the wicked do be blind?

MARY DOUL. If it is you'd have a right to speak a big, terrible word would make the water not cure us at all.

MARTIN DOUL. What way would I find a big, terrible word, and I shook with the fear; and if I did itself, who'd know rightly if it's good words or bad would save us this day from himself?

MARY DOUL. They're coming. I hear their feet on the stones.

[*The Saint comes in on right, with Timmy and Molly Byrne in holiday clothes, the others as before.*]

TIMMY. I've heard tell Martin Doul and Mary Doul were seen this day about on the road, holy father, and we were thinking you'd have pity on them and cure them again.

SAINT. I would, maybe, but where are they at all? I have little time left when I have the two of you wed in the church.

MAT SIMON (*at their seat*). There are the rushes they do have lying round on the stones. It's not far off they'll be, surely.

MOLLY BYRNE (*pointing with astonishment*). Look beyond, Timmy.

[*They all look over and see Martin Doul.*]

TIMMY. Well, Martin's a lazy fellow to be lying in there at the height of the day. (*He goes over shouting.*) Let you get up out of that. You were near losing a great chance by your sleepiness this day, Martin Doul. . . . The two of them's in it, God help us all!

MARTIN DOUL (*scrambling up with Mary Doul*). What is it you want, Timmy, that you can't leave us in peace?

TIMMY. The Saint's come to marry the two of us, and I'm after speaking a word for yourselves, the way he'll be curing you now; for if you're a foolish man itself, I do be pitying you, for I've a kind heart, when I think of you sitting dark again, and you after seeing a while and working for your bread.

[*Martin Doul takes Mary Doul's hand and tries to grope his way off right; he has lost his hat, and they are both covered with dust and grass seeds.*]

PEOPLE. You're going wrong. It's this way, Martin Doul.

[*They push him over in front of the Saint, near centre. Martin Doul and Mary Doul stand with piteous hang-dog dejection.*]

SAINT. Let you not be afeard, for there's great pity with the Lord.

MARTIN DOUL. We aren't afeard, holy father.

SAINT. It's many a time those that are cured with the well of the four beauties of God lose their sight when a time is gone, but those I cure a second time go on seeing till the hour of death. (*He takes the cover from his can.*) I've a few drops only left of the water, but, with the help of God, it'll be enough for the two of you, and let you kneel down now upon the road.

[*Martin Doul wheels round with Mary Doul and tries to get away.*]

SAINT. You can kneel down here, I'm saying, we'll not trouble this time going to the church.

TIMMY (*turning Martin Doul round, angrily*). Are you going mad in your head, Martin Doul? It's here you're to kneel. Did you not hear his reverence, and he speaking to you now?

SAINT. Kneel down, I'm saying, the ground's dry at your feet.

MARTIN DOUL (*with distress*). Let you go on your own way, holy father. We're not calling you at all.

SAINT. I'm not saying a word of penance, or fasting itself, for I'm thinking the Lord has brought you great teaching in the blindness of your eyes; so you've no call now to be fearing me, but let you kneel down till I give you your sight.

MARTIN DOUL (*more troubled*). We're not asking our sight, holy father, and let you walk on your own way, and be fasting, or praying, or doing anything that you will, but leave us here in our peace, at the crossing of the roads, for it's best we are this way, and we're not asking to see.

SAINT (*to the People*). Is his mind gone that he's no wish to be cured this day, or to be living or working, or looking on the wonders of the world?

MARTIN DOUL. It's wonders enough I seen in a short space for the life of one man only.

SAINT (*severely*). I never heard tell of any person wouldn't have great joy to be looking on the earth, and the image of the Lord thrown upon men.

MARTIN DOUL (*raising his voice*). Them is great sights, holy father. . . . What was it I seen when I first opened my eyes but your own bleeding feet, and they cut with the stones? That was a great sight, maybe, of the image of God. . . . And what was it I seen my last day but the villainy of hell looking out from the eyes of the girl you're coming to marry—the Lord forgive you—with Timmy the smith. That was a great sight, maybe. And wasn't it great sights I seen on the roads when the north winds would be driving, and the skies would be harsh, till you'd see the horses and the asses, and the dogs itself, maybe, with their heads hanging, and they closing their eyes—

SAINT. And did you never hear tell of the summer, and the fine spring, and the places where the holy men of Ireland have built up churches to the Lord? No man isn't a madman, I'm thinking, would be talking the like of that, and wishing to be closed up and seeing no sight of the grand glittering seas, and the furze that is opening above, and will soon have the hills shining as if it was fine creels of gold they were, rising to the sky.

MARTIN DOUL. Is it talking now you are of Knock and Ballavore? Ah, it's ourselves had finer sights than the like of them, I'm telling you, when we were sitting a while back hearing the birds and bees humming in every weed of the ditch, or when we'd be smelling the sweet, beautiful smell does be rising in the warm nights, when you do hear the swift flying things racing in the air, till we'd be looking up in our own minds into a grand sky, and seeing lakes, and big rivers, and fine hills for taking the plough.

SAINT (*to People*). There's little use talking with the like of him.

MOLLY BYRNE. It's lazy he is, holy father, and not wanting to work; for a while before you had him cured he was always talking, and wishing, and longing for his sight.

MARTIN DOUL (*turning on her*). I was longing, surely, for sight; but I seen my fill in a short while with the look of my wife, and the look of yourself, Molly Byrne, when you'd the queer wicked grin in your eyes you do have the time you're making game with a man.

MOLLY BYRNE. Let you not mind him, holy father; for it's bad things he was saying to me a while back—bad things for a married man, your reverence—and you'd do right surely to leave him in darkness, if it's that is best fitting the villainy of his heart.

TIMMY (*to Saint*). Would you cure Mary Doul, your reverence, who is a quiet poor woman, never did hurt to any, or said a hard word, saving only when she'd be vexed with himself, or with young girls would be making game of her below?

SAINT (*to Mary Doul*). If you have any sense, Mary, kneel down at my feet, and I'll bring the sight again into your eyes.

MARTIN DOUL (*more defiantly*). You will not, holy father. Would you have her looking on me, and saying hard words to me, till the hour of death?

SAINT (*severely*). If she's wanting her sight I wouldn't have the like of you stop her at all. (*To Mary Doul.*) Kneel down, I'm saying.

MARY DOUL (*doubtfully*). Let us be as we are, holy father, and then we'll be known again in a short while as the people is happy and blind, and he having an easy time, with no trouble to live, and we getting halfpence on the road.

MOLLY BYRNE. Let you not be a raving fool, Mary Doul. Kneel down now, and let him give you your sight, and himself can be sitting here if he likes it best, and taking halfpence on the road.

TIMMY. That's the truth, Mary; and if it's choosing a wilful blindness you are, I'm thinking there isn't any-one in this place will ever be giving you a hand's turn or a hap'orth of meal, or be doing the little things you need to keep you at all living in the world.

MAT SIMON. If you had your sight, Mary, you could be walking up for him and down with him, and be stitch-ing his clothes, and keeping a watch on him day and night the way no other woman would come near him at all.

MARY DOUL (*half persuaded*). That's the truth, may-be—

SAINT. Kneel down now, I'm saying, for it's in haste I am to be going on with the marriage and be walking my own way before the fall of night.

THE PEOPLE. Kneel down, Mary! Kneel down when you're bid by the Saint!

MARY DOUL (*looking uneasily towards Martin Doul*). Maybe it's right they are, and I will if you wish it, holy father.

[*She kneels down. The Saint takes off his hat and gives it to some one near him. All the men take off their hats. He goes forward a step to take Martin Doul's hand away from Mary Doul.*]

SAINT (*to Martin Doul*). Go aside now; we're not wanting you here.

MARTIN DOUL (*pushes him away roughly, and stands with his left hand on Mary Doul's shoulder*). Keep off yourself, holy father, and let you not be taking my rest from me in the darkness of my wife. . . . What call has the like of you to be coming between married people —that you're not understanding at all—and be making a great mess with the holy water you have, and the length of your prayers? Go on now, I'm saying, and leave us here on the road.

SAINT. If it was a seeing man I heard talking to me the like of that I'd put a black curse on him would weigh down his soul till it'd be falling to hell; but you're a poor blind sinner, God forgive you, and I don't mind you at all. (*He raises his can.*) Go aside now till I give the blessing to your wife, and if you won't go with your own will, there are those standing by will make you, surely.

MARTIN DOUL (*pulling Mary Doul*). Come along now, and don't mind him at all.

SAINT (*imperiously, to the People*). Let you take that man and drive him down upon the road.

[*Some men seize Martin Doul.*]

MARTIN DOUL (*struggling and shouting*). Make them leave me go, holy father! Make them leave me go, I'm saying, and you may cure her this day, or do anything that you will.

SAINT (*to People*). Let him be. . . . Let him be if his sense is come to him at all.

MARTIN DOUL (*shakes himself loose, feels for Mary Doul, sinking his voice to a plausible whine*). You may cure herself, surely, holy father; I wouldn't stop you at all—and it's great joy she'll have looking on your face —but let you cure myself along with her, the way I'll see when it's lies she's telling, and be looking out day and night upon the holy men of God.

[*He kneels down a little before Mary Doul.*]

SAINT (*speaking half to the People*). Men who are dark a long while and thinking over queer thoughts in their heads, aren't the like of simple men, who do be working every day, and praying, and living like ourselves; so if he has found a right mind at the last minute itself, I'll cure him, if the Lord will, and not be thinking of the hard, foolish words he's after saying this day to us all.

MARTIN DOUL (*listening eagerly*). I'm waiting now, holy father.

SAINT (*with can in his hand, close to Martin Doul*). With the power of the water from the grave of the four beauties of God, with the power of this water, I'm saying, that I put upon your eyes—

[*He raises can.*]

MARTIN DOUL (*with a sudden movement strikes the can from the Saint's hand and sends it rocketing across stage. He stands up; People murmur loudly*). If I'm a poor dark sinner I've sharp ears, God help me, and have left you with a big head on you and it's well I heard the little splash of the water you had there in the can. Go on now, holy father, for if you're a fine Saint itself, it's more sense is in a blind man, and more power maybe than you're thinking at all. Let you walk on now with your worn feet, and your welted knees, and your fasting, holy ways a thin pitiful arm. (*The Saint looks at him for a moment severely, then turns away and picks up his can. He pulls Mary Doul up.*) For if it's a right some of you have to be working and sweating the like of Timmy the smith, and a right some of you have to be fasting and praying and talking holy talk the like of yourself, I'm thinking it's a good right ourselves have to be sitting blind, hearing a soft wind turning round the little leaves of the spring and feeling the sun, and we not tormenting our souls with the sight of the gray days, and the holy men, and the dirty feet is trampling the world.

[*He gropes towards his stone with Mary Doul.*]

MAT SIMON. It'd be an unlucky fearful thing, I'm thinking, to have the like of that man living near us at all in the townland of Grianan. Wouldn't he bring down a curse upon us, holy father, from the heavens of God?

SAINT (*tying his girdle*). God has great mercy, but great wrath for them that sin.

THE PEOPLE. Go on now, Martin Doul. Go on from this place. Let you not be bringing great storms or droughts on us maybe from the power of the Lord.

[*Some of them throw things at him.*]

MARTIN DOUL (*turning round defiantly and picking up a stone*). Keep off now, the yelping lot of you, or it's more than one maybe will get a bloody head on him with the pitch of my stone. Keep off now, and let you not be afeard; for we're going on the two of us to the towns of the south, where the people will have kind voices maybe, and we won't know their bad looks or their villainy at all. (*He takes Mary Doul's hand again.*) Come along now and we'll be walking to the south, for we've seen too much of everyone in this place, and it's small joy we'd have living near them, or hearing the lies they do be telling from the gray of dawn till the night.

MARY DOUL (*despondingly*). That's the truth, surely; and we'd have a right to be gone, if it's a long way itself, as I've heard them say, where you do have to be walking with a slough of wet on the one side and a slough of wet on the other, and you going a stony path with a north wind blowing behind.

[*They go out.*]

TIMMY. There's a power of deep rivers with floods in them where you do have to be lepping the stones and you going to the south, so I'm thinking the two of them will be drowned together in a short while, surely.

SAINT. They have chosen their lot, and the Lord have mercy on their souls. (*He rings his bell.*) And let the two of you come up now into the church, Molly Byrne and Timmy the smith, till I make your marriage and put my blessing on you all.

[*He turns to the church; procession forms, and the curtain comes down, as they go slowly into the church.*]

THE TINKER'S WEDDING

PREFACE

THE drama is made serious—in the French sense of the word—not by the degree in which it is taken up with problems that are serious in themselves, but by the degree in which it gives the nourishment, not very easy to define, on which our imaginations live. We should not go to the theatre as we go to a chemist's, or a dram-shop, but as we go to a dinner, where the food we need is taken with pleasure and excitement. This was nearly always so in Spain and England and France when the drama was at its richest—the infancy and decay of the drama tend to be didactic—but in these days the play-house is too often stocked with the drugs of many seedy problems, or with the absinthe or vermouth of the last musical comedy.

The drama, like the symphony, does not teach or prove anything. Analysts with their problems, and teachers with their systems, are soon as old-fashioned as the pharmacopœia of Galen,—look at Ibsen and the Germans—but the best plays of Ben Jonson and Molière can no more go out of fashion than the blackberries on the hedges.

Of the things which nourish the imagination humour is one of the most needful, and it is dangerous to limit or destroy it. Baudelaire calls laughter the greatest sign of the Satanic element in man; and where a country loses its humour, as some towns in Ireland are doing, there will be morbidity of mind, as Baudelaire's mind was morbid.

In the greater part of Ireland, however, the whole people, from the tinkers to the clergy, have still a life, and view of life, that are rich and genial and humorous. I do not think that these country people, who have so much humour themselves, will mind being laughed at without malice, as the people in every country have been laughed at in their own comedies.

J. M. S.

December 2, 1907

THE TINKER'S WEDDING

A PLAY IN TWO ACTS

PERSONS IN THE PLAY

MICHAEL BYRNE (*a tinker*)

MARY BYRNE (*an old woman, his mother*)

SARAH CASEY (*a young tinker woman*)

A PRIEST

THE TINKER'S WEDDING

ACT I

SCENE. *A Village roadside after nightfall. A fire of sticks is burning near the ditch a little to the right. Michael is working beside it. In the background, on the left, a sort of tent and ragged clothes drying on the hedge. On the right a chapel-gate.*

SARAH CASEY (*coming in on right, eagerly*). We'll see his reverence this place, Michael Byrne, and he passing backward to his house to-night.

MICHAEL (*grimly*). That'll be a sacred and a sainted joy!

SARAH (*sharply*). It'll be small joy for yourself if you aren't ready with my wedding ring. (*She goes over to him.*) Is it near done this time, or what way is it at all?

MICHAEL. A poor way only, Sarah Casey, for it's the divil's job making a ring, and you'll be having my hands destroyed in a short while the way I'll not be able to make a tin can at all maybe at the dawn of day.

SARAH (*sitting down beside him and throwing sticks on the fire*). If it's the divil's job, let you mind it, and leave your speeches that would choke a fool.

MICHAEL (*slowly and glumly*). And it's you'll go talking of fools, Sarah Casey, when no man did ever hear a lying story even of your like unto this mortal day. You to be going beside me a great while, and rearing a lot of them, and then to be setting off with your talk of getting married, and your driving me to it, and I not asking it at all.

181

[*Sarah turns her back to him and arranges something in the ditch.*]

MICHAEL (*angrily*). Can't you speak a word when I'm asking what is it ails you since the moon did change?

SARAH (*musingly*). I'm thinking there isn't anything ails me, Michael Byrne; but the spring-time is a queer time, and it's queer thoughts maybe I do think at whiles.

MICHAEL. It's hard set you'd be to think queerer than welcome, Sarah Casey; but what will you gain dragging me to the priest this night, I'm saying, when it's new thoughts you'll be thinking at the dawn of day?

SARAH (*teasingly*). It's at the dawn of day I do be thinking I'd have a right to be going off to the rich tinker's do be travelling from Tibradden to the Tara Hill; for it'd be a fine life to be driving with young Jaunting Jim, where there wouldn't be any big hills to break the back of you, with walking up and walking down.

MICHAEL (*with dismay*). It's the like of that you do be thinking!

SARAH. The like of that, Michael Byrne, when there is a bit of sun in it, and a kind air, and a great smell coming from the thorn trees is above your head.

MICHAEL (*looks at her for a moment with horror, and then hands her the ring*). Will that fit you now?

SARAH (*trying it on*). It's making it tight you are, and the edges sharp on the tin.

MICHAEL (*looking at it carefully*). It's the fat of your own finger, Sarah Casey; and isn't it a mad thing I'm saying again that you'd be asking marriage of me, or making a talk of going away from me, and you thriving and getting your good health by the grace of the Almighty God?

SARAH (*giving it back to him*). Fix it now, and it'll do, if you're wary you don't squeeze it again.

MICHAEL (*moodily, working again*). It's easy saying be wary; there's many things easy said, Sarah Casey, you'd wonder a fool even would be saying at all. (*He starts violently.*) The divil mend you, I'm scalded again!

SARAH (*scornfully*). If you are, it's a clumsy man you are this night, Michael Byrne (*raising her voice*); and let you make haste now, or herself will be coming with the porter.

MICHAEL (*defiantly, raising his voice*). Let me make haste? I'll be making haste maybe to hit you a great clout; for I'm thinking it's the like of that you want. I'm thinking on the day I got you above at Rathvanna, and the way you began crying out and we coming down off the hill, crying out and saying, "I'll go back to my ma," and I'm thinking on the way I came behind you that time, and hit you a great clout in the lug, and how quiet and easy it was you came along with me from that hour to this present day.

SARAH (*standing up and throwing all her sticks into the fire*). And a big fool I was too, maybe; but we'll be seeing Jaunting Jim to-morrow in Ballinaclash, and he after getting a great price for his white foal in the horse-fair of Wicklow, the way it'll be a great sight to see him squandering his share of gold, and he with a grand eye for a fine horse, and a grand eye for a woman.

MICHAEL (*working again with impatience*). The divil do him good with the two of them.

SARAH (*kicking up the ashes with her foot*). Ah, he's a great lad, I'm telling you, and it's proud and happy I'll be to see him, and he the first one called me the Beauty of Ballinacree, a fine name for a woman.

MICHAEL (*with contempt*). It's the like of that name they do be putting on the horses they have below racing in Arklow. It's easy pleased you are, Sarah Casey, easy pleased with a big word, or the liar speaks it.

SARAH. Liar!

MICHAEL. Liar, surely.

SARAH (*indignantly*). Liar, is it? Didn't you ever hear tell of the peelers followed me ten miles along the Glen Malure, and they talking love to me in the dark night, or of the children you'll meet coming from school and they saying one to the other, "It's this day we seen Sarah Casey, the Beauty of Ballinacree, a great sight surely."

MICHAEL. God help the lot of them!

SARAH. It's yourself you'll be calling God to help, in two weeks or three, when you'll be waking up in the dark night and thinking you see me coming with the sun on me, and I driving a high cart with Jaunting Jim going behind. It's lonesome and cold you'll be feeling the ditch where you'll be lying down that night, I'm telling you, and you hearing the old woman making a great noise in her sleep, and the bats squeaking in the trees.

MICHAEL. Whist. I hear some one coming the road.

SARAH (*looking out right*). It's some one coming forward from the doctor's door.

MICHAEL. It's often his reverence does be in there playing cards, or drinking a sup, or singing songs, until the dawn of day.

SARAH. It's a big boast of a man with a long step on him and a trumpeting voice. It's his reverence surely; and if you have the ring done, it's a great bargain we'll make now and he after drinking his glass.

MICHAEL (*going to her and giving her the ring*). There's your ring, Sarah Casey; but I'm thinking he'll walk by and not stop to speak with the like of us at all.

SARAH (*tidying herself, in great excitement*). Let you be sitting here and keeping a great blaze, the way he can look on my face; and let you seem to be working, for it's great love the like of him have to talk of work.

MICHAEL (*moodily, sitting down and beginning to work at a tin can*). Great love surely.

SARAH (*eagerly*). Make a great blaze now, Michael Byrne.

[*The priest comes in on right; she comes forward in front of him.*]

SARAH (*in a very plausible voice*). Good evening, your reverence. It's a grand fine night, by the grace of God.

PRIEST. The Lord have mercy on us! What kind of a living woman is it that you are at all?

SARAH. It's Sarah Casey I am, your reverence, the Beauty of Ballinacree, and it's Michael Byrne is below in the ditch.

PRIEST. A holy pair, surely! Let you get out of my way.

[*He tries to pass by.*]

SARAH (*keeping in front of him*). We are wanting a little word with your reverence.

PRIEST. I haven't a halfpenny at all. Leave the road I'm saying.

SARAH. It isn't a halfpenny we're asking, holy father; but we were thinking maybe we'd have a right to be getting married; and we were thinking it's yourself would marry us for not a halfpenny at all; for you're a kind man, your reverence, a kind man with the poor.

PRIEST (*with astonishment*). Is it marry you for nothing at all?

SARAH. It is, your reverence; and we were thinking maybe you'd give us a little small bit of silver to pay for the ring.

PRIEST (*loudly*). Let you hold your tongue; let you be quiet, Sarah Casey. I've no silver at all for the like of you; and if you want to be married, let you pay your pound. I'd do it for a pound only, and that's making it a sight cheaper than I'd make it for one of my own pairs is living here in the place.

SARAH. Where would the like of us get a pound, your reverence?

PRIEST. Wouldn't you easy get it with your selling asses, and making cans, and your stealing east and west in Wicklow and Wexford and the County Meath? (*He tries to pass her.*) Let you leave the road, and not be plaguing me more.

SARAH (*pleadingly, taking money from her pocket*). Wouldn't you have a little mercy on us, your reverence? (*Holding out money.*) Wouldn't you marry us for a half a sovereign, and it a nice shiny one with a view on it of the living king's mamma?

PRIEST. If it's ten shillings you have, let you get ten more the same way, and I'll marry you then.

SARAH (*whining*). It's two years we are getting that bit, your reverence, with our pence and our halfpence and an odd threepenny bit; and if you don't marry us now, himself and the old woman, who has a great drouth, will be drinking it to-morrow in the fair (*she puts her apron to her eyes, half sobbing*), and then I won't be married any time, and I'll be saying till I'm an old woman: "It's a cruel and a wicked thing to be bred poor."

PRIEST (*turning up towards the fire*). Let you not be crying, Sarah Casey. It's a queer woman you are to be crying at the like of that, and you your whole life walking the roads.

SARAH (*sobbing*). It's two years we are getting the gold, your reverence, and now you won't marry us for that bit, and we hard-working poor people do be making cans in the dark night, and blinding our eyes with the black smoke from the bits of twigs we do be burning.

[*An old woman is heard singing tipsily on the left.*]

PRIEST (*looking at the can Michael is making*). When will you have that can done, Michael Byrne?

MICHAEL. In a short space only, your reverence, for I'm putting the last dab of solder on the rim.

PRIEST. Let you get a crown along with the ten shillings and the gallon can, Sarah Casey, and I will wed you so.

MARY (*suddenly shouting behind, tipsily*). Larry was a fine lad, I'm saying; Larry was a fine lad, Sarah Casey—

MICHAEL. Whist, now, the two of you. There's my mother coming, and she'd have us destroyed if she heard the like of that talk the time she's been drinking her fill.

MARY (*comes in singing*).

And when we asked him what way he'd die,
    And he hanging unrepented,
"Begob," says Larry, "that's all in my eye,
    By the clergy first invented."

SARAH. Give me the jug now, or you'll have it spilt in the ditch.

MARY (*holding the jug with both her hands, in a stilted voice*). Let you leave me easy, Sarah Casey. I won't spill it, I'm saying. God help you; are you thinking it's frothing full to the brim it is at this hour of the night, and I after carrying it in my two hands a long step from Jemmy Neill's?

MICHAEL (*anxiously*). Is there a sup left at all?

SARAH (*looking into the jug*). A little small sup only I'm thinking.

MARY (*sees the priest, and holds out jug towards him*). God save your reverence. I'm after bringing down a smart drop; and let you drink it up now, for it's a middling drouthy man you are at all times, God forgive you, and this night is cruel dry.

[*She tries to go towards him. Sarah holds her back.*]

PRIEST (*waving her away*). Let you not be falling to the flames. Keep off, I'm saying.

MARY (*persuasively*). Let you not be shy of us, your reverence. Aren't we all sinners, God help us! Drink a sup now, I'm telling you; and we won't let on a word about it till the Judgment Day.

[*She takes up a tin mug, pours some porter into it, and gives it to him.*]

MARY (*singing, and holding the jug in her hand*).

A lonesome ditch in Ballygan
The day you're beating a tenpenny can;
A lonesome bank in Ballyduff
The time . . .

[*She breaks off.*]

It's a bad, wicked song, Sarah Casey; and let you put me down now in the ditch, and I won't sing it till himself will be gone; for it's bad enough he is, I'm thinking, without ourselves making him worse.

SARAH (*putting her down, to the priest, half laughing*). Don't mind her at all, your reverence. She's no shame the time she's a drop taken; and if it was the Holy Father from Rome was in it, she'd give him a little sup out of her mug, and say the same as she'd say to yourself.

MARY (*to the priest*). Let you drink it up, holy father. Let you drink it up, I'm saying, and not be letting on you wouldn't do the like of it, and you with a stack of pint bottles above, reaching the sky.

PRIEST (*with resignation*). Well, here's to your good health, and God forgive us all.

[*He drinks.*]

MARY. That's right now, your reverence, and the blessing of God be on you. Isn't it a grand thing to see you sitting down, with no pride in you, and drinking a sup with the like of us, and we the poorest, wretched, starving creatures you'd see any place on the earth?

PRIEST. If it's starving you are itself, I'm thinking it's well for the like of you that do be drinking when there's drouth on you, and lying down to sleep when your legs are stiff. (*He sighs gloomily.*) What would you do if it was the like of myself you were, saying Mass with your mouth dry, and running east and west for a sick call maybe, and hearing the rural people again and they saying their sins?

MARY (*with compassion*). It's destroyed you must be hearing the sins of the rural people on a fine spring.

PRIEST (*with despondency*). It's a hard life, I'm telling you, a hard life, Mary Byrne; and there's the bishop coming in the morning, and he an old man, would have you destroyed if he seen a thing at all.

MARY (*with great sympathy*). It'd break my heart to hear you talking and sighing the like of that, your reverence. (*She pats him on the knee.*) Let you rouse up, now, if it's a poor, single man you are itself, and I'll be singing you songs unto the dawn of day.

PRIEST (*interrupting her*). What is it I want with your songs when it'd be better for the like of you, that'll soon die, to be down on your two knees saying prayers to the Almighty God?

MARY. If it's prayers I want, you'd have a right to say one yourself, holy father; for we don't have them at all, and I've heard tell a power of times it's that you're for. Say one now, your reverence, for I've heard a power of queer things and I walking the world, but there's one thing I never heard any time, and that's a real priest saying a prayer.

PRIEST. The Lord protect us!

MARY. It's no lie, holy father. I often heard the rural people making a queer noise and they going to rest; but who'd mind the like of them? And I'm thinking it should be great game to hear a scholar, the like of you, speaking Latin to the saints above.

PRIEST (*scandalized*). Stop your talking, Mary Byrne; you're an old flagrant heathen, and I'll stay no more with the lot of you.

[*He rises.*]

MARY (*catching hold of him*). Stop till you say a prayer, your reverence; stop till you say a little prayer, I'm tell-

ing you, and I'll give you my blessing and the last sup
from the jug.

PRIEST (*breaking away*). Leave me go, Mary Byrne;
for I have never met your like for hard abominations
the score and two years I'm living in the place.

MARY (*innocently*). Is that the truth?

PRIEST. It is, then, and God have mercy on your soul.

[*The priest goes towards the left, and Sarah follows
him.*]

SARAH (*in a low voice*). And what time will you do the
thing I'm asking, holy father? for I'm thinking you'll
do it surely, and not have me growing into an old,
wicked heathen like herself.

MARY (*calling out shrilly*). Let you be walking back
here, Sarah Casey, and not be talking whisper-talk with
the like of him in the face of the Almighty God.

SARAH (*to the priest*). Do you hear her now, your reverence? Isn't it true, surely, she's an old, flagrant
heathen, would destroy the world?

PRIEST (*to Sarah, moving off*). Well, I'll be coming
down early to the chapel, and let you come to me a
while after you see me passing, and bring the bit of gold
along with you, and the tin can. I'll marry you for them
two, though it's a pitiful small sum; for I wouldn't be
easy in my soul if I left you growing into an old, wicked
heathen the like of her.

SARAH (*following him out*). The blessing of the Almighty God be on you, holy father, and that He may reward and watch you from this present day.

MARY (*nudging Michael*). Did you see that, Michael
Byrne? Didn't you hear me telling you she's flighty a
while back since the change of the moon? With her

fussing for marriage, and she making whisper-talk with one man or another man along by the road.

MICHAEL. Whist now, or she'll knock the head of you the time she comes back.

MARY. Ah, it's a bad, wicked way the world is this night, if there's a fine air in it itself. You'd never have seen me, and I a young woman, making whisper-talk with the like of him, and he the fearfulest old fellow you'd see any place walking the world.

[*Sarah comes back quickly.*]

MARY (*calling out to her*). What is it you're after whispering above with himself?

SARAH (*exultingly*). Lie down, and leave us in peace.

[*She whispers with Michael.*]

MARY (*poking out her pipe with a straw, sings*).

She'd whisper with one, and she'd whisper with
    two—

(*She breaks off coughing.*) My singing voice is gone for this night, Sarah Casey. (*She lights her pipe.*) But if it's flighty you are itself, you're a grand handsome woman, the glory of tinkers, the pride of Wicklow, the Beauty of Ballinacree. I wouldn't have you lying down and you lonesome to sleep this night in a dark ditch when the spring is coming in the trees; so let you sit down there by the big bough, and I'll be telling you the finest story you'd hear any place from Dundalk to Ballinacree, with great queens in it, making themselves matches from the start to the end, and they with shiny silks on them the length of the day, and white shifts for the night.

MICHAEL (*standing up with the tin can in his hand*). Let you go asleep, and not have us destroyed.

MARY (*lying back sleepily*). Don't mind him, Sarah

Casey. Sit down now, and I'll be telling you a story would be fit to tell a woman the like of you in the spring-time of the year.

SARAH (*taking the can from Michael, and tying it up in a piece of sacking*). That'll not be rusting now in the dews of night. I'll put it up in the ditch the way it will be handy in the morning; and now we've that done, Michael Byrne, I'll go along with you and welcome for Tim Flaherty's hens.

[*She puts the can in the ditch.*]

MARY (*sleepily*). I've a grand story of the great queens of Ireland with white necks on them the like of Sarah Casey, and fine arms would hit you a slap the way Sarah Casey would hit you.

SARAH (*beckoning on the left*). Come along now, Michael, while she's falling asleep.

[*He goes towards left. Mary sees that they are going, starts up suddenly, and turns over on her hands and knees.*]

MARY (*piteously*). Where is it you're going? Let you walk back here, and not be leaving me lonesome when the night is fine.

SARAH. Don't be waking the world with your talk when we're going up through the back wood to get two of Tim Flaherty's hens are roosting in the ash-tree above at the well.

MARY. And it's leaving me lone you are? Come back here, Sarah Casey. Come back here, I'm saying; or if it's off you must go, leave me the two little coppers you have, the way I can walk up in a short while, and get another pint for my sleep.

SARAH. It's too much you have taken. Let you stretch

yourself out and take a long sleep; for isn't that the best thing any woman can do, and she an old drinking heathen like yourself.

[*She and Michael go out left.*]

MARY (*standing up slowly*). It's gone they are, and I with my feet that weak under me you'd knock me down with a rush, and my head with a noise in it the like of what you'd hear in a stream and it running between two rocks and rain falling. (*She goes over to the ditch where the can is tied in sacking, and takes it down.*) What good am I this night, God help me? What good are the grand stories I have when it's few would listen to an old woman, few but a girl maybe would be in great fear the time her hour was come, or a little child wouldn't be sleeping with the hunger on a cold night? (*She takes the can from the sacking and fits in three empty bottles and straw in its place, and ties them up.*) Maybe the two of them have a good right to be walking out the little short while they'd be young; but if they have itself, they'll not keep Mary Byrne from her full pint when the night's fine, and there's a dry moon in the sky. (*She takes up the can, and puts the package back in the ditch.*) Jemmy Neill's a decent lad; and he'll give me a good drop for the can; and maybe if I keep near the peelers to-morrow for the first bit of the fair, herself won't strike me at all; and if she does itself, what's a little stroke on your head beside sitting lonesome on a fine night, hearing the dogs barking, and the bats squeaking, and you saying over, it's a short while only till you die.

[*She goes out singing "The night before Larry was stretched."*]

CURTAIN

ACT II

SCENE. *The same. Early morning. Sarah is washing her face in an old bucket; then plaits her hair. Michael is tidying himself also. Mary Byrne is asleep against the ditch.*

SARAH (*to Michael, with pleased excitement*). Go over, now, to the bundle beyond, and you'll find a kind of a red handkerchief to put upon your neck, and a green one for myself.

MICHAEL (*getting them*). You're after spending more money on the like of them. Well, it's a power we're losing this time, and we not gaining a thing at all. (*With the handkerchiefs.*) Is it them two?

SARAH. It is, Michael. (*She takes one of them.*) Let you tackle that one round under your chin; and let you not forget to take your hat from your head when we go up into the church. I asked Biddy Flynn below, that's after marrying her second man, and she told me it's the like of that they do.

[*Mary yawns, and turns over in her sleep.*]

SARAH (*with anxiety*). There she is waking up on us, and I thinking we'd have the job done before she'd know of it at all.

MICHAEL. She'll be crying out now, and making game of us, and saying it's fools we are surely.

SARAH. I'll send her to sleep again, or get her out of it one way or another; for it'd be a bad case to have a divil's scholar the like of her turning the priest against us maybe with her godless talk.

MARY (*waking up, and looking at them with curiosity, blandly*). That's fine things you have on you, Sarah Casey; and it's a great stir you're making this day, washing your face. I'm that used to the hammer, I wouldn't hear it at all, but washing is a rare thing, and you're after waking me up, and I having a great sleep in the sun.

[*She looks around cautiously at the bundle in which she has hidden the bottles.*]

SARAH (*coaxingly*). Let you stretch out again for a sleep, Mary Byrne, for it'll be a middling time yet before we go to the fair.

MARY (*with suspicion*). That's a sweet tongue you have, Sarah Casey; but if sleep's a grand thing, it's a grand thing to be waking up a day the like of this, when there's a warm sun in it, and a kind air, and you'll hear the cuckoos singing and crying out on the top of the hills.

SARAH. If it's that gay you are, you'd have a right to walk down and see would you get a few halfpence from the rich men do be driving early to the fair.

MARY. When rich men do be driving early, it's queer tempers they have, the Lord forgive them; the way it's little but bad words and swearing out you'd get from them all.

SARAH (*losing her temper and breaking out fiercely*). Then if you'll neither beg nor sleep, let you walk off from this place where you're not wanted, and not have us waiting for you maybe at the turn of day.

MARY (*rather uneasy, turning to Michael*). God help our spirits, Michael; there she is again rousing cranky from the break of dawn. Oh! isn't she a terror since the moon did change? (*She gets up slowly.*) And I'd best be going forward to sell the gallon can.

[*She goes over and takes up the bundle.*]

SARAH (*crying out angrily*). Leave that down, Mary Byrne. Oh! aren't you the scorn of women to think that you'd have that drouth and roguery on you that you'd go drinking the can and the dew not dried from the grass?

MARY (*in a feigned tone of pacification, with the bundle still in her hand*). It's not a drouth but a heartburn I have this day, Sarah Casey, so I'm going down to cool my gullet at the blessed well; and I'll sell the can to the parson's daughter below, a harmless poor creature would fill your hand with shillings for a brace of lies.

SARAH. Leave down the tin can, Mary Byrne, for I hear the drouth upon your tongue to-day.

MARY. There's not a drink-house from this place to the fair, Sarah Casey; the way you'll find me below with the full price, and not a farthing gone.

[*She turns to go off left.*]

SARAH (*jumping up, and picking up the hammer threateningly*). Put down that can, I'm saying.

MARY (*looking at her for a moment in terror, and putting down the bundle in the ditch*). Is it raving mad you're going, Sarah Casey, and you the pride of women to destroy the world?

SARAH (*going up to her, and giving her a push off left*). I'll show you if it's raving mad I am. Go on from this place, I'm saying, and be wary now.

MARY (*turning back after her*). If I go, I'll be telling old and young you're a weathered heathen savage, Sarah Casey, the one did put down a head of the parson's cabbage to boil in the pot with your clothes (*the priest comes in behind her, on the left, and listens*), and quenched the flaming candles on the throne of God the time your shadow fell within the pillars of the chapel door.

[*Sarah turns on her, and she springs round nearly into the priest's arms. When she sees him, she claps her shawl over her mouth, and goes up towards the ditch, laughing to herself.*]

PRIEST (*going to Sarah, half terrified at the language that he has heard*). Well, aren't you a fearful lot? I'm thinking it's only humbug you were making at the fall of night, and you won't need me at all.

SARAH (*with anger still in her voice*). Humbug is it! Would you be turning back upon your spoken promise in the face of God?

PRIEST (*dubiously*). I'm thinking you were never christened, Sarah Casey; and it would be a queer job to go dealing Christian sacraments unto the like of you. (*Persuasively feeling in his pocket.*) So it would be best, maybe, I'd give you a shilling for to drink my health, and let you walk on, and not trouble me at all.

SARAH. That's your talking, is it? If you don't stand to your spoken word, holy father, I'll make my own complaint to the mitred bishop in the face of all.

PRIEST. You'd do that!

SARAH. I would surely, holy father, if I walked to the city of Dublin with blood and blisters on my naked feet.

PRIEST (*uneasily scratching his ear*). I wish this day was done, Sarah Casey; for I'm thinking it's a risky thing getting mixed up in any matters with the like of you.

SARAH. Be hasty then, and you'll have us done with before you'd think at all.

PRIEST (*giving in*). Well, maybe it's right you are, and let you come up to the chapel when you see me looking from the door.

[*He goes up into the chapel.*]

SARAH (*calling after him*). We will, and God preserve you, holy father.

MARY (*coming down to them, speaking with amazement and consternation, but without anger*). Going to the chapel! It's at marriage you're fooling again, maybe? (*Sarah turns her back on her.*) It was for that you were washing your face, and you after sending me for porter at the fall of night the way I'd drink a good half from the jug? (*Going round in front of Sarah.*) Is it at marriage you're fooling again?

SARAH (*triumphantly*). It is, Mary Byrne. I'll be married now in a short while; and from this day there will no one have a right to call me a dirty name and I selling cans in Wicklow or Wexford or the city of Dublin itself.

MARY (*turning to Michael*). And it's yourself is wedding her, Michael Byrne?

MICHAEL (*gloomily*). It is, God spare us.

MARY (*looks at Sarah for a moment, and then bursts out into a laugh of derision*). Well, she's a tight, hardy girl, and it's no lie; but I never knew till this day it was a black born fool I had for a son. You'll breed asses, I've heard them say, and poaching dogs, and horses'd go licking the wind, but it's a hard thing, God help me, to breed sense in a son.

MICHAEL (*gloomily*). If I didn't marry her, she'd be walking off to Jaunting Jim maybe at the fall of night; and it's well yourself knows there isn't the like of her for getting money and selling songs to the men.

MARY. And you're thinking it's paying gold to his reverence would make a woman stop when she's a mind to go?

SARAH (*angrily*). Let you not be destroying us with your talk when I've as good a right to a decent marriage as any speckled female does be sleeping in the black hovels above, would choke a mule.

MARY (*soothingly*). It's as good a right you have surely, Sarah Casey, but what good will it do? Is it putting that ring on your finger will keep you from getting an aged woman and losing the fine face you have, or be easing your pains, when it's the grand ladies do be married in silk dresses, with rings of gold, that do pass any woman with their share of torment in the hour of birth, and do be paying the doctors in the city of Dublin a great price at that time, the like of what you'd pay for a good ass and a cart?

[*She sits down.*]

SARAH (*puzzled*). Is that the truth?

MARY (*pleased with the point she has made*). Wouldn't any know it's the truth? Ah, it's a few short years you are yet in the world, Sarah Casey, and it's little or nothing at all maybe you know about it.

SARAH (*vehement but uneasy*). What is it yourself knows of the fine ladies when they wouldn't let the like of you go near them at all?

MARY. If you do be drinking a little sup in one town and another town, it's soon you get great knowledge and a great sight into the world. You'll see men there, and women there, sitting up on the ends of barrels in the dark night, and they making great talk would soon have the like of you, Sarah Casey, as wise as a March hare.

MICHAEL (*to Sarah*). That's the truth she's saying, and maybe if you've sense in you at all, you'd have a right still to leave your fooling, and not be wasting our gold.

SARAH (*decisively*). If it's wise or fool I am, I've made a good bargain and I'll stand to it now.

MARY. What is it he's making you give?

MICHAEL. The ten shillings in gold, and the tin can is above tied in the sack.

MARY (*looking at the bundle with surprise and dread*). The bit of gold and the tin can, is it?

MICHAEL. The half a sovereign, and the gallon can.

MARY (*scrambling to her feet quickly*). Well, I think I'll be walking off the road to the fair the way you won't be destroying me going too fast on the hills. (*She goes a few steps towards the left, then turns and speaks to Sarah very persuasively*). Let you not take the can from the sack, Sarah Casey; for the people is coming above would be making game of you, and pointing their fingers if they seen you do the like of that. Let you leave it safe in the bag, I'm saying, Sarah darling. It's that way will be best.

[*She goes towards left, and pauses for a moment, looking about her with embarrassment.*]

MICHAEL (*in a low voice*). What ails her at all?

SARAH (*anxiously*). It's real wicked she does be when you hear her speaking as easy as that.

MARY (*to herself*). I'd be safer in the chapel, I'm thinking; for if she caught me after on the road, maybe she would kill me then.

[*She comes hobbling back towards the right.*]

SARAH. Where is it you're going? It isn't that way we'll be walking to the fair.

MARY. I'm going up into the chapel to give you my blessing and hear the priest saying his prayers. It's a lonesome road is running below to Greenane, and a woman would never know the things might happen her and she walking single in a lonesome place.

[*As she reaches the chapel-gate, the priest comes to it in his surplice.*]

PRIEST (*crying out*). Come along now. It is the whole day you'd keep me here saying my prayers, and I getting my death with not a bit in my stomach, and my breakfast in ruins, and the Lord Bishop maybe driving on the road to-day?

SARAH. We're coming now, holy father.

PRIEST. Give me the bit of gold into my hand.

SARAH. It's here, holy father.

[*She gives it to him. Michael takes the bundle from the ditch and brings it over, standing a little behind Sarah. He feels the bundle, and looks at Mary with a meaning look.*]

PRIEST (*looking at the gold*). It's a good one, I'm thinking, wherever you got it. And where is the can?

SARAH (*taking the bundle*). We have it here in a bit of clean sack, your reverence. We tied it up in the inside of that to keep it from rusting in the dews of night, and let you not open it now or you'll have the people making game of us and telling the story on us, east and west to the butt of the hills.

PRIEST (*taking the bundle*). Give it here into my hand, Sarah Casey. What is it any person would think of a tinker making a can.

[*He begins opening the bundle.*]

SARAH. It's a fine can, your reverence, for if it's poor simple people we are, it's fine cans we can make, and himself, God help him, is a great man surely at the trade.

[*Priest opens the bundle; the three empty bottles fall out.*]

SARAH. Glory to the saints of joy!

PRIEST. Did ever any man see the like of that? To think you'd be putting deceit on me, and telling lies to me, and I going to marry you for a little sum wouldn't marry a child.

SARAH (*crestfallen and astonished*). It's the divil did it, your reverence, and I wouldn't tell you a lie. (*Raising her hands.*) May the Lord Almighty strike me dead if the divil isn't after hooshing the tin can from the bag.

PRIEST (*vehemently*). Go along now, and don't be swearing your lies. Go along now, and let you not be thinking I'm big fool enough to believe the like of that, when it's after selling it you are or making a swap for drink of it, maybe, in the darkness of the night.

MARY (*in a peacemaking voice, putting her hand on the priest's left arm*). She wouldn't do the like of that, your reverence, when she hasn't a decent standing drouth on her at all; and she's setting great store on her marriage the way you'd have a right to be taking her easy, and not minding the can. What differ would an empty can make with a fine, rich, hardy man the like of you?

SARAH (*imploringly*). Marry us, your reverence, for the ten shillings in gold, and we'll make you a grand can in the evening—a can would be fit to carry water for the holy man of God. Marry us now and I'll be saying fine prayers for you, morning and night, if it'd be raining itself, and it'd be in two black pools I'd be setting my knees.

PRIEST (*loudly*). It's a wicked, thieving, lying, scheming lot you are, the pack of you. Let you walk off now and take every stinking rag you have there from the ditch.

MARY (*putting her shawl over her head*). Marry her, your reverence, for the love of God, for there'll be queer doings below if you send her off the like of that and she swearing crazy on the road.

SARAH (*angrily*). It's the truth she's saying; for it's herself, I'm thinking, is after swapping the tin can for a pint, the time she was raging mad with the drouth, and ourselves above walking the hill.

MARY (*crying out with indignation*). Have you no shame, Sarah Casey, to tell lies unto a holy man?

SARAH (*to Mary, working herself into a rage*). It's making game of me you'd be, and putting a fool's head on me in the face of the world; but if you were thinking to be mighty cute walking off, or going up to hide in the church, I've got you this time, and you'll not run from me now.

[*She seizes up one of the bottles.*]

MARY (*hiding behind the priest*). Keep her off, your

reverence, keep her off for the love of the Almighty God. What at all would the Lord Bishop say if he found me here lying with my head broken across, or the two of yous maybe digging a bloody grave for me at the door of the church?

PRIEST (*waving Sarah off*). Go along, Sarah Casey. Would you be doing murder at my feet? Go along from me now, and wasn't I a big fool to have to do with you when it's nothing but distraction and torment I get from the kindness of my heart?

SARAH (*shouting*). I've bet a power of strong lads east and west through the world, and are you thinking I'd turn back from a priest? Leave the road now, or maybe I would strike yourself.

PRIEST. You would not, Sarah Casey. I've no fear for the lot of you; but let you walk off, I'm saying, and not be coming where you've no business, and screeching tumult and murder at the doorway of the church.

SARAH. I'll not go a step till I have her head broke, or till I'm wed with himself. If you want to get shut of us, let you marry us now, for I'm thinking the ten shillings in gold is a good price for the like of you, and you near burst with the fat.

PRIEST. I wouldn't have you coming in on me and soiling my church; for there's nothing at all, I'm thinking, would keep the like of you from hell. (*He throws down the ten shillings on the ground.*) Gather up your gold now, and begone from my sight, for if ever I set an eye on you again you'll hear me telling the peelers who it was stole the black ass belonging to Philly O'Cullen, and whose hay it is the grey ass does be eating.

SARAH. You'd do that?

PRIEST. I would, surely.

SARAH. If you do, you'll be getting all the tinkers from Wicklow and Wexford, and the County Meath, to put up block tin in the place of glass to shield your windows where you do be looking out and blinking at the girls. It's hard set you'll be that time, I'm telling you, to fill the depth of your belly the long days of Lent; for we wouldn't leave a laying pullet in your yard at all.

PRIEST (*losing his temper finally*). Go on, now, or I'll send the Lords of Justice a dated story of your villainies —burning, stealing, robbing, raping to this mortal day. Go on now, I'm saying, if you'd run from Kilmainham or the rope itself.

MICHAEL (*taking off his coat*). Is it run from the like of you, holy father? Go up to your own shanty, or I'll beat you with the ass's reins till the world would hear you roaring from this place to the coast of Clare.

PRIEST. Is it lift your hand upon myself when the Lord would blight your members if you'd touch me now? Go on from this.

[*He gives him a shove.*]

MICHAEL. Blight me is it? Take it then, your reverence, and God help you so.

[*He runs at him with the reins.*]

PRIEST (*runs up to ditch crying out*). There are the peelers passing by the grace of God—hey, below!

MARY (*clapping her hand over his mouth*). Knock him down on the road; they didn't hear him at all.

[*Michael pulls him down.*]

SARAH. Gag his jaws.

MARY. Stuff the sacking in his teeth.

[*They gag him with the sack that had the can in it.*]

SARAH. Tie the bag around his head, and if the peelers come, we'll put him head-first in the boghole is beyond the ditch.

[*They tie him up in some sacking.*]

MICHAEL (*to Mary*). Keep him quiet, and the rags tight on him for fear he'd screech. (*He goes back to their camp.*) Hurry with the things, Sarah Casey. The peelers aren't coming this way, and maybe we'll get off from them now.

[*They bundle the things together in wild haste, the priest wriggling and struggling about on the ground, with old Mary trying to keep him quiet.*]

MARY (*patting his head*). Be quiet, your reverence. What is it ails you, with your wrigglings now? Is it choking maybe? (*She puts her hand under the sack, and feels his mouth, patting him on the back.*) It's only letting on you are, holy father, for your nose is blowing back and forward as easy as an east wind on an April day. (*In a soothing voice.*) There now, holy father, let you stay easy, I'm telling you, and learn a little sense and patience, the way you'll not be so airy again going to rob poor sinners of their scraps of gold. (*He gets quieter.*) That's a good boy you are now, your reverence, and let you not be uneasy, for we wouldn't hurt you at all. It's sick and sorry we are to tease you; but what did you want meddling with the like of us, when it's a long time we are going our own ways—father and son, and his son after him, or mother and daughter, and her own daughter again—and it's little need we ever had of going up into a church and swearing—I'm told there's swearing with it—a word no man would believe, or with drawing rings on our fingers, would be cutting our skins maybe when we'd be taking the ass from the shafts, and pulling the straps the time they'd be slippy with going around beneath the heavens in rains falling.

MICHAEL (*who has finished bundling up the things, comes over to Sarah*). We're fixed now; and I have a mind to run him in a boghole the way he'll not be tattling to the peelers of our games to-day.

SARAH. You'd have a right too, I'm thinking.

MARY (*soothingly*). Let you not be rough with him, Sarah Casey, and he after drinking his sup of porter with us at the fall of night. Maybe he'd swear a mighty oath he wouldn't harm us, and then we'd safer loose him; for if we went to drown him, they'd maybe hang the batch of us, man and child and woman, and the ass itself.

MICHAEL. What would he care for an oath?

MARY. Don't you know his like do live in terror of the wrath of God? (*Putting her mouth to the priest's ear in the sacking.*) Would you swear an oath, holy father, to leave us in our freedom, and not talk at all? (*Priest nods in sacking.*) Didn't I tell you? Look at the poor fellow nodding his head off in the bias of the sacks. Strip them off from him, and he'll be easy now.

MICHAEL (*as if speaking to a horse*). Hold up, holy father.

[*He pulls the sacking off, and shows the priest with his hair on end. They free his mouth.*]

MARY. Hold him till he swears.

PRIEST (*in a faint voice*). I swear surely. If you let me go in peace, I'll not inform against you or say a thing at all, and may God forgive me for giving heed unto your like to-day.

SARAH (*puts the ring on his finger*). There's the ring, holy father, to keep you minding of your oath until the end of time; for my heart's scalded with your fooling; and it'll be a long day till I go making talk of marriage or the like of that.

MARY (*complacently, standing up slowly*). She's vexed now, your reverence; and let you not mind her at all, for she's right surely, and it's little need we ever had of the like of you to get us our bit to eat, and our bit to drink, and our time of love when we were young men and women, and were fine to look at.

MICHAEL. Hurry on now. He's a great man to have kept us from fooling our gold; and we'll have a great time drinking that bit with the trampers on the green of Clash.

[*They gather up their things. The priest stands up.*]

PRIEST (*lifting up his hand*). I've sworn not to call the hand of man upon your crimes to-day; but I haven't sworn I wouldn't call the fire of heaven from the hand of the Almighty God.

[*He begins saying a Latin malediction in a loud ecclesiastical voice.*]

MARY. There's an old villain.

ALL (*together*). Run, run. Run for your lives.

[*They rush out, leaving the priest master of the situation.*]

CURTAIN

DEIRDRE OF THE SORROWS

A PLAY IN THREE ACTS

PERSONS IN THE PLAY

*First performed at the Abbey Theatre, Dublin,
Thursday, January 13, 1910.*

LAVARCHAM (*Deirdre's nurse*)   Sara Allgood

OLD WOMAN (*Lavarcham's servant*)
                              Eileen O'Doherty

OWEN (*Conchubor's attendant and spy*)
                              J. A. O'Rourke

CONCHUBOR (*High King of Ulster*)   Arthur Sinclair

FERGUS (*Conchubor's friend*)   Sydney J. Morgan

DEIRDRE   Maire O'Neill

NAISI (*Deirdre's lover*)   Fred O'Donovan

AINNLE (*Naisi's brother*)   J. M. Kerrigan

ARDAN (*Naisi's brother*)   John Carrick

TWO SOLDIERS   { Ambrose Power
                       { Harry Young

DEIRDRE OF THE SORROWS

ACT I

SCENE. *Lavarcham's house on Slieve Fuadh. There is a door to inner room on the left, and a door to open air on the right. Window at back and a frame with a half-finished piece of tapestry. There are also a large press and heavy oak chest near the back wall. The place is neat and clean but bare. Lavarcham, woman of fifty, is working at tapestry frame. Old Woman comes in from left.*

OLD WOMAN. She hasn't come yet, is it, and it falling to the night?

LAVARCHAM. She has not. . . . (*Concealing her anxiety.*) It's dark with the clouds are coming from the west and south, but it isn't later than the common.

OLD WOMAN. It's later, surely, and I hear tell the Sons of Usna, Naisi and his brothers, are above chasing hares for two days or three, and the same awhile since when the moon was full.

LAVARCHAM (*more anxiously*). The gods send they don't set eyes on her—(*with a sign of helplessness*) yet if they do itself, it wasn't my wish brought them or could send them away.

OLD WOMAN (*reprovingly*). If it wasn't, you'd do well to keep a check on her, and she turning a woman that was meant to be a queen.

LAVARCHAM. Who'd check her like was meant to have her pleasure only, the way if there were no warnings told about her you'd see troubles coming when an old king is taking her, and she without a thought but for her beauty and to be straying the hills.

OLD WOMAN. The gods help the lot of us. . . . Shouldn't she be well pleased getting the like of Conchubor, and he middling settled in his years itself? I don't know what he wanted putting her this wild place to be breaking her in, or putting myself to be roasting her supper and she with no patience for her food at all.

[*She looks out.*]

LAVARCHAM. Is she coming from the glen?

OLD WOMAN. She is not. But whisht—there's two men leaving the furze—(*crying out*) it's Conchubor and Fergus along with him. Conchubor'll be in a blue stew this night and herself abroad.

LAVARCHAM (*settling room hastily*). Are they close by?

OLD WOMAN. Crossing the stream, and there's herself on the hillside with a load of twigs. Will I run out and put her in order before they'll set eyes on her at all?

LAVARCHAM. You will not. Would you have him see you, and he a man would be jealous of a hawk would fly between her and the rising sun. (*She looks out.*) Go up to the hearth and be as busy as if you hadn't seen them at all.

OLD WOMAN (*sitting down to polish vessel*). There'll be trouble this night, for he should be in his tempers from the way he's stepping out, and he swinging his hands.

LAVARCHAM (*wearied with the whole matter*). It'd be best of all, maybe, if he got in tempers with herself, and made an end quickly, for I'm in a poor way between the pair of them. (*Going back to tapestry frame.*) There they are now at the door.

[*Conchubor and Fergus come in.*]

CONCHUBOR AND FERGUS. The gods save you.

LAVARCHAM (*getting up and curtseying*). The gods save and keep you kindly, and stand between you and all harm for ever.

CONCHUBOR (*looking around*). Where is Deirdre?

LAVARCHAM (*trying to speak with indifference*). Abroad upon Slieve Fuadh. She does be all times straying around picking flowers or nuts, or sticks itself; but so long as she's gathering new life I've a right not to heed her, I'm thinking, and she taking her will.

[*Fergus talks to Old Woman.*]

CONCHUBOR (*stiffly*). A night with thunder coming is no night to be abroad.

LAVARCHAM (*more uneasily*). She's used to every track and pathway, and the lightning itself wouldn't let down its flame to singe the beauty of her like.

FERGUS (*cheerfully*). She's right, Conchubor, and let you sit down and take your ease, (*he takes a wallet from under his cloak*) and I'll count out what we've brought, and put it in the presses within.

[*He goes into the inner room with the Old Woman.*]

CONCHUBOR (*sitting down and looking about*). Where are the mats and hangings and the silver skillets I sent up for Deirdre?

LAVARCHAM. The mats and hangings are in this press, Conchubor. She wouldn't wish to be soiling them, she said, running out and in with mud and grasses on her feet, and it raining since the night of Samhain. The silver skillets and the golden cups we have beyond locked in the chest.

CONCHUBOR. Bring them out and use them from this day.

LAVARCHAM. We'll do it, Conchubor.

CONCHUBOR (*getting up and going to frame*). Is this hers?

LAVARCHAM (*pleased to speak of it*). It is, Conchubor. All say there isn't her match at fancying figures and throwing purple upon crimson, and she edging them all times with her greens and gold.

CONCHUBOR (*a little uneasily*). Is she keeping wise and busy since I passed before, and growing ready for her life in Emain?

LAVARCHAM (*dryly*). That is a question will give small pleasure to yourself or me. (*Making up her mind to speak out.*) If it's the truth I'll tell you, she's growing too wise to marry a big king and she a score only. Let you not be taking it bad, Conchubor, but you'll get little good seeing her this night, for with all my talking it's wilfuller she's growing these two months or three.

CONCHUBOR (*severely, but relieved things are no worse*). Isn't it a poor thing you're doing so little to school her to meet what is to come?

LAVARCHAM. I'm after serving you two score of years, and I'll tell you this night, Conchubor, she's little call to mind an old woman when she has the birds to school her, and the pools in the rivers where she goes bathing in the sun. I'll tell you if you seen her that time, with her white skin, and her red lips, and the blue water and the ferns about her, you'd know, maybe, and you greedy itself, it wasn't for your like she was born at all.

CONCHUBOR. It's little I heed for what she was born; she'll be my comrade, surely.

[*He examines her workbox.*]

LAVARCHAM (*sinking into sadness again*). I'm in dread

so they were right saying she'd bring destruction on the world, for it's a poor thing when you see a settled man putting the love he has for a young child, and the love he has for a full woman, on a girl the like of her; and it's a poor thing, Conchubor, to see a High King, the way you are this day, prying after her needles and numbering her lines of thread.

CONCHUBOR (*getting up*). Let you not be talking too far and you old itself. (*Walks across room and back.*) Does she know the troubles are foretold?

LAVARCHAM (*in the tone of the earlier talk*). I'm after telling her one time and another, but I'd do as well speaking to a lamb of ten weeks and it racing the hills. . . . It's not the dread of death or troubles that would tame her like.

CONCHUBOR (*looks out*). She's coming now, and let you walk in and keep Fergus till I speak with her a while.

LAVARCHAM (*going left*). If I'm after vexing you itself, it'd be best you weren't taking her hasty or scolding her at all.

CONCHUBOR (*very stiffly*). I've no call to. I'm well pleased she's light and airy.

LAVARCHAM (*offended at his tone*). Well pleased, is it? (*With a snort of irony.*) It's a queer thing the way the likes of me do be telling the truth, and the wise are lying all times.

[*She goes into room on left. Conchubor arranges himself before a mirror for a moment, then goes a little to the left and waits. Deirdre comes in poorly dressed, with a little bag and a bundle of twigs in her arms. She is astonished for a moment when she sees Conchubor; then she makes a curtsey to him, and goes to the hearth without any embarrassment.*]

CONCHUBOR. The gods save you, Deirdre. I have come up bringing you rings and jewels from Emain Macha.

DEIRDRE. The gods save you.

CONCHUBOR. What have you brought from the hills?

DEIRDRE (*quite self-possessed*). A bag of nuts, and twigs for our fires at the dawn of day.

CONCHUBOR (*showing annoyance in spite of himself*). And it's that way you're picking up the manners will fit you to be Queen of Ulster?

DEIRDRE (*made a little defiant by his tone*). I have no wish to be a queen.

CONCHUBOR (*almost sneeringly*). You'd wish to be dressing in your duns and grey, and you herding your geese or driving your calves to their shed—like the common lot scattered in the glens.

DEIRDRE (*very defiant*). I would not, Conchubor. (*She goes to tapestry and begins to work.*) A girl born the way I'm born is more likely to wish for a mate who'd be her likeness. . . . A man with his hair like the raven, maybe, and his skin like the snow and his lips like blood spilt on it.

CONCHUBOR (*sees his mistake, and after a moment takes a flattering tone, looking at her work*). Whatever you wish, there's no queen but would be well pleased to have your skill at choosing colours and making pictures on the cloth. (*Looking closely.*) What is it you're figuring?

DEIRDRE (*deliberately*). Three young men and they chasing in the green gap of a wood.

CONCHUBOR (*now almost pleading*). It's soon you'll have dogs with silver chains to be chasing in the woods of Emain, for I have white hounds rearing up for you, and grey horses, that I've chosen from the finest in Ulster and Britain and Gaul.

DEIRDRE (*unmoved as before*). I've heard tell, in Ulster and Britain and Gaul, Naisi and his brothers have no match and they chasing in the woods.

CONCHUBOR (*very gravely*). Isn't it a strange thing you'd be talking of Naisi and his brothers, or figuring them either, when you know the things that are foretold about themselves and you? Yet you've little knowledge, and I'd do wrong taking it bad when it'll be my share from this out to keep you the way you'll have little call to trouble for knowledge, or its want either.

DEIRDRE. Yourself should be wise, surely.

CONCHUBOR. The like of me has a store of knowledge that's a weight and terror. It's for that we do choose out the like of yourself that are young and glad only. . . . I'm thinking you are gay and lively each day in the year?

DEIRDRE. I don't know if that's true, Conchubor. There are lonesome days and bad nights in this place like another.

CONCHUBOR. You should have as few sad days, I'm thinking, as I have glad and good ones.

DEIRDRE. What is it has you that way ever coming this place, when you'd hear the old woman saying a good child's as happy as a king?

CONCHUBOR. How would I be happy seeing age coming on me each year, when the dry leaves are blowing back and forward at the gate of Emain? And yet this last while I'm saying out, when I see the furze breaking and the daws sitting two and two on ash-trees by the duns of Emain, Deirdre's a year nearer her full age when she'll be my mate and comrade, and then I'm glad surely.

DEIRDRE (*almost to herself*). I will not be your mate in Emain.

CONCHUBOR (*not heeding her*). It's there you'll be proud and happy and you'll learn that, if young men are great hunters, yet it's with the like of myself you'll find a knowledge of what is priceless in your own like. What we all need is a place is safe and splendid, and it's that you'll get in Emain in two days or three.

DEIRDRE (*aghast*). Two days!

CONCHUBOR. I have the rooms ready, and in a little while you'll be brought down there, to be my queen and queen of the five parts of Ireland.

DEIRDRE (*standing up frightened and pleading*). I'd liefer stay this place, Conchubor. . . . Leave me this place, where I'm well used to the tracks and pathways and the people of the glens. . . . It's for this life I'm born, surely.

CONCHUBOR. You'll be happier and greater with myself in Emain. It is I will be your comrade, and will stand between you and the great troubles are foretold.

DEIRDRE. I will not be your queen in Emain when it's my pleasure to be having my freedom on the edges of the hills.

CONCHUBOR. It's my wish to have you quickly; I'm sick and weary thinking of the day you'll be brought down to me, and seeing you walking into my big, empty halls. I've made all sure to have you, and yet all said there's a fear in the back of my mind I'd miss you and have great troubles in the end. It's for that, Deirdre, I'm praying that you'll come quickly; and you may take the word of a man has no lies, you'll not find, with any other, the like of what I'm bringing you in wildness and confusion in my own mind.

DEIRDRE. I cannot go, Conchubor.

CONCHUBOR (*taking a triumphant tone*). It is my pleasure to have you, and I a man is waiting a long while on the throne of Ulster. Wouldn't you liefer be my comrade, growing up the like of Emer and Maeve, than to be in this place and you a child always?

DEIRDRE. You don't know me and you'd have little joy taking me, Conchubor. . . . I'm a long while watching the days getting a great speed passing me by. I'm too long taking my will, and it's that way I'll be living always.

CONCHUBOR (*dryly*). Call Fergus to come with me. This is your last night upon Slieve Fuadh.

DEIRDRE (*now pleadingly*). Leave me a short space longer, Conchubor. Isn't it a poor thing I should be hastened away, when all these troubles are foretold? Leave me a year, Conchubor; it isn't much I'm asking.

CONCHUBOR. It's much to have me two score and two weeks waiting for your voice in Emain, and you in this place growing lonesome and shy. I'm a ripe man and in great love, and yet, Deirdre, I'm the King of Ulster. (*He gets up.*) I'll call Fergus, and we'll make Emain ready in the morning.

[*He goes towards door on left.*]

DEIRDRE (*clinging to him*). Do not call him, Conchubor. . . . Promise me a year of quiet. . . . It's one year I'm asking only.

CONCHUBOR. You'd be asking a year next year, and the years that follow. (*Calling.*) Fergus! Fergus! (*To Deirdre.*) Young girls are slow always; it is their lovers that must say the word. (*Calling.*) Fergus!

[*Deirdre springs away from him as Fergus comes in with Lavarcham and the Old Woman.*]

CONCHUBOR (*to Fergus*). There is a storm coming, and we'd best be going to our people when the night is young.

FERGUS (*cheerfully*). The gods shield you, Deirdre. (*To Conchubor.*) We're late already, and it's no work the High King to be slipping on stepping-stones and hilly pathways when the floods are rising with the rain.

[*He helps Conchubor into his cloak.*]

CONCHUBOR (*glad that he has made his decision—to Lavarcham*). Keep your rules a few days longer, and you'll be brought down to Emain, you and Deirdre with you.

LAVARCHAM (*obediently*). Your rules are kept always.

CONCHUBOR. The gods shield you.

[*He goes out with Fergus. Old Woman bolts door.*]

LAVARCHAM (*looking at Deirdre, who has covered her face*). Wasn't I saying you'd do it? You've brought your marriage a sight nearer not heeding those are wiser than yourself.

DEIRDRE (*with agitation*). It wasn't I did it. Will you take me from this place, Lavarcham, and keep me safe in the hills?

LAVARCHAM. He'd have us tracked in the half of a day, and then you'd be his queen in spite of you, and I and mine would be destroyed for ever.

DEIRDRE (*terrified with the reality that is before her*). Are there none can go against Conchubor?

LAVARCHAM. Maeve of Connaught only, and those that are her like.

DEIRDRE. Would Fergus go against him?

LAVARCHAM. He would, maybe, and his temper roused.

DEIRDRE (*in a lower voice with sudden excitement*). Would Naisi and his brothers?

LAVARCHAM (*impatiently*). Let you not be dwelling on Naisi and his brothers. . . . In the end of all there is none can go against Conchubor, and it's folly that we're talking, for if any went against Conchubor it's sorrow he'd earn and the shortening of his day of life.

[*She turns away, and Deirdre stands up stiff with excitement and goes and looks out of the window.*]

DEIRDRE. Are the stepping-stones flooding, Lavarcham? Will the night be stormy in the hills?

LAVARCHAM (*looking at her curiously*). The stepping-stones are flooding, surely, and the night will be the worst, I'm thinking, we've seen these years gone by.

DEIRDRE (*tearing open the press and pulling out clothes and tapestries*). Lay these mats and hangings by the windows, and at the tables for our feet, and take out the skillets of silver, and the golden cups we have, and our two flasks of wine.

LAVARCHAM. What ails you?

DEIRDRE (*gathering up a dress*). Lay them out quickly, Lavarcham, we've no call dawdling this night. Lay them out quickly; I'm going into the room to put on the rich dresses and jewels have been sent from Emain.

LAVARCHAM. Putting on dresses at this hour, and it dark and drenching with the weight of rain! Are you away in your head?

DEIRDRE (*gathering her things together with an outburst of excitement*). I will dress like Emer in Dundealgan, or Maeve in her house in Connaught. If Conchubor'll make me a queen, I'll have the right of a queen who is a master, taking her own choice and making a stir to the edges of the seas. . . . Lay out your mats and hangings where I can stand this night and look about me. Lay out the skins of the rams of Connaught and of the goats of the west. I will not be a child or plaything; I'll put on my robes that are the richest, for I will not be brought down to Emain as Cuchulain brings his horse to the yoke, or Conall Cearneach puts his shield upon his arm; and maybe from this day I will turn the men of Ireland like a wind blowing on the heath.

[*She goes into room. Lavarcham and Old Woman look at each other, then the Old Woman goes over, looks in at Deirdre through chink of the door, and then closes it carefully.*]

OLD WOMAN (*in a frightened whisper*). She's thrown off the rags she had about her, and there she is in her skin; she's putting her hair in shiny twists. Is she raving, Lavarcham, or has she a good right turning to a queen like Maeve?

LAVARCHAM (*putting up hanging very anxiously*). It's more than raving's in her mind, or I'm the more astray; and yet she's as good a right as another, maybe, having her pleasure, though she'd spoil the world.

OLD WOMAN (*helping her*). Be quick before she'll come back. . . . Who'd have thought we'd run before her, and she so quiet till to-night. Will the High King get the better of her, Lavarcham? If I was Conchubor, I wouldn't marry with her like at all.

LAVARCHAM. Hang that by the window. That should please her, surely. When all's said, it's her like will be the master till the end of time.

OLD WOMAN (*at the window*). There's a mountain of

blackness in the sky, and the greatest rain falling has been these long years on the earth. The gods help Conchubor. He'll be a sorry man this night, reaching his dun, and he with all his spirits, thinking to himself he'll be putting his arms around her in two days or three.

LAVARCHAM. It's more than Conchubor'll be sick and sorry, I'm thinking, before this story is told to the end.

[*Loud knocking on door at the right.*]

LAVARCHAM (*startled*). Who is that?

NAISI (*outside*). Naisi and his brothers.

LAVARCHAM. We are lonely women. What is it you're wanting in the blackness of the night?

NAISI. We met a young girl in the woods who told us we might shelter this place if the rivers rose on the pathways and the floods gathered from the butt of the hills.

[*Old Woman clasps her hands in horror.*]

LAVARCHAM (*with great alarm*). You cannot come in. . . . There is no one let in here, and no young girl with us.

NAISI. Let us in from the great storm. Let us in and we will go further when the cloud will rise.

LAVARCHAM. Go round east to the shed and you'll have shelter. You cannot come in.

NAISI (*knocking loudly*). Open the door or we will burst it. (*The door is shaken.*)

OLD WOMAN (*in a timid whisper*). Let them in, and keep Deirdre in her room to-night.

AINNLE AND ARDAN (*outside*). Open! Open!

LAVARCHAM (*to Old Woman*). Go in and keep her.

OLD WOMAN. I couldn't keep her. I've no hold on her. Go in yourself and I will free the door.

LAVARCHAM. I must stay and turn them out. (*She pulls her hair and cloak over her face.*) Go in and keep her.

OLD WOMAN. The gods help us.

[*She runs into the inner room.*]

VOICES. Open!

LAVARCHAM (*opening the door*). Come in then and ill-luck if you'll have it so.

[*Naisi and Ainnle and Ardan come in and look round with astonishment.*]

NAISI. It's a rich man has this place, and no herd at all.

LAVARCHAM (*sitting down with her head half covered*). It is not, and you'd best be going quickly.

NAISI (*hilariously, shaking rain from his clothes*). When we've had the pick of luck finding princely comfort in the darkness of the night! Some rich man of Ulster should come here and he chasing in the woods. May we drink? (*He takes up flask.*) Whose wine is this that we may drink his health?

LAVARCHAM. It's no one's that you've call to know.

NAISI. Your own health then and length of life. (*Pouring out wine for the three. They drink.*)

LAVARCHAM (*very crossly*). You're great boys taking a welcome where it isn't given, and asking questions where you've no call to. . . . If you'd a quiet place settled up to be playing yourself, maybe, with a gentle queen, what'd you think of young men prying around and carrying tales? When I was a bit of a girl the big men of Ulster had better manners, and they the like of your three selves, in the top folly of youth. That'll be a story to tell out in Tara that Naisi is a tippler and stealer, and Ainnle the drawer of a stranger's cork.

NAISI (*quite cheerfully, sitting down beside her*). At your age you should know there are nights when a king like Conchubor will spit upon his arm ring, and queens will stick their tongues out at the rising moon. We're that way this night, and it's not wine we're asking only. Where is the young girl told us we might shelter here?

LAVARCHAM. Asking me you'd be? We're decent people, and I wouldn't put you tracking a young girl, not if you gave me the gold clasp you have hanging on your coat.

NAISI (*giving it to her*). Where is she?

LAVARCHAM (*in confidential whisper, putting her hand on his arm*). Let you walk back into the hills and turn up by the second cnuceen where there are three together. You'll see a path running on the rocks and then you'll hear the dogs barking in the houses, and their noise will guide you till you come to a bit of cabin at the foot of an ash-tree. It's there there is a young and flighty girl that I'm thinking is the one you've seen.

NAISI (*hilariously*). Here's health, then, to herself and you!

ARDAN. Here's to the years when you were young as she!

AINNLE (*in a frightened whisper*). Naisi!

[*Naisi looks up and Ainnle beckons to him. He goes over and Ainnle points to something on the golden mug he holds in his hand.*]

NAISI (*looking at it in astonishment*). This is the High King's. . . . I see his mark on the rim. Does Conchubor come lodging here?

LAVARCHAM (*jumping up with extreme annoyance*). Who says it's Conchubor's? How dare young fools the like of you—(*speaking with vehement insolence*) come prying around, running the world into troubles for some slip of a girl? What brings you this place straying from Emain? (*Very bitterly.*) Though you think, maybe, young men can do their fill of foolery and there is none to blame them.

NAISI (*very soberly*). Is the rain easing?

ARDAN. The clouds are breaking. . . . I can see Orion in the gap of the glen.

NAISI (*still cheerfully*). Open the door and we'll go forward to the little cabin between the ash-tree and the rocks. Lift the bolt and pull it.

[*Deirdre comes in on left royally dressed and very beautiful. She stands for a moment, and then as the door opens she calls softly.*]

DEIRDRE. Naisi! Do not leave me, Naisi. I am Deirdre of the Sorrows.

NAISI (*transfixed with amazement*). And it is you who go around in the woods making the thrushes bear a grudge against the heavens for the sweetness of your voice singing.

DEIRDRE. It is with me you've spoken, surely. (*To Lavarcham and Old Woman.*) Take Ainnle and Ardan, these two princes, into the little hut where we eat, and serve them with what is best and sweetest. I have many things for Naisi only.

LAVARCHAM (*overawed by her tone*). I will do it, and I ask their pardon. I have fooled them here.

DEIRDRE (*to Ainnle and Ardan*). Do not take it badly that I am asking you to walk into our hut for a little. You will have a supper that is cooked by the cook of

Conchubor, and Lavarcham will tell you stories of
Maeve and Nessa and Rogh.

AINNLE. We'll ask Lavarcham to tell us stories of yourself, and with that we'll be well pleased to be doing your
wish.

[*They all go out except Deirdre and Naisi.*]

DEIRDRE (*sitting in the high chair in the centre*). Come
to this stool, Naisi (*pointing to the stool*). If it's low
itself the High King would sooner be on it this night
than on the throne of Emain Macha.

NAISI (*sitting down*). You are Fedlimid's daughter that
Conchubor has walled up from all the men of Ulster.

DEIRDRE. Do many know what is foretold, that Deirdre
will be the ruin of the Sons of Usna, and have a little
grave by herself, and a story will be told for ever?

NAISI. It's a long while men have been talking of Deirdre, the child who had all gifts, and the beauty that has
no equal; there are many know it, and there are kings
would give a great price to be in my place this night and
you grown to a queen.

DEIRDRE. It isn't many I'd call, Naisi. . . . I was in the
woods at the full moon and I heard a voice singing.
Then I gathered up my skirts, and I ran on a little path
I have to the verge of a rock, and I saw you pass by
underneath, in your crimson cloak, singing a song, and
you standing out beyond your brothers are called the
Flower of Ireland.

NAISI. It's for that you called us in the dusk?

DEIRDRE (*in a low voice*). Since that, Naisi, I have been
one time the like of a ewe looking for a lamb that had
been taken away from her, and one time seeing new

gold on the stars, and a new face on the moon, and all times dreading Emain.

NAISI (*pulling himself together and beginning to draw back a little*). Yet it should be a lonesome thing to be in this place and you born for great company.

DEIRDRE (*softly*). This night I have the best company in the whole world.

NAISI (*still a little formally*). It is I who have the best company, for when you're queen in Emain you will have none to be your match or fellow.

DEIRDRE. I will not be queen in Emain.

NAISI. Conchubor has made an oath you will, surely.

DEIRDRE. It's for that maybe I'm called Deirdre, the girl of many sorrows . . . for it's a sweet life you and I could have, Naisi. . . . It should be a sweet thing to have what is best and richest, if it's for a short space only.

NAISI (*very distressed*). And we've a short space only to be triumphant and brave.

DEIRDRE. You must not go, Naisi, and leave me to the High King, a man is aging in his dun, with his crowds round him, and his silver and gold. (*More quickly.*) I will not live to be shut up in Emain, and wouldn't we do well paying, Naisi, with silence and a near death. (*She stands up and walks away from him.*) I'm a long while in the woods with my own self, and I'm in little dread of death, and it earned with riches would make the sun red with envy, and he going up the heavens; and the moon pale and lonesome, and she wasting away. (*She comes to him and puts her hands on his shoulders.*) Isn't it a small thing is foretold about the ruin of ourselves, Naisi, when all men have age coming and great ruin in the end?

NAISI. Yet it's a poor thing it's I should bring you to a tale of blood and broken bodies, and the filth of the grave. . . . Wouldn't we do well to wait, Deirdre, and I each twilight meeting you on the sides of the hills?

DEIRDRE (*despondently*). His messengers are coming.

NAISI. Messengers are coming?

DEIRDRE. To-morrow morning or the next, surely.

NAISI. Then we'll go away. It isn't I will give your like to Conchubor, not if the grave was dug to be my lodging when a week was by. (*He looks out.*) The stars are out, Deirdre, and let you come with me quickly, for it is the stars will be our lamps many nights and we abroad in Alban, and taking our journeys among the little islands in the sea. There has never been the like of the joy we'll have, Deirdre, you and I, having our fill of love at the evening and the morning till the sun is high.

DEIRDRE. And yet I'm in dread leaving this place, where I have lived always. Won't I be lonesome and I thinking on the little hill beyond, and the apple-trees do be budding in the spring-time by the post of the door? (*A little shaken by what has passed.*) Won't I be in great dread to bring you to destruction, Naisi, and you so happy and young?

NAISI. Are you thinking I'd go on living after this night, Deirdre, and you with Conchubor in Emain? Are you thinking I'd go out after hares when I've had your lips in my sight?

[*Lavarcham comes in as they cling to each other.*]

LAVARCHAM. Are you raving, Deirdre? Are you choosing this night to destroy the world?

DEIRDRE (*very deliberately*). It's Conchubor has chosen this night calling me to Emain. (*To Naisi.*) Bring in

Ainnle and Ardan, and take me from this place, where I'm in dread from this out of the footsteps of a hare passing.

[*He goes.*]

DEIRDRE (*clinging to Lavarcham*). Do not take it bad I'm going, Lavarcham. It's you have been a good friend and given me great freedom and joy, and I living on Slieve Fuadh; and maybe you'll be well pleased one day saying you have nursed Deirdre.

LAVARCHAM (*moved*). It isn't I'll be well pleased and I far away from you. Isn't it a hard thing you're doing, but who can help it? Birds go mating in the spring of the year, and ewes at the leaves falling, but a young girl must have her lover in all the courses of the sun and moon.

DEIRDRE. Will you go to Emain in the morning?

LAVARCHAM. I will not. I'll go to Brandon in the south; and in the course of a piece, maybe, I'll be sailing back and forward on the seas to be looking on your face and the little ways you have that none can equal.

[*Naisi comes back with Ainnle and Ardan and Old Woman.*]

DEIRDRE (*taking Naisi's hand*). My two brothers, I am going with Naisi to Alban and the north to face the troubles are foretold. Will you take word to Conchubor in Emain?

AINNLE. We will go with you.

ARDAN. We will be your servants and your huntsmen, Deirdre.

DEIRDRE. It isn't one brother only of you three is brave and courteous. Will you wed us, Lavarcham? You have the words and customs.

LAVARCHAM. I will not, then. What would I want meddling in the ruin you will earn?

NAISI. Let Ainnle wed us. . . . He has been with wise men and he knows their ways.

AINNLE (*joining their hands*). By the sun and moon and the whole earth, I wed Deirdre to Naisi. (*He steps back and holds up his hands.*) May the air bless you, and water and the wind, the sea, and all the hours of the sun and moon.

CURTAIN

ACT II

SCENE. *Alban. Early morning in the beginning of winter. A wood outside the tent of Deirdre and Naisi. Lavarcham comes in muffled in a cloak.*

LAVARCHAM (*calling*). Deirdre. . . . Deirdre. . . .

DEIRDRE (*coming from tent*). My welcome, Lavarcham. . . . Whose curagh is rowing from Ulster? I saw the oars through the tops of the trees, and I thought it was you were coming towards us.

LAVARCHAM. I came in the shower was before dawn.

DEIRDRE. And who is coming?

LAVARCHAM (*mournfully*). Let you not be startled or taking it bad, Deirdre. It's Fergus bringing messages of peace from Conchubor to take Naisi and his brother back to Emain.

[*Sitting down.*]

DEIRDRE (*lightly*). Naisi and his brothers are well

pleased with this place; and what would take them back to Conchubor in Ulster?

LAVARCHAM. Their like would go any place where they'd see death standing. (*With more agitation.*) I'm in dread Conchubor wants to have yourself and to kill Naisi, and that that'll be the ruin of the Sons of Usna. I'm silly, maybe, to be dreading the like, but those have a great love for yourself have a right to be in dread always.

DEIRDRE (*more anxiously*). Emain should be no safe place for myself and Naisi. And isn't it a hard thing they'll leave us no peace, Lavarcham, and we so quiet in the woods?

LAVARCHAM (*impressively*). It's a hard thing, surely; but let you take my word and swear Naisi, by the earth, and the sun over it, and the four quarters of the moon, he'll not go back to Emain—for good faith or bad faith—the time Conchubor's keeping the high throne of Ireland. . . . It's that would save you, surely.

DEIRDRE (*without hope*). There's little power in oaths to stop what's coming, and little power in what I'd do, Lavarcham, to change the story of Conchubor and Naisi and the things old men foretold.

LAVARCHAM (*aggressively*). Was there little power in what you did the night you dressed in your finery and ran Naisi off along with you, in spite of Conchubor and the big nobles did dread the blackness of your luck? It was power enough you had that night to bring distress and anguish; and now I'm pointing you a way to save Naisi, you'll not stir stick or straw to aid me.

DEIRDRE (*a little haughtily*). Let you not raise your voice against me, Lavarcham, if you have will itself to guard Naisi.

LAVARCHAM (*breaking out in anger*). Naisi is it? I didn't care if the crows were stripping his thigh-bones at the dawn of day. It's to stop your own despair and wailing, and you waking up in a cold bed, without the man you have your heart on, I am raging now. (*Starting up with temper.*) Yet there is more men than Naisi in it; and maybe I was a big fool thinking his dangers, and this day, would fill you up with dread.

DEIRDRE (*sharply*). Let you end; such talking is a fool's only, when it's well you know if a thing harmed Naisi it isn't I would live after him. (*With distress.*) It's well you know it's this day I'm dreading seven years, and I fine nights watching the heifers walking to the haggard with long shadows on the grass; (*with emotion*) or the time I've been stretched in the sunshine, when I've heard Ainnle and Ardan stepping lightly, and they saying: Was there ever the like of Deirdre for a happy and sleepy queen?

LAVARCHAM (*not fully pacified*). And yet you'll go, and welcome is it, if Naisi chooses?

DEIRDRE. I've dread going or staying, Lavarcham. It's lonesome this place, having happiness like ours, till I'm asking each day will this day match yesterday, and will to-morrow take a good place beside the same day in the year that's gone, and wondering all times is it a game worth playing, living on until you're dried and old, and our joy is gone for ever.

LAVARCHAM. If it's that ails you, I tell you there's little hurt getting old, though young girls and poets do be storming at the shapes of age. (*Passionately.*) There's little hurt getting old, saving when you're looking back, the way I'm looking this day, and seeing the young you have a love for breaking up their hearts with folly.

(*Going to Deirdre.*) Take my word and stop Naisi, and the day'll come you'll have more joy having the senses of an old woman and you with your little grandsons shrieking round you, than I'd have this night putting on the red mouth and the white arms you have, to go walking lonesome byways with a gamey king.

DEIRDRE. It's little joy of a young woman, or an old woman, I'll have from this day, surely. But what use is in our talking when there's Naisi on the foreshore, and Fergus with him?

LAVARCHAM (*despairingly*). I'm late so with my warnings, for Fergus'd talk the moon over to take a new path in the sky. (*With reproach.*) You'll not stop him this day, and isn't it a strange story you were a plague and torment, since you were that height, to those did hang their lifetimes on your voice. (*Overcome with trouble; gathering her cloak about her.*) Don't think bad of my crying. I'm not the like of many and I'd see a score of naked corpses and not heed them at all, but I'm destroyed seeing yourself in your hour of joy when the end is coming surely.

[*Owen comes in quickly, rather ragged, bows to Deirdre.*]

OWEN (*to Lavarcham*). Fergus's men are calling you. You were seen on the path, and he and Naisi want you for their talk below.

LAVARCHAM (*looking at him with dislike*). Yourself's an ill-lucky thing to meet a morning is the like of this. Yet if you are a spy itself I'll go and give my word that's wanting surely.

[*Goes out.*]

OWEN (*to Deirdre*). So I've found you alone, and I

after waiting three weeks getting ague and asthma in the chill of the bogs, till I saw Naisi caught with Fergus.

DEIRDRE. I've heard news of Fergus; what brought you from Ulster?

OWEN (*who has been searching, finds a loaf and sits down eating greedily, and cutting it with a large knife.*) The full moon, I'm thinking, and it squeezing the crack in my skull. Was there ever a man crossed nine waves after a fool's wife and he not away in his head?

DEIRDRE (*absently*). It should be a long time since you left Emain, where there's civility in speech with queens.

OWEN. It's a long while, surely. It's three weeks I am losing my manners beside the Saxon bull-frogs at the head of the bog. Three weeks is a long space, and yet you're seven years spancelled with Naisi and the pair.

DEIRDRE (*beginning to fold up her silks and jewels*). Three weeks of your days might be long, surely, yet seven years are a short space for the like of Naisi and myself.

OWEN (*derisively*). If they're a short space there aren't many the like of you. Wasn't there a queen in Tara had to walk out every morning till she'd meet a stranger and see the flame of courtship leaping up within his eye? Tell me now, (*leaning towards her*) are you well pleased that length with the same man snorting next you at the dawn of day?

DEIRDRE (*very quietly*). Am I well pleased seven years seeing the same sun throwing light across the branches at the dawn of day? It's a heartbreak to the wise that it's for a short space we have the same things only.

(*With contempt.*) Yet the earth itself is a silly place, maybe, when a man's a fool and talker.

OWEN (*sharply*). Well, go, take your choice. Stay here and rot with Naisi or go to Conchubor in Emain. Conchubor's a wrinkled fool with a swelling belly on him, and eyes falling downward from his shining crown; Naisi should be stale and weary. Yet there are many roads, Deirdre, and I tell you I'd liefer be bleaching in a bog-hole than living on without a touch of kindness from your eyes and voice. It's a poor thing to be so lonesome you'd squeeze kisses on a cur dog's nose.

DEIRDRE. Are there no women like yourself could be your friends in Emain?

OWEN (*vehemently*). There are none like you, Deirdre. It's for that I'm asking are you going back this night with Fergus?

DEIRDRE. I will go where Naisi chooses.

OWEN (*with a burst of rage*). It's Naisi, Naisi, is it? Then, I tell you, you'll have great sport one day seeing Naisi getting a harshness in his two sheep's eyes and he looking on yourself. Would you credit it, my father used to be in the broom and heather kissing Lavarcham, with a little bird chirping out above their heads, and now she'd scare a raven from a carcase on a hill. (*With a sad cry that brings dignity into his voice.*) Queens get old, Deirdre, with their white and long arms going from them, and their backs hooping. I tell you it's a poor thing to see a queen's nose reaching down to scrape her chin.

DEIRDRE (*looking out, a little uneasy*). Naisi and Fergus are coming on the path.

OWEN. I'll go so, for if I had you seven years I'd be

jealous of the midges and the dust is in the air. (*Muffles himself in his cloak; with a sort of warning in his voice.*) I'll give you a riddle, Deirdre: Why isn't my father as ugly and old as Conchubor? You've no answer? . . . It's because Naisi killed him. (*With curious expression.*) Think of that and you awake at night, hearing Naisi snoring, or the night you hear strange stories of the things I'm doing in Alban or in Ulster either.

[*He goes out, and in a moment Naisi and Fergus come in on the other side.*]

NAISI (*gaily*). Fergus has brought messages of peace from Conchubor.

DEIRDRE (*greeting Fergus*). He is welcome. Let you rest, Fergus, you should be hot and thirsty after mounting the rocks.

FERGUS. It's a sunny nook you've found in Alban; yet any man would be well pleased mounting higher rocks to fetch yourself and Naisi back to Emain.

DEIRDRE (*with keenness*). They've answered? They would go?

FERGUS (*benignly*). They have not, but when I was a young man we'd have given a lifetime to be in Ireland a score of weeks; and to this day the old men have nothing so heavy as knowing it's in a short while they'll lose the high skies are over Ireland, and the lonesome mornings with birds crying on the bogs. Let you come this day, for there's no place but Ireland where the Gael can have peace always.

NAISI (*gruffly*). It's true, surely. Yet we're better this place while Conchubor's in Emain Macha.

FERGUS (*giving him parchments*). There are your

sureties and Conchubor's seal. (*To Deirdre.*) I am your surety with Conchubor. You'll not be young always, and it's time you were making yourselves ready for the years will come, building up a homely dun beside the seas of Ireland, and getting in your children from the princes' wives. It's little joy wandering till age is on you and your youth is gone away, so you'd best come this night, for you'd have great pleasure putting out your foot and saying, "I am in Ireland, surely."

DEIRDRE. It isn't pleasure I'd have while Conchubor is king in Emain.

FERGUS (*almost annoyed*). Would you doubt the seals of Conall Cearneach and the kings of Meath? (*He gets parchments from his cloak and gives them to Naisi. More gently.*) It's easy being fearful and you alone in the woods, yet it would be a poor thing if a timid woman (*taunting her a little*) could turn away the Sons of Usna from the life of kings. Let you be thinking on the years to come, Deirdre, and the way you'd have a right to see Naisi a high and white-haired justice beside some king of Emain. Wouldn't it be a poor story if a queen the like of you should have no thought but to be scraping up her hours dallying in the sunshine with the sons of kings?

DEIRDRE (*turning away a little haughtily*). I leave the choice to Naisi. (*Turning back towards Fergus.*) Yet you'd do well, Fergus, to go on your own way, for the sake of your own years, so you'll not be saying till your hour of death, maybe, it was yourself brought Naisi and his brothers to a grave was scooped by treachery.

[*Goes into tent.*]

FERGUS. It is a poor thing to see a queen so lonesome and afraid. (*He watches till he is sure Deirdre cannot hear him.*) Listen now to what I'm saying. You'd do well to come back to men and women are your match and comrades, and not be lingering until the day that you'll grow weary, and hurt Deirdre showing her the hardness will grow up within your eyes. . . . You're here years and plenty to know it's truth I'm saying.

[*Deirdre comes out of tent with a horn of wine, she catches the beginning of Naisi's speech and stops with stony wonder.*]

NAISI (*very thoughtfully*). I'll not tell you a lie. There have been days a while past when I've been throwing a line for salmon or watching for the run of hares, that I've a dread upon me a day'd come I'd weary of her voice, (*very slowly*) and Deirdre'd see I'd wearied.

FERGUS (*sympathetic but triumphant*). I knew it, Naisi. . . . And take my word, Deirdre's seen your dread and she'll have no peace from this out in the woods.

NAISI (*with confidence*). She's not seen it. . . . Deirdre's no thought of getting old or wearied; it's that puts wonder in her ways, and she with spirits would keep bravery and laughter in a town with plague.

[*Deirdre drops the horn of wine and crouches down where she is.*]

FERGUS. That humour'll leave her. But we've no call going too far, with one word borrowing another. Will you come this night to Emain Macha?

NAISI. I'll not go, Fergus. I've had dreams of getting old and weary, and losing my delight in Deirdre; but my dreams were dreams only. What are Conchubor's seals and all your talk of Emain and the fools of Meath beside one evening in Glen Masain? We'll stay this place till our lives and time are worn out. It's that word you may take in your curagh to Conchubor in Emain.

FERGUS (*gathering up his parchments*). And you won't go, surely.

NAISI. I will not. . . . I've had dread, I tell you, dread winter and summer, and the autumn and the spring-time, even when there's a bird in every bush making his own stir till the fall of night; but this talk's brought me ease, and I see we're as happy as the leaves on the young trees, and we'll be so ever and always, though we'd live the age of the eagle and the salmon and the crow of Britain.

FERGUS (*with anger*). Where are your brothers? My message is for them also.

NAISI. You'll see them above chasing otters by the stream.

FERGUS (*bitterly*). It isn't much I was mistaken, think-ing you were hunters only.

[*He goes. Naisi turns towards tent and sees Deirdre crouching down with her cloak round her face. Deirdre comes out.*]

NAISI. You've heard my words to Fergus? (*She does not answer. A pause. He puts his arm round her.*) Leave troubling, and we'll go this night to Glen da Ruadh, where the salmon will be running with the tide.

[*Crosses and sits down.*]

DEIRDRE (*in a very low voice*). With the tide in a little while we will be journeying again, or it is our own blood maybe will be running away. (*She turns and clings to him.*) The dawn and evening are a little while, the winter and the summer pass quickly, and what way would you and I, Naisi, have joy for ever?

NAISI. We'll have the joy is highest till our age is come, for it isn't Fergus's talk of great deeds could take us back to Emain.

DEIRDRE. It isn't to great deeds you're going but to near troubles, and the shortening of your days the time that they are bright and sunny; and isn't it a poor thing that I, Deirdre, could not hold you away?

NAISI. I've said we'd stay in Alban always.

DEIRDRE. There's no place to stay always. . . . It's a long time we've had, pressing the lips together, going up and down, resting in our arms, Naisi, waking with the smell of June in the tops of the grasses, and listening to the birds in the branches that are highest. . . . It's a long time we've had, but the end has come, surely.

NAISI. Would you have us go to Emain, though if any ask the reason we do not know it, and we journeying as the thrushes come from the north, or young birds fly out on a dark sea?

DEIRDRE. There's reason all times for an end that's come. And I'm well pleased, Naisi, we're going forward in the winter the time the sun has a low place, and the moon has her mastery in a dark sky, for it's you and I are well lodged our last day, where there is a light behind the clear trees, and the berries on the thorns are a red wall.

NAISI. If our time in this place is ended, come away without Ainnle and Ardan to the woods of the east, for it's right to be away from all people when two lovers have their love only. Come away and we'll be safe always.

DEIRDRE (broken-hearted). There's no safe place, Naisi, on the ridge of the world. . . . And it's in the quiet woods I've seen them digging our grave, throwing out the clay on leaves are bright and withered.

NAISI (*still more eagerly*). Come away, Deirdre, and it's little we'll think of safety or the grave beyond it, and we resting in a little corner between the daytime and the long night.

DEIRDRE (*clearly and gravely*). It's this hour we're between the daytime and a night where there is sleep for ever, and isn't it a better thing to be following on to a near death, than to be bending the head down, and dragging with the feet, and seeing one day a blight showing upon love where it is sweet and tender?

NAISI (*his voice broken with distraction*). If a near death is coming what will be my trouble losing the earth and the stars over it, and you, Deirdre, are their flame and bright crown? Come away into the safety of the woods.

DEIRDRE (*shaking her head slowly*). There are as many ways to wither love as there are stars in a night of Samhain; but there is no way to keep life, or love with it, a short space only. . . . It's for that there's nothing lonesome like a love is watching out the time most lovers do be sleeping. . . . It's for that we're setting out for Emain Macha when the tide turns on the sand.

NAISI (*giving in*). You're right, maybe. It should be a poor thing to see great lovers and they sleepy and old.

DEIRDRE (*with a more tender intensity*). We're seven years without roughness or growing weary; seven years so sweet and shining, the gods would be hard set to give us seven days the like of them. It's for that we're going to Emain, where there'll be a rest for ever, or a place for forgetting, in great crowds and they making a stir.

NAISI (*very softly*). We'll go, surely, in place of keeping a watch on a love had no match and it wasting away. (*They cling to each other for a moment, then Naisi looks up.*) There are Fergus and Lavarcham and my two brothers.

[*Deirdre goes. Naisi sits with his head bowed. Owen runs in stealthily, comes behind Naisi and seizes him round the arms. Naisi shakes him off and whips out his sword.*]

OWEN (*screaming with derisive laughter and showing his empty hands*). Ah, Naisi, wasn't it well I didn't kill you that time? There was a fright you got! I've been watching Fergus above—don't be frightened—and I've come down to see him getting the cold shoulder, and going off alone.

[*Fergus and others come in. They are all subdued like men at a queen's wake.*]

NAISI (*putting up his sword*). There he is. (*Goes to Fergus.*) We are going back when the tide turns, I and Deirdre with yourself.

ALL. Going back!

AINNLE. And you'll end your life with Deirdre, though she has no match for keeping spirits in a little company is far away by itself?

ARDAN. It's seven years myself and Ainnle have been servants and bachelors for yourself and Deirdre. Why will you take her back to Conchubor?

NAISI. I have done what Deirdre wishes and has chosen.

FERGUS. You've made a choice wise men will be glad of in the five ends of Ireland.

OWEN. Wise men is it, and they going back to Conchubor? I could stop them only Naisi put in his sword among my father's ribs, and when a man's done that he'll not credit your oath. Going to Conchubor! I could tell of plots and tricks, and spies were well paid for their play. (*He throws up a bag of gold.*) Are you paid, Fergus?

[*He scatters gold pieces over Fergus.*]

FERGUS. He is raving. . . . Seize him.

OWEN (*flying between them*). You won't. Let the lot of you be off to Emain, but I'll be off before you. . . . Dead men, dead men! Men who'll die for Deirdre's beauty; I'll be before you in the grave!

[*Runs out with his knife in his hand. They all run after him except Lavarcham, who looks out and then clasps her hands. Deirdre comes out to her in a dark cloak.*]

DEIRDRE. What has happened?

LAVARCHAM. It's Owen's gone raging mad, and he's after splitting his gullet beyond at the butt of the stone. There was ill luck this day in his eye. And he knew a power if he'd said it all.

[*Naisi comes back quickly, followed by the others.*]

AINNLE (*coming in very excited*). That man knew plots of Conchubor's. We'll not go to Emain, where Conchubor may love her and have hatred for yourself.

FERGUS. Would you mind a fool and raver?

AINNLE. It's many times there's more sense in madmen than the wise. We will not obey Conchubor.

NAISI. I and Deirdre have chosen; we will go back with Fergus.

ARDAN. We will not go back. We will burn your curaghs by the sea.

FERGUS. My sons and I will guard them.

AINNLE. We will blow the horn of Usna and our friends will come to aid us.

NAISI. It is my friends will come.

AINNLE. Your friends will bind your hands, and you out of your wits.

[*Deirdre comes forward quickly and comes between Ainnle and Naisi.*]

DEIRDRE (*in a low voice*). For seven years the Sons of Usna have not raised their voices in a quarrel.

AINNLE. We will not take you to Emain.

ARDAN. It is Conchubor has broken our peace.

AINNLE (*to Deirdre*). Stop Naisi going. What way would we live if Conchubor should take you from us?

DEIRDRE. There is no one could take me from you. I have chosen to go back with Fergus. Will you quarrel with me, Ainnle, though I have been your queen these seven years in Alban?

AINNLE (*subsiding suddenly*). Naisi has no call to take you.

ARDAN. Why are you going?

DEIRDRE (*to both of them and the others*). It is my wish. . . . It may be I will not have Naisi growing an old man in Alban with an old woman at his side, and young girls pointing out and saying, "that is Deirdre and Naisi had great beauty in their youth." It may be we do well putting a sharp end to the day is brave and glorious, as our fathers put a sharp end to the days of the kings of Ireland; or that I'm wishing to set my foot on Slieve Fuadh, where I was running one time and leaping the streams, (*to Lavarcham*) and that I'd be well pleased to see our little apple-trees, Lavarcham, behind our cabin on the hill; or that I've learned, Fergus, it's a lonesome thing to be away from Ireland always.

AINNLE (*giving in*). There is no place but will be lonesome to us from this out, and we thinking on our seven years in Alban.

DEIRDRE (*to Naisi*). It's in this place we'd be lonesome in the end. . . . Take down Fergus to the sea. He has been a guest had a hard welcome and he bringing messages of peace.

FERGUS. We will make your curagh ready and it fitted for the voyage of a king.

[*He goes with Naisi.*]

DEIRDRE. Take your spears, Ainnle and Ardan, and go down before me, and take your horse-boys to be carrying my cloaks are on the threshold.

AINNLE (*obeying*). It's with a poor heart we'll carry your things this day we have carried merrily so often, and we hungry and cold.

[*They gather up things and go out.*]

DEIRDRE (*to Lavarcham*). Go you, too, Lavarcham. You are old, and I will follow quickly.

LAVARCHAM. I'm old, surely, and the hopes I had my pride in are broken and torn.

[*She goes out, with a look of awe at Deirdre.*]

DEIRDRE (*clasping her hands*). Woods of Cuan, woods of Cuan, dear country of the east! It's seven years we've had a life was joy only, and this day we're going west, this day we're facing death, maybe, and death should be a poor, untidy thing, though it's a queen that dies.

[*She goes out slowly.*]

CURTAIN

ACT III

SCENE. *Tent below Emain, with shabby skins and benches. There is an opening at each side and at back, the latter closed. Old Woman comes in with food and fruits and arranges them on table. Conchubor comes in on right.*

CONCHUBOR (*sharply*). Has no one come with news for me?

OLD WOMAN. I've seen no one at all, Conchubor.

CONCHUBOR (*watches her working for a moment, then makes sure opening at back is closed*). Go up then to Emain, you're not wanting here. (*A noise heard left.*) Who is that?

OLD WOMAN (*going left*). It's Lavarcham coming again. She's a great wonder for jogging back and forward through the world, and I made certain she'd be off to meet them; but she's coming alone, Conchubor, my dear child Deirdre isn't with her at all.

CONCHUBOR. Go up so and leave us.

OLD WOMAN (*pleadingly*). I'd be well pleased to set my eyes on Deirdre if she's coming this night, as we're told.

CONCHUBOR (*impatiently*). It's not long till you'll see her. But I've matters with Lavarcham, and let you go now, I'm saying.

[*He shows her out right, as Lavarcham comes in on the left.*]

LAVARCHAM (*looking round her with suspicion*). This is a queer place to find you, and it's a queer place to be lodging Naisi and his brothers, and Deirdre with them, and the lot of us tired out with the long way we have been walking.

CONCHUBOR. You've come along with them the whole journey?

LAVARCHAM. I have, then, though I've no call now to be wandering that length to a wedding or a burial, or the two together. (*She sits down wearily.*) It's a poor thing the way me and you is getting old, Conchubor, and I'm thinking you yourself have no call to be loitering this place getting your death, maybe, in the cold of night.

CONCHUBOR. I'm waiting only to know is Fergus stopped in the north.

LAVARCHAM (*more sharply*). He's stopped, surely, and that's a trick has me thinking you have it in mind to bring trouble this night on Emain and Ireland and the big world's east beyond them. (*She goes to him.*) And yet you'd do well to be going to your dun, and not putting shame on her meeting the High King, and she seamed and sweaty and in great disorder from the dust of many roads. (*Laughing derisively*). Ah, Conchubor, my lad, beauty goes quickly in the woods, and you'd let a great gasp, I tell you, if you set your eyes this night on Deirdre.

CONCHUBOR (*fiercely*). It's little I care if she's white and worn, for it's I did rear her from a child. I should have a good right to meet and see her always.

LAVARCHAM. A good right, is it? Haven't the blind a good right to be seeing, and the lame to be dancing, and the dummies singing tunes? It's that right you have to be looking for gaiety on Deirdre's lips. (*Coaxingly.*) Come on to your dun, I'm saying, and leave her quiet for one night itself.

CONCHUBOR (*with sudden anger*). I'll not go, when it's long enough I am above in my dun stretching east and west without a comrade, and I more needy, maybe, than the thieves of Meath. . . . You think I'm old and wise, but I tell you the wise know the old must die, and they'll leave no chance for a thing slipping from them they've set their blood to win.

LAVARCHAM (*nodding her head*). If you're old and wise, it's I'm the same, Conchubor, and I'm telling you you'll not have her though you're ready to destroy mankind and skin the gods to win her. There's things a king can't have, Conchubor, and if you go rampaging this night you'll be apt to win nothing but death for many, and a sloppy face of trouble on your own self before the day will come.

CONCHUBOR. It's too much talk you have. (*Goes right.*) Where is Owen? Did you see him no place and you coming the road?

LAVARCHAM. I seen him surely. He went spying on Naisi, and now the worms is spying on his own inside.

CONCHUBOR (*exultingly*). Naisi killed him?

LAVARCHAM. He did not, then. It was Owen destroyed himself running mad because of Deirdre. Fools and kings and scholars are all one in a story with her like, and Owen thought he'd be a great man, being the first corpse in the game you'll play this night in Emain.

CONCHUBOR. It's yourself should be the first corpse, but my other messengers are coming, men from the clans that hated Usna.

LAVARCHAM (*drawing back hopelessly*). Then the gods have pity on us all!

[*Men with weapons come in.*]

CONCHUBOR (*to Soldiers*). Are Ainnle and Ardan separate from Naisi?

MEN. They are, Conchubor. We've got them off, saying they were needed to make ready Deirdre's house.

CONCHUBOR. And Naisi and Deirdre are coming?

SOLDIER. Naisi's coming, surely, and a woman with him is putting out the glory of the moon is rising and the sun is going down.

CONCHUBOR (*looking at Lavarcham*). That's your story that she's seamed and ugly?

SOLDIER. I have more news. (*Pointing to Lavarcham.*) When that woman heard you were bringing Naisi this place, she sent a horse-boy to call Fergus from the north.

CONCHUBOR (*to Lavarcham*). It's for that you've been playing your tricks, but what you've won is a nearer death for Naisi. (*To Soldiers.*) Go up and call my fighters, and take that woman up to Emain.

LAVARCHAM. I'd liefer stay this place. I've done my best, but if a bad end is coming, surely it would be a good thing maybe I was here to tend her.

CONCHUBOR (*fiercely*). Take her to Emain; it's too many tricks she's tried this day already. (*A Soldier goes to her.*)

LAVARCHAM. Don't touch me. (*She puts her cloak round her and catches Conchubor's arm.*) I thought to stay your hand with my stories till Fergus would come to be beside them, the way I'd save yourself, Conchubor, and Naisi and Emain Macha; but I'll walk up now into your halls, and I'll say (*with a gesture*) it's here nettles will be growing, and beyond thistles and docks. I'll go into your high chambers, where you've been figuring yourself stretching out your neck for the kisses of a queen of women; and I'll say it's here there'll be deer stirring and goats scratching, and sheep waking and coughing when there is a great wind from the north. (*Shaking herself loose. Conchubor makes a sign to Soldiers.*) I'm going, surely. In a short space I'll be sitting up with many listening to the flames crackling, and the beams breaking, and I looking on the great blaze will be the end of Emain.

[*She goes out.*]

CONCHUBOR (*looking out*). I see two people in the trees; it should be Naisi and Deirdre. (*To Soldier.*) Let you tell them they'll lodge here to-night.

[*Conchubor goes out right. Naisi and Deirdre come in on left, very weary.*]

NAISI (*to Soldiers*). Is it this place he's made ready for myself and Deirdre?

SOLDIER. The Red Branch House is being aired and swept and you'll be called there when a space is by; till then you'd find fruits and drink on this table, and so the gods be with you.

[*Goes out right.*]

NAISI (*looking round*). It's a strange place he's put us camping and we come back as his friends.

DEIRDRE. He's likely making up a welcome for us, having curtains shaken out and rich rooms put in order; and it's right he'd have great state to meet us, and you his sister's son.

NAISI (*gloomily*). It's little we want with state or rich rooms or curtains, when we're used to the ferns only and cold streams and they making a stir.

DEIRDRE (*roaming round room*). We want what is our right in Emain (*looking at hangings*), and though he's riches in store for us it's a shabby, ragged place he's put us waiting, with frayed rugs and skins are eaten by the moths.

NAISI (*a little impatiently*). There are few would worry over skins and moths on this first night that we've come back to Emain.

DEIRDRE (*brightly*). You should be well pleased it's for that I'd worry all times, when it's I have kept your tent these seven years as tidy as a bee-hive or a linnet's nest. If Conchubor'd a queen like me in Emain he'd not have stretched these rags to meet us. (*She pulls hanging, and it opens.*) There's new earth on the ground and a trench dug. . . . It's a grave, Naisi, that is wide and deep.

NAISI (*goes over and pulls back curtain showing grave*). And that'll be our home in Emain. . . . He's dug it wisely at the butt of a hill, with fallen trees to hide it. He'll want to have us killed and buried before Fergus comes.

DEIRDRE. Take me away. . . . Take me to hide in the rocks, for the night is coming quickly.

NAISI (*pulling himself together*). I will not leave my brothers.

DEIRDRE (*vehemently*). It's of us two he's jealous. Come away to the places where we're used to have our company. . . . Wouldn't it be a good thing to lie hid in the high ferns together? (*She pulls him left.*) I hear strange words in the trees.

NAISI. It should be the strange fighters of Conchubor. I saw them passing as we came.

DEIRDRE (*pulling him towards the right*). Come to this side. Listen, Naisi!

NAISI. There are more of them. . . . We are shut in,

and I have not Ainnle and Ardan to stand near me. Isn't it a hard thing that we three who have conquered many may not die together?

DEIRDRE (*sinking down*). And isn't it a hard thing that you and I are in this place by our opened grave; though none have lived had happiness like ours those days in Alban that went by so quick?

NAISI. It's a hard thing, surely, we've lost those days for ever; and yet it's a good thing, maybe, that all goes quick, for when I'm in that grave it's soon a day'll come you'll be too wearied to be crying out, and that day'll bring you ease.

DEIRDRE. I'll not be here to know if that is true.

NAISI. It's our three selves he'll kill to-night, and then in two months or three you'll see him walking down for courtship with yourself.

DEIRDRE. I'll not be here.

NAISI (*hard*). You'd best keep him off, maybe, and then, when the time comes, make your way to some place west in Donegal, and it's there you'll get used to stretching out lonesome at the fall of night, and waking lonesome for the day.

DEIRDRE. Let you not be saying things are worse than death.

NAISI (*a little recklessly*). I've one word left. If a day comes in the west that the larks are cocking their crests on the edge of the clouds, and the cuckoos making a stir, and there's a man you'd fancy, let you not be thinking that day I'd be well pleased you'd go on keening always.

DEIRDRE (*turning to look at him*). And if it was I that

died, Naisi, would you take another woman to fill up my place?

NAISI (*very mournfully*). It's little I know, saving only that it's a hard and bitter thing leaving the earth, and a worse and harder thing leaving yourself alone and desolate to be making lamentation on its face always.

DEIRDRE. I'll die when you do, Naisi. I'd not have come here from Alban but I knew I'd be along with you in Emain, and you living or dead. . . . Yet this night it's strange and distant talk you're making only.

NAISI. There's nothing, surely, the like of a new grave of open earth for putting a great space between two friends that love.

DEIRDRE. If there isn't, it's that grave when it's closed will make us one for ever, and we two lovers have had great space without weariness or growing old or any sadness of the mind.

CONCHUBOR (*coming in on right*). I'd bid you welcome, Naisi.

NAISI (*standing up*). You're welcome, Conchubor. I'm well pleased you've come.

CONCHUBOR (*blandly*). Let you not think bad of this place where I've put you till other rooms are readied.

NAISI (*breaking out*). We know the room you've readied. We know what stirred you to send your seals and Fergus into Alban and stop him in the north, (*opening curtain and pointing to the grave*) and dig that grave before us. Now I ask what brought you here?

CONCHUBOR. I've come to look on Deirdre.

NAISI. Look on her. You're a knacky fancier, and it's well you chose the one you'd lure from Alban. Look on her, I tell you, and when you've looked I've got ten fingers will squeeze your mottled goose neck, though you're king itself.

DEIRDRE (*coming between them*). Hush, Naisi! Maybe Conchubor'll make peace. . . . Do not mind him, Conchubor; he has cause to rage.

CONCHUBOR. It's little I heed his raging, when a call would bring my fighters from the trees. . . . But what do you say, Deirdre?

DEIRDRE. I'll say so near that grave we seem three lonesome people, and by a new made grave there's no man will keep brooding on a woman's lips, or on the man he hates. It's not long till your own grave will be dug in Emain, and you'd go down to it more easy if you'd let call Ainnle and Ardan, the way we'd have a supper all together, and fill that grave, and you'll be well pleased from this out, having four new friends the like of us in Emain.

CONCHUBOR (*looking at her for a moment*). That's the first friendly word I've heard you speaking, Deirdre. A game the like of yours should be the proper thing for softening the heart and putting sweetness in the tongue; and yet this night when I hear you I've small blame left for Naisi that he stole you off from Ulster.

DEIRDRE (*to Naisi*). Now, Naisi, answer gently, and we'll be friends to-night.

NAISI (*doggedly*). I have no call but to be friendly. I'll answer what you will.

DEIRDRE (*taking Naisi's hand*). Then you'll call Conchubor your friend and king, the man who reared me up upon Slieve Fuadh.

[*As Conchubor is going to clasp Naisi's hand cries are heard behind.*]

CONCHUBOR. What noise is that?

AINNLE (*behind*). Naisi. . . . Naisi! Come to us; we are betrayed and broken.

NAISI. It's Ainnle crying out in a battle.

CONCHUBOR. I was near won this night, but death's between us now.

[*He goes out.*]

DEIRDRE (*clinging to Naisi*). There is no battle. . . . Do not leave me, Naisi.

NAISI. I must go to them.

DEIRDRE (*beseechingly*). Do not leave me, Naisi. Let us creep up in the darkness behind the grave. If there's a battle, maybe the strange fighters will be destroyed, when Ainnle and Ardan are against them.

[*Cries heard.*]

NAISI (*wildly*). I hear Ardan crying out. Do not hold me from my brothers.

DEIRDRE. Do not leave me, Naisi. Do not leave me broken and alone.

NAISI. I cannot leave my brothers when it is I who have defied the king.

DEIRDRE. I will go with you.

NAISI. You cannot come. Do not hold me from the fight.

[*He throws her aside almost roughly.*]

DEIRDRE (*with restraint*). Go to your brothers. For seven years you have been kindly, but the hardness of death has come between us.

NAISI (*looking at her aghast*). And you'll have me meet death with a hard word from your lips in my ear?

DEIRDRE. We've had a dream, but this night has waked us surely. In a little while we've lived too long, Naisi, and isn't it a poor thing we should miss the safety of the grave, and we trampling its edge?

AINNLE (*behind*). Naisi, Naisi, we are attacked and ruined!

DEIRDRE. Let you go where they are calling. (*She looks at him for an instant coldly.*) Have you no shame loitering and talking, and a cruel death facing Ainnle and Ardan in the woods?

NAISI (*frantic*). They'll not get a death that's cruel, and they with men alone. It's women that have loved are cruel only; and if I went on living from this day I'd be putting a curse on the lot of them I'd meet walking in the east or west, putting a curse on the sun that gave them beauty, and on the madder and the stonecrop put red upon their cloaks.

DEIRDRE (*bitterly*). I'm well pleased there's no one in this place to make a story that Naisi was a laughing-stock the night he died.

NAISI. There'd not be many'd make a story, for that mockery is in your eyes this night will spot the face of Emain with a plague of pitted graves.

[*He goes out.*]

CONCHUBOR (*outside*). That is Naisi. Strike him! (*Tumult. Deirdre crouches down on Naisi's cloak. Conchubor comes in hurriedly.*) They've met their death—the three that stole you, Deirdre, and from this out you'll be my queen in Emain.

[*A keen of men's voices is heard behind.*]

DEIRDRE (*bewildered and terrified*). It is not I will be a queen.

CONCHUBOR. Make your lamentation a short while if you will, but it isn't long till a day'll come when you begin pitying a man is old and desolate, and High King also. . . . Let you not fear me, for it's I'm well pleased you have a store of pity for the three that were your friends in Alban.

DEIRDRE. I have pity, surely. . . . It's the way pity has me this night, when I think of Naisi, that I could set my teeth into the heart of a king.

CONCHUBOR. I know well pity's cruel, when it was my pity for my own self destroyed Naisi.

DEIRDRE (*more wildly*). It was my words without pity gave Naisi a death will have no match until the ends of life and time. (*Breaking out into a keen.*) But who'll pity Deirdre has lost the lips of Naisi from her neck and from her cheek for ever? Who'll pity Deirdre has lost the twilight in the woods with Naisi, when beech-trees were silver and copper, and ash-trees were fine gold?

CONCHUBOR (*bewildered*). It's I'll know the way to pity and care you, and I with a share of troubles has me thinking this night it would be a good bargain if it was I was in the grave, and Deirdre crying over me, and it was Naisi who was old and desolate.

[*Keen heard.*]

DEIRDRE (*wild with sorrow*). It is I who am desolate; I, Deirdre, that will not live till I am old.

CONCHUBOR. It's not long you'll be desolate, and I seven years saying, "It's a bright day for Deirdre in the woods of Alban"; or saying again, "What way will Deirdre be sleeping this night, and wet leaves and branches driving from the north?" Let you not break the thing I've set my life on, and you giving yourself up to your sorrow when it's joy and sorrow do burn out like straw blazing in an east wind.

DEIRDRE (*turning on him*). Was it that way with your sorrow, when I and Naisi went northward from Slieve Fuadh and let raise our sails for Alban?

CONCHUBOR. There's one sorrow has no end surely— that's being old and lonesome. (*With extraordinary pleading.*) But you and I will have a little peace in Emain, with harps playing, and old men telling stories at the fall of night. I've let build rooms for our two selves, Deirdre, with red gold upon the walls and ceilings that are set with bronze. There was never a queen in the east had a house the like of your house, that's waiting for yourself in Emain.

SOLDIER (*running in*). Emain is in flames. Fergus has come back and is setting fire to the world. Come up, Conchubor, or your state will be destroyed!

CONCHUBOR (*angry and regal again*). Are the Sons of Usna buried?

SOLDIER. They are in their grave, but no earth is thrown.

CONCHUBOR. Let me see them. Open the tent! (*Soldier opens back of tent and shows grave.*) Where are my fighters?

SOLDIER. They are gone to Emain.

CONCHUBOR (*to Deirdre*). There are none to harm you. Stay here until I come again.

[*Goes out with Soldier. Deirdre looks round for a moment, then goes up slowly and looks into grave. She crouches down and begins swaying herself backwards and forwards, keening softly. At first her words are not heard, then they become clear.*]

DEIRDRE. It's you three will not see age or death coming—you that were my company when the fires on the hill-tops were put out and the stars were our friends only. I'll turn my thoughts back from this night, that's pitiful for want of pity, to the time it was your rods and cloaks made a little tent for me where there'd be a birch tree making shelter and a dry stone; though from this day my own fingers will be making a tent for me, spreading out my hairs and they knotted with the rain.

[*Lavarcham and Old Woman come in stealthily on right.*]

DEIRDRE (*not seeing them*). It is I, Deirdre, will be crouching in a dark place; I, Deirdre, that was young with Naisi, and brought sorrow to his grave in Emain.

OLD WOMAN. Is that Deirdre broken down that was so light and airy?

LAVARCHAM. It is, surely, crying out over their grave.

[*She goes to Deirdre.*]

DEIRDRE. It will be my share from this out to be making lamentation on this stone always, and I crying for a love will be the like of a star shining on a little harbour by the sea.

LAVARCHAM (*coming forward*). Let you rise up, Deirdre, and come off while there are none to heed us, the way I'll find you shelter and some friend to guard you.

DEIRDRE. To what place would I go away from Naisi? What are the woods without Naisi or the sea shore?

LAVARCHAM (*very coaxingly*). If it is that way you'd be, come till I find you a sunny place where you'll be a great wonder they'll call the queen of sorrows; and you'll begin taking a pride to be sitting up pausing and dreaming when the summer comes.

DEIRDRE. It was the voice of Naisi that was strong in summer—the voice of Naisi that was sweeter than pipes playing, but from this day will be dumb always.

LAVARCHAM (*to Old Woman*). She doesn't heed us at all. We'll be hard set to rouse her.

OLD WOMAN. If we don't the High King will rouse her, coming down beside her with the rage of battle in his blood, for how could Fergus stand against him?

LAVARCHAM (*touching Deirdre with her hand*). There's a score of woman's years in store for you, and you'd best choose will you start living them beside the man you hate, or being your own mistress in the west or south?

DEIRDRE. It is not I will go on living after Ainnle and after Ardan. After Naisi I will not have a lifetime in the world.

OLD WOMAN (*with excitement*). Look, Lavarcham! There's a light leaving the Red Branch. Conchubor and his lot will be coming quickly with a torch of bog-deal for her marriage, throwing a light on her three comrades.

DEIRDRE (*startled*). Let us throw down clay on my three comrades. Let us cover up Naisi along with Ainnle and Ardan, they that were the pride of Emain. (*Throwing in clay.*) There is Naisi was the best of three, the choicest of the choice of many. It was a clean death was your share, Naisi; and it is not I will quit your head, when it's many a dark night among the snipe and plover that you and I were whispering together. It is not I will quit your head, Naisi, when it's many a night we saw the stars among the clear trees of Glen da Ruadh, or the moon pausing to rest her on the edges of the hills.

OLD WOMAN. Conchubor is coming, surely. I see the glare of flames throwing a light upon his cloak.

LAVARCHAM (*eagerly*). Rise up, Deirdre, and come to Fergus, or be the High King's slave for ever!

DEIRDRE (*imperiously*). I will not leave Naisi, who has left the whole world scorched and desolate. I will not go away when there is no light in the heavens, and no flower in the earth under them, but is saying to me that it is Naisi who is gone for ever.

CONCHUBOR (*behind*). She is here. Stay a little back. (*Lavarcham and Old Woman go into the shadow on left as Conchubor comes in. With excitement, to Deirdre.*) Come forward and leave Naisi the way I've left charred timber and a smell of burning in Emain Macha, and a heap of rubbish in the storehouse of many crowns.

DEIRDRE (*more awake to what is round her*). What are crowns and Emain Macha, when the head that gave them glory is this place, Conchubor, and it stretched upon the gravel will be my bed to-night?

CONCHUBOR. Make an end of talk of Naisi, for I've come to bring you to Dundealgan since Emain is destroyed.

[*Conchubor makes a movement towards her.*]

DEIRDRE (*with a tone that stops him*). Draw a little back from Naisi, who is young for ever. Draw a little back from the white bodies I am putting under a mound of clay and grasses that are withered—a mound will have a nook for my own self when the end is come.

CONCHUBOR (*roughly*). Let you rise up and come along with me in place of growing crazy with your wailings here.

DEIRDRE. It's yourself has made a crazy story, and let you go back to your arms, Conchubor, and to councils where your name is great, for in this place you are an old man and a fool only.

CONCHUBOR. If I've folly, I've sense left not to lose the thing I've bought with sorrow and the deaths of many.

[*He moves towards her.*]

DEIRDRE. Do not raise a hand to touch me.

CONCHUBOR. There are other hands to touch you. My fighters are set round in among the trees.

DEIRDRE. Who'll fight the grave, Conchubor, and it opened on a dark night?

LAVARCHAM (*eagerly*). There are steps in the wood. I hear the call of Fergus and his men.

CONCHUBOR (*furiously*). Fergus cannot stop me. I am more powerful than he is, though I am defeated and old.

FERGUS (*comes in to Deirdre; a red glow is seen behind the grove*). I have destroyed Emain, and now I'll guard you all times, Deirdre, though it was I, without knowledge, brought Naisi to his grave.

CONCHUBOR. It's not you will guard her, for my whole armies are gathering. Rise up, Deirdre, for you are mine surely.

FERGUS (*coming between them*). I am come between you.

CONCHUBOR (*wildly*). When I've killed Naisi and his

brothers, is there any man that I will spare? And is it you will stand against me, Fergus, when it's seven years you've seen me getting my death with rage in Emain?

FERGUS. It's I, surely, will stand against a thief and a traitor.

DEIRDRE (*stands up and sees the light from Emain*). Draw a little back with the squabbling of fools when I am broken up with misery. (*She turns round.*) I see the flames of Emain starting upward in the dark night; and because of me there will be weasels and wild cats crying on a lonely wall where there were queens and armies and red gold, the way there will be a story told of a ruined city and a raving king and a woman will be young for ever. (*She looks round.*) I see the trees naked and bare, and the moon shining. Little moon, little moon of Alban, it's lonesome you'll be this night, and to-morrow night, and long nights after, and you pacing the woods beyond Glen Laoi, looking every place for Deirdre and Naisi, the two lovers who slept so sweetly with each other.

FERGUS (*going to Conchubor's right and whispering*). Keep back, or you will have the shame of pushing a bolt on a queen who is out of her wits.

CONCHUBOR. It is I who am out of my wits, with Emain in flames, and Deirdre raving, and my own heart gone within me.

DEIRDRE (*in a high and quiet tone*). I have put away sorrow like a shoe that is worn out and muddy, for it is I have had a life that will be envied by great companies. It was not by a low birth I made kings uneasy, and they sitting in the halls of Emain. It was not a low thing to be chosen by Conchubor, who was wise, and Naisi had no match for bravery. It is not a small thing to be rid of grey hairs, and the loosening of the teeth. (*With a sort of triumph.*) It was the choice of lives we had in the clear woods, and in the grave, we're safe, surely. . . .

CONCHUBOR. She will do herself harm.

DEIRDRE (*showing Naisi's knife*). I have a little key to unlock the prison of Naisi you'd shut upon his youth for ever. Keep back, Conchubor; for the High King who is your master has put his hands between us. (*She half turns to the grave.*) It was sorrows were foretold, but great joys were my share always; yet it is a cold place I must go to be with you, Naisi; and it's cold your arms will be this night that were warm about my neck so often. . . . It's a pitiful thing to be talking out when your ears are shut to me. It's a pitiful thing, Conchubor, you have done this night in Emain; yet a thing will be a joy and triumph to the ends of life and time.

[*She presses knife into her heart and sinks into the grave. Conchubor and Fergus go forward. The red glow fades, leaving stage very dark.*]

FERGUS. Four white bodies are laid down together; four clear lights are quenched in Ireland. (*He throws his sword into the grave.*) There is my sword that could not shield you—my four friends that were the dearest always. The flames of Emain have gone out: Deirdre is dead and there is none to keen her. That is the fate of Deirdre and the children of Usna, and for this night, Conchubor, our war is ended.

[*He goes out.*]

LAVARCHAM. I have a little hut where you can rest, Conchubor; there is a great dew falling.

CONCHUBOR (*with the voice of an old man*). Take me with you. I'm hard set to see the way before me.

OLD WOMAN. This way, Conchubor.

[*They go out.*]

LAVARCHAM (*beside the grave*). Deirdre is dead, and Naisi is dead; and if the oaks and stars could die for sorrow, it's a dark sky and a hard and naked earth we'd have this night in Emain.

CURTAIN

POEMS AND TRANSLATIONS

PREFACE

I HAVE often thought that at the side of the poetic diction, which everyone condemns, modern verse contains a great deal of poetic material, using poetic in the same special sense. The poetry of exaltation will be always the highest; but when men lose their poetic feeling for ordinary life, and cannot write poetry of ordinary things, their exalted poetry is likely to lose its strength of exaltation, in the way men cease to build beautiful churches when they have lost happiness in building shops.

Many of the older poets, such as Villon and Herrick and Burns, used the whole of their personal life as their material, and the verse written in this way was read by strong men, and thieves, and deacons, not by little cliques only. Then, in the town writing of the eighteenth century, ordinary life was put into verse that was not poetry, and when poetry came back with Coleridge and Shelley, it went into verse that was not always human.

In these days poetry is usually a flower of evil or good; but it is the timber of poetry that wears most surely, and there is no timber that has not strong roots among the clay and worms.

Even if we grant that exalted poetry can be kept successful by itself, the strong things of life are needed in poetry also, to show that what is exalted and tender is not made by feeble blood. It may almost be said that before verse can be human again it must learn to be brutal.

The poems which follow were written at different times during the last sixteen or seventeen years, most of them before the views just stated, with which they have little to do, had come into my head.

The translations are sometimes free, and sometimes almost literal, according as seemed most fitting with the form of language I have used.

J. M. S.

Glenageary, December, 1908

POEMS

QUEENS

Seven dog-days we let pass,
Naming Queens in Glenmacnass,
All the rare and royal names
Wormy sheepskin yet retains:
Etain, Helen, Maeve, and Fand,
Golden Deirdre's tender hand;
Bert, the big-foot, sung by Villon,
Cassandra, Ronsard found in Lyon.
Queen of Sheba, Meath and Connaught,
Coifed with crown, or gaudy bonnet;
Queen whose finger once did stir men,
Queens were eaten of fleas and vermin,
Queens men drew like Monna Lisa,
Or slew with drugs in Rome and Pisa.
We named Lucrezia Crivelli,
And Titian's lady with amber belly,
Queens acquainted in learned sin,
Jane of Jewry's slender shin:
Queens who cut the bogs of Glanna,
Judith of Scripture, and Gloriana,
Queens who wasted the East by proxy,
Or drove the ass-cart, a tinker's doxy.
Yet these are rotten—I ask their pardon—
And we've the sun on rock and garden;
These are rotten, so you're the Queen
Of all are living, or have been.

IN KERRY

We heard the thrushes by the shore and sea,
And saw the golden stars' nativity,
Then round we went the lane by Thomas Flynn,
Across the church where bones lie out and in;
And there I asked beneath a lonely cloud
Of strange delight, with one bird singing loud,
What change you'd wrought in graveyard, rock and sea,
This new wild paradise to wake for me....
Yet knew no more than knew those merry sins
Had built this stack of thigh-bones, jaws and shins.

A WISH

May seven tears in every week
Touch the hollow of your cheek,
That I—signed with such a dew—
For a lion's share may sue
Of the roses ever curled
Round the May-pole of the world.

Heavy riddles lie in this,
Sorrow's sauce for every kiss.

THE 'MERGENCY MAN

He was lodging above in Coom,
And he'd the half of the bailiff's room.

Till a black night came in Coomasaharn
A night of rains you'd swamp a star in.

"To-night," says he, "with the devil's weather
The hares itself will quit the heather.

"I'll catch my boys with a latch on the door,
And serve my process on near a score."

The night was black at the fording place,
And the flood was up in a whitened race,
But devil a bit he'd turn his face.

Then the peelers said, "Now mind your lepping,
How can you see the stones for stepping?

"We'll wash our hands of your bloody job."
"Wash and welcome," says he, "begob."

He made two leps with a run and dash,
Then the peelers heard a yell and splash;

And the 'mergency man in two days and a bit
Was found in the ebb tide stuck in a net.

DANNY

One night a score of Erris men,
A score I'm told and nine,
Said, "We'll get shut of Danny's noise
Of girls and widows dyin'.

"There's not his like from Binghamstown
To Boyle and Ballycroy,
At playing hell on decent girls,
At beating man and boy.

"He's left two pairs of female twins
Beyond in Killacreest,
And twice in Crossmolina fair
He's struck the parish priest.

"But we'll come round him in the night
A mile beyond the Mullet;
Ten will quench his bloody eyes,
And ten will choke his gullet."

It wasn't long till Danny came,
From Bangor making way,
And he was damning moon and stars
And whistling grand and gay.

Till in a gap of hazel glen—
And not a hare in sight—
Out lepped the nine-and-twenty lads
Along his left and right.

Then Danny smashed the nose on Byrne,
He split the lips on three,
And bit across the right hand thumb
On one Red Shawn Magee.

But seven tripped him up behind,
And seven kicked before,
And seven squeezed around his throat
Till Danny kicked no more.

Then some destroyed him with their heels,
Some tramped him in the mud,
Some stole his purse and timber pipe,
And some washed off the blood.

.   .   .

And when you're walking out the way
From Bangor to Belmulet,
You'll see a flat cross on a stone
Where men choked Danny's gullet.

PATCH-SHANEEN

Shaneen and Maurya Prendergast
Lived west in Carnareagh,
And they'd a cur-dog, cabbage plot,
A goat, and cock of hay.

He was five foot one or two,
Herself was four foot ten,
And he went travelling asking meal
Above through Caragh Glen.

She'd pick her bag of carrageen
Or perries through the surf,
Or loan an ass of Foxy Jim
To fetch her creel of turf.

Till on one windy Samhain night,
When there's stir among the dead,
He found her perished stiff and stark,
Beside him in the bed.

And now when Shaneen travels far
From Droum to Ballyhyre
The women lay him sacks of straw,
Beside the seed of fire.

And when the grey cocks crow and flap,
And winds are in the sky,
"Oh, Maurya, Maurya, are you dead?"
You'll hear Patch-Shaneen cry.

ON AN ISLAND

You've plucked a curlew, drawn a hen,
Washed the shirts of seven men,
You've stuffed my pillow, stretched the sheet,
And filled the pan to wash your feet,
You've cooped the pullets, wound the clock,
And rinsed the young men's drinking crock;
And now we'll dance to jigs and reels,
Nailed boots chasing girls' naked heels,
Until your father'll start to snore,
And Jude, now you're married, will stretch on the floor.

BEG-INNISH

Bring Kateen-beug and Maurya Jude
To dance in Beg-Innish,
And when the lads (they're in Dunquin)
Have sold their crabs and fish,
Wave fawny shawls and call them in,
And call the little girls who spin,
And seven weavers from Dunquin,
To dance in Beg-Innish.

I'll play you jigs, and Maurice Kean,
Where nets are laid to dry,
I've silken strings would draw a dance
From girls are lame or shy;
Four strings I've brought from Spain and France
To make your long men skip and prance,
Till stars look out to see the dance
Where nets are laid to dry.

We'll have no priest or peeler in
To dance in Beg Innish;
But we'll have drink from M'riarty Jim
Rowed round while gannets fish,
A keg with porter to the brim,
That every lad may have his whim,
Till we up sails with M'riarty Jim
And sail from Beg-Innish.

EPITAPH

After reading Ronsard's lines from Rabelais

If fruits are fed on any beast
Let vine-roots suck this parish priest,
For while he lived, no summer sun
Went up but he'd a bottle done,
And in the starlight beer and stout
Kept his waistcoat bulging out.

Then Death that changes happy things
Damned his soul to water springs.

THE PASSING OF THE SHEE

After looking at one of A. E.'s pictures

Adieu, sweet Angus, Maeve, and Fand,
Ye plumed yet skinny Shee,
That poets played with hand in hand
To learn their ecstasy.

We'll stretch in Red Dan Sally's ditch,
And drink in Tubber fair,
Or poach with Red Dan Philly's bitch
The badger and the hare.

ON AN ANNIVERSARY

After reading the dates in a book of Lyrics

With Fifteen-ninety or Sixteen-sixteen
We end Cervantes, Marot, Nashe or Green:
Then Sixteen-thirteen till two score and nine,
Is Crashaw's niche, that honey-lipped divine.
And so when all my little work is done
They'll say I came in Eighteen-seventy-one,
And died in Dublin. . . . What year will they write
For my poor passage to the stall of night?

TO THE OAKS OF GLENCREE

My arms are around you, and I lean
Against you, while the lark
Sings over us, and golden lights, and green
Shadows are on your bark.

There'll come a season when you'll stretch
Black boards to cover me:
Then in Mount Jerome I will lie, poor wretch,
With worms eternally

A QUESTION

I asked if I got sick and died, would you
With my black funeral go walking too,
If you'd stand close to hear them talk or pray
While I'm let down in that steep bank of clay.

And, No, you said, for if you saw a crew
Of living idiots pressing round that new
Oak coffin—they alive, I dead beneath
That board—you'd rave and rend them with your teeth.

DREAD

Beside a chapel I'd a room looked down,
Where all the women from the farms and town,
On Holy-days and Sundays used to pass.
To marriages, and christenings, and to Mass.

Then I sat lonely watching score and score,
Till I turned jealous of the Lord next door. . . .
Now by this window, where there's none can see,
The Lord God's jealous of yourself and me.

IN GLENCULLEN

Thrush, linnet, stare and wren,
Brown lark beside the sun,
Take thought of kestril, sparrow-hawk,
Birdlime and roving gun.

You great-great-grand-children
Of birds I've listened to,
I think I robbed your ancestors
When I was young as you.

I'VE THIRTY MONTHS

I've thirty months, and that's my pride,
Before my age's a double score,
Though many lively men have died
At twenty-nine or little more.

I've left a long and famous set
Behind some seven years or three,
But there are millions I'd forget
Will have their laugh at passing me.

EPITAPH

A silent sinner, nights and days,
No human heart to him drew nigh,
Alone he wound his wonted ways,
Alone and little loved did die.

And autumn Death for him did choose,
A season dank with mists and rain,
And took him, while the evening dews
Were settling o'er the fields again.

PRELUDE

Still south I went and west and south again,
Through Wicklow from the morning till the night,
And far from cities, and the sights of men,
Lived with the sunshine and the moon's delight.

I knew the stars, the flowers, and the birds,
The grey and wintry sides of many glens,
And did but half remember human words,
In converse with the mountains, moors, and fens.

IN MAY

In a nook
That opened south,
You and I
Lay mouth to mouth.

A snowy gull
And sooty daw
Came and looked
With many a caw;

"Such," I said,
"Are I and you,
When you've kissed me
Black and blue!"

ON A BIRTHDAY

Friend of Ronsard, Nashe, and Beaumont,
Lark of Ulster, Meath, and Thomond,
Heard from Smyrna and Sahara
To the surf of Connemara,
Lark of April, June, and May,
Sing loudly this my Lady-day.

WINTER

With little money in a great city

There's snow in every street
Where I go up and down,
And there's no woman, man, or dog
That knows me in the town.

I know each shop, and all
These Jews and Russian Poles,
For I go walking night and noon
To spare my sack of coals.

THE CURSE

To a sister of an enemy of the author's
who disapproved of "The Playboy."

Lord, confound this surly sister,
Blight her brow with blotch and blister,
Cramp her larynx, lung, and liver,
In her guts a galling give her.

Let her live to earn her dinners
In Mountjoy with seedy sinners:
Lord, this judgment quickly bring,
And I'm your servant, J. M. Synge.

TRANSLATIONS FROM PETRARCH

SONNETS FROM "LAURA IN DEATH"

LAURA BEING DEAD, PETRARCH FINDS TROUBLE IN ALL THE THINGS OF THE EARTH

Life is flying from me, not stopping an hour, and Death is making great strides following my track. The days about me and the days passed over me, are bringing me desolation, and the days to come will be the same surely.

All things that I am bearing in mind, and all things I am in dread of, are keeping me in troubles, in this way one time, in that way another time, so that if I wasn't taking pity on my own self it's long ago I'd have given up my life.

If my dark heart has any sweet thing it is turned away from me, and then farther off I see the great winds where I must be sailing. I see my good luck far away in the harbor, but my steersman is tired out, and the masts and the ropes on them are broken, and the beautiful lights where I would be always looking are quenched.

HE ASKS HIS HEART TO RAISE ITSELF UP TO GOD

What is it you're thinking, lonesome heart? For what is it you're turning back ever and always to times that are gone away from you? For what is it you're throwing sticks on the fire when it is your own self that is burning?

The little looks and sweet words you've taken one by

one and written down among your songs, are gone up into the Heavens, and it's late, you know well, to go seeking them on the face of the earth.

Let you not be giving new life every day to your own destruction, and following a fool's thoughts for ever. Let you seek Heaven when there is nothing left pleasing on the earth, and it a poor thing if a great beauty, the like of her, would be destroying your peace and she living or dead.

HE WISHES HE MIGHT DIE AND FOLLOW LAURA

In the years of her age the most beautiful and the most flowery—the time Love has his mastery—Laura, who was my life, has gone away leaving the earth stripped and desolate. She has gone up into the Heavens, living and beautiful and naked, and from that place she is keeping her Lordship and her rein upon me, and I crying out: Ohone, when will I see that day breaking that will be my first day with herself in Paradise?

My thoughts are going after her, and it is that way my soul would follow her, lightly, and airily, and happily, and I would be rid of all my great troubles. But what is delaying me is the proper thing to lose me utterly, to make me a greater weight on my own self.

Oh, what a sweet death I might have died this day three years to-day!

LAURA IS EVER PRESENT TO HIM

If the birds are making lamentation, or the green banks are moved by a little wind of summer, or you can hear the waters making a stir by the shores that are green and flowery.

That's where I do be stretched out thinking Heaven shows me though hidden in the earth of love, writing my songs, and itself that I set my eyes on, and hear the way that she feels my sighs and makes an answer to me.

"Alas," I hear her say, "why are you using yourself up before the time is come, and pouring out a stream of tears so sad and doleful?

"You'd do right to be glad rather, for in dying I won days that have no ending, and when you saw me shutting up my eyes I was opening them on the light that is eternal."

HE CEASES TO SPEAK OF HER GRACES AND HER VIRTUES WHICH ARE NO MORE

The eyes that I would be talking of so warmly, and the arms, and the hands, and the feet, and the face that are after calling me away from myself, and making me a lonesome man among all people.

The hair that was of shining gold, and brightness of the smile that was the like of an angel's surely, and was making a paradise of the earth, are turned to a little dust that knows nothing at all.

And yet I myself am living; it is for this I am making a complaint to be left without the light I had such a great love for, in good fortune and bad, and this will be the end of my songs of love, for the vein where I had cleverness is dried up, and everything I have is turned to complaint only.

HE IS JEALOUS OF THE HEAVENS AND
THE EARTH

What a grudge I am bearing the earth that has its arms about her, and is holding that face away from me, where I was finding peace from great sadness.

What a grudge I am bearing the Heavens that are after taking her, and shutting her in with greediness, the Heavens that do push their bolt against so many.

What a grudge I am bearing the blessed saints that have got her sweet company, that I am always seeking; and what a grudge I am bearing against Death, that is standing in her two eyes, and will not call me with a word.

THE FINE TIME OF THE YEAR
INCREASES PETRARCH'S SORROW

The south wind is coming back, bringing the fine season, and the flowers, and the grass, her sweet family, along with her. The swallow and the nightingale are making a stir, and the spring is turning white and red in every place.

There is a cheerful look on the meadows, and peace in the sky, and the sun is well pleased, I'm thinking, looking downward, and the air and the waters and the earth herself are full of love, and every beast is turning back looking for its mate.

And what is coming to me is great sighing and trouble, which herself is drawing out of my deep heart, herself that has taken the key of it up to Heaven.

And it is this way I am, that the singing birds, and the flowers of the earth, and the sweet ladies, with their grace and comeliness, are the like of a desert to me, and wild beasts astray in it.

HE UNDERSTANDS THE GREAT
CRUELTY OF DEATH

My flowery and green age was passing away, and I feeling a chill in the fires had been wasting my heart, for I was drawing near the hillside that is above the grave.

Then my sweet enemy was making a start, little by little, to give over her great wariness, the way she was wringing a sweet thing out of my sharp sorrow. The time was coming when Love and Decency can keep company, and lovers may sit together and say out all things are in their hearts. But Death had his grudge against me, and he got up in the way, like an armed robber, with a pike in his hand.

THE SIGHT OF LAURA'S HOUSE
REMINDS HIM OF THE GREAT
HAPPINESS HE HAS LOST

Is this the nest in which my Phœnix put on her feathers of gold and purple, my Phœnix that did hold me under her wing, and she drawing out sweet words and sighs from me? Oh, root of my sweet misery, where is that beautiful face, where light would be shining out, the face that did keep my heart like a flame burning? She was without a match upon the earth, I hear them say, and now she is happy in the Heavens.

And she has left me after her dejected and lonesome, turning back all times to the place I do be making much of for her sake only, and I seeing the night on the little hills where she took her last flight up into the Heavens, and where one time her eyes would make sunshine and it night itself.

HE SENDS HIS RHYMES TO THE TOMB OF LAURA TO PRAY HER TO CALL HIM TO HER

Let you go down, sorrowful rhymes, to the hard rock is covering my dear treasure, and then let you call out till herself that is in the Heavens will make answer, though her dead body is lying in a shady place.

Let you say to her that it is tired out I am with being alive, with steering in bad seas, but I am going after step by step, gathering up what she let fall behind her.

It is of her only I do be thinking, and she living and dead, and now I have made her with my songs so that the whole world may know her, and give her the love that is her due.

May it please her to be ready for my own passage that is getting near; may she be there to meet me, herself, in the Heavens, that she may call me, and draw me after her.

ONLY HE WHO MOURNS HER AND HEAVEN THAT POSSESSES HER KNEW HER WHILE SHE LIVED

Ah, Death, it is you that have left the world cold and shady, with no sun over it. It's you have left Love without eyes or arms to him, you've left liveliness stripped, and beauty without a shape to her, and all courtesy in chains, and honesty thrown down into a hole. I am making lamentation alone, though it isn't myself only has a cause to be crying out; since you, Death, have crushed the first seed of goodness in the whole world, and with it gone what place will we find a second?

The air and the earth and seas would have a good right to be crying out and they pitying the race of men that is left without herself, like a meadow without flowers or a ring robbed of jewellery.

The world didn't know her the time she was in it, but I myself knew her—and I left now to be weeping in this place; and the Heavens knew her, the Heavens that are giving an ear this day to my crying out.

LAURA WAITS FOR HIM IN HEAVEN

The first day she passed up and down through the Heavens, gentle and simple were left standing, and they in great wonder, saying one to the other:

"What new light is that? What new beauty at all? The like of herself hasn't risen up these long years from the common world."

And herself, well pleased with the Heavens, was going forward, matching herself with the most perfect that were before her, yet one time and another, waiting a little, and turning her head back to see if myself was coming after her. It's for that I'm lifting up all my thoughts and will into the Heavens, because I do hear her praying that I should be making haste for ever.

THE ARAN ISLANDS

AUTHOR'S FOREWORD

THE geography of the Aran Islands is very simple, yet it may need a word to itself. There are three islands: Aranmor, the north island, about nine miles long; Inishmaan, the middle island, about three miles and a half across, and nearly round in form; and the south island, Inishere—in Irish, east island,—like the middle island but slightly smaller. They lie about thirty miles from Galway, up the centre of the bay, but they are not far from the cliffs of County Clare, on the south, or the corner of Connemara on the north.

Kilronan, the principal village on Aranmor, has been so much changed by the fishing industry, developed there by the Congested Districts Board, that it has now very little to distinguish it from any fishing village on the west coast of Ireland. The other islands are more primitive, but even on them many changes are being made, that it was not worth while to deal with in the text.

In the pages that follow I have given a direct account of my life on the islands, and of what I met with among them, inventing nothing, and changing nothing that is essential. As far as possible, however, I have disguised the identity of the people I speak of, by making changes in their names, and in the letters I quote, and by altering some local and family relationships. I have had nothing to say about them that was not wholly in their favour, but I have made this disguise to keep them from ever feeling that a too direct use had been made of their kindness, and friendship, for which I am more grateful than it is easy to say.

THE ARAN ISLANDS

PART I

I AM in Aranmor, sitting over a turf fire, listening to a murmur of Gaelic that is rising from a little public-house under my room.

The steamer which comes to Aran sails according to the tide, and it was six o'clock this morning when we left the quay of Galway in a dense shroud of mist.

A low line of shore was visible at first on the right between the movement of the waves and fog, but when we came further it was lost sight of, and nothing could be seen but the mist curling in the rigging, and a small circle of foam.

There were few passengers; a couple of men going out with young pigs tied loosely in sacking, three or four young girls who sat in the cabin with their heads completely twisted in their shawls, and a builder, on his way to repair the pier at Kilronan, who walked up and down and talked with me.

In about three hours Aran came in sight. A dreary rock appeared at first sloping up from the sea into the fog; then, as we drew nearer, a coast-guard station and the village.

A little later I was wandering out along the one good roadway of the island, looking over low walls on either side into small flat fields of naked rock. I have seen nothing so desolate. Grey floods of water were weeping everywhere upon the limestone, making at times a wild torrent of the road, which twined continually over low hills and cavities in the rock or passed between a few small fields of potatoes or grass hidden away in corners that had shelter. Whenever the cloud lifted I could see the edge of the sea below me on the right, and the naked ridge of the island above me on the other side. Occasionally I passed a lonely chapel or schoolhouse, or a line of stone pillars with crosses above them and inscriptions asking a prayer for the soul of the person they commemorated.

I met few people; but here and there a band of tall girls passed me on their way to Kilronan, and called out to me with humorous wonder, speaking English with a slight foreign intonation that differed a good deal from the brogue of Galway. The rain and cold seemed to have no influence on their vitality, and as they hurried past me with eager laughter and great talking in Gaelic, they left the wet masses of rock more desolate than before.

A little after midday when I was coming back one old half-blind man spoke to me in Gaelic, but, in general, I was surprised at the abundance and fluency of the foreign tongue.

In the afternoon the rain continued, so I sat here in the inn looking out through the mist at a few men who were unlading hookers that had come in with turf from Connemara, and at the long-legged pigs that were playing in the surf. As the fishermen came in and out of the public-house underneath my room, I could hear through the broken panes that a number of them still used the Gaelic, though it seems to be falling out of use among the younger people of this village.

The old woman of the house had promised to get me a teacher of the language, and after a while I heard shuffling on the stairs, and the old dark man I had spoken to in the morning groped his way into the room.

I brought him over to the fire, and we talked for many hours. He told me that he had known Petrie an

Sir William Wilde, and many living antiquarians, and had taught Irish to Dr. Finck and Dr. Pedersen, and given stories to Mr. Curtin of America. A little after middle age he had fallen over a cliff, and since then he had had little eyesight, and a trembling of his hands and head.

As we talked he sat huddled together over the fire, shaking and blind, yet his face was indescribably pliant, lighting up with an ecstasy of humour when he told me anything that had a point of wit or malice, and growing sombre and desolate again when he spoke of religion or the fairies.

He had great confidence in his own powers and talent, and in the superiority of his stories over all other stories in the world. When we were speaking of Mr. Curtin, he told me that this gentleman had brought out a volume of his Aran stories in America, and made five hundred pounds by the sale of them.

'And what do you think he did then?' he continued; 'he wrote a book of his own stories after making that lot of money with mine. And he brought them out, and the divil a halfpenny did he get for them. Would you believe that?'

Afterwards he told me how one of his children had been taken by the fairies.

One day a neighbour was passing, and she said, when she saw it on the road, 'That's a fine child.'

Its mother tried to say 'God bless it,' but something choked the words in her throat.

A while later they found a wound on its neck, and for three nights the house was filled with noises.

'I never wear a shirt at night,' he said, 'but I got up out of my bed, all naked as I was, when I heard the noises in the house, and lighted a light, but there was nothing in it.'

Then a dummy came and made signs of hammering nails in a coffin.

The next day the seed potatoes were full of blood, and the child told his mother that he was going to America.

That night it died, and 'Believe me,' said the old man, 'the fairies were in it.'

When he went away, a little bare-footed girl was sent up with turf and the bellows to make a fire that would last for the evening.

She was shy, yet eager to talk, and told me that she had good spoken Irish, and was learning to read it in the school, and that she had been twice to Galway, though there are many grown women in the place who have never set a foot upon the mainland.

The rain has cleared off, and I have had my first real introduction to the island and its people.

I went out through Killeany—the poorest village in Aranmor—to a long neck of sandhill that runs out into the sea towards the south-west. As I lay there on the grass the clouds lifted from the Connemara mountains and, for a moment, the green undulating foreground, backed in the distance by a mass of hills, reminded me of the country near Rome. Then the dun top-sail of a hooker swept above the edge of the sandhill and re-vealed the presence of the sea.

As I moved on a boy and a man came down from the next village to talk to me, and I found that here, at least, English was imperfectly understood. When I asked them if there were any trees in the island they held a hurried consultation in Gaelic, and then the man asked if 'tree' meant the same thing as 'bush,' for if so there were a few in sheltered hollows to the east.

They walked on with me to the sound which separates this island from Inishmaan—the middle island of the group—and showed me the roll from the Atlantic running up between two walls of cliff.

They told me that several men had stayed on Inishmaan to learn Irish, and the boy pointed out a line of hovels where they had lodged running like a belt of straw round the middle of the island. The place looked hardly fit for habitation. There was no green to be seen, and no sign of the people except these beehive-like roofs, and the outline of a Dun that stood out above them against the edge of the sky.

After a while my companions went away and two other boys came and walked at my heels, till I turned and made them talk to me. They spoke at first of their poverty, and then one of them said—

'I dare say you do have to pay ten shillings a week in the hotel?'

'More,' I answered.

'Twelve?'

'More.'

'Fifteen?'

'More still.'

Then he drew back and did not question me any further, either thinking that I had lied to check his curiosity, or too awed by my riches to continue.

Repassing Killeany I was joined by a man who had spent twenty years in America, where he had lost his health and then returned, so long ago that he had forgotten English and could hardly make me understand him. He seemed hopeless, dirty, and asthmatic, and after going with me for a few hundred yards he stopped and asked for coppers. I had none left, so I gave him a fill of tobacco, and he went back to his hovel.

When he was gone, two little girls took their place behind me and I drew them in turn into conversation.

They spoke with a delicate exotic intonation that was full of charm, and told me with a sort of chant how they guide 'ladies and gintlemins' in the summer to all that is worth seeing in their neighbourhood, and sell them pampooties and maidenhair ferns, which are common among the rocks.

We were now in Kilronan, and as we parted they showed me holes in their own pampooties, or cowskin sandals, and asked me the price of new ones. I told them that my purse was empty, and then with a few quaint words of blessing they turned away from me and went down to the pier.

All this walk back had been extraordinarily fine. The intense insular clearness one sees only in Ireland, and after rain, was throwing out every ripple in the sea and sky, and every crevice in the hills beyond the bay.

This evening an old man came to see me, and said he had known a relative of mine who passed some time on this island forty-three years ago.

'I was standing under the pier-wall mending nets,' he said, 'when you came off the steamer, and I said to myself in that moment, if there is a man of the name of Synge left walking the world, it is that man yonder will be he.'

He went on to complain in curiously simple yet dignified language of the changes that have taken place here since he left the island to go to sea before the end of his childhood.

'I have come back,' he said, 'to live in a bit of a house

with my sister. The island is not the same at all to what it was. It is little good I can get from the people who are in it now, and anything I have to give them they don't care to have.'

From what I hear this man seems to have shut himself up in a world of individual conceits and theories, and to live aloof at his trade of net-mending, regarded by the other islanders with respect and half-ironical sympathy.

A little later when I went down to the kitchen I found two men from Inishmaan who had been benighted on the island. They seemed a simpler and perhaps a more interesting type than the people here, and talked with careful English about the history of the Duns, and the Book of Ballymote, and the Book of Kells, and other ancient MSS., with the names of which they seemed familiar.

In spite of the charm of my teacher, the old blind man I met the day of my arrival, I have decided to move on to Inishmaan, where Gaelic is more generally used, and the life is perhaps the most primitive that is left in Europe.

I spent all this last day with my blind guide, looking at the antiquities that abound in the west or north-west of the island.

As we set out I noticed among the groups of girls who smiled at our fellowship—old Mourteen says we are like the cuckoo with its pipit—a beautiful oval face with the singularly spiritual expression that is so marked in one type of the West Ireland women. Later in the day, as the old man talked continually of the fairies and the women they have taken, it seemed that there was a possible link between the wild mythology that is accepted on the islands and the strange beauty of the women.

At midday we rested near the ruins of a house, and two beautiful boys came up and sat near us. Old Mourteen asked them why the house was in ruins, and who had lived in it.

'A rich farmer built it a while since,' they said, 'but after two years he was driven away by the fairy host.'

The boys came on with us some distance to the north to visit one of the ancient beehive dwellings that is still in perfect preservation. When we crawled in on our hands and knees, and stood up in the gloom of the interior, old Mourteen took a freak of earthly humour and began telling what he would have done if he could have come in there when he was a young man and a young girl along with him.

Then he sat down in the middle of the floor and began to recite old Irish poetry, with an exquisite purity of intonation that brought tears to my eyes though I understood but little of the meaning.

On our way home he gave me the Catholic theory of the fairies.

When Lucifer saw himself in the glass he thought himself equal with God. Then the Lord threw him out of Heaven, and all the angels that belonged to him. While He was 'chucking them out,' an archangel asked Him to spare some of them, and those that were falling are in the air still, and have power to wreck ships, and to work evil in the world.

From this he wandered off into tedious matters of theology, and repeated many long prayers and sermons in Irish that he had heard from the priests.

A little further on we came to a slated house, and I asked him who was living in it.

'A kind of a schoolmistress,' he said; then his old face puckered with a gleam of pagan malice.

'Ah, master,' he said, 'wouldn't it be fine to be in there, and to be kissing her?'

A couple of miles from this village we turned aside to look at an old ruined church of the Ceathair Aluinn (The Four Beautiful Persons), and a holy well near it that is famous for cures of blindness and epilepsy.

As we sat near the well a very old man came up from a cottage near the road, and told me how it had become famous.

'A woman of Sligo had a son who was born blind, and one night she dreamed that she saw an island with a blessed well in it that could cure her son. She told her dream in the morning, and an old man said it was of Aran she was after dreaming.

'She brought her son down by the coast of Galway, and came out in a curagh, and landed below where you see a bit of a cove.

'She walked up then to the house of my father— God rest his soul—and she told them what she was looking for.

'My father said that there was a well like what she had dreamed of, and that he would send a boy along with her to show her the way.

' "There's no need, at all," said she; "haven't I seen it all in my dream?"

'Then she went out with the child and walked up to this well, and she kneeled down and began saying her prayers. Then she put her hand out for the water, and put it on his eyes, and the moment it touched him he called out: "O mother, look at the pretty flowers!" '

After that Mourteen described the feats of poteen drinking and fighting that he did in his youth, and went on to talk of Diarmid, who was the strongest man after Samson, and of one of the beds of Diarmid and Grainne, which is on the east of the island. He says that Diarmid was killed by the druids, who put a burning shirt on him,—a fragment of mythology that may connect Diarmid with the legend of Hercules, if it is not due to the 'learning' in some hedge-school master's ballad.

Then we talked about Inishmaan.

'You'll have an old man to talk with you over there,' he said, 'and tell you stories of the fairies, but he's walking about with two sticks under him this ten year. Did ever you hear what it is goes on four legs when it is young, and on two legs after that, and on three legs when it does be old?'

I gave him the answer.

'Ah, master,' he said, 'you're a cute one, and the blessing of God be on you. Well, I'm on three legs this minute, but the old man beyond is back on four; I don't know if I'm better than the way he is; he's got his sight and I'm only an old dark man.'

I am settled at last on Inishmaan in a small cottage with a continual drone of Gaelic coming from the kitchen that opens into my room.

Early this morning the man of the house came over for me with a four-oared curagh—that is, a curagh with four rowers and four oars on either side, as each man uses two—and we set off a little before noon.

It gave me a moment of exquisite satisfaction to find myself moving away from civilisation in this rude canvas canoe of a model that has served primitive races since men first went on the sea.

We had to stop for a moment at a hulk that is anchored in the bay, to make some arrangements for the fish-curing of the middle island, and my crew called out as soon as we were within earshot that they had a man with them who had been in France a month from this day.

When we started again, a small sail was run up in the bow, and we set off across the sound with a leaping oscillation that had no resemblance to the heavy movement of a boat.

The sail is only used as an aid, so the men continued to row after it had gone up, and as they occupied the four cross-seats I lay on the canvas at the stern and the frame of slender laths, which bent and quivered as the waves passed under them.

When we set off it was a brilliant morning of April, and the green, glittering waves seemed to toss the canoe among themselves, yet as we drew nearer this island a sudden thunderstorm broke out behind the rocks we were approaching, and lent a momentary tumult to this still vein of the Atlantic.

We landed at a small pier, from which a rude track leads up to the village between small fields and bare sheets of rock like those in Aranmor. The youngest son of my boatman, a boy of about seventeen, who is to be my teacher and guide, was waiting for me at the pier and guided me to his house, while the men settled the curagh and followed slowly with my baggage.

My room is at one end of the cottage, with a boarded floor and ceiling, and two windows opposite each other. Then there is the kitchen with earth floor and open rafters, and two doors opposite each other opening into the open air, but no windows. Beyond it there are two small rooms of half the width of the kitchen with one window apiece.

The kitchen itself, where I will spend most of my time, is full of beauty and distinction. The red dresses of the women who cluster round the fire on their stools give a glow of almost Eastern richness, and the walls have been toned by the turf-smoke to a soft brown that blends with the grey earth-colour of the floor. Many sorts of fishing-tackle, and the nets and oil-skins of the men, are hung upon the walls or among the open rafters; and right overhead, under the thatch, there is a whole cowskin from which they make pampooties.

Every article on these islands has an almost personal character, which gives this simple life, where all art is unknown, something of the artistic beauty of mediæval life. The curaghs and spinning-wheels, the tiny wooden barrels that are still much used in the place of earthenware, the home-made cradles, churns, and baskets, are all full of individuality, and being made from materials that are common here, yet to some extent peculiar to the island, they seem to exist as a natural link between the people and the world that is about them.

The simplicity and unity of the dress increases in another way the local air of beauty. The women wear red petticoats and jackets of the island wool stained with madder, to which they usually add a plaid shawl twisted round their chests and tied at their backs. When it rains they throw another petticoat over their heads with the waistband round their faces, or, if they are young, they use a heavy shawl like those worn in Galway. Occasionally other wraps are worn, and during the thunderstorm I arrived in I saw several girls with men's waistcoats buttoned round their bodies. Their skirts do not come much below the knee, and show their powerful legs in the heavy indigo stockings with which they are all provided.

The men wear three colours: the natural wool, indigo, and a grey flannel that is woven of alternate threads of indigo and the natural wool. In Aranmor many of the younger men have adopted the usual fisherman's jersey, but I have only seen one on this island.

As flannel is cheap—the women spin the yarn from the wool of their own sheep, and it is then woven by a weaver in Kilronan for fourpence a yard—the men seem to wear an indefinite number of waistcoats and woollen drawers one over the other. They are usually surprised at the lightness of my own dress, and one old man I spoke to for a minute on the pier, when I came ashore, asked me if I was not cold with 'my little clothes.'

As I sat in the kitchen to dry the spray from my coat, several men who had seen me walking up came in to me to talk to me, usually murmuring on the threshold, 'The blessing of God on this place,' or some similar words.

The courtesy of the old woman of the house is singularly attractive, and though I could not understand much of what she said—she has no English—I could see with how much grace she motioned each visitor to a chair, or stool, according to his age, and said a few words to him till he drifted into our English conversation.

For the moment my own arrival is the chief subject of interest, and the men who come in are eager to talk to me.

Some of them express themselves more correctly than the ordinary peasant, others use the Gaelic idioms continually and substitute 'he' or 'she' for 'it,' as the neuter pronoun is not found in modern Irish.

A few of the men have a curiously full vocabulary,

others know only the commonest words in English, and are driven to ingenious devices to express their meaning. Of all the subjects we can talk of war seems their favourite, and the conflict between America and Spain is causing a great deal of excitement. Nearly all the families have relations who have had to cross the Atlantic, and all eat of the flour and bacon that is brought from the United States, so they have a vague fear that 'if anything happened to America,' their own island would cease to be habitable.

Foreign languages are another favourite topic, and as these men are bilingual they have a fair notion of what it means to speak and think in many different idioms. Most of the strangers they see on the islands are philological students, and the people have been led to conclude that linguistic studies, particularly Gaelic studies, are the chief occupation of the outside world.

'I have seen Frenchmen, and Danes, and Germans,' said one man, 'and there does be a power of Irish books along with them, and they reading them better than ourselves. Believe me there are few rich men now in the world who are not studying the Gaelic.'

They sometimes ask me the French for simple phrases, and when they have listened to the intonation for a moment, most of them are able to reproduce it with admirable precision.

When I was going out this morning to walk round the island with Michael, the boy who is teaching me Irish, I met an old man making his way down to the cottage. He was dressed in miserable black clothes which seemed to have come from the mainland, and was so bent with rheumatism that, at a little distance, he looked more like a spider than a human being.

Michael told me it was Pat Dirane, the story-teller old Mourteen had spoken of on the other island. I wished to turn back, as he appeared to be on his way to visit me, but Michael would not hear of it.

'He will be sitting by the fire when we come in,' he said; 'let you not be afraid, there will be time enough to be talking to him by and by.'

He was right. As I came down into the kitchen some hours later old Pat was still in the chimney-corner, blinking with the turf smoke.

He spoke English with remarkable aptness and fluency, due, I believe, to the months he spent in the English provinces working at the harvest when he was a young man.

After a few formal compliments he told me how he had been crippled by an attack of the 'old hin' (*i.e.* the influenza), and had been complaining ever since in addition to his rheumatism.

While the old woman was cooking my dinner he asked me if I liked stories, and offered to tell one in English, though he added, it would be much better if I could follow the Gaelic. Then he began:—

There were two farmers in County Clare. One had a son, and the other, a fine rich man, had a daughter.

The young man was wishing to marry the girl, and his father told him to try and get her if he thought well, though a power of gold would be wanting to get the like of her.

'I will try,' said the young man.

He put all his gold into a bag. Then he went over to the other farm, and threw in the gold in front of him.

'Is that all gold?' said the father of the girl.

'All gold,' said O'Conor (the young man's name was O'Conor).

'It will not weigh down my daughter,' said the father.

'We'll see that,' said O'Conor.

Then they put them in the scales, the daughter in one side and the gold in the other. The girl went down against the ground, so O'Conor took his bag and went out on the road.

As he was going along he came to where there was a little man, and he standing with his back against the wall.

'Where are you going with the bag?' said the little man.

'Going home,' said O'Conor.

'Is it gold you might be wanting?' said the man.

'It is, surely,' said O'Conor.

'I'll give you what you are wanting,' said the man, 'and we can bargain in this way—you'll pay me back in a year the gold I give you, or you'll pay me with five pounds cut off your own flesh.'

That bargain was made between them. The man gave a bag of gold to O'Conor, and he went back with it, and was married to the young woman.

They were rich people, and he built her a grand castle on the cliffs of Clare, with a window that looked out straight over the wild ocean.

One day when he went up with his wife to look out over the wild ocean, he saw a ship coming in on the rocks, and no sails on her at all. She was wrecked on the rocks, and it was tea that was in her, and fine silk.

O'Conor and his wife went down to look at the wreck, and when the lady O'Conor saw the silk she said she wished a dress of it.

They got the silk from the sailors, and when the Captain came up to get the money for it, O'Conor asked him to come again and take his dinner with them. They had a grand dinner, and they drank after it, and the Captain was tipsy. While they were still drinking, a letter came to O'Conor, and it was in the letter that a friend of his was dead, and that he would have to go away on a long journey. As he was getting ready the Captain came to him.

'Are you fond of your wife?' said the Captain.

'I am fond of her,' said O'Conor.

'Will you make me a bet of twenty guineas no man comes near her while you'll be away on the journey?' said the Captain.

'I will bet it,' said O'Conor; and he went away.

There was an old hag who sold small things on the road near the castle, and the lady O'Conor allowed her to sleep up in her room in a big box. The Captain went down on the road to the old hag.

'For how much will you let me sleep one night in your box?' said the Captain.

'For no money at all would I do such a thing,' said the hag.

'For ten guineas?' said the Captain.

'Not for ten guineas,' said the hag.

'For twelve guineas?' said the Captain.

'Not for twelve guineas,' said the hag.

'For fifteen guineas?' said the Captain.

'For fifteen I will do it,' said the hag.

Then she took him up and hid him in the box. When night came the lady O'Conor walked up into her room, and the Captain watched her through a hole that was in the box. He saw her take off her two rings and put them on a kind of a board that was over her head like a chimney-piece, and take off her clothes, except her shift, and go up into her bed.

As soon as she was asleep the Captain came out of his box, and he had some means of making a light, for he lit the candle. He went over to the bed where she was sleeping without disturbing her at all, or doing any bad thing, and he took the two rings off the board, and blew out the light, and went down again into the box.

He paused for a moment, and a deep sigh of relief rose from the men and women who had crowded in while the story was going on, till the kitchen was filled with people.

As the Captain was coming out of his box the girls, who had appeared to know no English, stopped their spinning and held their breath with expectation.

The old man went on—

When O'Conor came back the Captain met him, and told him that he had been a night in his wife's room, and gave him the two rings.

O'Conor gave him the twenty guineas of the bet. Then he went up into the castle, and he took his wife up to look out of the window over the wild ocean. While she was looking he pushed her from behind, and she fell down over the cliff into the sea.

An old woman was on the shore, and she saw her falling. She went down then to the surf and pulled her out all wet and in great disorder, and she took the wet clothes off her, and put on some old rags belonging to herself.

When O'Conor had pushed his wife from the window he went away into the land.

After a while the lady O'Conor went out searching for him, and when she had gone here and there a long time in the country, she heard that he was reaping in a field with sixty men.

She came to the field and she wanted to go in, but the gate-man would not open the gate for her. Then the owner came by, and she told him her story. He brought her in, and her husband was there, reaping, but he never gave any sign of knowing her. She showed him to the owner, and he made the man come out and go with his wife.

Then the lady O'Conor took him out on the road where there were horses, and they rode away.

When they came to the place where O'Conor had met the little man, he was there on the road before them.

'Have you my gold on you?' said the man.

'I have not,' said O'Conor.

'Then you'll pay me the flesh off your body,' said the man.

They went into a house, and a knife was brought, and a clean white cloth was put on the table, and O'Conor was put upon the cloth.

Then the little man was going to strike the lancet into him, when says lady O'Conor—

'Have you bargained for five pounds of flesh?'

'For five pounds of flesh,' said the man.

'Have you bargained for any drop of his blood?' said lady O'Conor.

'For no blood,' said the man.

'Cut out the flesh,' said lady O'Conor, 'but if you spill one drop of his blood I'll put that through you.' And she put a pistol to his head.

The little man went away and they saw no more of him.

When they got home to their castle they made a

great supper, and they invited the Captain and the old hag, and the old woman that had pulled the lady O'Conor out of the sea.

After they had eaten well the lady O'Conor began, and she said they would all tell their stories. Then she told how she had been saved from the sea, and how she had found her husband.

Then the old woman told her story, the way she had found the lady O'Conor wet, and in great disorder, and had brought her in and put on her some old rags of her own.

The lady O'Conor asked the Captain for his story, but he said they would get no story from him. Then she took her pistol out of her pocket, and she put it on the edge of the table, and she said that any one that would not tell his story would get a bullet into him.

Then the Captain told the way he had got into the box, and come over to her bed without touching her at all, and had taken away the rings.

Then the lady O'Conor took the pistol and shot the hag through the body, and they threw her over the cliff into the sea.

That is my story.

It gave me a strange feeling of wonder to hear this illiterate native of a wet rock in the Atlantic telling a story that is so full of European associations.

The incident of the faithful wife takes us beyond Cymbeline to the sunshine on the Arno, and the gay company who went out from Florence to tell narratives of love. It takes us again to the low vineyards of Würzburg on the Main, where the same tale was told in the middle ages, of the 'Two Merchants and the Faithful Wife of Ruprecht von Würzburg.'

The other portion, dealing with the pound of flesh, has a still wider distribution, reaching from Persia and Egypt to the *Gesta Romanorum*, and the *Pecorone* of Ser Giovanni, a Florentine notary.

The present union of the two tales has already been found among the Gaels, and there is a somewhat similar version in Campbell's *Popular Tales of the Western Highlands*.

Michael walks so fast when I am out with him that I cannot pick my steps, and the sharp-edged fossils which abound in the limestone have cut my shoes to pieces.

The family held a consultation on them last night, and in the end it was decided to make me a pair of pampooties, which I have been wearing to-day among the rocks.

They consist simply of a piece of raw cowskin, with the hair outside, laced over the toe and round the heel with two ends of fishing-line that work round and are tied above the instep.

In the evening, when they are taken off, they are placed in a basin of water, as the rough hide cuts the foot and stocking if it is allowed to harden. For the same reason the people often step into the surf during the day, so that their feet are continually moist.

At first I threw my weight upon my heels, as one does naturally in a boot, and was a good deal bruised, but after a few hours I learned the natural walk of man, and could follow my guide in any portion of the island.

In one district below the cliffs, towards the north, one goes for nearly a mile jumping from one rock to another without a single ordinary step; and here I realised that toes have a natural use, for I found myself jump-

ing towards any tiny crevice in the rock before me, and
clinging with an eager grip in which all the muscles of
my feet ached from their exertion.

The absence of the heavy boot of Europe has preserved to these people the agile walk of the wild animal,
while the general simplicity of their lives has given them
many other points of physical perfection. Their way of
life has never been acted on by anything much more
artificial than the nests and burrows of the creatures
that live round them, and they seem, in a certain sense,
to approach more nearly to the finer types of our aris-
tocracies—who are bred artificially to a natural ideal
—than to the labourer or citizen, as the wild horse re-
sembles the thoroughbred rather than the hack or cart-
horse. Tribes of the same natural development are, perhaps, frequent in half-civilised countries, but here a
touch of the refinement of old societies is blended, with
singular effect, among the qualities of the wild animal.

While I am walking with Michael some one often
comes to me to ask the time of day. Few of the people,
however, are sufficiently used to modern time to understand in more than a vague way the convention of the
hours, and when I tell them what o'clock it is by my
watch they are not satisfied, and ask how long is left
them before the twilight.

The general knowledge of time on the island de-
pends, curiously enough, on the direction of the wind.
Nearly all the cottages are built, like this one, with two
doors opposite each other, the more sheltered of which
lies open all day to give light to the interior. If the wind
is northerly the south door is opened, and the shadow of
the door-post moving across the kitchen floor indicates
the hour; as soon, however, as the wind changes to the

south the other door is opened, and the people, who never think of putting up a primitive dial, are at a loss.

This system of doorways has another curious result. It usually happens that all the doors on one side of the village pathway are lying open with women sitting about on the thresholds, while on the other side the doors are shut and there is no sign of life. The moment the wind changes everything is reversed, and sometimes when I come back to the village after an hour's walk there seems to have been a general flight from one side of the way to the other.

In my own cottage the change of the doors alters the whole tone of the kitchen, turning it from a brilliantly-lighted room looking out on a yard and laneway to a sombre cell with a superb view of the sea.

When the wind is from the north the old woman manages my meals with fair regularity, but on the other days she often makes my tea at three o'clock instead of six. If I refuse it she puts it down to simmer for three hours in the turf, and then brings it in at six o'clock full of anxiety to know if it is warm enough.

The old man is suggesting that I should send him a clock when I go away. He'd like to have something from me in the house, he says, the way they wouldn't forget me, and wouldn't a clock be as handy as another thing, and they'd be thinking on me whenever they'd look on its face.

The general ignorance of any precise hours in the day makes it impossible for the people to have regular meals.

They seem to eat together in the evening, and some-times in the morning, a little after dawn, before they scatter for their work, but during the day they simply drink a cup of tea and eat a piece of bread, or some potatoes, whenever they are hungry.

For men who live in the open air they eat strangely little. Often when Michael has been out weeding potatoes for eight or nine hours without food, he comes in and eats a few slices of home-made bread, and then he is ready to go out with me and wander for hours about the island.

They use no animal food except a little bacon and salt fish. The old woman says she would be very ill if she ate fresh meat.

Some years ago, before tea, sugar, and flour had come into general use, salt fish was much more the staple article of diet than at present, and, I am told, skin diseases were very common, though they are now rare on the islands.

No one who has not lived for weeks among these grey clouds and seas can realise the joy with which the eye rests on the red dresses of the women, especially when a number of them are to be found together, as happened early this morning.

I heard that the young cattle were to be shipped for a fair on the mainland, which is to take place in a few days, and I went down on the pier, a little after dawn, to watch them.

The bay was shrouded in the greys of coming rain, yet the thinness of the cloud threw a silvery light on the sea, and an unusual depth of blue to the mountains of Connemara.

As I was going across the sandhills one dun-sailed hooker glided slowly out to begin her voyage, and another beat up to the pier. Troops of red cattle, driven mostly by the women, were coming up from several di-

rections, forming, with the green of the long tract of
grass that separates the sea from the rocks, a new unity
of colour.

The pier itself was crowded with bullocks and a great
number of the people. I noticed one extraordinary girl
in the throng who seemed to exert an authority on all
who came near her. Her curiously formed nostrils and
narrow chin gave her a witch-like expression, yet the
beauty of her hair and skin made her singularly attractive.

When the empty hooker was made fast its deck was
still many feet below the level of the pier, so the animals were slung down by a rope from the mast-head,
with much struggling and confusion. Some of them
made wild efforts to escape, nearly carrying their owners
with them into the sea, but they were handled with
wonderful dexterity, and there was no mishap.

When the open hold was filled with young cattle,
packed as tightly as they could stand, the owners with
their wives or sisters, who go with them to prevent extravagance in Galway, jumped down on the deck, and
the voyage was begun. Immediately afterwards a rickety
old hooker beat up with turf from Connemara, and
while she was unlading all the men sat along the edge of
the pier and made remarks upon the rottenness of her
timber till the owners grew wild with rage.

The tide was now too low for more boats to come to
the pier, so a move was made to a strip of sand towards
the south-east, where the rest of the cattle were shipped
through the surf. Here the hooker was anchored about
eighty yards from the shore, and a curagh was rowed
round to tow out the animals. Each bullock was caught
in its turn and girded with a sling of rope by which it
could be hoisted on board. Another rope was fastened

to the horns and passed out to a man in the stern of the curagh. Then the animal was forced down through the surf and out of its depth before it had much time to struggle. Once fairly swimming, it was towed out to the hooker and dragged on board in a half-drowned condition.

The freedom of the sand seemed to give a stronger spirit of revolt, and some of the animals were only caught after a dangerous struggle. The first attempt was not always successful, and I saw one three-year-old lift two men with his horns, and drag another fifty yards along the sand by his tail before he was subdued.

While this work was going on a crowd of girls and women collected on the edge of the cliff and kept shouting down a confused babble of satire and praise.

When I came back to the cottage I found that among the women who had gone to the mainland was a daughter of the old woman's, and that her baby of about nine months had been left in the care of its grandmother.

As I came in she was busy getting ready my dinner, and old Pat Dirane, who usually comes at this hour, was rocking the cradle. It is made of clumsy wicker-work, with two pieces of rough wood fastened underneath to serve as rockers, and all the time I am in my room I can hear it bumping on the floor with extraordinary violence. When the baby is awake it sprawls on the floor, and the old woman sings it a variety of inarticulate lullabies that have much musical charm.

Another daughter, who lives at home, has gone to the fair also, so the old woman has both the baby and myself to take care of as well as a crowd of chickens that live in a hole beside the fire. Often when I want tea, or when the old woman goes for water, I have to take my own turn at rocking the cradle.

One of the largest Duns, or pagan forts, on the islands, is within a stone's throw of my cottage, and I often stroll up there after a dinner of eggs or salt pork, to smoke drowsily on the stones. The neighbours know my habit, and not infrequently some one wanders up to ask what news there is in the last paper I have received, or to make inquiries about the American war. If no one comes I prop my book open with stones touched by the Fir-bolgs, and sleep for hours in the delicious warmth of the sun. The last few days I have almost lived on the round walls, for, by some miscalculation, our turf has come to an end, and the fires are kept up with dried cow-dung—a common fuel on the island—the smoke from which filters through into my room and lies in blue layers above my table and bed.

Fortunately the weather is fine, and I can spend my days in the sunshine. When I look round from the top of these walls I can see the sea on nearly every side, stretching away to distant ranges of mountains on the north and south. Underneath me to the east there is the one inhabited district of the island, where I can see red figures moving about the cottages, sending up an occasional fragment of conversation or of old island melodies.

The baby is teething, and has been crying for several days. Since his mother went to the fair they have been feeding him with cow's milk, often slightly sour, and giving him, I think, more than he requires.

This morning, however, he seemed so unwell they sent out to look for a foster-mother in the village, and before long a young woman, who lives a little way to the east, came in and restored him his natural food.

A few hours later, when I came into the kitchen to

talk to old Pat, another woman performed the same
kindly office, this time a person with a curiously whimsical expression.

Pat told me a story of an unfaithful wife, which I
will give further down, and then broke into a moral
dispute with the visitor, which caused immense delight
to some young men who had come down to listen to the
story. Unfortunately it was carried on so rapidly in
Gaelic that I lost most of the points.

This old man talks usually in a mournful tone about
his ill-health, and his death, which he feels to be approaching, yet he has occasional touches of humour that
remind me of old Mourteen on the north island. To-day
a grotesque twopenny doll was lying on the floor near
the old woman. He picked it up and examined it as if
comparing it with her. Then he held it up: 'Is it you is
after bringing that thing into the world,' he said, 'woman of the house?'

Here is the story:——

One day I was travelling on foot from Galway to
Dublin, and the darkness came on me and I ten miles
from the town I was wanting to pass the night in. Then
a hard rain began to fall and I was tired walking, so
when I saw a sort of a house with no roof on it up
against the road, I got in the way the walls would give
me shelter.

As I was looking round I saw a light in some trees
two perches off, and thinking any sort of a house would
be better than where I was, I got over a wall and went
up to the house to look in at the window.

I saw a dead man laid on a table, and candles lighted,
and a woman watching him. I was frightened when I
saw him, but it was raining hard, and I said to myself,

if he was dead he couldn't hurt me. Then I knocked on the door and the woman came and opened it.

'Good evening, ma'am,' says I.

'Good evening kindly, stranger,' says she. 'Come in out of the rain.'

Then she took me in and told me her husband was after dying on her, and she was watching him that night.

'But it's thirsty you'll be, stranger,' says she. 'Come into the parlour.'

Then she took me into the parlour—and it was a fine clean house—and she put a cup, with a saucer under it, on the table before me with fine sugar and bread.

When I'd had a cup of tea I went back into the kitchen where the dead man was lying, and she gave me a fine new pipe off the table with a drop of spirits.

'Stranger,' says she, 'would you be afeard to be alone with himself?'

'Not a bit in the world, ma'am,' says I; 'he that's dead can do no hurt.'

Then she said she wanted to go over and tell the neighbours the way her husband was after dying on her, and she went out and locked the door behind her.

I smoked one pipe, and I leaned out and took another off the table. I was smoking it with my hand on the back of my chair—the way you are yourself this minute, God bless you—and I looking on the dead man, when he opened his eyes as wide as myself and looked at me.

'Don't be afraid, stranger,' said the dead man; 'I'm not dead at all in the world. Come here and help me up and I'll tell you all about it.'

Well, I went up and took the sheet off of him, and I saw that he had a fine clean shirt on his body, and fine flannel drawers.

He sat up then, and says he——

'I've got a bad wife, stranger, and I let on to be dead the way I'd catch her goings on.'

Then he got two fine sticks he had to keep down his wife, and he put them at each side of his body, and he laid himself out again as if he was dead.

In half an hour his wife came back and a young man along with her. Well, she gave him his tea, and she told him he was tired, and he would do right to go and lie down in the bedroom.

The young man went in and the woman sat down to watch by the dead man. A while after she got up and 'Stranger,' says she, 'I'm going in to get the candle out of the room; I'm thinking the young man will be asleep by this time.' She went into the bedroom, but the divil a bit of her came back.

Then the dead man got up, and he took one stick, and he gave the other to myself. We went in and saw them lying together with her head on his arm.

The dead man hit him a blow with the stick so that the blood out of him leapt up and hit the gallery.

That is my story.

In stories of this kind he always speaks in the first person, with minute details to show that he was actually present at the scenes that are described.

At the beginning of this story he gave me a long account of what had made him be on his way to Dublin on that occasion, and told me about all the rich people he was going to see in the finest streets of the city.

A week of sweeping fogs has passed over and given me a strange sense of exile and desolation. I walk round the island nearly every day, yet I can see nothing anywhere but a mass of wet rock, a strip of surf, and then a tumult of waves.

The slaty limestone has grown black with the water that is dripping on it, and wherever I turn there is the same grey obsession twining and wreathing itself among the narrow fields, and the same wail from the wind that shrieks and whistles in the loose rubble of the walls.

At first the people do not give much attention to the wilderness that is round them, but after a few days their voices sink in the kitchen, and their endless talk of pigs and cattle falls to the whisper of men who are telling stories in a haunted house.

The rain continues; but this evening a number of young men were in the kitchen mending nets, and the bottle of poteen was drawn from its hiding-place.

One cannot think of these people drinking wine on the summit of this crumbling precipice, but their grey poteen, which brings a shock of joy to the blood, seems predestined to keep sanity in men who live forgotten in these worlds of mist.

I sat in the kitchen part of the evening to feel the gaiety that was rising, and when I came into my own room after dark, one of the sons came in every time the bottle made its round, to pour me out my share.

It has cleared, and the sun is shining with a luminous warmth that makes the whole island glisten with the splendour of a gem, and fills the sea and sky with a radiance of blue light.

I have come out to lie on the rocks where I have the black edge of the north island in front of me, Galway Bay, too blue almost to look at, on my right, the Atlantic on my left, a perpendicular cliff under my ankles, and over me innumerable gulls that chase each other in a white cirrus of wings.

A nest of hooded crows is somewhere near me, and one of the old birds is trying to drive me away by letting itself fall like a stone every few moments, from about forty yards above me to within reach of my hand.

Gannets are passing up and down above the sound, swooping at times after a mackerel, and further off I can see the whole fleet of hookers coming out from Kilronan for a night's fishing in the deep water to the west.

As I lie here hour after hour, I seem to enter into the wild pastimes of the cliff, and to become a companion of the cormorants and crows.

Many of the birds display themselves before me with the vanity of barbarians, performing in strange evolutions as long as I am in sight, and returning to their ledge of rock when I am gone. Some are wonderfully expert, and cut graceful figures for an inconceivable time without a flap of their wings, growing so absorbed in their own dexterity that they often collide with one another in their flight, an incident always followed by a wild outburst of abuse. Their language is easier than Gaelic, and I seem to understand the greater part of their cries, though I am not able to answer. There is one plaintive note which they take up in the middle of their usual babble with extraordinary effect, and pass on from one to another along the cliff with a sort of an inarticulate wail, as if they remembered for an instant the horror of the mist.

On the low sheets of rock to the east I can see a number of red and grey figures hurrying about their work. The continual passing in this island between the misery of last night and the splendour of to-day, seems to create an affinity between the moods of these people and the moods of varying rapture and dismay that are frequent in artists, and in certain forms of alienation. Yet it is only in the intonation of a few sentences or some old fragment of melody that I catch the real spirit of the island, for in general the men sit together and talk with endless iteration of the tides and fish, and of the price of kelp in Connemara.

After Mass this morning an old woman was buried. She lived in the cottage next mine, and more than once before noon I heard a faint echo of the keen. I did not go to the wake for fear my presence might jar upon the mourners, but all last evening I could hear the strokes of a hammer in the yard, where, in the middle of a little crowd of idlers, the next of kin laboured slowly at the coffin. To-day, before the hour for the funeral, poteen was served to a number of men who stood about upon the road, and a portion was brought to me in my room. Then the coffin was carried out sewn loosely in sailcloth, and held near the ground by three cross-poles lashed upon the top. As we moved down to the low eastern portion of the island, nearly all the men, and all the oldest women, wearing petticoats over their heads, came out and joined in the procession.

While the grave was being opened the women sat down among the flat tombstones, bordered with a pale fringe of early bracken, and began the wild keen, or crying for the dead. Each old woman, as she took her turn in the leading recitative, seemed possessed for the moment with a profound ecstasy of grief, swaying to and fro, and bending her forehead to the stone before her, while she called out to the dead with a perpetually recurring chant of sobs.

All round the graveyard other wrinkled women, looking out from under the deep red petticoats that cloaked them, rocked themselves with the same rhythm, and intoned the inarticulate chant that is sustained by all as an accompaniment.

The morning had been beautifully fine, but as they lowered the coffin into the grave, thunder rumbled overhead and hailstones hissed among the bracken.

In Inishmaan one is forced to believe in a sympathy between man and nature, and at this moment when the thunder sounded a death-peal of extraordinary grandeur above the voices of the women, I could see the faces near me stiff and drawn with emotion.

When the coffin was in the grave, and the thunder had rolled away across the hills of Clare, the keen broke out again more passionately than before.

This grief of the keen is no personal complaint for the death of one woman over eighty years, but seems to contain the whole passionate rage that lurks somewhere in every native of the island. In this cry of pain the inner consciousness of the people seems to lay itself bare for an instant, and to reveal the mood of beings who feel their isolation in the face of a universe that wars on them with winds and seas. They are usually silent, but in the presence of death all outward show of indifference or patience is forgotten, and they shriek with pitiable despair before the horror of the fate to which they all are doomed.

Before they covered the coffin an old man kneeled down by the grave and repeated a simple prayer for the dead.

There was an irony in these words of atonement and Catholic belief spoken by voices that were still hoarse with the cries of pagan desperation.

A little beyond the grave I saw a line of old women who had recited in the keen sitting in the shadow of a wall beside the roofless shell of the church. They were still sobbing and shaken with grief, yet they were beginning to talk again of the daily trifles that veil from them the terror of the world.

When we had all come out of the graveyard, and two men had rebuilt the hole in the wall through which the coffin had been carried in, we walked back to the village, talking of anything, and joking of anything, as if merely coming from the boat-slip, or the pier.

One man told me of the poteen drinking that takes place at some funerals.

'A while since,' he said, 'there were two men fell down in the graveyard while the drink was on them. The sea was rough that day, the way no one could go to bring the doctor, and one of the men never woke again, and found death that night.'

The other day the men of this house made a new field. There was a slight bank of earth under the wall of the yard, and another in the corner of the cabbage garden. The old man and his eldest son dug out the clay, with the care of men working in a gold-mine, and Michael packed it in panniers—there are no wheeled vehicles on this island—for transport to a flat rock in a sheltered corner of their holding, where it was mixed with sand and seaweed and spread out in a layer upon the stone.

Most of the potato-growing of the island is carried on in fields of this sort—for which the people pay a considerable rent—and if the season is at all dry, their hope of a fair crop is nearly always disappointed.

It is now nine days since rain has fallen, and the people are filled with anxiety, although the sun has not yet been hot enough to do harm.

The drought is also causing a scarcity of water. There are a few springs on this side of the island, but they come only from a little distance, and in hot weather are not to be relied on. The supply for this house is carried up in a water-barrel by one of the women. If it is drawn off at once it is not very nauseous, but if it has lain, as it often does, for some hours in the barrel, the smell, colour, and taste are unendurable. The water for washing is also coming short, and as I walk round the edges of the sea, I often come on a girl with her petticoats tucked up round her, standing in a pool left by the tide and washing her flannels among the sea-anemones and crabs. Their red bodices and white tapering legs make them as beautiful as tropical sea-birds, as they stand in a frame of seaweeds against the brink of the Atlantic. Michael, however, is a little uneasy when they are in sight, and I cannot pause to watch them. This habit of using the sea water for washing causes a good deal of rheumatism on the island, for the salt lies in the clothes and keeps them continually moist.

The people have taken advantage of this dry moment to begin the burning of the kelp, and all the islands are lying in a volume of grey smoke. There will not be a very large quantity this year, as the people are discouraged by the uncertainty of the market, and do not care to undertake the task of manufacture without a certainty of profit.

The work needed to form a ton of kelp is considerable. The seaweed is collected from the rocks after the storms of autumn and winter, dried on fine days, and then made up into a rick, where it is left till the beginning of June.

It is then burnt in low kilns on the shore, an affair that takes from twelve to twenty-four hours of continuous hard work, though I understand the people here do not manage well and spoil a portion of what they produce by burning it more than is required.

The kiln holds about two tons of molten kelp, and when full it is loosely covered with stones, and left to cool. In a few days the substance is as hard as the limestone, and has to be broken with crowbars before it can be placed in curaghs for transport to Kilronan, where it is tested to determine the amount of iodine it contains, and is paid for accordingly. In former years good kelp would bring seven pounds a ton, now four pounds are not always reached.

In Aran even manufacture is of interest. The low flame-edged kiln, sending out dense clouds of creamy smoke, with a band of red and grey clothed workers moving in the haze, and usually some petticoated boys and women who come down with drink, forms a scene with as much variety and colour as any picture from the East.

The men feel in a certain sense the distinction of their island, and show me their work with pride. One of them said to me yesterday, 'I'm thinking you never saw the like of this work before this day?'

'That is true,' I answered, 'I never did.'

'Bedad, then,' he said, 'isn't it a great wonder that you've seen France and Germany, and the Holy Father, and never seen a man making kelp till you come to Inishmaan.'

All the horses from this island are put out on grass among the hills of Connemara from June to the end of

September, as there is no grazing here during the summer.

Their shipping and transport is even more difficult than that of the horned cattle. Most of them are wild Connemara ponies, and their great strength and timidity make them hard to handle on the narrow pier, while in the hooker itself it is not easy to get them safely on their feet in the small space that is available. They are dealt with in the same way as the bullocks I have spoken of already, but the excitement becomes much more intense, and the storm of Gaelic that rises the moment a horse is shoved from the pier, till it is safely in its place, is indescribable. Twenty boys and men howl and scream with agitation, cursing and exhorting, without knowing, most of the time, what they are saying.

Apart, however, from this primitive babble, the dexterity and power of the men are displayed to more advantage than in anything I have seen hitherto. I noticed particularly the owner of a hooker from the north island that was loaded this morning. He seemed able to hold up a horse by his single weight when it was swinging from the masthead, and preserved a humorous calm even in moments of the wildest excitement. Sometimes a large mare would come down sideways on the backs of the other horses, and kick there till the hold seemed to be filled with a mass of struggling centaurs, for the men themselves often leap down to try and save the foals from injury. The backs of the horses put in first are often a good deal cut by the shoes of the others that arrive on top of them, but otherwise they do not seem to be much the worse, and as they are not on their way to a fair, it is not of much consequence in what condition they come to land.

There is only one bit and saddle in the island, which

are used by the priest, who rides from the chapel to the pier when he has held the service on Sunday.

The islanders themselves ride with a simple halter and a stick, yet sometimes travel, at least in the larger island, at a desperate gallop. As the horses usually have panniers, the rider sits sideways over the withers, and if the panniers are empty they go at full speed in this position without anything to hold to.

More than once in Aranmor I met a party going out west with empty panniers from Kilronan. Long before they came in sight I could hear a clatter of hoofs, and then a whirl of horses would come round a corner at full gallop with their heads out, utterly indifferent to the slender halter that is their only check. They generally travel in single file with a few yards between them, and as there is no traffic there is little fear of an accident.

Sometimes a woman and a man ride together, but in this case the man sits in the usual position, and the woman sits sideways behind him, and holds him round the waist.

Old Pat Dirane continues to come up every day to talk to me, and at times I turn the conversation to his experiences of the fairies.

He has seen a good many of them, he says, in different parts of the island, especially in the sandy districts north of the slip. They are about a yard high with caps like the 'peelers' pulled down over their faces. On one occasion he saw them playing ball in the evening just above the slip, and he says I must avoid that place in the morning or after nightfall for fear they might do me mischief.

He has seen two women who were 'away' with them, one a young married woman, the other a girl. The woman was standing by a wall, at a spot he described to me with great care, looking out towards the north.

Another night he heard a voice crying out in Irish, 'mháthair tá mé marbh' ('O mother, I'm killed'), and in the morning there was blood on the wall of his house, and a child in a house not far off was dead.

Yesterday he took me aside, and said he would tell me a secret he had never yet told to any person in the world.

'Take a sharp needle,' he said, 'and stick it in under the collar of your coat, and not one of them will be able to have power on you.'

Iron is a common talisman with barbarians, but in this case the idea of exquisite sharpness was probably present also, and, perhaps, some feeling for the sanctity of the instrument of toil, a folk-belief that is common in Brittany.

The fairies are more numerous in Mayo than in any other county, though they are fond of certain districts in Galway, where the following story is said to have taken place.

'A farmer was in great distress as his crops had failed, and his cow had died on him. One night he told his wife to make him a fine new sack for flour before the next morning; and when it was finished he started off with it before the dawn.

'At that time there was a gentleman who had been taken by the fairies, and made an officer among them, and it was often people would see him and her riding on a white horse at dawn and in the evening.

'The poor man went down to the place where they used to see the officer, and when he came by on his horse, he asked the loan of two hundred and a half of flour, for he was in great want.

'The officer called the fairies out of a hole in the rocks where they stored their wheat, and told them to give the poor man what he was asking. Then he told him to come back and pay him in a year, and rode away.

'When the poor man got home he wrote down the day on a piece of paper, and that day year he came back and paid the officer.'

When he had ended his story the old man told me that the fairies have a tenth of all the produce of the country, and make stores of it in the rocks.

It is a Holy Day, and I have come up to sit on the Dun while the people are at Mass.

A strange tranquillity has come over the island this morning, as happens sometimes on Sunday, filling the two circles of sea and sky with the quiet of a church.

The one landscape that is here lends itself with singular power to this suggestion of grey luminous cloud. There is no wind, and no definite light. Aranmor seems to sleep upon a mirror, and the hills of Connemara look so near that I am troubled by the width of the bay that lies before them, touched this morning with individual expression one sees sometimes in a lake.

On these rocks, where there is no growth of vegetable or animal life, all the seasons are the same, and this June day is so full of autumn that I listen unconsciously for the rustle of dead leaves.

The first group of men are coming out of the chapel, followed by a crowd of women, who divide at the gate and troop off in different directions, while the men linger on the road to gossip.

The silence is broken; I can hear far off, as if over water, a faint murmur of Gaelic.

In the afternoon the sun came out and I was rowed over for a visit to Kilronan.

As my men were bringing round the curagh to take me off a headland near the pier, they struck a sunken rock, and came ashore shipping a quantity of water. They plugged the hole with a piece of sacking torn from a bag of potatoes they were taking over for the priest, and we set off with nothing but a piece of torn canvas between us and the Atlantic.

Every few hundred yards one of the rowers had to stop and bail, but the hole did not increase.

When we were about half way across the sound we met a curagh coming towards us with its sails set. After some shouting in Gaelic, I learned that they had a packet of letters and tobacco for myself. We sidled up as near as was possible with the roll, and my goods were thrown to me wet with spray.

After my weeks in Inishmaan, Kilronan seemed an imposing centre of activity. The half-civilised fishermen of the larger island are inclined to despise the simplicity of the life here, and some of them who were standing about when I landed asked me how at all I passed my time with no decent fishing to be looking at.

I turned in for a moment to talk to the old couple in the hotel, and then moved on to pay some other visits in the village.

Later in the evening I walked out along the northern road, where I met many of the natives of the outlying villages, who had come down to Kilronan for the Holy Day, and were now wandering home in scattered groups.

The women and girls, when they had no men with them, usually tried to make fun with me.

'Is it tired you are, stranger?' said one girl. I was

walking very slowly, to pass the time before my return to the east.

'Bedad, it is not, little girl,' I answered in Gaelic, 'it is lonely I am.'

'Here is my little sister, stranger, who will give you her arm.'

And so it went. Quiet as these woman are on ordinary occasions, when two or three of them are gathered together in their holiday petticoats and shawls, they are as wild and capricious as the women who live in towns.

About seven o'clock I got back to Kilronan, and beat up my crew from the public-houses near the bay. With their usual carelessness they had not seen to the leak in the curagh, nor to an oar that was losing the brace that holds it to the toll-pin, and we moved off across the sound at an absurd pace with a deepening pool at our feet.

A superb evening light was lying over the island, which made me rejoice at our delay. Looking back there was a golden haze behind the sharp edges of the rock, and a long wake from the sun, which was making jewels of the bubbling left by the oars.

The men had had their share of porter and were unusually voluble, pointing out things to me that I had already seen, and stopping now and then to make me notice the oily smell of mackerel that was rising from the waves.

They told me that an evicting party is coming to the island to-morrow morning, and gave me a long account of what they make and spend in a year, and of their trouble with the rent.

'The rent is hard enough for a poor man,' said one of them, 'but this time we didn't pay, and they're after serving processes on every one of us. A man will have to pay his rent now, and a power of money with it for the process, and I'm thinking the agent will have money enough out of them processes to pay for his servant-girl and his man all the year.'

I asked afterwards who the island belonged to.

'Bedad,' they said, 'we've always heard it belonged to Miss ———, and she is dead.'

When the sun passed like a lozenge of gold flame into the sea the cold became intense. Then the men began to talk among themselves, and losing the thread, I lay half in a dream looking at the pale oily sea about us, and the low cliffs of the island sloping up past the village with its wreath of smoke to the outline of Dun Conor.

Old Pat was in the house when I arrived, and he told a long story after supper:—

There was once a widow living among the woods, and her only son living along with her. He went out every morning through the trees to get sticks, and one day as he was lying on the ground he saw a swarm of flies flying over what the cow leaves behind her. He took up his sickle and hit one blow at them, and hit that hard he left no single one of them living.

That evening he said to his mother that it was time he was going out into the world to seek his fortune, for he was able to destroy a whole swarm of flies at one blow, and he asked her to make him three cakes the way he might take them with him in the morning.

He started the next day a while after the dawn, with his three cakes in his wallet, and he ate one of them near ten o'clock.

He got hungry again by midday and ate the second, and when night was coming on him he ate the third.

After that he met a man on the road who asked him where he was going.

'I'm looking for some place where I can work for my living,' said the young man.

'Come with me,' said the other man, 'and sleep to-night in the barn, and I'll give you work to-morrow to see what you're able for.'

The next morning the farmer brought him out and showed him his cows and told him to take them out to graze on the hills, and to keep good watch that no one should come near them to milk them. The young man drove out the cows into the fields, and when the heat of the day came on he lay down on his back and looked up into the sky. A while after he saw a black spot in the north-west, and it grew larger and nearer till he saw a great giant coming towards him.

He got up on to his feet and he caught the giant round the legs with his two arms, and he drove him down into the hard ground above his ankles, the way he was not able to free himself. Then the giant told him to do him no hurt, and gave him his magic rod, and told him to strike on the rock, and he would find his beautiful black horse, and his sword and his fine suit.

The young man struck the rock and it opened before him, and he found the beautiful black horse, and the giant's sword and the suit lying before him. He took out the sword alone, and he struck one blow with it and struck off the giant's head. Then he put back the sword into the rock, and went out again to his cattle, till it was time to drive them home to the farmer.

When they came to milk the cows they found a power of milk in them, and the farmer asked the young man if he had seen nothing out on the hills, for the other cow-boys had been bringing home the cows with no drop of milk in them. And the young man said he had seen nothing.

The next day he went out again with the cows. He lay down on his back in the heat of the day, and after a while he saw a black spot in the north-west, and it grew larger and nearer, till he saw it was a great giant coming to attack him.

'You killed my brother,' said the giant; 'come here, till I make a garter of your body.'

The young man went to him and caught him by the legs and drove him down into the hard ground up to his ankles.

Then he hit the rod against the rock, and took out the sword and struck off the giant's head.

That evening the farmer found twice as much milk in the cows as the evening before, and he asked the young man if he had seen anything. The young man said that he had seen nothing.

The third day the third giant came to him and said, 'You have killed my two brothers; come here, till I make a garter of your body.'

And he did with this giant as he had done with the other two, and that evening there was so much milk in the cows it was dropping out of their udders on the pathway.

The next day the farmer called him and told him he might leave the cows in the stalls that day, for there was a great curiosity to be seen, namely, a beautiful king's daughter that was to be eaten by a great fish, if there was no one in it that could save her. But the young man said such a sight was all one to him, and he went out with the cows on to the hills. When he came to the rock he hit it with his rod and brought out the suit and put it on him, and brought out the sword and

strapped it on his side, like an officer, and he got on the
black horse and rode faster than the wind till he came to
where the beautiful king's daughter was sitting on the
shore in a golden chair, waiting for the great fish.

When the great fish came in on the sea, bigger than
a whale, with two wings on the back of it, the young
man went down into the surf and struck at it with his
sword and cut off one of its wings. All the sea turned
red with the bleeding out of it, till it swam away and
left the young man on the shore.

Then he turned his horse and rode faster than the
wind till he came to the rock, and he took the suit off
him and put it back in the rock, with the giant's sword
and the black horse, and drove the cows down to the
farm.

The man came out before him and said he had missed
the greatest wonder ever was, and that a noble person
was after coming down with a fine suit on him and cutting off one of the wings from the great fish.

'And there'll be the same necessity on her for two
mornings more,' said the farmer, 'and you'd do right to
come and look on it.'

But the young man said he would not come.

The next morning he went out with his cows, and he
took the sword and the suit and the black horse out of
the rock, and he rode faster than the wind till he came
where the king's daughter was sitting on the shore.
When the people saw him coming there was great wonder on them to know if it was the same man they had
seen the day before. The king's daughter called out to
him to come and kneel before her, and when he kneeled
down she took her scissors and cut off a lock of hair
from the back of his head and hid it in her clothes.

Then the great fish came in from the sea, and he

went down into the surf and cut the other wing off
from it. All the sea turned red with the bleeding out of
it, till it swam away and left them.

That evening the farmer came out before him and
told him of the great wonder he had missed, and asked
him would he go the next day and look on it. The young
man said he would not go.

The third day he came again on the black horse to
where the king's daughter was sitting on a golden chair
waiting for the great fish. When it came in from the
sea the young man went down before it, and every time
it opened its mouth to eat him, he struck into its mouth,
till his sword went out through its neck, and it rolled
back and died.

Then he rode off faster than the wind, and he put
the suit and the sword and the black horse into the rock,
and drove home the cows.

The farmer was there before him and he told him
that there was to be a great marriage feast held for three
days, and on the third day the king's daughter would be
married to the man that killed the great fish, if they
were able to find him.

A great feast was held, and men of great strength
came and said it was themselves were after killing the
great fish.

But on the third day the young man put on the suit,
and strapped the sword to his side like an officer, and
got on the black horse and rode faster than the wind,
till he came to the palace.

The king's daughter saw him, and she brought him
in and made him kneel down before her. Then she
looked at the back of his head and she saw the place
where she had cut off the lock with her own hand. She

led him in to the king, and they were married, and the young man was given all the estate.

That is my story.

Two recent attempts to carry out evictions on the island came to nothing, for each time a sudden storm rose, by, it is said, the power of a native witch, when the steamer was approaching, and made it impossible to land.

This morning, however, broke beneath a clear sky of June, and when I came into the open air the sea and rocks were shining with wonderful brilliancy. Groups of men, dressed in their holiday clothes, were standing about, talking with anger and fear, yet showing a lurking satisfaction at the thought of the dramatic pageant that was to break the silence of the seas.

About half-past nine the steamer came in sight, on the narrow line of sea-horizon that is seen in the centre of the bay, and immediately a last effort was made to hide the cows and sheep of the families that were most in debt.

Till this year no one on the island would consent to act as bailiff, so that it was impossible to identify the cattle of the defaulters. Now, however, a man of the name of Patrick has sold his honour, and the effort of concealment is practically futile.

This falling away from the ancient loyalty of the island has caused intense indignation, and early yesterday morning, while I was dreaming on the Dun, this letter was nailed on the doorpost of the chapel:—

'Patrick, the devil, a revolver is waiting for you. If you are missed with the first shot, there will be five more that will hit you.

'Any man that will talk with you, or work with you,

or drink a pint of porter in your shop, will be done with the same way as yourself.'

As the steamer drew near I moved down with the men to watch the arrival, though no one went further than about a mile from the shore.

Two curaghs from Kilronan with a man who was to give help in identifying the cottages, the doctor, and the relieving officer, were drifting with the tide, unwilling to come to land without the support of the larger party. When the anchor had been thrown it gave me a strange throb of pain to see the boats being lowered, and the sunshine gleaming on the rifles and helmets of the constabulary who crowded into them.

Once on shore the men were formed in close marching order, a word was given, and the heavy rhythm of their boots came up over the rocks. We were collected in two straggling bands on either side of the roadway, and a few moments later the body of magnificent armed men passed close to us, followed by a low rabble, who had been brought to act as drivers for the sheriff.

After my weeks spent among primitive men this glimpse of the newer types of humanity was not reassuring. Yet these mechanical police, with the commonplace agents and sheriffs, and the rabble they had hired, represented aptly enough the civilisation for which the homes of the island were to be desecrated.

A stop was made at one of the first cottages in the village, and the day's work began. Here, however, and at the next cottage, a compromise was made, as some relatives came up at the last moment and lent the money that was needed to gain a respite.

In another case a girl was ill in the house, so the doctor interposed, and the people were allowed to remain after a merely formal eviction. About midday,

however, a house was reached where there was no pretext for mercy, and no money could be procured. At a
sign from the sheriff the work of carrying out the beds
and utensils was begun in the middle of a crowd of
natives who looked on in absolute silence, broken only
by the wild imprecations of the woman of the house.
She belonged to one of the most primitive families on
the island, and she shook with uncontrollable fury as
she saw the strange armed men who spoke a language
she could not understand driving her from the hearth she
had brooded on for thirty years. For these people the outrage to the hearth is the supreme catastrophe. They live
here in a world of grey, where there are wild rains and
mists every week in the year, and their warm chimney
corners, filled with children and young girls, grow
into the consciousness of each family in a way it is not
easy to understand in more civilised places.

The outrage to a tomb in China probably gives no
greater shock to the Chinese than the outrage to a hearth
in Inishmaan gives to the people.

When the few trifles had been carried out, and the
door blocked with stones, the old woman sat down by
the threshold and covered her head with her shawl.

Five or six other women who lived close by sat down
in a circle round her, with mute sympathy. Then the
crowd moved on with the police to another cottage
where the same scene was to take place, and left the
group of desolate women sitting by the hovel.

There were still no clouds in the sky, and the heat
was intense. The police when not in motion lay sweating and gasping under the walls with their tunics un-
buttoned. They were not attractive, and I kept comparing them with the islandmen, who walked up and
down as cool and fresh-looking as the sea-gulls.

When the last eviction had been carried out a division was made: half the party went off with the bailiff to search the inner plain of the island for the cattle that had been hidden in the morning, the other half remained on the village road to guard some pigs that had already been taken possession of.

After a while two of these pigs escaped from the drivers and began a wild race up and down the narrow road. The people shrieked and howled to increase their terror, and at last some of them became so excited that the police thought it time to interfere. They drew up in double line opposite the mouth of a blind laneway where the animals had been shut up. A moment later the shrieking began again in the west and the two pigs came in sight, rushing down the middle of the road with the drivers behind them.

They reached the line of the police. There was a slight scuffle, and then the pigs continued their mad rush to the east, leaving three policemen lying in the dust.

The satisfaction of the people was immense. They shrieked and hugged each other with delight, and it is likely that they will hand down these animals for generations in the tradition of the island.

Two hours later the other party returned, driving three lean cows before them, and a start was made for the slip. At the public-house the policemen were given a drink while the dense crowd that was following waited in the lane. The island bull happened to be in a field close by, and he became wildly excited at the sight of the cows and of the strangely-dressed men. Two young islanders sidled up to me in a moment or two as I was resting on a wall, and one of them whispered in my ear—

'Do you think they could take fines of us if we let out the bull on them?'

In face of the crowd of women and children, I could only say it was probable, and they slunk off.

At the slip there was a good deal of bargaining, which ended in all the cattle being given back to their owners. It was plainly of no use to take them away, as they were worth nothing.

When the last policeman had embarked, an old woman came forward from the crowd and, mounting on a rock near the slip, began a fierce rhapsody in Gaelic, pointing at the bailiff and waving her withered arms with extraordinary rage.

'This man is my own son,' she said; 'it is I that ought to know him. He is the first ruffian in the whole big world.'

Then she gave an account of his life, coloured with a vindictive fury I cannot reproduce. As she went on the excitement became so intense I thought the man would be stoned before he could get back to his cottage.

On these islands the women live only for their children, and it is hard to estimate the power of the impulse that made this old woman stand out and curse her son.

In the fury of her speech I seem to look again into the strangely reticent temperament of the islanders, and to feel the passionate spirit that expresses itself, at odd moments only, with magnificent words and gestures.

Old Pat has told me a story of the goose that lays the golden eggs, which he calls the Phœnix:—

A poor widow had three sons and a daughter. One day when her sons were out looking for sticks in the wood they saw a fine speckled bird flying in the trees. The next day they saw it again, and the eldest son told his brothers to go and get sticks by themselves, for he was going after the bird.

He went after it, and brought it in with him when he came home in the evening. They put it in an old hen-coop, and they gave it some of the meal they had for themselves;—I don't know if it ate the meal, but they divided what they had themselves; they could do no more.

That night it laid a fine spotted egg in the basket. The next night it laid another.

At that time its name was in the papers and many heard of the bird that laid the golden eggs, for the eggs were of gold, and there's no lie in it.

When the boys went down to the shop the next day to buy a stone of meal, the shopman asked if he could buy the bird of them. Well, it was arranged in this way. The shopman would marry the boys' sister—a poor simple girl without a stitch of good clothes—and get the bird with her.

Some time after that one of the boys sold an egg of the bird to a gentleman that was in the country. The gentleman asked him if he had the bird still. He said that the man who had married his sister was after getting it.

'Well,' said the gentleman, 'the man who eats the heart of that bird will find a purse of gold beneath him every morning, and the man who eats its liver will be king of Ireland.'

The boy went out—he was a simple poor fellow—and told the shopman.

Then the shopman brought in the bird and killed it,

and he ate the heart himself and he gave the liver to his wife.

When the boy saw that, there was great anger on him, and he went back and told the gentleman.

'Do what I'm telling you,' said the gentleman. 'Go down now and tell the shopman and his wife to come up here to play a game of cards with me, for it's lonesome I am this evening.'

When the boy was gone he mixed a vomit and poured the lot of it into a few naggins of whiskey, and he put a strong cloth on the table under the cards.

The man came up with his wife and they began to play.

The shopman won the first game and the gentleman made them drink a sup of the whiskey.

They played again and the shopman won the second game. Then the gentleman made him drink a sup more of the whiskey.

As they were playing the third game the shopman and his wife got sick on the cloth, and the boy picked it up and carried it into the yard, for the gentleman had let him know what he was to do. Then he found the heart of the bird and he ate it, and the next morning when he turned in his bed there was a purse of gold under him.

That is my story.

When the steamer is expected I rarely fail to visit the boat-slip, as the men usually collect when she is in the offing, and lie arguing among their curaghs till she has made her visit to the south island, and is seen coming towards us.

This morning I had a long talk with an old man who

was rejoicing over the improvement he had seen here during the last ten or fifteen years.

Till recently there was no communication with the mainland except by hookers, which were usually slow, and could only make the voyage in tolerably fine weather, so that if an islander went to a fair it was often three weeks before he could return. Now, however, the steamer comes here twice in the week, and the voyage is made in three or four hours.

The pier on this island is also a novelty, and is much thought of, as it enables the hookers that still carry turf and cattle to discharge and take their cargoes directly from the shore. The water round it, however, is only deep enough for a hooker when the tide is nearly full, and will never float the steamer, so passengers must still come to land in curaghs. The boat-slip at the corner next the south island is extremely useful in calm weather, but it is exposed to a heavy roll from the south, and is so narrow that the curaghs run some danger of missing it in the tumult of the surf.

In bad weather four men will often stand for nearly an hour at the top of the slip with a curagh in their hands, watching a point of rock towards the south where they can see the strength of the waves that are coming in.

The instant a break is seen they swoop down to the surf, launch their curagh, and pull out to sea with incredible speed. Coming to land is attended with the same difficulty, and, if their moment is badly chosen, they are likely to be washed sideways and swamped among the rocks.

This continual danger, which can only be escaped by extraordinary personal dexterity, has had considerable influence on the local character, as the waves have made it impossible for clumsy, foolhardy, or timid men to live on these islands.

When the steamer is within a mile of the slip, the curaghs are put out and range themselves—there are usually from four to a dozen—in two lines at some distance from the shore.

The moment she comes in among them there is a short but desperate struggle for good places at her side. The men are lolling on their oars talking with the dreamy tone which comes with the rocking of the waves. The steamer lies to, and in an instant their faces become distorted with passion, while the oars bend and quiver with the strain. For one minute they seem utterly indifferent to their own safety and that of their friends and brothers. Then the sequence is decided, and they begin to talk again with the dreamy tone that is habitual to them, while they make fast and clamber up into the steamer.

While the curaghs are out I am left with a few women and very old men who cannot row. One of these old men, whom I often talk with, has some fame as a bone-setter, and is said to have done remarkable cures, both here and on the mainland. Stories are told of how he has been taken off by the quality in their carriages through the hills of Connemara, to treat their sons and daughters, and come home with his pockets full of money.

Another old man, the oldest on the island, is fond of telling me anecdotes—not folk-tales—of things that have happened here in his lifetime.

He often tells me about a Connaught man who killed his father with the blow of a spade when he was in passion, and then fled to this island and threw himself on the mercy of some of the natives with whom he was said to be related. They hid him in a hole—which the old man has shown me—and kept him safe for weeks, though the police came and searched for him, and he could hear their boots grinding on the stones over his head. In spite of a reward which was offered, the island was incorruptible, and after much trouble the man was safely shipped to America.

This impulse to protect the criminal is universal in the west. It seems partly due to the association between justice and the hated English jurisdiction, but more directly to the primitive feeling of these people, who are never criminals yet always capable of crime, that a man will not do wrong unless he is under the influence of a passion which is as irresponsible as a storm on the sea. If a man has killed his father, and is already sick and broken with remorse, they can see no reason why he should be dragged away and killed by the law.

Such a man, they say, will be quiet all the rest of his life, and if you suggest that punishment is needed as an example, they ask, 'Would any one kill his father if he was able to help it?'

Some time ago, before the introduction of police, all the people of the islands were as innocent as the people here remain to this day. I have heard that at that time the ruling proprietor and magistrate of the north island used to give any man who had done wrong a letter to a jailer in Galway, and send him off by himself to serve a term of imprisonment.

As there was no steamer, the ill-doer was given a passage in some chance hooker to the nearest point on the mainland. Then he walked for many miles along a desolate shore till he reached the town. When his time had been put through he crawled back along the same route, feeble and emaciated, and had often to wait many weeks before he could regain the island. Such at least is the story.

It seems absurd to apply the same laws to these people and to the criminal classes of a city. The most intelligent man on Inishmaan has often spoken to me of his contempt of the law, and of the increase of crime the police have brought to Aranmor. On this island, he says, if men have a little difference, or a little fight, their friends take care it does not go too far, and in a little time it is forgotten. In Kilronan there is a band of men paid to make out cases for themselves; the moment a blow is struck they come down and arrest the man who gave it. The other man he quarrelled with has to give evidence against him; whole families come down to the court and swear against each other till they become bitter enemies. If there is a conviction the man who is convicted never forgives. He waits his time, and before the year is out there is a cross summons, which the other man in turn never forgives. The feud continues to grow, till a dispute about the colour of a man's hair may end in a murder, after a year's forcing by the law. The mere fact that it is impossible to get reliable evidence in the island—not because the people are dishonest, but because they think the claim of kinship more sacred than the claims of abstract truth—turns the whole system of sworn evidence into a demoralising farce, and it is easy to believe that law dealings on this false basis must lead to every sort of injustice.

While I am discussing these questions with the old men the curaghs begin to come in with cargoes of salt, and flour, and porter.

To-day a stir was made by the return of a native who had spent five years in New York. He came on shore with half a dozen people who had been shopping on the mainland, and walked up and down on the slip in his neat suit, looking strangely foreign to his birthplace, while his old mother of eighty-five ran about on the slippery seaweed, half crazy with delight, telling every one the news.

When the curaghs were in their places the men crowded round him to bid him welcome. He shook hands with them readily enough, but with no smile of recognition.

He is said to be dying.

Yesterday—a Sunday—three young men rowed me over to Inisheer, the south island of the group.

The stern of the curagh was occupied, so I was put in the bow with my head on a level with the gunnel. A considerable sea was running in the sound, and when we came out from the shelter of this island, the curagh rolled and vaulted in a way not easy to describe.

At one moment, as we went down into the furrow, green waves curled and arched themselves above me; then in an instant I was flung up into the air and could look down on the heads of the rowers, as if we were sitting on a ladder, or out across a forest of white crests to the black cliff of Inishmaan.

The men seemed excited and uneasy, and I thought for a moment that we were likely to be swamped. In a little while, however, I realised the capacity of the curagh to raise its head among the waves, and the motion became strangely exhilarating. Even, I thought, if we were dropped into the blue chasm of the waves, this death, with the fresh sea saltness in one's teeth, would be better than most deaths one is likely to meet.

When we reached the other island, it was raining heavily, so that we could not see anything of the antiquities or people.

For the greater part of the afternoon we sat on the tops of empty barrels in the public-house, talking of the destiny of Gaelic. We were admitted as travellers, and the shutters of the shop were closed behind us, letting in only a glimmer of grey light, and the tumult of the storm. Towards evening it cleared a little and we came home in a calmer sea, but with a dead head-wind that gave the rowers all they could do to make the passage.

On calm days I often go out fishing with Michael. When we reach the space above the slip where the curaghs are propped, bottom upwards, on the limestone, he lifts the prow of the one we are going to embark in, and I slip underneath and set the centre of the foremost seat upon my neck. Then he crawls under the stern and stands up with the last seat upon his shoulders. We start for the sea. The long prow bends before me so that I see nothing but a few yards of shingle at my feet. A quivering pain runs from the top of my spine to the sharp stones that seem to pass through my pampooties, and grate upon my ankles. We stagger and groan beneath the weight; but at last our feet reach the slip, and we run down with a half-trot like the pace of barefooted children.

A yard from the sea we stop and lower the curagh to the right. It must be brought down gently—a difficult task for our strained and aching muscles—and sometimes as the gunnel reaches the slip I lose my balance and roll in among the seats.

Yesterday we went out in the curagh that had been damaged on the day of my visit to Kilronan, and as we were putting in the oars the freshly-tarred patch stuck to the slip which was heated with the sunshine. We carried up water in the bailer—the 'supeen,' a shallow wooden vessel like a soup-plate—and with infinite pains we got free and rode away. In a few minutes, however, I found the water spouting up at my feet.

The patch had been misplaced, and this time we had no sacking. Michael borrowed my pocket scissors, and with admirable rapidity cut a square of flannel from the tail of his shirt and squeezed it into the hole, making it fast with a splint which he hacked from one of the oars.

During our excitement the tide had carried us to the brink of the rocks, and I admired again the dexterity with which he got his oars into the water and turned us out as we were mounting on a wave that would have hurled us to destruction.

With the injury to our curagh we did not go far from the shore. After a while I took a long spell at the oars, and gained a certain dexterity, though they are not easy to manage. The handles overlap by about six inches —in order to gain leverage, as the curagh is narrow— and at first it was almost impossible to avoid striking the upper oar against one's knuckles. The oars are rough and square, except at the ends, so one cannot do so with impunity. Again, a curagh with two light people in it floats on the water like a nut-shell, and the slightest inequality in the stroke throws the prow round at least a right angle from its course. In the first half-hour I found myself more than once moving towards the point I had come from, greatly to Michael's satisfaction.

This morning we were out again near the pier on the north side of the island. As we paddled slowly with the tide, trolling for pollock, several curaghs, weighed to the gunnel with kelp, passed us on their way to Kilronan.

An old woman, rolled in red petticoats, was sitting on a ledge of rock that runs into the sea at the point where the curaghs were passing from the south, hailing them in quavering Gaelic, and asking for a passage to Kilronan.

The first one that came round without a cargo turned in from some distance and took her away.

The morning had none of the supernatural beauty that comes over the island so often in rainy weather, so we basked in the vague enjoyment of the sunshine, looking down at the wild luxuriance of the vegetation beneath the sea, which contrasts strangely with the nakedness above it.

Some dreams I have had in this cottage seem to give strength to the opinion that there is a psychic memory attached to certain neighbourhoods.

Last night, after walking in a dream among buildings with strangely intense light on them, I heard a faint rhythm of music beginning far away on some stringed instrument.

It came closer to me, gradually increasing in quickness and volume with an irresistibly definite progression. When it was quite near the sound began to move in my nerves and blood, and to urge me to dance with them.

I knew that if I yielded I would be carried away to some moment of terrible agony, so I struggled to remain quiet, holding my knees together with my hands.

The music increased continually, sounding like the strings of harps, tuned to a forgotten scale, and having a resonance as searching as the strings of the 'cello.

Then the luring excitement became more powerful than my will, and my limbs moved in spite of me.

In a moment I was swept away in a whirlwind of notes. My breath and my thoughts and every impulse of my body, became a form of the dance, till I could not distinguish between the instruments and the rhythm and my own person or consciousness.

For a while it seemed an excitement that was filled with joy, then it grew into an ecstasy where all existence was lost in a vortex of movement. I could not think there had ever been a life beyond the whirling of the dance.

Then with a shock the ecstasy turned to an agony and rage. I struggled to free myself, but seemed only to increase the passion of the steps I moved to. When I shrieked I could only echo the notes of the rhythm.

At last with a moment of uncontrollable frenzy I broke back to consciousness and awoke.

I dragged myself trembling to the window of the cottage and looked out. The moon was glittering across the bay, and there was no sound anywhere on the island.

I am leaving in two days, and old Pat Dirane has bidden me good-bye. He met me in the village this morning and took me into 'his little tint,' a miserable hovel where he spends the night.

I sat for a long time on his threshold, while he leaned on a stool behind me, near his bed, and told me the last story I shall have from him—a rude anecdote not worth recording. Then he told me with careful emphasis how he had wandered when he was a young man, and lived in a fine college, teaching Irish to the young priests!

They say on the island that he can tell as many lies as four men: perhaps the stories he has learned have strengthened his imagination.

When I stood up in the doorway to give him God's blessing, he leaned over on the straw that forms his bed, and shed tears. Then he turned to me again, lifting up one trembling hand, with the mitten worn to a hole on the palm, from the rubbing of his crutch.

'I'll not see you again,' he said, with tears trickling on his face, 'and you're a kindly man. When you come back next year I won't be in it. I won't live beyond the winter. But listen now to what I'm telling you; let you put insurance on me in the city of Dublin, and it's five hundred pounds you'll get on my burial.'

This evening, my last in the island, is also the evening of the 'Pattern'—a festival something like 'Pardons' of Brittany.

I waited especially to see it, but a piper who was expected did not come, and there was no amusement. A few friends and relations came over from the other island and stood about the public-house in their best clothes, but without music dancing was impossible.

I believe on some occasions when the piper is present there is a fine day of dancing and excitement, but the Galway piper is getting old, and is not easily induced to undertake the voyage.

Last night, St. John's Eve, the fires were lighted and boys ran about with pieces of the burning turf, though I could not find out if the idea of lighting the house fires from the bonfires is still found on the island.

I have come out of an hotel full of tourists and commercial travellers, to stroll along the edge of Galway bay, and look out in the direction of the islands. The sort of yearning I feel towards those lonely rocks is indescribably acute. This town, that is usually so full of wild human interest, seems in my present mood a tawdry medley of all that is crudest in modern life. The nullity of the rich and the squalor of the poor give me the same pang of wondering disgust; yet the islands are fading already and I can hardly realise that the smell of the seaweed and the drone of the Atlantic are still moving round them.

One of my island friends has written to me:—

DEAR JOHN SYNGE,—I am for a long time expecting a letter from you and I think you are forgetting this island altogether.

Mr. —— died a long time ago on the big island and his boat was on anchor in the harbour and the wind blew her to Black Head and broke her up after his death.

Tell me are you learning Irish since you went. We have a branch of the Gaelic League here now and the people is going on well with the Irish and reading.

I will write the next letter in Irish to you. Tell me will you come to see us next year and if you will you'll write a letter before you. All your loving friends is well in health.—*Mise do chara go buan.*

Another boy I sent some baits to has written to me also, beginning his letter in Irish and ending it in English:—

DEAR JOHN,—I got your letter four days ago, and there was pride and joy on me because it was written in Irish, and a fine, good, pleasant letter it was. The baits you sent are very good, but I lost two of them and half my line. A big fish came and caught the bait, and the line was bad and half of the line and the baits went away. My sister has come back from America, but I'm thinking it won't be long till she goes away again, for it is lonesome and poor she finds the island now.—I am your friend. . . .

Write soon and let you write in Irish, if you don't I won't look on it.

PART II

THE evening before I returned to the west I wrote to Michael—who had left the islands to earn his living on the mainland—to tell him that I would call at the house where he lodged the next morning, which was a Sunday.

A young girl with fine western features, and little English, came out when I knocked at the door. She seemed to have heard all about me, and was so filled with the importance of her message that she could hardly speak it intelligibly.

'She got your letter,' she said, confusing the pronouns, as is often done in the west, 'she is gone to Mass, and she'll be in the square after that. Let your honour go now and sit in the square and Michael will find you.'

As I was returning up the main street I met Michael wandering down to meet me, as he had got tired of waiting.

He seemed to have grown a powerful man since I had seen him, and was now dressed in the heavy brown flannels of the Connaught labourer. After a little talk we turned back together and went out on the sandhills above the town. Meeting him here a little beyond the threshold of my hotel I was singularly struck with the refinement of his nature, which has hardly been influenced by his new life, and the townsmen and sailors he has met with.

'I do often come outside the town on Sunday,' he said while we were talking, 'for what is there to do in a town in the middle of all the people when you are not at your work?'

A little later another Irish-speaking labourer—a

friend of Michael's—joined us, and we lay for hours talking and arguing on the grass. The day was unbearably sultry, and the sand and the sea near us were crowded with half-naked women, but neither of the young men seemed to be aware of their presence. Before we went back to the town a man came out to ring a young horse on the sand close to where we were lying, and then the interest of my companions was intense.

Late in the evening I met Michael again, and we wandered round the bay, which was still filled with bathing women, until it was quite dark. I shall not see him again before my return from the islands, as he is busy to-morrow, and on Tuesday I go out with the steamer.

I returned to the middle island this morning, in the steamer to Kilronan, and on here in a curagh that had gone over with salt fish. As I came up from the slip the doorways in the village filled with women and children, and several came down on the roadway to shake hands and bid me a thousand welcomes.

Old Pat Dirane is dead, and several of my friends have gone to America; that is all the news they have to give me after an absence of many months.

When I arrived at the cottage I was welcomed by the old people, and great excitement was made by some little presents I had bought them—a pair of folding scissors for the old woman, a strop for her husband, and some other trifles.

Then the youngest son, Columb, who is still at home, went into the inner room and brought out the alarm clock I sent them last year when I went away.

'I am very fond of this clock,' he said, patting it on the back; 'it will ring for me any morning when I want to go out fishing. Bedad, there are no two clocks in the island that would be equal to it.'

I had some photographs to show them that I took here last year, and while I was sitting on a little stool near the door of the kitchen, showing them to the family, a beautiful young woman I had spoken to a few times last year slipped in, and after a wonderfully simple and cordial speech of welcome, she sat down on the floor beside me to look on also.

The complete absence of shyness or self-consciousness in most of these people gives them a peculiar charm, and when this young and beautiful woman leaned across my knees to look nearer at some photograph that pleased her, I felt more than ever the strange simplicity of the island life.

Last year when I came here everything was new, and the people were a little strange with me, but now I am familiar with them and their way of life, so that their qualities strike me more forcibly than before.

When my photographs of this island had been examined with immense delight, and every person in them had been identified—even those who only showed a hand or a leg—I brought out some I had taken in County Wicklow. Most of them were fragments, showing fairs in Rathdrum or Aughrim, men cutting turf on the hills, or other scenes of inland life, yet they gave the greatest delight to these people who are wearied of the sea.

This year I see a darker side of life in the islands. The sun seldom shines, and day after day a cold southwestern wind blows over the cliffs, bringing up showers of hail and dense masses of cloud.

The sons who are at home stay out fishing whenever

it is tolerably calm, from about three in the morning
till after nightfall, yet they earn little, as fish are not
plentiful.

The old man fishes also with a long rod and ground-
bait, but as a rule has even smaller success.

When the weather breaks completely, fishing is abandoned, and they both go down and dig potatoes in the
rain. The women sometimes help them, but their usual
work is to look after the calves and do their spinning
in the house.

There is a vague depression over the family this year,
because of the two sons who have gone away, Michael
to the mainland, and another son, who was working in
Kilronan last year, to the United States.

A letter came yesterday from Michael to his mother.
It was written in English, as he is the only one of the
family who can read or write in Irish, and I heard it
being slowly spelled out and translated as I sat in my
room. A little later the old woman brought it in for
me to read.

He told her first about his work, and the wages he is
getting. Then he said that one night he had been walking in the town, and had looked up among the streets,
and thought to himself what a grand night it would be
on the Sandy Head of this island—not, he added, that
he was feeling lonely or sad. At the end he gave an
account, with the dramatic emphasis of the folk-tale,
of how he had met me on the Sunday morning, and,
'believe me,' he said, 'it was the fine talk we had for
two hours or three.' He told them also of a knife I had
given him that was so fine, no one on the island 'had
ever seen the like of her.'

Another day a letter came from the son who is in
America, to say that he had had a slight accident to one

of his arms, but was well again, and that he was leaving New York and going a few hundred miles up the country.

All the evening afterwards the old woman sat on her stool at the corner of the fire with her shawl over her head, keening piteously to herself. America appeared far away, yet she seems to have felt that, after all, it was only the other edge of the Atlantic, and now when she hears them talking of railroads and inland cities where there is no sea, things she cannot understand, it comes home to her that her son is gone for ever. She often tells me how she used to sit on the wall behind the house last year and watch the hooker he worked in coming out of Kilronan and beating up the sound, and what company it used to be to her the time they'd all be out.

The maternal feeling is so powerful on these islands that it gives a life of torment to the women. Their sons grow up to be banished as soon as they are of age, or to live here in continual danger on the sea; their daughters go away also, or are worn out in their youth with bearing children that grow up to harass them in their own turn a little later.

There has been a storm for the last twenty-four hours, and I have been wandering on the cliffs till my hair is stiff with salt. Immense masses of spray were flying up from the base of the cliff, and were caught at times by the wind and whirled away to fall at some distance from the shore. When one of these happened to fall on me, I had to crouch down for an instant, wrapped and blinded by a white hail of foam.

The waves were so enormous that when I saw one more than usually large coming towards me, I turned

instinctively to hide myself, as one blinks when struck
upon the eyes.

After a few hours the mind grows bewildered with
the endless change and struggle of the sea, and an utter
despondency replaces the first moment of exhilaration.

At the south-west corner of the island I came upon
a number of people gathering the seaweed that is now
thick on the rocks. It was raked from the surf by the
men, and then carried up to the brow of the cliff by a
party of young girls.

In addition to their ordinary clothing these girls wore
a raw sheepskin on their shoulders, to catch the oozing
sea-water, and they looked strangely wild and seal-like
with the salt caked upon their lips and wreaths of seaweed in their hair.

For the rest of my walk I saw no living thing but one
flock of curlews, and a few pipits hiding among the
stones.

About the sunset the clouds broke and the storm
turned to a hurricane. Bars of purple cloud stretched
across the sound where immense waves were rolling
from the west, wreathed with snowy phantasies of
spray. Then there was the bay full of green delirium,
and the Twelve Pins touched with mauve and scarlet
in the east.

The suggestion from this world of inarticulate
power was immense, and now at midnight, when the
wind is abating, I am still trembling and flushed with
exultation.

I have been walking through the wet lanes in my
pampooties in spite of the rain, and I have brought on a
feverish cold.

The wind is terrific. If anything serious should happen to me I might die here and be nailed in my box, and shoved down into a wet crevice in the graveyard before any one could know it on the mainland.

Two days ago a curagh passed from the south island —they can go out when we are weather-bound because of a sheltered cove in their island—it was thought in search of the doctor. It became too rough afterwards to make the return journey, and it was only this morning we saw them repassing towards the south-east in a terrible sea.

A four-oared curagh with two men in her besides the rowers—probably the priest and the doctor—went first, followed by the three-oared curagh from the south island, which ran more danger. Often when they go for the doctor in weather like this, they bring the priest also, as they do not know if it will be possible to go for him if he is needed later.

As a rule there is little illness, and the women often manage their confinements among themselves without any trained assistance. In most cases all goes well, but at times a curagh is sent off in desperate haste for the priest and the doctor when it is too late.

The baby that spent some days here last year is now established in the house; I suppose the old woman has adopted him to console herself for the loss of her own sons.

He is now a well-grown child, though not yet able to say more than a few words of Gaelic. His favourite amusement is to stand behind the door with a stick, waiting for any wandering pig or hen that may chance to come in, and then to dash out and pursue them. There are two young kittens in the kitchen also, which he ill-treats, without meaning to do them harm.

Whenever the old woman comes into my room with

turf for the fire, he walks in solemnly behind her with
a sod under each arm, deposits them on the back of the
fire with great care, and then flies off round the corner
with his long petticoats trailing behind him.

He has not yet received any official name on the island, as he has not left the fireside, but in the house
they usually speak of him as 'Michaeleen beug' (*i.e.*
'little small-Michael').

Now and then he is slapped, but for the most part
the old woman keeps him in order with stories of 'the
long-toothed hag,' that lives in the Dun and eats children who are not good. He spends half his day eating
cold potatoes and drinking very strong tea, yet seems
in perfect health.

An Irish letter has come to me from Michael. I will
translate it literally.

DEAR NOBLE PERSON,—I write this letter with joy
and pride that you found the way to the house of my
father the day you were on the steamship. I am thinking
there will not be loneliness on you, for there will be
the fine beautiful Gaelic League and you will be learning powerfully.

I am thinking there is no one in life walking with
you now but your own self from morning till night,
and great is the pity.

What way are my mother and my three brothers and
my sisters, and do not forget white Michael, and the
poor little child and the old grey woman, and Rory. I
am getting a forgetfulness on all my friends and kindred.—I am your friend . . .

It is curious how he accuses himself of forgetfulness
after asking for all his family by name. I suppose the

first home-sickness is wearing away and he looks on his independent wellbeing as a treason towards his kindred.

One of his friends was in the kitchen when the letter was brought to me, and, by the old man's wish, he read it out loud as soon as I had finished it. When he came to the last sentence he hesitated for a moment, and then omitted it altogether.

This young man had come up to bring me a copy of the 'Love Songs of Connaught,' which he possesses, and I persuaded him to read, or rather chant me some of them. When he had read a couple I found that the old woman knew many of them from her childhood, though her version was often not the same as what was in the book. She was rocking herself on a stool in the chimney corner beside a pot of indigo, in which she was dyeing wool, and several times when the young man finished a poem she took it up again and recited the verses with exquisite musical intonation, putting a wistfulness and passion into her voice that seemed to give it all the cadences that are sought in the profoundest poetry.

The lamp had burned low, and another terrible gale was howling and shrieking over the island. It seemed like a dream that I should be sitting here among these men and women listening to this rude and beautiful poetry that is filled with the oldest passions of the world.

The horses have been coming back for the last few days from their summer's grazing in Connemara. They are landed at the sandy beach where the cattle were shipped last year, and I went down early this morning to watch their arrival through the waves. The hooker was anchored at some distance from the shore, but I could see a horse standing at the gunnel surrounded by men shouting and flipping at it with bits of rope. In a moment it jumped over into the sea, and some men, who were waiting for it in a curagh, caught it by the halter and towed it to within twenty yards of the surf. Then the curagh turned back to the hooker, and the horse was left to make its own way to the land.

As I was standing about a man came up to me and asked after the usual salutations:—

'Is there any war in the world at this time, noble person?'

I told him something of the excitement in the Transvaal, and then another horse came near the waves and I passed on and left him.

Afterwards I walked round the edge of the sea to the pier, where a quantity of turf has recently been brought in. It is usually left for some time stacked on the sandhills, and then carried up to the cottages in panniers slung on donkeys or any horses that are on the island.

They have been busy with it the last few weeks, and the track from the village to the pier has been filled with lines of red-petticoated boys driving their donkeys before them, or cantering down on their backs when the panniers are empty.

In some ways these men and women seem strangely far away from me. They have the same emotions that I have, and the animals have, yet I cannot talk to them when there is much to say, more than to the dog that whines beside me in a mountain fog.

There is hardly an hour I am with them that I do not feel the shock of some inconceivable idea, and then again the shock of some vague emotion that is familiar to them and to me. On some days I feel this island as a

perfect home and resting place; on other days I feel
that I am a waif among the people. I can feel more
with them than they can feel with me, and while I
wander among them, they like me sometimes, and laugh
at me sometimes, yet never know what I am doing.

In the evenings I sometimes meet with a girl who is
not yet half through her 'teens, yet seems in some ways
more consciously developed than any one else that I
have met here. She has passed part of her life on the
mainland, and the disillusion she found in Galway has
coloured her imagination.

As we sit on stools on either side of the fire I hear
her voice going backwards and forwards in the same
sentence from the gaiety of a child to the plaintive intonation of an old race that is worn with sorrow. At
one moment she is a simple peasant, at another she seems
to be looking out at the world with a sense of prehistoric
disillusion and to sum up in the expression of her grey-
blue eyes the whole external despondency of the clouds
and sea.

Our conversation is usually disjointed. One evening
we talked of a town on the mainland.

'Ah, it's a queer place,' she said: 'I wouldn't choose
to live in it. It's a queer place, and indeed I don't know
the place that isn't.'

Another evening we talked of the people who live
on the island or come to visit it.

'Father —— is gone,' she said; 'he was a kind man
but a queer man. Priests is queer people, and I don't
know who isn't.'

Then after a long pause she told me with seriousness,
as if speaking of a thing that surprised herself, and
should surprise me, that she was very fond of the boys.

In our talk, which is sometimes full of the innocent

realism of childhood, she is always pathetically eager to say the right thing and be engaging.

One evening I found her trying to light a fire in the little side room of her cottage, where there is an ordinary fireplace. I went in to help her and showed her how to hold up a paper before the mouth of the chimney to make a draught, a method she had never seen. Then I told her of men who live alone in Paris and make their own fires that they may have no one to bother them. She was sitting in a heap on the floor staring into the turf, and as I finished she looked up with surprise.

'They're like me so,' she said; 'would anyone have thought that!'

Below the sympathy we feel there is still a chasm between us.

'Musha,' she muttered as I was leaving her this evening, 'I think it's to hell you'll be going by and by.'

Occasionally I meet her also in a kitchen where young men go to play cards after dark and a few girls slip in to share the amusement. At such times her eyes shine in the light of the candles, and her cheeks flush with the first tumult of youth, till she hardly seems the same girl who sits every evening droning to herself over the turf.

A branch of the Gaelic League has been started here since my last visit, and every Sunday afternoon three little girls walk through the village ringing a shrill hand-bell, as a signal that the women's meeting is to be held,—here it would be useless to fix an hour, as the hours are not recognised.

Soon afterwards bands of girls—of all ages from five to twenty-five begin to troop down to the schoolhouse in their reddest Sunday petticoats. It is remarkable that these young women are willing to spend their one afternoon of freedom in laborious studies of orthography for no reason but a vague reverence for the Gaelic. It is true that they owe this reverence, or most of it, to the influence of some recent visitors, yet the fact that they feel such an influence so keenly is itself of interest.

In the older generation that did not come under the influence of the recent language movement, I do not see any particular affection for Gaelic. Whenever they are able, they speak English to their children, to render them more capable of making their way in life. Even the young men sometimes say to me—

'There's very hard English on you, and I wish to God I had the like of it."

The women are the great conservative force in this matter of the language. They learn a little English in school and from their parents, but they rarely have occasion to speak with any one who is not a native of the islands, so their knowledge of the foreign tongue remains rudimentary. In my cottage I have never heard a word of English from the women except when they were speaking to the pigs or to the dogs, or when the girl was reading a letter in English. Women, however, with a more assertive temperament, who have had, apparently, the same opportunities, often attain a considerable fluency, as is the case with one, a relative of the old woman of the house, who often visits here.

In the boys' school, where I sometimes look in, the children surprise me by their knowledge of English, though they always speak in Irish among themselves. The school itself is a comfortless building in a terribly bleak position. In cold weather the children arrive in the morning with a sod of turf tied up with their books,

a simple toll which keeps the fire well supplied, yet, I believe, a more modern method is soon to be introduced.

I am in the north island again, looking out with a
singular sensation to the cliffs across the sound. It is
hard to believe that those hovels I can just see in the
south are filled with people whose lives have the strange
quality that is found in the oldest poetry and legend.
Compared with them the falling off that has come with
the increased prosperity of this island is full of discour-
agement. The charm which the people over there share
with the birds and flowers has been replaced here by
the anxiety of men who are eager for gain. The eyes and
expression are different, though the faces are the same,
and even the children here seem to have an indefinable
modern quality that is absent from the men of Inishmaan.

My voyage from the middle island was wild. The
morning was so stormy, that in ordinary circumstances
I would not have attempted the passage, but as I had
arranged to travel with a curagh that was coming over
for the parish priest who is to hold stations on Inishmaan—I did not like to draw back.

I went out in the morning and walked up to the cliffs
as usual. Several men I fell in with shook their heads
when I told them I was going away, and said they
doubted if a curagh could cross the sound with the sea
that was in it.

When I went back to the cottage I found the curate
had just come across from the south island, and had had
a worse passage than any he had yet experienced.

The tide was to turn at two o'clock, and after that
it was thought the sea would be calmer, as the wind and

the waves would be running from the same point. We sat about in the kitchen all the morning, with men coming in every few minutes to give their opinion whether the passage should be attempted, and at what points the sea was likely to be at its worst.

At last it was decided we should go, and I started for the pier in a wild shower of rain with the wind howling in the walls. The schoolmaster and a priest who was to have gone with me came out as I was passing through the village and advised me not to make the passage; but my crew had gone on towards the sea, and I thought it better to go after them. The eldest son of the family was coming with me, and I considered that the old man, who knew the waves better than I did, would not send out his son if there was more than reasonable danger.

I found my crew waiting for me under a high wall below the village, and we went on together. The island had never seemed so desolate. Looking out over the black limestone through the driving rain to the gulf of struggling waves, an indescribable feeling of dejection came over me.

The old man gave me his view of the use of fear.

'A man who is not afraid of the sea will soon be drownded,' he said, 'for he will be going out on a day he shouldn't. But we do be afraid of the sea, and we do only be drownded now and again.'

A little crowd of neighbours had collected lower down to see me off, and as we crossed the sand hills we had to shout to each other to be heard above the wind.

The crew carried down the curagh and then stood under the lee of the pier tying on their hats with strings and drawing on their oilskins.

They tested the braces of the oars, and the oarpins,

and everything in the curagh with a care I had not seen them give to anything, then my bag was lifted in, and we were ready. Besides the four men of the crew a man was going with us who wanted a passage to this island. As he was scrambling into the bow, an old man stood forward from the crowd.

'Don't take that man with you,' he said. 'Last week they were taking him to Clare and the whole lot of them were near drowned. Another day he went to Inisheer and they broke three ribs of the curagh, and they coming back. There is not the like of him for ill-luck in the three islands.'

'The divil choke your old gob,' said the man, 'you will be talking.'

We set off. It was a four-oared curagh, and I was given the last seat so as to leave the stern for the man who was steering with an oar, worked at right angles to the others by an extra thole-pin in the stern gunnel.

When we had gone about a hundred yards they ran up a bit of a sail in the bow and the pace became extraordinarily rapid.

The shower had passed over and the wind had fallen, but large, magnificently brilliant waves were rolling down on us at right angles to our course.

Every instant the steersman whirled us round with a sudden stroke of his oar, the prow reared up and then fell into the next furrow with a crash, throwing up masses of spray. As it did so, the stern in its turn was thrown up, and both the steersman, who let go his oar and clung with both hands to the gunnel, and myself, were lifted high up above the sea.

The wave passed, we regained our course and rowed violently for a few yards, when the same manœuvre had to be repeated. As we worked out into the sound we began to meet another class of waves, that could be seen for some distance towering above the rest.

When one of these came in sight, the first effort was to get beyond its reach. The steersman began crying out in Gaelic 'Siubhal, siubhal' ('Run, run'), and sometimes, when the mass was gliding towards us with horrible speed, his voice rose to a shriek. Then the rowers themselves took up the cry, and the curagh seemed to leap and quiver with the frantic terror of a beast till the wave passed behind it or fell with a crash beside the stern.

It was in this racing with the waves that our chief danger lay. If the wave could be avoided, it was better to do so, but if it overtook us while we were trying to escape, and caught us on the broadside, our destruction was certain. I could see the steersman quivering with the excitement of his task, for any error in his judgment would have swamped us.

We had one narrow escape. A wave appeared high above the rest, and there was the usual moment of intense exertion. It was of no use, and in an instant the wave seemed to be hurling itself upon us. With a yell of rage the steersman struggled with his oar to bring our prow to meet it. He had almost succeeded, when there was a crash and rush of water round us. I felt as if I had been struck upon the back with knotted ropes. White foam gurgled round my knees and eyes. The curagh reared up, swaying and trembling for a moment, and then fell safely into the furrow.

This was our worst moment, though more than once, when several waves came so closely together that we had no time to regain control of the canoe between them, we had some dangerous work. Our lives depended upon the skill and courage of the men, as the life of the rider

or swimmer is often in his own hands, and the excitement was too great to allow time for fear.

I enjoyed the passage. Down in this shallow trough
of canvas that bent and trembled with the motion of
the men, I had a far more intimate feeling of the glory
and power of the waves than I have ever known in a
steamer.

Old Mourteen is keeping me company again, and I
am now able to understand the greater part of his Irish.

He took me out to-day to show me the remains of
some cloghauns, or beehive dwellings, that are left near
the central ridge of the island. After I had looked at
them we lay down in the corner of a little field, filled
with the autumn sunshine and the odour of withering
flowers, while he told me a long folk-tale which took
more than an hour to narrate.

He is so blind that I can gaze at him without dis-
courtesy, and after a while the expression of his face
made me forget to listen, and I lay dreamily in the sunshine letting the antique formulas of the story blend
with the suggestions from the prehistoric masonry I lay
on. The glow of childish transport that came over him
when he reached the nonsense ending—so common in
these tales—recalled me to myself, and I listened at-
tentively while he gabbled with delighted haste: 'They
found the path and I found the puddle. They were
drowned and I was found. If it's all one to me to-night,
it wasn't all one to them the next night. Yet, if it wasn't
itself, not a thing did they lose but an old back tooth'—
or some such gibberish.

As I led him home through the paths he described
to me—it is thus we get along—lifting him at times
over the low walls he is too shaky to climb, he brought

the conversation to the topic they are never weary of—
my views on marriage.

He stopped as we reached the summit of the island,
with the stretch of the Atlantic just visible behind him.

'Whisper, noble person,' he began, 'do you never be
thinking on the young girls? The time I was a young
man, the divil a one of them could I look on without
wishing to marry her.'

'Ah, Mourteen,' I answered, 'it's a great wonder
you'd be asking me. What at all do you think of me
yourself?'

'Bedad, noble person, I'm thinking it's soon you'll be
getting married. Listen to what I'm telling you: a man
who is not married is no better than an old jackass. He
goes into his sister's house, and into his brother's house;
he eats a bit in this place and a bit in another place, but
he has no home for himself; like an old jackass straying
on the rocks.'

I have left Aran. The steamer had a more than
usually heavy cargo, and it was after four o'clock when
we sailed from Kilronan.

Again I saw the three low rocks sink down into the
sea with a moment of inconceivable distress. It was a
clear evening, and as we came out into the bay the sun
stood like an aureole behind the cliffs of Inishmaan. A
little later a brilliant glow came over the sky, throwing
out the blue of the sea and of the hills of Connemara.

When it was quite dark, the cold became intense, and
I wandered about the lonely vessel that seemed to be
making her own way across the sea. I was the only
passenger, and all the crew, except one boy who was
steering, were huddled together in the warmth of the
engine-room.

Three hours passed, and no one stirred. The slowness of the vessel and the lamentation of the cold sea about her sides became almost unendurable. Then the lights of Galway came in sight, and the crew appeared as we beat up slowly to the quay.

Once on shore I had some difficulty in finding any one to carry my baggage to the railway. When I found a man in the darkness and got my bag on his shoulders, he turned out to be drunk, and I had trouble to keep him from rolling from the wharf with all my possessions. He professed to be taking me by a short cut into the town, but when we were in the middle of a waste of broken buildings and skeletons of ships he threw my bag on the ground and sat down on it.

'It's real heavy she is, your honour,' he said; 'I'm thinking it's gold there will be in it.'

'Divil a hap'worth is there in it at all but books,' I answered him in Gaelic.

'Bedad, is mor an truaghé' ('It's a big pity'), he said; 'if it was gold was in it it's the thundering spree we'd have together this night in Galway.'

In about half an hour I got my luggage once more on his back, and we made our way into the city.

Later in the day I went down towards the quay to look for Michael. As I turned into the narrow street where he lodges, some one seemed to be following me in the shadow, and when I stopped to find the number of his house I heard the 'Failte' (Welcome) of Inishmaan pronounced close to me.

It was Michael.

'I saw you in the street,' he said, 'but I was ashamed to speak to you in the middle of the people, so I followed you the way I'd see if you'd remember me.'

We turned back together and walked about the town

till he had to go to his lodgings. He was still just the same, with all his old simplicity and shrewdness; but the work he has here does not agree with him, and he is not contented.

It was the eve of the Parnell celebration in Dublin, and the town was full of excursionists waiting for a train which was to start at midnight. When Michael left me I spent some time in an hotel, and then wandered down to the railway.

A wild crowd was on the platform, surging round the train in every stage of intoxication. It gave me a better instance than I had yet seen of the half-savage temperament of Connaught. The tension of human excitement seemed greater in this insignificant crowd than anything I have felt among enormous mobs in Rome or Paris.

There were a few people from the islands on the platform, and I got in along with them to a third-class carriage. One of the women of the party had her niece with her, a young girl from Connaught who was put beside me; at the other end of the carriage there were some old men who were talking Irish, and a young man who had been a sailor.

When the train started there were wild cheers and cries on the platform, and in the train itself the noise was intense; men and women shrieking and singing and beating their sticks on the partitions. At several stations there was a rush to the bar, so the excitement increased as we proceeded.

At Ballinasloe there were some soldiers on the platform looking for places. The sailor in our compartment had a dispute with one of them, and in an instant the door was flung open and the compartment was filled with reeling uniforms and sticks. Peace was made after a moment of uproar and the soldiers got out, but as they did so a pack of their women followers thrust their bare heads and arms into the doorway, cursing and blaspheming with extraordinary rage.

As the train moved away a moment later, these women set up a frantic lamentation. I looked out and caught a glimpse of the wildest heads and figures I have ever seen, shrieking and screaming and waving their naked arms in the light of the lanterns.

As the night went on girls began crying out in the carriage next us, and I could hear the words of obscene songs when the train stopped at a station.

In our own compartment the sailor would allow no one to sleep, and talked all night with sometimes a touch of wit or brutality, and always with a beautiful fluency with wild temperament behind it.

The old men in the corner, dressed in black coats that had something of the antiquity of heirlooms, talked all night among themselves in Gaelic. The young girl beside me lost her shyness after a while, and let me point out the features of the country that were beginning to appear through the dawn as we drew nearer Dublin. She was delighted with the shadows of the trees—trees are rare in Connaught—and with the canal, which was beginning to reflect the morning light. Every time I showed her some new shadow she cried out with naïve excitement—

'Oh, it's lovely, but I can't see it.'

This presence at my side contrasted curiously with the brutality that shook the barrier behind us. The whole spirit of the west of Ireland, with its strange wildness and reserve, seemed moving in this single train to pay a last homage to the dead statesman of the east.

PART III

A LETTER has come from Michael while I am in Paris. It is in English.

MY DEAR FRIEND,—I hope that you are in good health since I have heard from you before, it's many a time I do think of you since and it was not forgetting you I was for the future.

I was at home in the beginning of March for a fort-night and was very bad with the Influence, but I took good care of myself.

I am getting good wages from the first of this year, and I am afraid I won't be able to stand with it, al-though it is not hard, I am working in a saw-mills and getting the money for the wood and keeping an account of it.

I am getting a letter and some news from home two or three times a week, and they are all well in health, and your friends in the island as well as if I mentioned them.

Did you see any of my friends in Dublin Mr.——— or any of those gentlemen or gentlewomen.

I think I soon try America but not until next year if I am alive.

I hope we might meet again in good and pleasant health.

It is now time to come to a conclusion, good-bye and not for ever, write soon.—I am your friend in Galway.

Write soon dear friend.

Another letter in a more rhetorical mood.

My dear Mr. S.,—I am for a long time trying to spare a little time for to write a few words to you.

Hoping that you are still considering good and pleasant health since I got a letter from you before.

I see now that your time is coming round to come to this place to learn your native language. There was a great Feis in this island two weeks ago, and there was a very large attendance from the South island, and not very many from the North.

Two cousins of my own have been in this house for three weeks or beyond it, but now they are gone, and there is a place for you if you wish to come, and you can write before you and we'll try and manage you as well as we can.

I am at home now for about two months, for the mill was burnt where I was at work. After that I was in Dublin, but I did not get my health in that city.— *Mise le mor mheas ort a chara.*

Soon after I received this letter I wrote to Michael to say that I was going back to them. This time I chose a day when the steamer went direct to the middle island, and as we came up between the two lines of curaghs that were waiting outside the slip, I saw Michael, dressed once more in his island clothes, rowing in one of them.

He made no sign of recognition, but as soon as they could get alongside he clambered on board and came straight up on the bridge to where I was.

'Bh-fuil tu go maith?' ('Are you well?') he said. 'Where is your bag?'

His curagh had got a bad place near the bow of the steamer, so I was slung down from a considerable height on top of some sacks of flour and my own bag, while the curagh swayed and battered itself against the side.

When we were clear I asked Michael if he had got my letter.

'Ah no,' he said, 'not a sight of it, but maybe it will come next week.'

Part of the slip had been washed away during the winter, so we had to land to the left of it, among the rocks, taking our turn with the other curaghs that were coming in.

As soon as I was on shore the men crowded round me to bid me welcome, asking me as they shook hands if I had travelled far in the winter, and seen many wonders, ending, as usual, with the inquiry if there was much war at present in the world.

It gave me a thrill of delight to hear their Gaelic blessings, and to see the steamer moving away, leaving me quite alone among them. The day was fine with a clear sky, and the sea was glittering beyond the limestone. Further off a light haze on the cliffs of the larger island, and on the Connaught hills, gave me the illusion that it was still summer.

A little boy was sent off to tell the old woman that I was coming, and we followed slowly talking, and carrying the baggage.

When I had exhausted my news they told me theirs. A power of strangers—four or five—a French priest among them, had been on the island in the summer; the potatoes were bad, but the rye had begun well, till a dry week came and then it had turned into oats.

'If you didn't know us so well,' said the man who was talking, 'you'd think it was a lie we were telling, but the sorrow a lie is in it. It grew straight and well till it

was high as your knee, then it turned into oats. Did ever
you see the like of that in County Wicklow?'

In the cottage everything was as usual, but Michael's
presence has brought back the old woman's humour and
contentment. As I sat down on my stool and lit my pipe
with the corner of a sod, I could have cried out with
the feeling of festivity that this return procured me.

This year Michael is busy in the daytime, but at present there is a harvest moon, and we spend most of the
evening wandering about the island, looking out over
the bay where the shadows of the clouds throw strange
patterns of gold and black. As we were returning
through the village this evening a tumult of revelry
broke out from one of the smaller cottages, and Michael
said it was the young boys and girls who have sport at
this time of the year. I would have liked to join them,
but feared to embarrass their amusement. When we
passed on again the groups of scattered cottages on each
side of the way reminded me of places I have sometimes
passed when travelling at night in France or Bavaria,
places that seemed so enshrined in the blue silence of
night one could not believe they would reawaken.

Afterwards we went up on the Dun, where Michael
said he had never been before after nightfall, though he
lives within a stone's-throw. The place gains unexpected
grandeur in this light, standing out like a corona of
prehistoric stone upon the summit of the island. We
walked round the top of the wall for some time looking
down on the faint yellow roofs, with the rocks glittering beyond them, and the silence of the bay. Though
Michael is sensible of the beauty of the nature round
him, he never speaks of it directly, and many of our

evening walks are occupied with long Gaelic discourses about the movements of the stars and moon.

These people make no distinction between the natural and the supernatural.

This afternoon—it was Sunday, when there is usually some interesting talk among the islanders—it rained, so I went into the schoolmaster's kitchen, which is a good deal frequented by the more advanced among the people. I know so little of their ways of fishing and farming that I do not find it easy to keep up our talk without reaching matters where they cannot follow me, and since the novelty of my photographs has passed off I have some difficulty in giving them the entertainment they seem to expect from my company. To-day I showed them some simple gymnastic feats and conjurer's tricks, which gave them great amusement.

'Tell us now,' said an old woman when I had finished, 'didn't you learn those things from the witches that do be out in the country?'

In one of the tricks I seemed to join a piece of string which was cut by the people, and the illusion was so complete that I saw one man going off with it into a corner and pulling at the apparent joining till he sank red furrows round his hands.

Then he brought it back to me.

'Bedad,' he said, 'this is the greatest wonder ever I seen. The cord is a taste thinner where you joined it but as strong as ever it was.'

A few of the younger men looked doubtful, but the older people, who have watched the rye turning into oats, seemed to accept the magic frankly, and did not show any surprise that 'a duine uasal' (a noble person) should be able to do like the witches.

My intercourse with these people has made me realise that miracles must abound wherever the new conception of law is not understood. On these islands alone miracles enough happen every year to equip a divine emissary. Rye is turned into oats, storms are raised to keep evictors from the shore, cows that are isolated on lonely rocks bring forth calves, and other things of the same kind are common.

The wonder is a rare expected event, like the thunderstorm or the rainbow, except that it is a little rarer and a little more wonderful. Often, when I am walking and get into conversation with some of the people, and tell them that I have received a paper from Dublin, they ask me—

'And is there any great wonder in the world at this time?'

When I had finished my feats of dexterity, I was surprised to find that none of the islanders, even the youngest and most agile, could do what I did. As I pulled their limbs about in my effort to teach them, I felt that the ease and beauty of their movements has made me think them lighter than they really are. Seen in their curaghs between these cliffs and the Atlantic, they appear lithe and small, but if they were dressed as we are and seen in an ordinary room, many of them would seem heavily and powerfully made.

One man, however, the champion dancer of the island, got up after a while and displayed the salmon leap—lying flat on his face and then springing up, horizontally, high in the air—and some other feats of extraordinary agility, but he is not young and we could not get him to dance.

In the evening I had to repeat my tricks here in the

kitchen, for the fame of them had spread over the island.

No doubt these feats will be remembered here for generations. The people have so few images for description that they seize on anything that is remarkable in their visitors and use it afterwards in their talk.

For the last few years when they are speaking of any one with fine rings they say: 'She had beautiful rings on her fingers like Lady ———,' a visitor to the island.

I have been down sitting on the pier till it was quite dark. I am only beginning to understand the nights of Inishmaan and the influence they have had in giving distinction to these men who do most of their work after nightfall.

I could hear nothing but a few curlews and other wild-fowl whistling and shrieking in the seaweed, and the low rustling of the waves. It was one of the dark sultry nights peculiar to September, with no light anywhere except the phosphorescence of the sea, and an occasional rift in the clouds that showed the stars behind them.

The sense of solitude was immense. I could not see or realise my own body, and I seemed to exist merely in my perception of the waves and of the crying birds, and of the smell of seaweed.

When I tried to come home I lost myself among the sandhills, and the night seemed to grow unutterably cold and dejected, as I groped among slimy masses of seaweed and wet crumbling walls.

After a while I heard a movement in the sand, and two grey shadows appeared beside me. They were two men who were going home from fishing. I spoke to them and knew their voices, and we went home together.

In the autumn season the threshing of the rye is one of the many tasks that fall to the men and boys. The sheaves are collected on a bare rock, and then each is beaten separately on a couple of stones placed on end one against the other. The land is so poor that a field hardly produces more grain than is needed for seed the following year, so the rye-growing is carried on merely for the straw, which is used for thatching.

The stooks are carried to and from the threshing fields, piled on donkeys that one meets everywhere at this season, with their black, unbridled heads just visible beneath a pinnacle of golden straw.

While the threshing is going on sons and daughters keep turning up with one thing and another till there is a little crowd on the rocks, and any one who is passing stops for an hour or two to talk on his way to the sea, so that, like the kelp-burning in the summer-time, this work is full of sociability.

When the threshing is over the straw is taken up to the cottages and piled up in an outhouse, or more often in a corner of the kitchen, where it brings a new liveliness of colour.

A few days ago when I was visiting a cottage where there are the most beautiful children on the island, the eldest daughter, a girl of about fourteen, went and sat down on a heap of straw by the doorway. A ray of sunlight fell on her and on a portion of the rye, giving her figure and red dress with the straw under it a curious relief against the nets and oilskins, and forming a natural picture of exquisite harmony and colour.

In our own cottage the thatching—it is done every year—has just been carried out. The rope-twisting was done partly in the lane, partly in the kitchen when the weather was uncertain. Two men usually sit together at this work, one of them hammering the straw with a heavy block of wood, the other forming the rope, the main body of which is twisted by a boy or girl with a bent stick specially formed for this employment.

In wet weather, when the work must be done indoors, the person who is twisting recedes gradually out of the door, across the lane, and sometimes across a field or two beyond it. A great length is needed to form the close network which is spread over the thatch, as each piece measures about fifty yards. When this work is in progress in half the cottages of the village, the road has a curious look, and one has to pick one's steps through a maze of twisting ropes that pass from the dark doorways on either side into the fields.

When four or five immense balls of rope have been completed, a thatching party is arranged, and before dawn some morning they come down to the house, and the work is taken in hand with such energy that it is usually ended within the day.

Like all work that is done in common on the island, the thatching is regarded as a sort of festival. From the moment a roof is taken in hand there is a whirl of laughter and talk till it is ended, and, as the man whose house is being covered is a host instead of an employer, he lays himself out to please the men who work with him.

The day our own house was thatched the large table was taken into the kitchen from my room, and high teas were given every few hours. Most of the people who came along the road turned down into the kitchen for a few minutes, and the talking was incessant. Once when I went into the window I heard Michael retailing my astronomical lectures from the apex of the gable, but usually their topics have to do with the affairs of the island.

It is likely that much of the intelligence and charm of these people is due to the absence of any division of labour, and to the correspondingly wide development of each individual, whose varied knowledge and skill necessitates a considerable activity of mind. Each man can speak two languages. He is a skilled fisherman, and can manage a curagh with extraordinary nerve and dexterity. He can farm simply, burn kelp, cut out pampooties, mend nets, build and thatch a house, and make a cradle or a coffin. His work changes with the seasons in a way that keeps him free from the dulness that comes to people who have always the same occupation. The danger of his life on the sea gives him the alertness of the primitive hunter, and the long nights he spends fishing in his curagh bring him some of the emotions that are thought peculiar to men who have lived with the arts.

As Michael is busy in the daytime, I have got a boy to come up and read Irish to me every afternoon. He is about fifteen, and is singularly intelligent, with a real sympathy for the language and the stories we read.

One evening when he had been reading to me for two hours, I asked him if he was tired.

'Tired?' he said, 'sure you wouldn't ever be tired reading!'

A few years ago this predisposition for intellectual things would have made him sit with old people and learn their stories, but now boys like him turn to books and to papers in Irish that are sent them from Dublin.

In most of the stories we read, where the English and

Irish are printed side by side, I see him looking across to the English in passages that are a little obscure, though he is indignant if I say that he knows English better than Irish. Probably he knows the local Irish better than English, and printed English better than printed Irish, as the latter has frequent dialectic forms he does not know.

A few days ago when he was reading a folk-tale from Douglas Hyde's *Beside the Fire*, something caught his eye in the translation.

'There's a mistake in the English,' he said, after a moment's hesitation, 'he's put "gold chair" instead of "golden chair." '

I pointed out that we speak of gold watches and gold pins.

'And why wouldn't we?' he said; 'but "golden chair" would be much nicer.'

It is curious to see how his rudimentary culture has given him the beginning of a critical spirit that occupies itself with the form of language as well as with ideas.

One day I alluded to my trick of joining string.

'You can't join a string, don't be saying it,' he said; 'I don't know what way you're after fooling us, but you didn't join that string, not a bit of you.'

Another day when he was with me the fire burned low and I held up a newspaper before it to make a draught. It did not answer very well, and though the boy said nothing I saw he thought me a fool.

The next day he ran up in great excitement.

'I'm after trying the paper over the fire,' he said, 'and it burned grand. Didn't I think, when I seen you doing it there was no good in it at all, but I put a paper over the master's (the schoolmaster's) fire and it flamed up. Then I pulled back the corner of the paper and I ran my head in, and believe me, there was a big cold wind blowing up the chimney that would sweep the head from you.'

We nearly quarrelled because he wanted me to take his photograph in his Sunday clothes from Galway, instead of his native homespuns that become him far better, though he does not like them as they seem to connect him with the primitive life of the island. With his keen temperament, he may go far if he can ever step out into the world.

He is constantly thinking.

One day he asked me if there was great wonder on their names out in the country.

I said there was no wonder on them at all.

'Well,' he said, 'there is great wonder on your name in the island, and I was thinking maybe there would be great wonder on our names out in the country.'

In a sense he is right. Though the names here are ordinary enough, they are used in a way that differs altogether from the modern system of surnames.

When a child begins to wander about the island, the neighbours speak of it by its Christian name, followed by the Christian name of its father. If this is not enough to identify it, the father's epithet—whether it is a nickname or the name of his own father—is added.

Sometimes when the father's name does not lend itself, the mother's Christian name is adopted as epithet for the children.

An old woman near this cottage is called 'Peggeen,' and her sons are 'Patch Pheggeen,' 'Seaghan Pheggeen,' etc.

Occasionally the surname is employed in its Irish form, but I have not heard them using the 'Mac' prefix when speaking Irish among themselves; perhaps the idea of a surname which it gives is too modern for them, perhaps they do use it at times that I have not noticed.

Sometimes a man is named from the colour of his hair. There is thus a Seaghan Ruadh (Red John), and his children are 'Mourteen Seaghan Ruadh,' etc.

Another man is known as 'an iasgaire' ('the fisher'), and his children are 'Maire an iasgaire' ('Mary daughter of the fisher'), and so on.

The schoolmaster tells me that when he reads out the roll in the morning the children repeat the local name all together in a whisper after each official name, and then the child answers. If he calls, for instance, 'Patrick O'Flaharty,' the children murmur, 'Patch Scaghan Dearg' or some such name, and the boy answers.

People who come to the island are treated in much the same way. A French Gaelic student was in the islands recently, and he is always spoken of as 'An Saggart Ruadh' ('the red priest') or as 'An Saggart Francach' ('the French priest'), but never by his name.

If an islander's name alone is enough to distinguish him it is used by itself, and I know one man who is spoken of as Eamonn. There may be other Edmunds on the island, but if so they have probably good nicknames or epithets of their own.

In other countries where the names are in a somewhat similar condition, as in modern Greece, the man's calling is usually one of the most common means of distinguishing him, but in this place, where all have the same calling, this means is not available.

Late this evening I saw a three-oared curagh with two old women in her besides the rowers, landing at the slip through a heavy roll. They were coming from Inishere, and they rowed up quickly enough till they were within a few yards of the surf-line, where they spun round and waited with the prow towards the sea, while wave after wave passed underneath them and broke on the remains of the slip. Five minutes passed; ten minutes; and still they waited with the oars just paddling in the water, and their heads turned over their shoulders.

I was beginning to think that they would have to give up and row round to the lee side of the island, when the curagh seemed suddenly to turn into a living thing. The prow was again towards the slip, leaping and hurling itself through the spray. Before it touched, the man in the bow wheeled round, two white legs came out over the prow like the flash of a sword, and before the next wave arrived he had dragged the curagh out of danger.

This sudden and united action in men without discipline shows well the education that the waves have given them. When the curagh was in safety the two old women were carried up through the surf and slippery seaweed on the backs of their sons.

In this broken weather a curagh cannot go out without danger, yet accidents are rare and seem to be nearly always caused by drink. Since I was here last year four men have been drowned on their way home from the large island. First a curagh belonging to the south island which put off with two men in her heavy with drink, came to shore here the next evening dry and uninjured, with the sail half set, and no one in her.

More recently a curagh from this island with three men, who were the worse for drink, was upset on its way home. The steamer was not far off, and saved two of the men, but could not reach the third.

Now a man has been washed ashore in Donegal with

one pampooty on him, and a striped shirt with a purse in one of the pockets, and a box for tobacco.

For three days the people have been trying to fix his identity. Some think it is the man from this island, others think that the man from the south answers the description more exactly. To-night as we were returning from the slip we met the mother of the man who was drowned from this island, still weeping and looking out over the sea. She stopped the people who had come over from the south island to ask them with a terrified whisper what is thought over there.

Later in the evening, when I was sitting in one of the cottages, the sister of the dead man came in through the rain with her infant, and there was a long talk about the rumours that had come in. She pieced together all she could remember about his clothes, and what his purse was like, and where he had got it, and the same for his tobacco box, and his stockings. In the end there seemed little doubt that it was her brother.

'Ah!' she said, 'it's Mike sure enough, and please God they'll give him a decent burial.'

Then she began to keen slowly to herself. She had loose yellow hair plastered round her head with the rain, and as she sat by the door suckling her infant, she seemed like a type of the women's life upon the islands.

For a while the people sat silent, and one could hear nothing but the lips of the infant, the rain hissing in the yard, and the breathing of four pigs that lay sleeping in one corner. Then one of the men began to talk about the new boats that have been sent to the south island, and the conversation went back to its usual round of topics.

The loss of one man seems a slight catastrophe to all except the immediate relatives. Often when an accident happens a father is lost with his two eldest sons, or in some other way all the active men of a household die together.

A few years ago three men of a family that used to make the wooden vessels—like tiny barrels—that are still used among the people, went to the big island together. They were drowned on their way home, and the art of making these little barrels died with them, at least on Inishmaan, though it still lingers in the north and south islands.

Another catastrophe that took place last winter gave a curious zest to the observance of holy days. It seems that it is not the custom for the men to go out fishing on the evening of a holy day, but one night last December some men, who wished to begin fishing early the next morning, rowed out to sleep in their hookers.

Towards morning a terrible storm rose, and several hookers with their crews on board were blown from their moorings and wrecked. The sea was so high that no attempt at rescue could be made, and the men were drowned.

'Ah!' said the man who told me the story, 'I'm thinking it will be a long time before men will go out again on a holy day. That storm was the only storm that reached into the harbour the whole winter, and I'm thinking there was something in it.'

To-day when I went down to the slip I found a pig-jobber from Kilronan with about twenty pigs that were to be shipped for the English market.

When the steamer was getting near, the whole drove was moved down on the slip and the curaghs were carried out close to the sea. Then each beast was caught in its turn and thrown on its side, while its legs were hitched together in a single knot, with a tag of rope remaining, by which it could be carried.

Probably the pain inflicted was not great, yet the animals shut their eyes and shrieked with almost human intonations, till the suggestion of the noise became so intense that the men and women who were merely looking on grew wild with excitement, and the pigs waiting their turn foamed at the mouth and tore each other with their teeth.

After a while there was a pause. The whole slip was covered with a mass of sobbing animals, with here and there a terrified woman crouching among the bodies, and patting some special favourite to keep it quiet while the curaghs were being launched.

Then the screaming began again while the pigs were carried out and laid in their places, with a waistcoat tied round their feet to keep them from damaging the canvas. They seemed to know where they were going, and looked up at me over the gunnel with an ignoble desperation that made me shudder to think that I had eaten of this whimpering flesh. When the last curagh went out I was left on the slip with a band of women and children, and one old boar who sat looking out over the sea.

The women were over-excited, and when I tried to talk to them they crowded round me and began jeering and shrieking at me because I am not married. A dozen screamed at a time, and so rapidly that I could not understand all they were saying, yet I was able to make out that they were taking advantage of the absence of their husbands to give me the full volume of their contempt. Some little boys who were listening threw themselves down, writhing with laughter among the seaweed, and the young girls grew red with embarrassment and stared down into the surf.

For a moment I was in confusion. I tried to speak to them, but I could not make myself heard, so I sat down on the slip and drew out my wallet of photographs. In an instant I had the whole band clambering round me, in their ordinary mood.

When the curaghs came back—one of them towing a large kitchen table that stood itself up on the waves and then turned somersaults in an extraordinary manner —word went round that the ceannuighe (pedlar) was arriving.

He opened his wares on the slip as soon as he landed, and sold a quantity of cheap knives and jewellery to the girls and younger women. He spoke no Irish, and the bargaining gave immense amusement to the crowd that collected round him.

I was surprised to notice that several women who professed to know no English could make themselves understood without difficulty when it pleased them.

'The rings is too dear at you, sir,' said one girl using the Gaelic construction; 'let you put less money on them and all the girls will be buying.'

After the jewellery he displayed some cheap religious pictures—abominable oleographs—but I did not see many buyers.

I am told that most of the pedlars who come here are Germans or Poles, but I did not have occasion to speak with this man by himself.

I have come over for a few days to the south island, and, as usual, my voyage was not favourable.

The morning was fine, and seemed to promise one of the peculiarly hushed, pellucid days that occur sometimes before rain in early winter. From the first gleam of dawn the sky was covered with white cloud, and the tranquillity was so complete that every sound seemed to float away by itself across the silence of the bay. Lines of blue smoke were going up in spirals over the village, and further off heavy fragments of rain-cloud were lying on the horizon. We started early in the day, and, although the sea looked calm from a distance, we met a considerable roll coming from the south-west when we got out from the shore.

Near the middle of the sound the man who was rowing in the bow broke his oar-pin, and the proper management of the canoe became a matter of some difficulty. We had only a three-oared curagh, and if the sea had gone much higher we should have run a good deal of danger. Our progress was so slow that clouds came up with a rise in the wind before we reached the shore, and rain began to fall in large single drops. The black curagh working slowly through this world of grey, and the soft hissing of the rain gave me one of the moods in which we realise with immense distress the short moment we have left us to experience all the wonder and beauty of the world.

The approach to the south island is made at a fine sandy beach on the north-west. This interval in the rocks is of great service to the people, but the tract of wet sand with a few hideous fishermen's houses, lately built on it, looks singularly desolate in broken weather.

The tide was going out when we landed, so we merely stranded the curagh and went up to the little hotel. The cess-collector was at work in one of the rooms, and there were a number of men and boys waiting about, who stared at us while we stood at the door and talked to the proprietor.

When we had had our drink I went down to the sea with my men, who were in a hurry to be off. Some time was spent in replacing the oar-pin, and then they set out, though the wind was still increasing. A good many fishermen came down to see the start, and long after the curagh was out of sight I stood and talked with them in Irish, as I was anxious to compare their language and temperament with what I knew of the other island.

The language seems to be identical, though some of these men speak rather more distinctly than any Irish speakers I have yet heard. In physical type, dress, and general character, however, there seems to be a considerable difference. The people on this island are more advanced than their neighbours, and the families here are gradually forming into different ranks, made up of the well-to-do, the struggling, and the quite poor and thriftless. These distinctions are present in the middle island also, but over there they have had no effect on the people, among whom there is still absolute equality.

A little later the steamer came in sight and lay to in the offing. While the curaghs were being put out I noticed in the crowd several men of the ragged, humorous type that was once thought to represent the real peasant of Ireland. Rain was now falling heavily, and as we looked out through the fog there was something nearly appalling in the shrieks of laughter kept up by one of these individuals, a man of extraordinary ugliness and wit.

At last he moved off toward the houses, wiping his eyes with the tail of his coat and moaning to himself 'Tá mé marbh,' ('I'm killed'), till some one stopped him and he began again pouring out a medley of rude puns and jokes that meant more than they said.

There is quaint humour, and sometimes wild humour, on the middle island, but never this half-sensual ecstasy of laughter. Perhaps a man must have a sense of intimate

misery, not known there, before he can set himself to
jeer and mock at the world. These strange men with
receding foreheads, high cheekbones, and ungovernable
eyes seem to represent some old type found on these few
acres at the extreme border of Europe, where it is only in
wild jests and laughter that they can express their loneliness and desolation.

The mode of reciting ballads in this island is singularly harsh. I fell in with a curious man to-day beyond
the east village, and we wandered out on the rocks
towards the sea. A wintry shower came on while we
were together, and we crouched down in the bracken,
under a loose wall. When we had gone through the usual
topics he asked me if I was fond of songs, and began
singing to show what he could do.

The music was much like what I have heard before
on the islands—a monotonous chant with pauses on the
high and low notes to mark the rhythm; but the harsh
nasal tone in which he sang was almost intolerable. His
performance reminded me in general effect of a chant
I once heard from a party of Orientals I was travelling
with in a third-class carriage from Paris to Dieppe, but
the islander ran his voice over a much wider range.

His pronunciation was lost in the rasping of his throat,
and, though he shrieked into my ear to make sure that
I understood him above the howling of the wind, I could
only make out that it was an endless ballad telling the
fortune of a young man who went to sea, and had many
adventures. The English nautical terms were employed
continually in describing his life on the ship, but the man
seemed to feel that they were not in their place, and
stopped short when one of them occurred to give me a
poke with his finger and explain gib, topsail, and bow-

sprit, which were for me the most intelligible features of the poem. Again, when the scene changed to Dublin, 'glass of whiskey,' 'public-house,' and such things were in English.

When the shower was over he showed me a curious cave hidden among the cliffs, a short distance from the sea. On our way back he asked me the three questions I am met with on every side—whether I am a rich man, whether I am married, and whether I have ever seen a poorer place than these islands.

When he heard that I was not married he urged me to come back in the summer so that he might take me over in a curagh to the Spa in County Clare, where there is 'spree mor agus go leor ladies' ('a big spree and plenty of ladies').

Something about the man repelled me while I was with him, and though I was cordial and liberal he seemed to feel that I abhorred him. We arranged to meet again in the evening, but when I dragged myself with an inexplicable loathing to the place of meeting, there was no trace of him.

It is characteristic that this man, who is probably a drunkard and shebeener and certainly in penury, refused the chance of a shilling because he felt that I did not like him. He had a curiously mixed expression of hardness and melancholy. Probably his character has given him a bad reputation on the island, and he lives here with the restlessness of a man who has no sympathy with his companions.

I have come over again to Inishmaan, and this time I had fine weather for my passage. The air was full of luminous sunshine from the early morning, and it was almost a summer's day when I set sail at noon with Michael and two other men who had come over for me in a curagh.

The wind was in our favour, so the sail was put up and Michael sat in the stern to steer with an oar while I rowed with the others.

We had had a good dinner and drink and were wrought up by this sudden revival of summer to a dreamy voluptuous gaiety, that made us shout with exultation to hear our voices passing out across the blue twinkling of the sea.

Even after the people of the south island, these men of the Inishmaan seemed to be moved by strange archaic sympathies with the world. Their mood accorded itself with wonderful fineness to the suggestions of the day, and their ancient Gaelic seemed so full of divine simplicity that I would have liked to turn the prow to the west and row with them for ever.

I told them I was going back to Paris in a few days to sell my books and my bed, and that then I was coming back to grow as strong and simple as they were among the islands of the west.

When our excitement sobered down, Michael told me that one of the priests had left his gun at our cottage and given me leave to use it till he returned to the island. There was another gun and a ferret in the house also, and he said that as soon as we got home he was going to take me out fowling on rabbits.

A little later in the day we set off, and I nearly laughed to see Michael's eagerness that I should turn out a good shot.

We put the ferret down in a crevice between two bare sheets of rock, and waited. In a few minutes we heard rushing paws underneath us, then a rabbit shot up straight into the air from the crevice at our feet and set off for a wall that was a few feet away. I threw up the gun and fired.

'Buail tu é,' screamed Michael at my elbow as he ran up the rock. I had killed it.

We shot seven or eight more in the next hour, and Michael was immensely pleased. If I had done badly I think I should have had to leave the islands. The people would have despised me. A 'duine uasal' who cannot shoot seems to these descendants of hunters a fallen type who is worse than an apostate.

The women of this island are before conventionality, and share some of the liberal features that are thought peculiar to the women of Paris and New York.

Many of them are too contented and too sturdy to have more than a decorative interest, but there are others full of curious individuality.

This year I have got to know a wonderfully humorous girl, who has been spinning in the kitchen for the last few days with the old woman's spinning-wheel. The morning she began I heard her exquisite intonation almost before I awoke, brooding and cooing over every syllable she uttered.

I have heard something similar in the voices of German and Polish women, but I do not think men—at least European men—who are always further than women from the simple, animal emotions, or any speakers who use languages with weak gutturals, like French or English, can produce this inarticulate chant in their ordinary talk.

She plays continual tricks with her Gaelic in the way girls are fond of, piling up diminutives and repeating adjectives with a humorous scorn of syntax. While she is here the talk never stops in the kitchen. To-day she has been asking me many questions about Germany, for it seems one of her sisters married a German husband in America some years ago, who kept her in great comfort, with a fine 'capull glas' ('grey horse') to ride on, and this girl has decided to escape in the same way from the drudgery of the island.

This was my last evening on my stool in the chimney corner, and I had a long talk with some neighbours who came in to bid me prosperity, and lay about on the floor with their heads on low stools and their feet stretched out to the embers of the turf. The old woman was at the other side of the fire, and the girl I have spoken of was standing at her spinning-wheel, talking and joking with every one. She says when I go away now I am to marry a rich wife with plenty of money, and if she dies on me I am to come back here and marry herself for my second wife.

I have never heard talk so simple and so attractive as the talk of these people. This evening they began disputing about their wives, and it appeared that the greatest merit they see in a woman is that she should be fruitful and bring them many children. As no money can be earned by children on the island this one attitude shows the immense difference between these people and the people of Paris.

The direct sexual instincts are not weak on the island, but they are so subordinated to the instincts of the family that they rarely lead to irregularity. The life here is still at an almost patriarchal stage, and the people are nearly as far from the romantic moods of love as they are from the impulsive life of the savage.

The wind was so high this morning that there was some doubt whether the steamer would arrive, and I spent half the day wandering about with Michael watching the horizon.

At last, when we had given her up, she came in sight far away to the north, where she had gone to have the wind with her where the sea was at its highest.

I got my baggage from the cottage and set off for the slip with Michael and the old man, turning into a cottage here and there to say good-bye.

In spite of the wind outside, the sea at the slip was as calm as a pool. The men who were standing about while the steamer was at the south island wondered for the last time whether I would be married when I came back to see them. Then we pulled out and took our place in the line. As the tide was running hard the steamer stopped a certain distance from the shore, and gave us a long race for good places at her side. In the struggle we did not come off well, so I had to clamber across two curaghs, twisting and fumbling with the roll, in order to get on board.

It seemed strange to see the curaghs full of well-known faces turning back to the slip without me, but the roll in the sound soon took off my attention. Some men were on board whom I had seen on the south island, and a good many Kilronan people on their way home from Galway, who told me that in one part of their passage in the morning they had come in for heavy seas.

As is usual on Saturday, the steamer had a large cargo of flour and porter to discharge at Kilronan, and, as it was nearly four o'clock before the tide could float her at the pier, I felt some doubt about our passage to Galway.

The wind increased as the afternoon went on, and when I came down in the twilight I found that the cargo was not yet all unladen, and that the captain feared to face the gale that was rising. It was some time before he came to a final decision, and we walked backwards and forwards from the village with heavy clouds flying overhead and the wind howling in the walls. At last he telegraphed to Galway to know if he was wanted the next day, and we went into a public-house to wait for the reply.

The kitchen was filled with men sitting closely on long forms ranged in lines at each side of the fire. A wild-looking but beautiful girl was kneeling on the hearth talking loudly to the men, and a few natives of Inishmaan were hanging about the door, miserably drunk. At the end of the kitchen the bar was arranged, with a sort of alcove beside it, where some older men were playing cards. Overhead there were the open rafters, filled with turf and tobacco smoke.

This is the haunt so much dreaded by the women of the other islands, where the men linger with their money till they go out at last with reeling steps and are lost in the sound. Without this background of empty curaghs, and bodies floating naked with the tide, there would be something almost absurd about the dissipation of this simple place where men sit, evening after evening, drinking bad whiskey and porter, and talking with endless repetition of fishing, and kelp, and of the sorrows of purgatory.

When we had finished our whiskey word came that the boat might remain.

With some difficulty I got my bags out of the steamer and carried them up through the crowd of women and donkeys that were still struggling on the quay in an inconceivable medley of flour-bags and cases of petroleum. When I reached the inn the old woman was in great good humour, and I spent some time talking by the

kitchen fire. Then I groped my way back to the harbour, where, I was told, the old net-mender, who came
to see me on my first visit to the islands, was spending
the night as watchman.

It was quite dark on the pier, and a terrible gale was
blowing. There was no one in the little office where I
expected to find him, so I groped my way further on
towards a figure I saw moving with a lantern.

It was the old man, and he remembered me at once
when I hailed him and told him who I was. He spent
some time arranging one of his lanterns, and then he
took me back to his office—a mere shed of planks and
corrugated iron, put up for the contractor of some work
which is in progress on the pier.

When we reached the light I saw that his head was
rolled up in an extraordinary collection of mufflers to
keep him from the cold, and that his face was much
older than when I saw him before, though still full of
intelligence.

He began to tell how he had gone to see a relative of
mine in Dublin when he first left the island as a cabin-
boy, between forty and fifty years ago.

He told his story with the usual detail:—

We saw a man walking about on the quay in Dublin,
and looking at us without saying a word. Then he came
down to the yacht.

'Are you the men from Aran?' said he.

'We are,' said we.

'You're to come with me so,' said he.

'Why?' said we.

Then he told us it was Mr. Synge had sent him and
we went with him. Mr. Synge brought us into his kitchen
and gave the men a glass of whiskey all round, and a half-

glass to me because I was a boy—though at that time and to this day I can drink as much as two men and not be the worse of it. We were some time in the kitchen, then one of the men said we should be going. I said it would not be right to go without saying a word to Mr. Synge. Then the servant-girl went up and brought him down, and he gave us another glass of whiskey, and he gave me a book in Irish because I was going to sea, and I was able to read in the Irish.

I owe it to Mr. Synge and that book that when I came back here, after not hearing a word of Irish for thirty years, I had as good Irish, or maybe better Irish, than any person on the island.

I could see all through his talk that the sense of superiority which his scholarship in this little-known language gave him above the ordinary seaman, had influenced his whole personality and been the central interest of his life.

On one voyage he had a fellow-sailor who often boasted that he had been at school and learned Greek, and this incident took place:—

One night we had a quarrel, and I asked him could he read a Greek book with all his talk of it.

'I can so,' said he.

'We'll see that,' said I.

Then I got the Irish book out of my chest, and I gave it into his hand.

'Read that to me,' said I, 'if you know Greek.'

He took it, and he looked at it this way, and that way, and not a bit of him could make it out.

'Bedad, I've forgotten my Greek,' said he.

'You're telling a lie,' said I.

'I'm not,' said he; 'it's the divil a bit I can read it.'

Then I took the book back into my hand, and said to him—

'It's the sorra a word of Greek you ever knew in your life, for there's not a word of Greek in that book, and not a bit of you knew.'

He told me another story of the only time he had heard Irish spoken during his voyages:—

One night I was in New York, walking in the streets with some other men, and we came upon two women quarrelling in Irish at the door of a public-house.

'What's that jargon?' said one of the men.

'It's no jargon,' said I.

'What is it?' said he.

'It's Irish,' said I.

Then I went up to them, and you know, sir, there is no language like the Irish for soothing and quieting. The moment I spoke to them they stopped scratching and swearing and stood there as quiet as two lambs.

Then they asked me in Irish if I wouldn't come in and have a drink, and I said I couldn't leave my mates.

'Bring them too,' said they.

Then we all had a drop together.

While we were talking another man had slipped in and sat down in the corner with his pipe, and the rain had become so heavy we could hardly hear our voices over the noise on the iron roof.

The old man went on telling of his experiences at sea and the places he had been to.

'If I had my life to live over again,' he said, 'there's no other way I'd spend it. I went in and out everywhere and saw everything. I was never afraid to take my glass, though I was never drunk in my life, and I was a great player of cards though I never played for money.'

'There's no diversion at all in cards if you don't play for money,' said the man in the corner.

'There was no use in my playing for money,' said the old man, 'for I'd always lose, and what's the use in playing if you always lose?'

Then our conversation branched off to the Irish language and the books written in it.

He began to criticise Archbishop MacHale's version of *Moore's Irish Melodies* with great severity and acuteness, citing whole poems both in the English and Irish, and then giving versions that he had made himself.

'A translation is no translation,' he said, 'unless it will give you the music of a poem along with the words of it. In my translation you won't find a foot or a syllable that's not in the English, yet I've put down all his words mean, and nothing but it. Archbishop MacHale's work is a most miserable production.'

From the verses he cited his judgment seemed perfectly justified, and even if he was wrong, it is interesting to note that this poor sailor and night-watchman was ready to rise up and criticise an eminent dignitary and scholar on rather delicate points of versification and the finer distinctions between old words of Gaelic.

In spite of his singular intelligence and minute observation his reasoning was mediæval.

I asked him what he thought about the future of the language on these islands.

'It can never die out,' said he, 'because there's no family in the place can live without a bit of a field for potatoes, and they have only the Irish words for all that they do in the fields. They sail their new boats—their hookers—in English, but they sail a curagh oftener in

Irish, and in the fields they have the Irish alone. It can never die out, and when the people begin to see it fallen very low, it will rise up again like the Phœnix from its own ashes.'

'And the Gaelic League?' I asked him.

'The Gaelic League! Didn't they come down here with their organisers and their secretaries, and their meetings and their speechifyings, and start a branch of it, and teach a power of Irish for five weeks and a half!'[1]

'What do we want here with their teaching Irish?' said the man in the corner; 'haven't we Irish enough?'

'You have not,' said the old man; 'there's not a soul in Aran can count up to nine hundred and ninety-nine without using an English word but myself.'

It was getting late, and the rain had lessened for a moment, so I groped my way back to the inn through the intense darkness of a late autumn night.

[1] This was written, it should be remembered, some years ago.

PART IV

No TWO journeys to these islands are alike. This morning I sail with the steamer a little after five o'clock in a cold night air, with the stars shining on the bay. A number of Claddagh fishermen had been out all night fishing not far from the harbour, and without thinking, or perhaps caring to think, of the steamer, they had put out their nets in the channel where she was to pass. Just before we started the mate sounded the steam whistle repeatedly to give them warning, saying as he did so—

'If you were out now in the bay, gentlemen, you'd hear some fine prayers being said.'

When we had gone a little way we began to see the light from the turf fires carried by the fishermen flickering on the water, and to hear a faint noise of angry voices. Then the outline of a large fishing-boat came in sight through the darkness, with the forms of three men who stood on the course. The captain feared to turn aside, as there are sandbanks near the channel, so the engines were stopped and we glided over the nets without doing them harm. As we passed close to the boat the crew could be seen plainly on the deck, one of them holding the bucket of red turf, and their abuse could be distinctly heard. It changed continually, from profuse Gaelic maledictions to the simpler curses they know in English. As they spoke they could be seen writhing and twisting themselves with passion against the light which was beginning to turn on the ripple of the sea. Soon afterwards another set of voices began in front of us, breaking out in strange contrast with the dwindling stars and the silence of the dawn.

Further on we passed many boats that let us go by

without a word, as their nets were not in the channel. Then day came on rapidly with cold showers that turned golden in the first rays from the sun, filling the troughs of the sea with curious transparencies and light.

This year I have brought my fiddle with me so that I may have something new to keep up the interest of the people. I have played for them several tunes, but as far as I can judge they do not feel modern music, though they listen eagerly from curiosity. Irish airs like 'Eileen Aroon' please them better, but it is only when I play some jig like the 'Black Rogue'—which is known on the island—that they seem to respond to the full meaning of the notes. Last night I played for a large crowd, which had come together for another purpose from all parts of the island.

About six o'clock I was going into the schoolmaster's house, and I heard a fierce wrangle going on between a man and a woman near the cottages to the west, that lie below the road. While I was listening to them several women came down to listen also from behind the wall, and told me that the people who were fighting were near relations who lived side by side and often quarrelled about trifles, though they were as good friends as ever the next day. The voices sounded so enraged that I thought mischief would come of it, but the women laughed at the idea. Then a lull came, and I said that they seemed to have finished at last.

'Finished!' said one of the women; 'sure they haven't rightly begun. It's only playing they are yet.'

It was just after sunset and the evening was bitterly cold, so I went into the house and left them.

An hour later the old man came down from my cottage to say that some of the lads and the 'fear lionta'

('the man of the nets'—a young man from Aranmor
who is teaching net-mending to the boys) were up at
the house, and had sent him down to tell me they would
like to dance, if I would come up and play for them.

I went out at once, and as soon as I came into the air
I heard the dispute going on still to the west more violently than ever. The news of it had gone about the
island, and little bands of girls and boys were running
along the lanes towards the scene of the quarrel as
eagerly as if they were going to a racecourse. I stopped
for a few minutes at the door of our cottage to listen to
the volume of abuse that was rising across the stillness of
the island. Then I went into the kitchen and began tun-
ing the fiddle, as the boys were impatient for my music.
At first I tried to play standing, but on the upward stroke
my bow came in contact with the salt-fish and oilskins
that hung from the rafters, so I settled myself at last on
a table in the corner, where I was out of the way, and
got one of the people to hold up my music before me, as
I had no stand. I played a French melody first, to get
myself used to the people and the qualities of the room,
which has little resonance between the earth floor and
the thatch overhead. Then I struck up the 'Black
Rogue,' and in a moment a tall man bounded out from
his stool under the chimney and began flying round the
kitchen with peculiarly sure and graceful bravado.

The lightness of the pampooties seems to make the
dancing on this island lighter and swifter than anything
I have seen on the mainland, and the simplicity of the
men enables them to throw a naïve extravagance into
their steps that is impossible in places where the people
are self-conscious.

The speed, however, was so violent that I had some
difficulty in keeping up, as my fingers were not in prac-

tice, and I could not take off more than a small part of my attention to watch what was going on. When I finished I heard a commotion at the door, and the whole body of people who had gone down to watch the quarrel filed into the kitchen and arranged themselves around the walls, the women and girls, as is usual, forming themselves in one compact mass crouching on their heels near the door.

I struck up another dance—'Paddy get up'—and the 'fear lionta' and the first dancer went through it together, with additional rapidity and grace, as they were excited by the presence of the people who had come in. Then word went round that an old man, known as Little Roger, was outside, and they told me he was once the best dancer on the island.

For a long time he refused to come in, for he said he was too old to dance, but at last he was persuaded, and the people brought him in and gave him a stool opposite me. It was some time longer before he would take his turn, and when he did so, though he was met with great clapping of hands, he only danced for a few moments. He did not know the dances in my book, he said, and did not care to dance to music he was not familiar with. When the people pressed him again he looked across to me.

'John,' he said, in shaking English, 'have you got "Larry Grogan," for it is an agreeable air?'

I had not, so some of the young men danced again to the 'Black Rogue,' and then the party broke up. The altercation was still going on at the cottage below us, and the people were anxious to see what was coming of it.

About ten o'clock a young man came in and told us that the fight was over.

'They have been at it for four hours,' he said, 'and

now they're tired. Indeed it is time they were, for you'd rather be listening to a man killing a pig than to the noise they were letting out of them.'

After the dancing and excitement we were too stirred up to be sleepy, so we sat for a long time round the embers of the turf, talking and smoking by the light of the candle.

From ordinary music we came to talk of the music or the fairies, and they told me this story, when I had told them some stories of my own:—

A man who lives in the other end of the village got his gun one day and went out to look for rabbits in a thicket near the small Dun. He saw a rabbit sitting up under a tree, and he lifted his gun to take aim at it, but just as he had it covered he heard a kind of music over his head, and he looked up into the sky. When he looked back for the rabbit, not a bit of it was to be seen.

He went on after that, and he heard the music again.

Then he looked over a wall, and he saw a rabbit sitting up by the wall with a sort of flute in its mouth, and it playing on it with its two fingers!

'What sort of rabbit was that?' said the old woman when they had finished. 'How could that be a right rabbit? I remember old Pat Dirane used to be telling us he was once out on the cliffs, and he saw a big rabbit sitting down in a hole under a flagstone. He called a man who was with him, and they put a hook on the end of a stick and ran it down into the hole. Then a voice called up to them—

' "Ah, Phaddrick, don't hurt me with the hook!" '

'Pat was a great rogue,' said the old man. 'Maybe you remember the bits of horns he had like handles on the end of his sticks? Well, one day there was a priest over and he said to Pat—

' "Is it the devil's horns you have on your sticks, Pat?"

' "I don't rightly know," said Pat, "but if it is, it's the devil's milk you've been drinking, since you've been able to drink, and the devil's flesh you've been eating and the devil's butter you've been putting on your bread, for I've seen the like of them horns on every old cow through the country." '

The weather has been rough, but early this afternoon the sea was calm enough for a hooker to come in with turf from Connemara, though while she was at the pier the roll was so great that the men had to keep a watch on the waves and loosen the cable whenever a large one was coming in, so that she might ease up with the water.

There were only two men on board, and when she was empty they had some trouble in dragging in the cables, hoisting the sails, and getting out of the harbour before they could be blown on the rocks.

A heavy shower came on soon afterwards, and I lay down under a stack of turf with some people who were standing about, to wait for another hooker that was coming in with horses. They began talking and laughing about the dispute last night and the noise made at it.

'The worst fights do be made here over nothing,' said an old man next me. 'Did Mourteen or any of them on the big island ever tell you of the fight they had there three-score years ago when they were killing each other with knives out on the strand?'

'They never told me,' I said.

'Well,' said he, 'they were going down to cut weed, and a man was sharpening his knife on a stone before he

went. A young boy came into the kitchen, and he said to
the man—

' "What are you sharpening that knife for?"

' "To kill your father with," said the man, and they
the best of friends all the time. The young boy went back
to his house and told his father there was a man sharpening a knife to kill him.

' "Bedad," said the father, "if he has a knife I'll have
one too."

'He sharpened his knife after that, and they went
down to the strand. Then the two men began making
fun about their knives, and from that they began raising
their voices, and it wasn't long before there were ten
men fighting with their knives, and they never stopped
till there were five of them dead.

'They buried them the day after, and when they were
coming home, what did they see but the boy who began
the work playing about with the son of the other man,
and their two fathers down in their graves.'

When he stopped, a gust of wind came and blew up a
bundle of dry seaweed that was near us, right over our
heads.

Another old man began to talk.

'That was a great wind,' he said. 'I remember one
time there was a man in the south island who had a lot
of wool up in shelter against the corner of a wall. He
was after washing it, and drying it, and turning it, and
he had it all nice and clean the way they could card it.
Then a wind came down and the wool began blowing
all over the wall. The man was throwing out his arms
on it and trying to stop it, and another man saw him.

' "The devil mend your head!" says he, "the like of
that wind is too strong for you."

' "If the devil himself is in it," said the other man, "I'll hold on to it while I can."

'Then whether it was because of the word or not I don't know, but the whole of the wool went up over his head and blew all over the island, yet, when his wife came to spin afterwards she had all they expected, as if that lot was not lost on them at all.'

'There was more than that in it,' said another man, 'for the night before a woman had a great sight out to the west in this island, and saw all the people that were dead a while back in this island and the south island, and they all talking with each other. There was a man over from the other island that night, and he heard the woman talking of what she had seen. The next day he went back to the south island, and I think he was alone in the curagh. As soon as he came near the other island he saw a man fishing from the cliffs, and this man called out to him—

' "Make haste now and go up and tell your mother to hide the poteen"—his mother used to sell poteen—"for I'm after seeing the biggest party of peelers and yeomanry passing by on the rocks was ever seen on the island." It was at that time the wool was taken with the other man above, under the hill, and no peelers in the island at all.'

A little after that the old men went away, and I was left with some young men between twenty and thirty, who talked to me of different things. One of them asked me if ever I was drunk, and another told me I would be right to marry a girl out of this island, for they were nice women in it, fine fat girls, who would be strong, and have plenty of children, and not be wasting my money on me.

When the horses were coming ashore a curagh that was far out after lobster-pots came hurrying in, and a man out of her ran up the sandhills to meet a little girl who was coming down with a bundle of Sunday clothes. He changed on the sand and then went out to the hooker, and went off to Connemara to bring back his horses.

A young married woman I used often to talk with is dying of a fever—typhus I am told—and her husband and brothers have gone off in a curagh to get the doctor and the priest from the north island, though the sea is rough.

I watched them from the Dun for a long time after they had started. Wind and rain were driving through the sound, and I could see no boats or people anywhere except this one black curagh splashing and struggling through the waves. When the wind fell a little I could hear people hammering below me to the east. The body of a young man who was drowned a few weeks ago came ashore this morning, and his friends have been busy all day making a coffin in the yard of the house where he lived.

After a while the curagh went out of sight into the mist, and I came down to the cottage shuddering with cold and misery.

The old woman was keening by the fire.

'I have been to the house where the young man is,' she said, 'but I couldn't go to the door with the air was coming out of it. They say his head isn't on him at all, and indeed it isn't any wonder and he three weeks in the sea. Isn't it great danger and sorrow is over every one on this island?'

I asked her if the curagh would soon be coming back with the priest.

'It will not be coming soon or at all to-night,' she said. 'The wind has gone up now, and there will come no curagh to this island for maybe two days or three. And wasn't it a cruel thing to see the haste was on them, and they in danger all the time to be drowned themselves?'

Then I asked her how the woman was doing.

'She's nearly lost,' said the old woman; 'she won't be alive at all to-morrow morning. They have no boards to make her a coffin, and they'll want to borrow the boards that a man below has had this two years to bury his mother, and she alive still. I heard them saying there are two more women with the fever, and a child that's not three. The Lord have mercy on us all!'

I went out again to look over the sea, but night had fallen and the hurricane was howling over the Dun. I walked down the lane and heard the keening in the house where the young man was. Further on I could see a stir about the door of the cottage that had been last struck by typhus. Then I turned back again in the teeth of the rain, and sat over the fire with the old man and woman talking of the sorrows of the people till it was late in the night.

This evening the old man told me a story he had heard long ago on the mainland:—

There was a young woman, he said, and she had a child. In a little time the woman died and they buried her the day after. That night another woman—a woman of the family—was sitting by the fire with the child on her lap, giving milk to it out of a cup. Then the woman they were after burying opened the door, and came into the house. She went over to the fire, and she took a stool and sat down before the other woman. Then she put out her hand and took the child on her lap, and gave it her breast. After that she put the child in the cradle and went over to the dresser and took milk and potatoes off it, and ate them. Then she went out. The other woman was frightened, and she told the man of the house when he came back, and two young men. They said they would be there the next night, and if she came back they would catch hold of her. She came the next night and gave the child her breast, and when she got up to go to the dresser, the man of the house caught hold of her, but he fell down on the floor. Then the two young men caught hold of her and they held her. She told them she was away with the fairies, and they could not keep her that night, though she was eating no food with the fairies, the way she might be able to come back to her child. Then she told them they would all be leaving that part of the country on the Oidhche Shamhna, and that there would be four or five hundred of them riding on horses, and herself would be on a grey horse, riding behind a young man. And she told them to go down to a bridge they would be crossing that night, and to wait at the head of it, and when she would be coming up she would slow the horse and they would be able to throw something on her and on the young man, and they would fall over on the ground and be saved.

She went away then, and on the Oidhche Shamhna the men went down and got her back. She had four children after that, and in the end she died.

It was not herself they buried at all the first time, but some old thing the fairies put in her place.

'There are people who say they don't believe in these things,' said the old woman, 'but there are strange things, let them say what they will. There was a woman

went to bed at the lower village a while ago, and her
child along with her. For a time they did not sleep, and
then something came to the window, and they heard a
voice and this is what it said—

' "It is time to sleep from this out."

'In the morning the child was dead, and indeed it is
many get their death that way on the island.'

The young man has been buried, and his funeral was
one of the strangest scenes I have met with. People
could be seen going down to his house from early in the
day, yet when I went there with the old man about the
middle of the afternoon, the coffin was still lying in front
of the door, with the men and women of the family
standing round beating it, and keening over it, in a great
crowd of people. A little later every one knelt down and
a last prayer was said. Then the cousins of the dead man
got ready two oars and some pieces of rope—the men of
his own family seemed too broken with grief to know
what they were doing—the coffin was tied up, and the
procession began. The old woman walked close behind
the coffin, and I happened to take a place just after them,
among the first of the men. The rough lane to the graveyard slopes away towards the east, and the crowd of
women going down before me in their red dresses,
cloaked with red petticoats, with the waistband that is
held round the head just seen from behind, had a strange
effect, to which the white coffin and the unity of colour
gave a nearly cloistral quietness.

This time the graveyard was filled with withered
grass and bracken instead of the early ferns that were to
be seen everywhere at the other funeral I have spoken
of, and the grief of the people was of a different kind, as
they had come to bury a young man who had died in his

first manhood, instead of an old woman of eighty. For this reason the keen lost a part of its formal nature, and was recited as the expression of intense personal grief by the young men and women of the man's own family.

When the coffin had been laid down, near the grave that was to be opened, two long switches were cut out from the brambles among the rocks, and the length and breadth of the coffin were marked on them. Then the men began their work, clearing off stones and thin layers of earth, and breaking up an old coffin that was in the place into which the new one had to be lowered. When a number of blackened boards and pieces of bone had been thrown up with the clay, a skull was lifted out, and placed upon a gravestone. Immediately the old woman, the mother of the dead man, took it up in her hands, and carried it away by herself. Then she sat down and put it in her lap—it was the skull of her own mother—and began keening and shrieking over it with the wildest lamentation.

As the pile of mouldering clay got higher beside the grave a heavy smell began to rise from it, and the men hurried with their work, measuring the hole repeatedly with the two rods of bramble. When it was nearly deep enough the old woman got up and came back to the coffin, and began to beat on it, holding the skull in her left hand. This last moment of grief was the most terrible of all. The young women were nearly lying among the stones, worn out with their passion of grief, yet raising themselves every few moments to beat with magnificent gestures on the boards of the coffin. The young men were worn out also, and their voices cracked continually in the wail of the keen.

When everything was ready the sheet was unpinned from the coffin, and it was lowered into its place. Then an old man took a wooden vessel with holy water in it, and a wisp of bracken, and the people crowded round him while he splashed the water over them. They seemed eager to get as much of it as possible, more than one old woman crying out with a humorous voice—

'Tabhair dham braon eile, a Mhourteen.' ('Give me another drop, Martin.')

When the grave was half filled in, I wandered round towards the north watching two seals that were chasing each other near the surf. I reached the Sandy Head as the light began to fail, and found some of the men I knew best fishing there with a sort of dragnet. It is a tedious process, and I sat for a long time on the sand watching the net being put out, and then drawn in again by eight men working together with a slow rhythmical movement.

As they talked to me and gave me a little poteen and a little bread when they thought I was hungry, I could not help feeling that I was talking with men who were under a judgment of death. I knew that every one of them would be drowned in the sea in a few years and battered naked on the rocks, or would die in his own cottage and be buried with another fearful scene in the graveyard I had come from.

When I got up this morning I found that the people had gone to Mass and latched the kitchen door from the outside, so that I could not open it to give myself light.

I sat for nearly an hour beside the fire with a curious feeling that I should be quite alone in this little cottage. I am so used to sitting here with the people that I have never felt the room before as a place where any man might live and work by himself. After a while as I waited, with just light enough from the chimney to let

me see the rafters and the greyness of the walls, I became
indescribably mournful, for I felt that this little corner
on the face of the world, and the people who live in it,
have a peace and dignity from which we are shut for
ever.

While I was dreaming, the old woman came in in a
great hurry and made tea for me and the young priest,
who followed her a little later drenched with rain and
spray.

The curate who has charge of the middle and south
islands has a wearisome and dangerous task. He comes
to this island or Inishere on Saturday night—whenever
the sea is calm enough—and has Mass the first thing on
Sunday morning. Then he goes down fasting and is
rowed across to the other island and has Mass again, so
that it is about midday when he gets a hurried breakfast
before he sets off again for Aranmore, meeting often on
both passages a rough and perilous sea.

A couple of Sundays ago I was lying outside the cottage in the sunshine smoking my pipe, when the curate,
a man of the greatest kindliness and humour, came up,
wet and worn out, to have his first meal. He looked at
me for a moment and then shook his head.

'Tell me,' he said, 'did you read your Bible this morning?'

I answered that I had not done so.

'Well, begob, Mr. Synge,' he went on, 'if you ever
go to Heaven, you'll have a great laugh at us.'

Although these people are kindly towards each other
and to their children, they have no feeling for the suf-
ferings of animals, and little sympathy for pain when the
person who feels it is not in danger. I have sometimes
seen a girl writhing and howling with toothache while

her mother sat at the other side of the fireplace pointing at her and laughing at her as if amused by the sight.

A few days ago, when we had been talking of the death of President McKinley, I explained the American way of killing murderers, and a man asked me how long the man who killed the President would be dying.

'While you'd be snapping your fingers,' I said.

'Well,' said the man, 'they might as well hang him so, and not be bothering themselves with all them wires. A man who would kill a King or a President knows he has to die for it, and it's only giving him the thing he bargained for if he dies easy. It would be right he should be three weeks dying, and there'd be fewer of those things done in the world.'

If two dogs fight at the slip when we are waiting for the steamer, the men are delighted and do all they can to keep up the fury of the battle.

They tie down donkeys' heads to their hoofs to keep them from straying, in a way that must cause horrible pain, and sometimes when I go into a cottage I find all the women of the place down on their knees plucking the feathers from live ducks and geese.

When the people are in pain themselves they make no attempt to hide or control their feelings. An old man who was ill in the winter took me out the other day to show me how far down the road they could hear him yelling 'the time he had a pain in his head.'

There was a great storm this morning, and I went up on the cliff to sit in the shanty they have made there for the men who watch for wrack. Soon afterwards a boy, who was out minding sheep, came up from the west, and we had a long talk.

He began by giving me the first connected account I

have had of the accident that happened some time ago, when the young man was drowned on his way to the south island.

'Some men from the south island,' he said, 'came over and bought some horses on this island, and they put them in a hooker to take across. They wanted a curagh to go with them to tow the horses on to the strand, and a young man said he would go, and they could give him a rope and tow him behind the hooker. When they were out in the sound a wind came down on them, and the man in the curagh couldn't turn her to meet the waves, because the hooker was pulling her and she began filling up with water.

'When the men in the hooker saw it they began crying out one thing and another thing without knowing what to do. One man called out to the man who was holding the rope: "Let go the rope now, or you'll swamp her."

'And the man with the rope threw it out on the water, and the curagh half-filled already, and I think only one oar in her. A wave came into her then, and she went down before them, and the young man began swimming about; then they let fall the sails in the hooker the way they could pick him up. And when they had them down they were too far off, and they pulled the sails up again the way they could tack back to him. He was there in the water swimming round, and swimming round, and before they got up with him again he sank the third time, and they didn't see any more of him.'

I asked if anyone had seen him on the island since he was dead.

'They have not,' he said, 'but there were queer things in it. Before he went out on the sea that day his dog came up and sat beside him on the rocks, and began crying.

When the horses were coming down to the slip an old woman saw her son, that was drowned a while ago, riding on one of them. She didn't say what she was after seeing, and this man caught the horse, he caught his own horse first, and then he caught this one, and after that he went out and was drowned. Two days after I dreamed they found him on the Ceann gaine (the Sandy Head) and carried him up to the house on the plain, and took his pampooties off him and hung them up on a nail to dry. It was there they found him afterwards as you'll have heard them say.'

'Are you always afraid when you hear a dog crying?' I said.

'We don't like it,' he answered; 'you will often see them on the top of the rocks looking up into the heavens, and they crying. We don't like it at all, and we don't like a cock or hen to break anything in the house, for we know then some one will be going away. A while before the man who used to live in that cottage below died in the winter, the cock belonging to his wife began to fight with another cock. The two of them flew up on the dresser and knocked the glass of the lamp off it, and it fell on the floor and was broken. The woman caught her cock after that and killed it, but she could not kill the other cock, for it was belonging to the man who lived in the next house. Then himself got a sickness and died after that.'

I asked him if he ever heard the fairy music on the island.

'I heard some of the boys talking in the school a while ago,' he said, 'and they were saying that their brothers and another man went out fishing a morning, two weeks ago, before the cock crew. When they were down near the Sandy Head they heard music near them, and it was the fairies were in it. I've heard of other things too. One time three men were out at night in a curagh, and they saw a big ship coming down on them. They were frightened at it, and they tried to get away, but it came on nearer them, till one of the men turned round and made the sign of the cross, and then they didn't see it any more.'

Then he went on in answer to another question:

'We do often see the people who do be away with them. There was a young man died a year ago, and he used to come to the window of the house where his brothers slept, and be talking to them in the night. He was married a while before that, and he used to be saying in the night he was sorry he had not promised the land to his son, and that it was to him it should go. Another time he was saying something about a mare, about her hoofs, or the shoes they should put on her. A little while ago Patch Ruadh saw him going down the road with broga arda (leather boots) on him and a new suit. Then two men saw him in another place.

'Do you see that straight wall of cliff?' he went on a few minutes later, pointing to a place below us. 'It is there the fairies do be playing ball in the night, and you can see the marks of their heels when you come in the morning, and three stones they have to mark the line, and another big stone they hop the ball on. It's often the boys have put away the three stones, and they will always be back again in the morning, and a while since the man who owns the land took the big stone itself and rolled it down and threw it over the cliff, yet in the morning it was back in its place before him.'

I am in the south island again, and I have come upon some old men with a wonderful variety of stories and

songs, the last, fairly often, both in English and Irish. I
went round to the house of one of them to-day, with a
native scholar who can write Irish, and we took down a
certain number, and heard others. Here is one of the
tales the old man told us at first before he had warmed
to his subject. I did not take it down, but it ran in this
way:—

There was a man of the name of Charley Lambert,
and every horse he would ride in a race he would come
in the first.

The people in the country were angry with him at
last, and this law was made, that he should ride no more
at races, and if he rode, any one who saw him would
have the right to shoot him. After that there was a gentleman from that part of the country over in England,
and he was talking one day with the people there, and he
said that the horses of Ireland were the best horses. The
English said it was the English horses were the best, and
at last they said there should be a race, and the English
horses would come over and race against the horses of
Ireland, and the gentleman put all his money on that
race.

Well, when he came back to Ireland he went to
Charley Lambert, and asked him to ride on his horse.
Charley said he would not ride, and told the gentleman
the danger he'd be in. Then the gentleman told him the
way he had put all his property on the horse, and at last
Charley asked where the races were to be, and the hour
and the day. The gentleman told him.

'Let you put a horse with a bridle and saddle on it
every seven miles along the road from here to the racecourse on that day,' said Lambert, 'and I'll be in it.'

When the gentleman was gone, Charley stripped off

his clothes and got into his bed. Then he sent for the doctor, and when he heard him coming he began throwing about his arms the way the doctor would think his pulse was up with the fever.

The doctor felt his pulse and told him to stay quiet till the next day, when he would see him again.

The next day it was the same thing, and so on till the day of the races. That morning Charley had his pulse beating so hard the doctor thought bad of him.

'I'm going to the races now, Charley,' said he, 'but I'll come in and see you again when I'll be coming back in the evening, and let you be very careful and quiet till you see me.'

As soon as he had gone Charley leapt up out of bed and got on his horse, and rode seven miles to where the first horse was waiting for him. Then he rode that horse seven miles, and another horse seven miles more, till he came to the racecourse.

He rode on the gentleman's horse and he won the race.

There were great crowds looking on, and when they saw him coming in they said it was Charley Lambert, or the devil was in it, for there was no one else could bring in a horse the way he did, for the leg was after being knocked off of the horse and he came in all the same.

When the race was over, he got up on the horse was waiting for him, and away with him for seven miles. Then he rode the other horse seven miles, and his own horse seven miles, and when he got home he threw off his clothes and lay down on his bed.

After a while the doctor came back and said it was a great race they were after having.

The next day the people were saying it was Charley Lambert was the man who rode the horse. An inquiry

was held, and the doctor swore that Charley was ill in
his bed, and he had seen him before the race and after it,
so the gentleman saved his fortune.

After that he told me another story of the same sort
about a fairy rider, who met a gentleman that was after
losing all his fortune but a shilling, and begged the shilling of him. The gentleman gave him the shilling, and
the fairy rider—a little red man—rode a horse for him
in a race, waving a red handkerchief to him as a signal
when he was to double the stakes, and made him a rich
man.

Then he gave us an extraordinary English doggerel
rhyme which I took down, though it seems singularly
incoherent when written out at length. These rhymes
are repeated by the old men as a sort of chant, and when
a line comes that is more than usually irregular they
seem to take a real delight in forcing it into the mould
of the recitative. All the time he was chanting the old
man kept up a kind of snakelike movement in his body,
which seemed to fit the chant and make it part of him.

THE WHITE HORSE

My horse he is white,
Though at first he was bay,
And he took great delight
In travelling by night
And by day.

His travels were great
If I could but half of them tell,
He was rode in the garden by Adam,
The day that he fell.

On Babylon plains
He ran with speed for the plate,
He was hunted next day
By Hannibal the great.

After that he was hunted
In the chase of a fox,
When Nebuchadnezzar ate grass,
In the shape of an ox.

We are told in the next verses of his going into the ark
with Noah, of Moses riding him through the Red Sea;
then

He was with king Pharaoh in Egypt
When fortune did smile,
And he rode him stately along
The gay banks of the Nile.

He was with king Saul and all
His troubles went through,
He was with king David the day
That Goliath he slew.

For a few verses he is with Juda and Maccabeus the
great, with Cyrus, and back again to Babylon. Next we
find him as the horse that came into Troy.

When (   ) came to Troy with joy,
My horse he was found,
He crossed over the walls and entered
The city I'm told.

.   .   .   .   .

I come on him again, in Spain,
And he in full bloom,
By Hannibal the great he was rode,
And he crossing the Alps into Rome.

The horse being tall
And the Alps very high,
His rider did fall
And Hannibal the great lost an eye.

Afterwards he carries young Sipho (Scipio), and then he is ridden by Brian when driving the Danes from Ireland, and by St. Ruth when he fell at the battle of Aughrim, and by Sarsfield at the siege of Limerick.

He was with king James who sailed
To the Irish shore,
But at last he got lame,
When the Boyne's bloody battle was o'er.

He was rode by the greatest of men
At famed Waterloo,
Brave Daniel O'Connell he sat
On his back it is true.

.   .   .   .   .

Brave Dan's on his back,
He's ready once more for the field.
He never will stop till the Tories,
He'll make them to yield.

Grotesque as this long rhyme appears, it has, as I said, a sort of existence when it is crooned by the old man at his fireside, and it has great fame in the island. The old man himself is hoping that I will print it, for it would not be fair, he says, that it should die out of the world, and he is the only man here who knows it, and none of them has ever heard it on the mainland. He has a couple more examples of the same kind of doggerel, but I have not taken them down.

Both in English and in Irish the songs are full of words the people do not understand themselves, and when they come to say the words slowly their memory is usually uncertain.

All the morning I have been digging maidenhair ferns with a boy I met on the rocks, who was in great sorrow because his father died suddenly a week ago of a pain in his heart.

'We wouldn't have chosen to lose our father for all the gold there is in the world,' he said, 'and it's great loneliness and sorrow there is in the house now.'

Then he told me that a brother of his who is a stoker in the Navy had come home a little while before his father died, and that he had spent all his money in having a fine funeral, with plenty of drink at it, and tobacco.

'My brother has been a long way in the world,' he said, 'and seen great wonders. He does be telling us of the people that do come out to them from Italy, and Spain, and Portugal, and that it is a sort of Irish they do be talking—not English at all—though it is only a word here and there you'd understand.'

When we had dug out enough of roots from the deep crannies in the rocks where they are only to be found, I gave my companion a few pence, and sent him back to his cottage.

The old man who tells me the Irish poems is curiously pleased with the translations I have made from
some of them.

He would never be tired, he says, listening while I
would be reading them, and they are much finer things
than his old bits of rhyme.

Here is one of them, as near the Irish as I am able
to make it:—

RUCARD MOR

I put the sorrow of destruction on the bad luck,
For it would be a pity ever to deny it,
It is to me it is stuck,
By loneliness my pain, my complaining.

It is the fairy-host
Put me a-wandering
And took from me my goods of the world.
At Mannistir na Ruaidthe
It is on me the shameless deed was done:
Finn Bheara and his fairy-host
Took my little horse on me from under the bag.

If they left me the skin
It would bring me tobacco for three months,
But they did not leave anything with me
But the old minister in its place.

Am not I to be pitied?
My bond and my note are on her,
And the price of her not yet paid,
My loneliness, my pain, my complaining.

The devil a hill or a glen, or highest fort
Ever was built in Ireland,
Is not searched on me for my mare,
And I am still at my complaining.

I got up in the morning,
I put a red spark in my pipe.
I went to the Cnoc-Maithe
To get satisfaction from them.

I spoke to them,
If it was in them to do a right thing,
To get me my little mare,
Or I would be changing my wits.

'Do you hear, Rucard Mor?
It is not here is your mare,
She is in Glenasmoil
With the fairy-men these three months.'

I ran on in my walking,
I followed the road straightly,
I was in Glenasmoil
Before the moon was ended.

I spoke to the fairy-man,
If it was in him to do a right thing,
To get me my little mare,
Or I would be changing my wits.

'Do you hear, Rucard Mor?
It is not here is your mare,
She is in Cnoc Bally Brishlawn
With the horseman of the music these three months.'

I ran off on my walking,
I followed the road straightly,
I was in Cnoc Bally Brishlawn
With the black fall of the night.

That is a place was a crowd
As it was seen by me,
All the weavers of the globe,
It is there you would have news of them.

I spoke to the horseman,
If it was in him to do the right thing,
To get me my little mare,
Or I would be changing my wits.

'Do you hear, Rucard Mor?
It is not here is your mare,
She is in Cnoc Cruachan,
In the back end of the palace.'

I ran off on my walking,
I followed the road straightly,
I made no rest or stop
Till I was in face of the palace.

That is the place was a crowd
As it appeared to me,
The men and women of the country,
And they all making merry.

Arthur Scoil (?) stood up
And began himself giving the lead,
It is joyful, light and active,
I would have danced the course with them.

They drew up on their feet
And they began to laugh,—
'Look at Rucard Mor,
And he looking for his little mare.'

I spoke to the man,
And he ugly and humpy,
Unless he would get me my mare
I would break a third of his bones.

'Do you hear, Rucard Mor?
It is not here is your mare,
She is in Alvin of Leinster,
On a halter with my mother.'

I ran off on my walking,
And I came to Alvin of Leinster.
I met the old woman—
On my word she was not pleasing.

I spoke to the old woman,
And she broke out in English:
'Get agone, you rascal,
I don't like your notions.'

'Do you hear, you old woman?
Keep away from me with your English,
But speak to me with the tongue
I hear from every person.'

'It is from me you will get word of her,
Only you come too late—
I made a hunting cap
For Conal Cath of her yesterday.'

I ran off on my walking,
Through roads that were cold and dirty,
I fell in with the fairy-man,
And he lying down on in the Ruadthe.

'I pity a man without a cow,
I pity a man without a sheep,
But in the case of a man without a horse
It is hard for him to be long in the world.'

This morning, when I had been lying for a long time on a rock near the sea watching some hooded crows that were dropping shell-fish on the rocks to break them, I saw one bird that had a large white object which it was dropping continually without any result. I got some stones and tried to drive it off when the thing had fallen, but several times the bird was too quick for me and made off with it before I could get down to him. At last, however, I dropped a stone almost on top of him and he flew away. I clambered down hastily, and found to my amazement a worn golf-ball! No doubt it had been brought out in some way or other from the links in County Clare, which are not far off, and the bird had been trying half the morning to break it.

Further on I had a long talk with a young man who is inquisitive about modern life, and I explained to him an elaborate trick or corner on the Stock Exchange that I heard of lately. When I got him to understand it fully, he shouted with delight and amusement.

'Well,' he said when he was quiet again, 'isn't it a great wonder to think that those rich men are as big rogues as ourselves?'

The old story-teller has given me a long rhyme about a man who fought with an eagle. It is rather irregular

and has some obscure passages, but I have translated it
with the scholar.

PHELIM AND THE EAGLE

On my getting up in the morning
And I bothered, on a Sunday,
I put my brogues on me,
And I going to Tierny
In the Glen of the Dead People.
It is there the big eagle fell in with me,
He like a black stack of turf sitting up stately.
I called him a lout and a fool,
The son of a female and a fool,
Of the race of the Clan Cleopas, the biggest rogues in
    the land.
That and my seven curses
And never a good day to be on you,
Who stole my little cock from me that could crow the
    sweetest.

'Keep your wits right in you
And don't curse me too greatly,
By my strength and my oath
I never took rent of you,
I didn't grudge what you would have to spare
In the house of the burnt pigeons,
It is always useful you were to men of business.

'But get off home
And ask Nora
What name was on the young woman that scalded his
    head.

The feathers there were on his ribs
Are burnt on the hearth,
And they eat him and they taking and it wasn't much
    were thankful.'

'You are a liar, you stealer,
They did not eat him, and they're taking
Nor a taste of the sort without being thankful,
You took him yesterday
As Nora told me,
And the harvest quarter will not be spent till I take a tax
    of you.'

'Before I lost the Fianna
It was a fine boy I was,
It was not about thieving was my knowledge,
But always putting spells,
Playing games and matches with the strength of Gol
    MacMorna,
And you are making me a rogue.
At the end of my life.'

'There is a part of my father's books with me,
Keeping in the bottom of a box,
And when I read them the tears fall down from me.
But I found out in history
That you are a son of the Dearg Mor,
If it is fighting you want and you won't be thankful.'

The Eagle dressed his bravery
With his share of arms and his clothes,
He had the sword that was the sharpest
Could be got anywhere.
I and my scythe with me,

And nothing on but my shirt,
We went at each other early in the day.

We were as two giants
Ploughing in a valley in a glen of the mountains.
We did not know for the while which was the better
    man.
You could hear the shakes that were on our arms under
    each other,
From that till the sunset,
Till it was forced on him to give up.

I wrote a 'challenge boxail' to him
On the morning of the next day,
To come till we would fight without doubt at the dawn
    of the day.
The second fist I drew on him
I struck him on the bone of his jaw,
He fell, and it is no lie there was a cloud in his head.

The Eagle stood up,
He took the end of my hand:—
'You are the finest man I ever saw in my life,
Go off home, my blessing will be on you for ever,
You have saved the fame of Eire for yourself till the
    Day of the Judgment.'

Ah! neighbours, did you hear
The goodness and power of Felim?
The biggest wild beast you could get,
The second fist he drew on it
He struck it on the jaw,
It fell, and it did not rise
Till the end of two days.

Well as I seem to know these people of the islands, there is hardly a day that I do not come upon some new primitive feature of their life.

Yesterday I went into a cottage where the woman was at work and very carelessly dressed. She waited for a while till I got into conversation with her husband, and then she slipped into the corner and put on a clean petticoat and a bright shawl round her neck. Then she came back and took her place at the fire.

This evening I was in another cottage till very late talking to the people. When the little boy—the only child of the house—got sleepy, the old grandmother took him on her lap and began singing to him. As soon as he was drowsy she worked his clothes off him by degrees, scratching him softly with her nails as she did so all over his body. Then she washed his feet with a little water out of a pot and put him into his bed.

When I was going home the wind was driving the sand into my face so that I could hardly find my way. I had to hold my hat over my mouth and nose, and my hand over my eyes while I groped along, with my feet feeling for rocks and holes in the sand.

I have been sitting all the morning with an old man who was making sugawn ropes for his house, and telling me stories while he worked. He was a pilot when he was young, and we had great talk at first about Germans, and Italians, and Russians, and the ways of seaport towns. Then he came round to talk of the middle island, and he told me this story which shows the curious jealousy that is between the islands:—

Long ago we used all to be pagans, and the saints used to be coming to teach us about God and the creation of the world. The people on the middle island were the last to keep a hold on the fire-worshipping, or whatever it was they had in those days, but in the long run a saint got in among them and they began listening to him, though they would often say in the evening they believed, and then say the morning after that, they did not believe. In the end the saint gained them over and they began building a church, and the saint had tools that were in use with them for working with the stones. When the church was half-way up the people held a kind of meeting one night among themselves, when the saint was asleep in his bed, to see if they did really believe and no mistake in it.

The leading man got up, and this is what he said: that they should go down and throw their tools over the cliff, for if there was such a man as God, and if the saint was as well known to Him as he said, then he would be as well able to bring up the tools out of the sea as they were to throw them in.

They went then and threw their tools over the cliff.

When the saint came down to the church in the morning the workmen were all sitting on the stones and no work doing.

'For what cause are you idle?' asked the saint.

'We have no tools,' said the men, and then they told him the story of what they had done.

He kneeled down and prayed God that the tools might come up out of the sea, and after that he prayed that no other people might ever be as great fools as the people on the middle island, and that God might preserve their dark minds of folly to them till the end of the world. And that is why no man out of that island can tell you a whole story without stammering, or bring any work to end without a fault in it.

I asked him if he had known old Pat Dirane on the middle island, and heard the fine stories he used to tell.

'No one knew him better than I did,' he said; 'for I do often be in that island making curaghs for the people. One day old Pat came down to me when I was after tarring a new curagh, and he asked me to put a little tar on the knees of his breeches the way the rain wouldn't come through on him.

'I took the brush in my hand, and I had him tarred down to his feet before he knew what I was at. "Turn round the other side now," I said, "and you'll be able to sit where you like." Then he felt the tar coming in hot against his skin and he began cursing my soul, and I was sorry for the trick I'd played on him.'

This old man was the same type as the genial, whimsical old men one meets all through Ireland, and had none of the local characteristics that are so marked on Inishmaan.

When we were tired talking I showed some of my tricks and a little crowd collected. When they were gone another old man who had come up began telling us about the fairies. One night when he was coming home from the lighthouse he heard a man riding on the road behind him, and he stopped to wait for him, but nothing came. Then he heard as if there was a man trying to catch a horse on the rocks, and in a little time he went on. The noise behind him got bigger as he went along as if twenty horses, and then as if a hundred or a thousand, were galloping after him. When he came to the stile where he had to leave the road and got out over it, something hit against him and threw him down on the rock, and a gun he had in his hand fell into the field beyond him.

'I asked the priest we had at that time what was in

it,' he said, 'and the priest told me it was the fallen angels; and I don't know but it was.

'Another time,' he went on, 'I was coming down where there is a bit of a cliff and a little hole under it, and I heard a flute playing in the hole or beside it, and that was before the dawn began. Whatever anyone says there are strange things. There was one night thirty years ago a man came down to get my wife to go up to his wife, for she was in childbed.

'He was something to do with the lighthouse or the coastguard, one of them Protestants who don't believe in any of these things and do be making fun of us. Well, he asked me to go down and get a quart of spirits while my wife would be getting herself ready, and he said he would go down along with me if I was afraid.

'I said I was not afraid, and I went by myself.

'When I was coming back there was something on the path, and wasn't I a foolish fellow, I might have gone to one side or the other over the sand, but I went on straight till I was near it—till I was too near it— then I remembered that I had heard them saying none of those creatures can stand before you and you saying the *De Profundis*, so I began saying it, and the thing ran off over the sand and I got home.

'Some of the people used to say it was only an old jackass that was on the path before me, but I never heard tell of an old jackass would run away from a man and he saying the *De Profundis*.'

I told him the story of the fairy ship which had disappeared when the man made the sign of the cross, as I had heard it on the middle island.

'There do be strange things on the sea,' he said. 'One night I was down there where you can see that green point, and I saw a ship coming in and I wondered what it would be doing coming so close to the rocks. It came straight on towards the place I was in, and then I got frightened and I ran up to the houses, and when the captain saw me running he changed his course and went away.

'Sometimes I used to go out as a pilot at that time—I went a few times only. Well, one Sunday a man came down and said there was a big ship coming into the sound. I ran down with two men and we went out in a curagh; we went round the point where they said the ship was, and there was no ship in it. As it was a Sunday we had nothing to do, and it was a fine, calm day, so we rowed out a long way looking for the ship, till I was further than I ever was before or after. When I wanted to turn back we saw a great flock of birds on the water and they all black, without a white bird through them. They had no fear of us at all, and the men with me wanted to go up to them, so we went further. When we were quite close they got up, so many that they blackened the sky, and they lit down again a hundred or maybe a hundred and twenty yards off. We went after them again, and one of the men wanted to kill one with a thole-pin, and the other man wanted to kill one with his rowing stick. I was afraid they would upset the curagh, but they would go after the birds.

'When we were quite close one man threw the pin and the other man hit at them with his rowing stick, and the two of them fell over in the curagh, and she turned on her side and only it was quite calm the lot of us were drowned.

'I think those black gulls and the ship were the same sort, and after that I never went out again as a pilot. It is often curaghs go out to ships and find there is no ship.

'A while ago a curagh went out to a ship from the big island, and there was no ship; and all the men in the curagh were drowned. A fine song was made about them after that, though I never heard it myself.

'Another day a curagh was out fishing from this island, and the men saw a hooker not far from them, and they rowed up to it to get a light for their pipes—at that time there were no matches—and when they up to the big boat it was gone out of its place, and they were in great fear.'

Then he told me a story he had got from the mainland about a man who was driving one night through the country, and met a woman who came up to him and asked him to take her into his cart. He thought something was not right about her, and he went on. When he had gone a little way he looked back, and it was a pig was on the road and not a woman at all.

He thought he was a done man, but he went on. When he was going through a wood further on, two men came out to him, one from each side of the road, and they took hold of the bridle of the horse and led it on between them. They were old stale men with frieze clothes on them, and the old fashions. When they came out of the wood he found people as if there was a fair on the road, with the people buying and selling and they not living people at all. The old men took him through the crowd, and then they left him. When he got home and told the old people of the two old men and the ways and fashions they had about them, the old people told him it was his two grandfathers had taken care of him, for they had had a great love for him and he a lad growing up.

This evening we had a dance in the inn parlour, where a fire had been lighted and the tables had been pushed into the corners. There was no master of the ceremonies, and when I had played two or three jigs and other tunes on my fiddle, there was a pause, as I did not know how much of my music the people wanted, or who else could be got to sing or play. For a moment a deadlock seemed to be coming, but a young girl I knew fairly well saw my difficulty, and took the management of our festivities into her hands. At first she asked a coastguard's daughter to play a reel on the mouth organ, which she did at once with admirable spirit and rhythm. Then the little girl asked me to play again, telling me what I should choose, and went on in the same way managing the evening till she thought it was time to go home. Then she stood up, thanked me in Irish, and walked out of the door, without looking at anybody, but followed almost at once by the whole party.

When they had gone I sat for a while on a barrel in the public-house talking to some young men who were reading a paper in Irish. Then I had a long evening with the scholar and two story-tellers—both old men who had been pilots—taking down stories and poems. We were at work for nearly six hours, and the more matter we got the more the old men seemed to remember.

'I was to go out fishing to-night,' said the younger as he came in, 'but I promised you to come, and you're a civil man, so I wouldn't take five pounds to break my word to you. And now'—taking up his glass of whiskey—'here's to your good health, and may you live till they make you a coffin out of a gooseberry bush, or till you die in childbed.'

They drank my health and our work began.

'Have you heard tell of the poet MacSweeny?' said the same man, sitting down near me.

'I have,' I said, 'in the town of Galway.'

'Well,' he said, 'I'll tell you his piece "The Big Wedding," for it's a fine piece and there aren't many that know it. There was a poor servant girl out in the country, and she got married to a poor servant boy. MacSweeny knew the two of them, and he was away at that time and it was a month before he came back. When he came back he went to see Peggy O'Hara—that was the name of the girl—and he asked her if they had had a great wedding. Peggy said it was only middling, but they hadn't forgotten him all the same, and she had a bottle of whiskey for him in the cupboard. He sat down by the fire and began drinking the whiskey. When he had a couple of glasses taken and was warm by the fire, he began making a song, and this was the song he made about the wedding of Peggy O'Hara.'

He had the poem both in English and Irish, but as it has been found elsewhere and attributed to another folk-poet, I need not give it.

We had another round of porter and whiskey, and then the old man who had MacSweeny's wedding gave us a bit of a drinking song, which the scholar took down and I translated with him afterwards:—

'This is what the old woman says at the Beulleaca when she sees a man without knowledge—

'Were you ever at the house of the Still, did you ever get a drink from it? Neither wine nor beer is as sweet as it is, but it is well I was not burnt when I fell down after a drink of it by the fire of Mr. Sloper.

'I praise Owen O'Hernon over all the doctors of

Ireland, it is he put drugs on the water, and it lying on the barley.

'If you gave but a drop of it to an old woman who does be walking the world with a stick, she would think for a week that it was a fine bed was made for her.'

After that I had to get out my fiddle and play some tunes for them while they finished their whiskey. A new stock of porter was brought in this morning to the little public-house underneath my room, and I could hear in the intervals of our talk that a number of men had come in to treat some neighbours from the middle island, and were singing many songs, some of them in English of the kind I have given, but most of them in Irish.

A little later when the party broke up downstairs my old men got nervous about the fairies—they live some distance away—and set off across the sandhills.

The next day I left with the steamer.

IN WICKLOW

AN AUTUMN NIGHT IN THE HILLS

A FEW years ago a pointer dog of my acquaintance was wounded by accident in a wild glen on the western slope of County Wicklow. He was left at the cottage of an under-keeper, or bailiff—the last cottage on the edge of two ranges of mountains that stretch on the north and west to the plain of Kildare—and a few weeks later I made my way there to bring him down to his master.

It was an afternoon of September, and some heavy rain of the night before had made the road which led up to the cottage through the middle of the glen as smooth as a fine beach, while the clearness of the air gave the granite that ran up on either side of the way a peculiar tinge that was nearly luminous against the shadow of the hills. Every cottage that I passed had a group of rowan trees beside it covered with scarlet berries that gave brilliant points of colour of curious effect.

Just as I came to the cottage the road turned across a swollen river which I had to cross on a range of slippery stones. Then, when I had gone a few yards further, I heard a bark of welcome, and the dog ran down to meet me. The noise he made brought two women to the door of the cottage, one a finely made girl, with an exquisitely open and graceful manner, the other a very old woman. A sudden shower had come up without any warning over the rim of the valley, so I went into the cottage and sat down on a sort of bench in the chimney-corner, at the end of a long low room with open rafters.

'You've come on a bad day,' said the old woman, 'for you won't see any of the lads or men about the place.'

'I suppose they went out to cut their oats,' I said, 'this morning while the weather was fine.'

'They did not,' she answered, 'but they're after going down to Aughrim for the body of Mary Kinsella, that is to be brought this night from the station. There will be a wake then at the last cottage you're after passing, where you saw all them trees with the red berries on them.'

She stopped for a moment while the girl gave me a drink of milk.

'I'm afraid it's a lot of trouble I'm giving you,' I said as I took it, 'and you busy, with no men in the place.'

'No trouble at all in the world,' said the girl, 'and if it was itself, wouldn't any one be glad of it in the lonesome place we're in?'

The old woman began talking again:

'You saw no sign or trace on the road of the people coming with the body?'

'No sign,' I said, 'and who was she at all?'

'She was a fine young woman with two children,' she went on, 'and a year and a half ago she went wrong in her head, and they had to send her away. And then up there in the Richmond asylum maybe they thought the sooner they were shut of her the better, for she died two days ago this morning, and now they're bringing her up to have a wake, and they'll bury her beyond at the churches, far as it is, for it's there are all the people of the two families.'

While we talked I had been examining a wound in the dog's side near the end of his lung.

'He'll do rightly now,' said the girl who had come in again and was putting tea-things on the table. 'He'll do rightly now. You wouldn't know he'd been hurted at all only for a kind of a cough he'll give now and again. Did they ever tell you the way he was hit?' she added, going down on her knees in the chimney-corner with some dry twigs in her hand and making a little fire on the flag-stone a few inches from the turf.

I told her I had heard nothing but the fact of his wound.

'Well,' she said, 'a great darkness and storm came down that night and they all out on the hill. The rivers rose, and they were there groping along by the turf track not minding the dogs. Then an old rabbit got up and run before them, and a man put up his gun and shot across it. When he fired that dog run out from behind a rock, and one grain of the shot cut the scruff off his nose, and another went in there where you were looking, at the butt of his ribs. He dropped down bleeding and howling, and they thought he was killed. The night was falling and they had no way they could carry him, so they made a kind of a shelter for him with sticks and turf, and they left him while they would be going for a sack.'

She stopped for a moment to knead some dough and put down a dozen hot cakes—cut out with the mouth of a tumbler—in a frying pan on the little fire she had made with the twigs. While she was doing so the old woman took up the talk.

'Ah,' she said, 'there do be queer things them nights out on the mountains and in the lakes among them. I was reared beyond in the valley where the mines used to be, in the valley of the Lough Nahanagan, and it's many a queer story I've heard of the spirit does be in that lake.'

'I have sometimes been there fishing till it was dark,' I said when she paused, 'and heard strange noises in the cliff.'

'There was an uncle of mine,' she continued, 'and he was there the same way as yourself, fishing with a big fly in the darkness of the night, and the spirit came down out of the clouds and rifted the waters asunder. He was afeared then and he run down to the houses trembling and shaking. There was another time,' she went on, 'a man came round to this county who was after swimming through the water of every lake in Ireland. He went up to swim in that lake, and a brother of my own went up along with him. The gentleman had heard tell of the spirit but not a bit would he believe in it. He went down on the bank, and he had a big black dog with him, and he took off his clothes.

' "For the love of God," said my brother, "put that dog in before you go in yourself, the way you'll see if he ever comes out of it." The gentleman said he would do that and they threw in a stick or a stone and the dog leapt in and swam out to it. Then he turned round again and he swam and he swam, and not a bit nearer did he come.

' "He's a long time swimming back," said the gentleman.

' "I'm thinking your honour'll have a grey beard before he comes back," said my brother, and before the word was out of his mouth the dog went down out of their sight, and the inside out of him came up on the top of the water.'

By this time the cakes were ready and the girl put them on a plate for me at the table, and poured out a cup of tea from the tea-pot, putting the milk and sugar herself into my cup as is the custom with the cottage people of Wicklow. Then she put the tea-pot down in the embers of the turf and sat down in the place I had left.

'Well,' she said, 'I was telling you the story of that night. When they got back here they sent up two lads for the dog, with a sack to carry him on if he was alive and a spade to bury him if he was dead. When they came to the turf where they left him they saw him near twenty yards down the path. The crathur thought they were after leaving him there to die, and he got that lonesome he dragged himself along like a Christian till he got too weak with the bleeding. James, the big lad, walked up again him first with the spade in his hand. When he seen the spade he let a kind of a groan out of him.

'That dog's as wise as a child, and he knew right well it was to bury him they brought the spade. Then Mike went up and laid down the sack on the ground, and the minute he seen it he jumped up and tumbled in on it himself. Then they carried him down, and the crathur getting his death with the cold and the great rain was falling. When they brought him in here you'd have thought he was dead. We put up a settle bed before the fire, and we put him into it. The heat roused him a bit, and he stretched out his legs and gave two groans out of him like an old man. Mike thought he'd drink some milk so we heated a cup of it over the fire. When he put down his tongue into it he began to cough and bleed, then he turned himself over in the settle bed and looked up at me like an old man. I sat up with him that night and it raining and blowing. At four in the morning I gave him a sup more of the milk and he was able to drink it.

'The next day he was stronger, and we gave him a little new milk every now and again. We couldn't keep him near the fire. So we put him in the little room beyond by the door and an armful of hay in along with him. In the afternoon the boys were out on the mountain and the old woman was gone somewhere else, and I was chopping sticks in the lane. I heard a sort of a noise and there he was with his head out through the window looking out on me in the lane. I was afraid he was lonesome in there all by himself, so I put in one of our old dogs to keep him company. Then I stuffed an old hat into the window and I thought they'd be quiet together.

'But what did they do but begin to fight in there all in the dark as they were. I opened the door and out runs that lad before I could stop him. Not a bit would he go in again, so I had to leave him running about beside me. He's that loyal to me now you wouldn't believe it. When I go for the cow he comes along with me, and when I go to make up a bit of hay on the hill he'll come and make a sort of bed for himself under a haycock, and not a bit of him will look at Mike or the boys.'

'Ah,' said the old woman, as the girl got up to pour me out another cup from the tea-pot, 'it's herself will be lonesome when that dog is gone, he's never out of her sight, and you'd do right to send her down a little dog all for herself.'

'You would so,' said the girl, 'but maybe he wouldn't be loyal to me, and I wouldn't give a thraneen for a dog as wasn't loyal.'

'Would you believe it,' said the old woman again, 'when the gentleman wrote down about that dog Mike went out to where she was in the haggard, and says "They're after sending me the prescription for that dog," says he, "to put on his tombstone." And she went down quite simple, and told the boys below in the bog, and it wasn't till they began making game of her that she seen the way she'd been humbugged.'

'That's the truth,' said the girl, 'I went down quite simple, and indeed it's a small wonder, that dog's as fit for a decent burial as many that gets it.'

Meanwhile the shower had turned to a dense torrent

of mountain rain, and although the evening was hardly coming on, it was so dark that the girl lighted a lamp and hung it at the corner of the chimney. The kitchen was longer than most that I have met with and had a skeleton staircase at the far end that looked vague and shadowy in the dim light. The old woman wore one of the old-fashioned caps with a white frill round the face, and entered with great fitness into the general scheme of the kitchen. I did not like leaving them to go into the raw night for a long walk on the mountains, and I sat down and talked to them for a long time, till the old woman thought I would be benighted.

'Go out now,' she said at last to the girl, 'go out now and see what water is coming over the fall above, for with this rain the water'll rise fast, and maybe he'll have to walk down to the bridge, a rough walk when the night is coming on.'

The girl came back in a moment.

'It's riz already,' she said. 'He'll want to go down to the bridge.' Then turning to me: 'If you'll come now I'll show you the way you have to go, and I'll wait below for the boys; it won't be long now till they come with the body of Mary Kinsella.'

We went out at once and she walked quickly before me through a maze of small fields and pieces of bog, where I would have soon lost the track if I had been alone.

The bridge, when we reached it, was a narrow wooden structure fastened up on iron bars which pierced large boulders in the bed of the river. An immense grey flood was struggling among the stones, looking dangerous and desolate in the half-light of the evening, while the wind was so great that the bridge wailed and quivered and whistled under our feet. A few paces

further on we came to a cottage where the girl wished
me a good journey and went in to wait for her brothers.

The daylight still lingered but the heavy rain and a
thick white cloud that had come down made everything
unreal and dismal to an extraordinary degree. I went
up a road where on one side I could see the trunks of
beech trees reaching up wet and motionless—with odd
sighs and movements when a gust caught the valley—
into a greyness overhead, where nothing could be distinguished. Between them there were masses of shadow,
and masses of half-luminous fog with black branches
across them. On the other side of the road flocks of sheep
I could not see coughed and choked with sad guttural
noises in the shelter of the hedge, or rushed away through
a gap when they felt the dog was near them. Above
everything my ears were haunted by the dead heavy
swish of the rain. When I came near the first village I
heard a loud noise and commotion. Many cars and gigs
were collected at the door of the public-house, and the
bar was filled with men who were drinking and making
a noise. Everything was dark and confused yet on one
car I was able to make out the shadow of a coffin,
strapped in the rain, with the body of Mary Kinsella.

SOME features of County Wicklow, such as the position of the principal workhouses and holiday places on either side of the coach road from Arklow to Bray, have made this district a favourite with the vagrants of Ireland. A few of these people have been on the road for generations; but fairly often they seem to have merely drifted out from the ordinary people of the villages, and do not differ greatly from the class they come from. Their abundance has often been regretted; yet in one sense it is an interesting sign, for wherever the labourer of a country has preserved his vitality, and begets an occasional temperament of distinction, a certain number of vagrants are to be looked for. In the middle classes the gifted son of a family is always the poorest—usually a writer or artist with no sense for speculation—and in a family of peasants, where the average comfort is just over penury, the gifted son sinks also, and is soon a tramp on the roadside.

In this life, however, there are many privileges. The tramp in Ireland is little troubled by the laws, and lives in out-of-door conditions that keep him in good-humour and fine bodily health. This is so apparent, in Wicklow at least, that these men rarely seek for charity on any plea of ill-health, but ask simply, when they beg: 'Would you help a poor fellow along the road?' or, 'Would you give me the price of a night's lodging, for I'm after walking a great way since the sun rose?'

The healthiness of this life, again, often causes these people to live to a great age, though it is not always easy to test the stories that are told of their longevity. One man, however, who died not long ago, claimed to have reached one hundred and two with a show of likeli-

hood; for several old people remember his first appearance in a certain district as a man of middle age, about
the year of the Famine, in 1847 or 1848. This man
could hardly be classed with ordinary tramps, for he was
married several times in different parts of the world,
and reared children of whom he seemed to have forgotten, in his old age, even the names and sex. In his
early life he spent thirty years at sea, where he sailed
with some one he spoke of afterwards as 'Il mio capi-
tane,' visiting India and Japan, and gaining odd words
and intonations that gave colour to his language. When
he was too old to wander in the world, he learned all
the paths of Wicklow, and till the end of his life he
could go the thirty miles from Dublin to the Seven
Churches without, as he said, 'putting out his foot on a
white road, or seeing any Christian but the hares and
moon.' When he was over ninety he married an old
woman of eighty-five. Before many days, however,
they quarrelled so fiercely that he beat her with his stick,
and came out again on the roads. In a few hours he was
arrested at her complaint, and sentenced to a month in
Kilmainham. He cared nothing for the plank-bed and
uncomfortable diet; but he always gathered himself together, and cursed with extraordinary rage, as he told
how they cut off the white hair which had grown down
upon his shoulders. All his pride and his half-conscious
feeling for the dignity of his age seemed to have set
themselves on this long hair, which marked him out
from the other people of this district; and I have often
heard him say to himself, as he sat beside me under a
ditch: 'What use is an old man without his hair? A man
has only his bloom like the trees; and what use is an
old man without his white hair?'

Among the country people of the East of Ireland the

tramps and tinkers who wander round from the West have a curious reputation for witchery and unnatural powers.

'There's great witchery in that country,' a man said to me once, on the side of a mountain to the east of Aughavanna, in Wicklow. 'There's great witchery in that country, and great knowledge of the fairies. I've had men lodging with me out of the West—men who would be walking the world looking for a bit of money —and every one of them would be talking of the wonders below in Connemara. I remember one time, a while after I was married, there was a tinker down there in the glen, and two women along with him. I brought him into my cottage to do a bit of a job, and my first child was there lying in the bed, and he covered up to his chin with the bed-clothes. When the tallest of the women came in, she looked around at him, and then she says—

' "That's a fine boy, God bless him."

' "How do you know it's a boy," says my woman, "when it's only the head of him you see?"

' "I know rightly," says the tinker, "and it's the first too."

'Then my wife was going to slate me for bringing in people to bewitch her child, and I had to turn the lot of them out to finish the job in the lane.'

I asked him where most of the tinkers came from that are met with in Wicklow.

'They come from every part,' he said. 'They're gallous lads for walking round through the world. One time I seen fifty of them above on the road to Rath-dangan, and they all match-making and marrying them-selves for the year that was to come. One man would take such a woman, and say he was going such roads and places, stopping at this fair and another fair, till he'd meet them again at such a place, when the spring was coming on. Another, maybe, would swap the woman he had with one from another man, with as much talk as if you'd be selling a cow. It's two hours I was there watching them from the bog underneath, where I was cutting turf, and the like of the crying and the kissing, and the singing and the shouting began when they went off this way and that way, you never heard in your life. Sometimes when a party would be gone a bit down over the hill, a girl would begin crying out and wanting to go back to her ma. Then the man would say: "Black hell to your soul, you've come with me now, and you'll go the whole way." I often seen tinkers before and since, but I never seen such a power of them as were in it that day.'

It need hardly be said that in all tramp life plaintive and tragic elements are common, even on the surface. Some are peculiar to Wicklow. In these hills the summer passes in a few weeks from a late spring, full of odour and colour, to an autumn that is premature and filled with the desolate splendour of decay; and it often happens that, in moments when one is most aware of this ceaseless fading of beauty, some incident of tramp life gives a local human intensity to the shadow of one's own mood.

One evening, on the high ground near the Avonbeg, I met a young tramp just as an extraordinary sunset had begun to fade, and a low white mist was rising from the bogs. He had a sort of table in his hands that he seemed to have made himself out of twisted rushes and a few branches of osier. His clothes were more than usually ragged, and I could see by his face that he was suffering from some terrible disease. When he was quite close, he held out the table.

'Would you give me a few pence for that thing?' he said. 'I'm after working at it all day by the river, and for the love of God give me something now, the way I can get a drink and lodging for the night.'

I felt in my pockets, and could find nothing but a shilling piece.

'I wouldn't wish to give you so much,' I said, holding it out to him, 'but it is all I have, and I don't like to give you nothing at all, and the darkness coming on. Keep the table; it's no use to me, and you'll maybe sell it for something in the morning.'

The shilling was more than he expected, and his eyes flamed with joy.

'May the Almighty God preserve you and watch over you and reward you for this night,' he said, 'but you'll take the table; I wouldn't keep it at all, and you after stretching out your hand with a shilling to me, and the darkness coming on.'

He forced it into my hands so eagerly that I could not refuse it, and set off down the road with tottering steps. When he had gone a few yards, I called after him: 'There's your table; take it and God speed you.'

Then I put down his table on the ground, and set off as quickly as I was able. In a few minutes he came up with me again, holding the table in his hands, and slipped round in front of me so that I could not get away.

'You wouldn't refuse it,' he said, 'and I after working at it all day below by the river.'

He was shaking with excitement and the exertion of overtaking me; so I took his table and let him go on his way. A quarter of a mile further on I threw it over the ditch in a desolate place, where no one was likely to find it.

In addition to the more genuine vagrants a number of wandering men and women are to be met with in the northern parts of the country, who walk out for ferns and flowers in bands of from four or five to a dozen. They usually set out in the evening, and sleep in some ditch or shed, coming home the next night with what they have gathered. If their sales are successful, both men and women drink heavily; so that they are always on the edge of starvation, and are miserably dressed, the women sometimes wearing nothing but an old petti-coat and shawl—a scantiness of clothing that is some-times met with also among the road-women of Kerry.

These people are nearly always at war with the po-lice, and are often harshly treated. Once after a holi-day, as I was walking home through a village on the border of Wicklow, I came upon several policemen, with a crowd round them, trying to force a drunken flower-woman out of the village. She did not wish to go, and threw herself down, raging and kicking, on the ground. They let her lie there for a few minutes, and then she propped herself up against the wall, scolding and storming at every one, till she became so outrageous the police renewed their attack. One of them walked up to her and hit her a sharp blow on the jaw with the back of his hand. Then two more of them seized her by the shoulders and forced her along the road for a few yards, till her clothes began to tear off with the violence of the struggle, and they let her go once more.

She sprang up at once when they did so.

'Let this be the barrack's yard, if you wish it,' she cried, tearing off the rags that still clung about her. 'Let this he the barrack's yard, and come on now, the lot of you.'

Then she rushed at them with extraordinary fury; but the police, to avoid scandal, withdrew into the town, and left her to be quieted by her friends.

Sometimes, it is fair to add, the police are generous and good-humoured. One evening, many years ago, when Whit Monday in Enniskerry was a very different thing from what it is now, I was looking out of a window in that village, watching the police, who had been brought in for the occasion, getting ready to start for Bray. As they were standing about, a young ballad-singer came along from the Dargle, and one of the policemen, who seemed to know him, asked him why a fine, stout lad the like of him wasn't earning his bread, instead of straying on the roads.

Immediately the young man drew up on the spot where he was, and began shouting a loud ballad at the top of his voice. The police tried to stop him; but he went on, getting faster and faster, till he ended, swinging his head from side to side, in a furious patter, of which I seem to remember—

Botheration
Take the nation,
Calculation,
In the stable,
Cain and Abel,
Tower of Babel,
And the Battle of Waterloo.

Then he pulled off his hat, dashed in among the police, and did not leave them till they had all given him the share of money he felt he had earned for his bread.

In all the circumstances of this tramp life there is a certain wildness that gives it romance and a peculiar value for those who look at life in Ireland with an eye that is aware of the arts also. In all the healthy movements of art, variations from the ordinary types of manhood are made interesting for the ordinary man, and in this way only the higher arts are universal. Besides this art, however, founded on the variations which are a condition and effect of all vigorous life, there is another art—sometimes confounded with it—founded on the freak of nature, in itself a mere sign of atavism or disease. This latter art, which is occupied with the antics of the freak, is of interest only to the variation from ordinary minds, and for this reason is never universal. To be quite plain, the tramp in real life, Hamlet and Faust in the arts, are variations; but the maniac in real life, and Des Esseintes and all his ugly crew in the arts, are freaks only.

IN WEST KERRY

IN WEST KERRY

At Tralee station—I was on my way to a village many miles beyond Dingle—I found a boy who carried my bag some way along the road to an open yard where the light railway starts for the west. There was a confused mass of peasants struggling on the platform, with all sort of baggage, which the people lifted into the train for themselves as well as they were able. The seats ran up either side of the cars, and the space between them was soon filled with sacks of flour, cases of porter, chairs rolled in straw, and other household goods. A drunken young man got in just before we started, and sang songs for a few coppers, telling us that he had spent all his money, and had nothing left to pay for his ticket. Then, when the carriage was closely packed, we moved slowly out of the station. At my side there was an old man who explained the Irish names of the places that we came to, and pointed out the Seven Pigs, a group of islands in the bay; Kerry Head, further off; and many distant mountains. Beyond him a dozen big women in shawls were crowded together; and just opposite me there was a young woman wearing a wedding ring, who was one of the peculiarly refined women of Kerry, with supreme charm in every movement and expression. The big woman talked to her about some elderly man who had been sick—her husband, it was likely—and some young man who had gone away to England, and was breaking his heart with loneliness.

'Ah, poor fellow!' she said; 'I suppose he will get used to it like another; and wouldn't he be worse off if he was beyond the seas in Saint Louis, or the towns of America?'

This woman seemed to unite the healthiness of the

country people with the greatest sensitiveness, and whenever there was any little stir or joke in the carriage, her
face and neck flushed with pleasure and amusement. As
we went on there were superb sights—first on the north,
towards Loop Head, and then when we reached the top
of the ridge, to the south also, to Drung Hill, Macgillicuddy's Reeks, and other mountains of South Kerry.
A little further on, nearly all the people got out at a
small station; and the young woman I had admired,
gathered up most of the household goods and got down
also, lifting heavy boxes with the power of a man. Then
two returned American girls got in, fine, stout-looking
women, with distress in their expression, and we started
again. Dingle Bay could now be seen through narrow
valleys on our left, and had extraordinary beauty in the
evening light. In the carriage next to ours a number of
herds and jobbers were travelling, and for the last hour
they kept up a furious altercation that seemed always on
the verge of breaking into a dangerous quarrel, but no
blows were given.

At the end of the line an old blue side-car was waiting to take me to the village where I was going. I was
some time fastening on my goods, with the raggedy boy
who was to drive me; and then we set off, passing
through the usual streets of a Kerry town, with public-
houses at the corners, till we left the town by a narrow
quay with a few sailing boats and a small steamer with
coal. Then we went over a bridge near a large water-
mill, where a number of girls were standing about, with
black shawls over their heads, and turned sharp to the
right, against the face of the mountains. At first we
went up hill for several miles, and got on slowly, though
the boy jumped down once or twice and gathered a
handful of switches to beat the tall mare he was driv-

ing. Just as the twilight was beginning to deepen we reached the top of the ridge and came out through a gap into sight of Smerwick Harbour, a wild bay with magnificent headlands beyond it, and a long stretch of the Atlantic. We drove on towards the west, sometimes very quickly, where the slope was gradual, and then slowly again when the road seemed to fall away under us, like the wall of a house. As the night fell the sea became like a piece of white silver on our right; and the mountains got black on our left, and heavy night smells began to come up out of the bogs. Once or twice I noticed a blue cloud over the edge of the road, and then I saw that we were nearly against the gables of a little village, where the houses were so closely packed together there was no light from any of them. It was now quite dark, and the boy got cautious in his driving, pulling the car almost into the ditch once or twice to avoid an enormous cavity where the middle of the road had settled down into the bogs. At last we came to another river and a public-house, and went up a hill, from which we could see the outline of a chapel; then the boy turned to me: 'Is it ten o'clock yet?' he said; 'for we're mostly now in the village.'

This morning, a Sunday, rain was threatening; but I went out west after my breakfast under Croagh Martin, in the direction of the Atlantic. At one of the first villages I came to I had a long talk with a man who was sitting on the ditch waiting till it was time for Mass. Before long we began talking about the Irish language.

'A few years ago,' he said, 'they were all for stopping it off; and when I was a boy they tied a gobban into my mouth for the whole afternoon because I was heard speaking Irish. Wasn't that great cruelty? And

now when I hear the same busybodies coming around
and telling us for the love of God to speak nothing but
Irish, I've a good mind to tell them to go to hell. There
was a priest out here a while since who was telling us
to stay always where we are, and to speak nothing but
Irish; but, I suppose, although the priests are learned
men, and great scholars, they don't understand the life
of the people the same as another man would. In this
place the land is poor—you can see that for yourself—
and the people have little else to live on; so that when
there is a long family, one son will stay at home and
keep on the farm, and the others will go away because
they must go. Then when they once pass out of the
Dingle station in Tralee they won't hear a word of
Irish, or meet anyone who'd understand it; so what
good, I ask you, is a man who hasn't got the English,
and plenty of it?'

After I left him I went on towards Dunquin, and
lay for a long time on the side of a magnificently wild
road under Croagh Martin, where I could see the
Blasket Islands and the end of Dunmore Head, the
most westerly point of Europe. It was a grey day with
a curious silence on the sea and sky and no sign of life
anywhere, except the sail of one curagh—or niavogue,
as they are called here—that was sailing in from the
islands. Now and then a cart passed me filled with old
people and children, who saluted me in Irish; then I
turned back myself. I got on a long road running
through a bog, with a smooth mountain on one side and
the sea on the other, and Brandon in front of me, partly
covered with clouds. As far as I could see there were
little groups of people on their way to the chapel in
Ballyferriter, the men in homespun and the women
wearing blue cloaks, or, more often, black shawls twisted

over their heads. This procession along the olive bogs, between the mountains and the sea, on this grey day of autumn seemed to wring me with the pang of emotion one meets everywhere in Ireland—an emotion that is partly local and patriotic, and partly a share of the desolation that is mixed everywhere with the supreme beauty of the world.

In the evening, when I was walking about the village, I fell in with a man who could read Gaelic, and was full of enthusiasm for the old language and of contempt for English.

'I can tell you,' he said, 'that the English I have is no more good to me than the cover of that pipe. Buyers come here from Dingle and Cork and Clare, and they have good Irish, and so has everyone we meet with, for there is no one can do business in this place who hasn't the language on his tongue.'

Then I asked him about the young men who go away to America.

'Many go away,' he said, 'who could stay if they wished to, for it is a fine place for fishing, and a man will get more money and better health for himself, and rear a better family, in this place than in many another. It's a good place to be in, and now, with the help of God, the little children will all learn to read and write in Irish, and that is a great thing, for how can people do any good, or make a song even, if they cannot write? You will be often three weeks making a song, and there will be times when you will think of good things to put into it that could never be beaten in the whole world; but if you cannot write them down you will forget them, maybe, by the next day, and then what good will be your song?'

After a while we went upstairs to a large room in the inn, where a number of young men and girls were dancing jigs and reels. These young people, although they are as Irish-speaking as the people of Connemara, are pushing forward in their ways of living and dress; so that this group of dancers could hardly have been known, by their appearance, from any Sunday party in Limerick or Cork. After a long four-hand reel, my friend, who was dressed in homespun, danced a jig to the whistling of a young man with great energy and spirit. Then he sat down beside me in the corner, and we talked about spring trawling and the price of nets. I told him about the ways of Aran and Connemara; and then he told me about the French trawlers who come to this neighbourhood in April and May.

'The Frenchmen from Fécamp,' he said, 'are Catholics and decent people; but those who come from Boulogne have no religion, and are little better than a wild beast would lep on you out of a wood. One night there was a drift of them below in the public-house, where there is a counter, as you've maybe seen, with a tin top on it. Well, they were talking together, and they had some little difference among themselves, and from that they went on raising their voices, till one of them out with his knife and drove it down through the tin into the wood! Wasn't that a dangerous fellow?'

Then he told me about their tobacco.

'The French do have two kinds of tobacco; one of them is called hay-tobacco, and if you give them a few eggs, or maybe nine little cabbage plants, they'll give you as much of it as would fill your hat. Then we get a pound of our own tobacco and mix the two of them together, and put them away in a pig's bladder—it's that way we keep our tobacco—and we have enough with that lot for the whole winter.'

This evening a circus was advertised in Dingle, for one night only; so I made my way there towards the end of the afternoon, although the weather was windy and threatening. I reached the town an hour too soon, so I spent some time watching the wild-looking fishermen and fisherwomen who stand about the quays. Then I wandered up and saw the evening train coming in with the usual number of gaily-dressed young women and half-drunken jobbers and merchants; and at last, about eight o'clock, I went to the circus field, just above the town, in a heavy splash of rain. The tent was set up in the middle of the field, and a little to the side of it a large crowd was struggling for tickets at one of the wheeled houses in which the acrobats live. I went round the tent in the hope of getting in by some easier means, and found a door in the canvas, where a man was calling out: 'Tickets, or money, this way,' and I passed in through a long winding passage. It was some time after the hour named for the show, but although the tent was almost filled there was no sign of the performers; so I stood back in a corner and watched the crowd coming in wet and dripping from the rain, which had turned to a downpour. The tent was lighted by a few flaring gas-jets round the central pole, with an opening above them, through which the rain shot down in straight whistling lines. The top of the tent was dripping and saturated, and the gas, shining sideways across, made it glitter in many places with the brilliancy of golden silk. When a sudden squall came with a rush from the narrow valleys behind the town, the whole structure billowed, and

flapped and strained, till one waited every moment to
see the canvas fall upon our heads. The people, who
looked strangely black and swarthy in the uncertain
light, were seated all round on three or four rows of
raised wooden seats, and many who were late were still
crushing forward, and standing in dense masses wherever there was room. At the entrance a rather riotous
crowd began to surge in so quickly that there was danger
of the place being rushed. Word was sent across the
ring, and in a moment three or four of the women performers, with long streaming ulsters buttoned over
their tights, ran out from behind the scenes and threw
themselves into the crowd, forcing back the wild hillside people, fishwomen and drunken sailors, in an extraordinary tumult of swearing, wrestling and laughter.
These women seemed to enjoy this part of their work,
and shrieked with amusement when two or three of
them fell on some enormous farmer or publican and
nearly dragged him to the ground. Here and there
among the people I could see a little party of squireens
and their daughters, in the fashions of five years ago,
trying, not always successfully, to reach the shilling seats.
The crowd was now so thick I could see little more than
the heads of the performers, who had at last come into
the ring, and many of the shorter women who were
near me must have seen nothing the whole evening, yet
they showed no sign of impatience. The performance
was begun by the usual dirty white horse, that was
brought out and set to gallop round, with a gaudy horse-
woman on his back who jumped through a hoop and did
the ordinary feats, the horse's hoofs splashing and poss-
ing all the time in the green slush of the ring. An old
door-mat was laid down near the entrance for the performers, and as they came out in turn they wiped the

mud from their feet before they got up on their horses.
A little later the clown came out, to the great delight of
the people. He was followed by some gymnasts, and
then the horse-people came out again in different dress
and make-up, and went through their old turns once
more. After that there was prolonged fooling between
the clown and the chief horseman, who made many
mediæval jokes, that reminded me of little circuses on
the outer Boulevards of Paris, and at last the horseman
sang a song which won great applause:—

> Here's to the man who kisses his wife,
> And kisses his wife alone;
> For there's many a man kissed another man's wife
> When he thought he kissed his own.

> Here's to the man who rocks his child,
> And rocks his child alone;
> For there's many a man rocked another man's child
> When he thought he rocked his own.

About ten o'clock there seemed to be a lull in the
storm, so I went out into the open air with two young
men who were going the road I had to travel. The rain
had stopped for a moment, but a high wind was blowing as we made our way to a public-house to get a few
biscuits and a glass of beer before we started. A sleepy
barmaid, who was lolling behind the counter with a
novel pricked up her ears when she heard us talking of
our journey.

'Surely you are not going to Ballydavid,' she said, 'at
such an hour of a night like this.'

We told her we were going to a place which was
further away.

'Well,' she said, 'I wouldn't go to that place to-night if you had a coach-and-four to drive me in, and gave me twenty pounds into the bargain! How at all will you get on in the darkness when the roads will be running with water, and you'll be likely to slip down every place into some drain or ditch?'

When we went out and began to make our way down the steep hill through the town, the night seemed darker than ever after the glare of the bar. Before we had gone many yards a woman's voice called out sharply from under the wall: 'Mind the horse.' I looked up and saw the black outline of a horse's head right above me. It was not plain in such darkness how we should get to the end of our ten-mile journey; but one of the young men borrowed a lantern from a chandler in the bottom of the town, and we made our way over the bridge and up the hill, going slowly and painfully with just light enough, when we kept close together, to avoid the slough of water and piles of stones on the roadway. By the time we reached the top of the ridge and began to work down carefully towards Smerwick, the rain stopped, and we reached the village without any mishap.

I go out often in the mornings to the site of Sybil Ferriter's Castle, on a little headland reached by a narrow strip of rocks. As I lie there I can watch whole flights of cormorants and choughs and seagulls that fly about under the cliffs, and beyond them a number of niavogues that are nearly always fishing in Ferriter's Cove. Further on there are Sybil Head and three rocky points, the Three Sisters; then Smerwick Harbour and Brandon far away, usually covered with white airy clouds. Between these headlands and the village there is a strip of sandhill grown over with sea-holly, and a low beach where scores of red bullocks lie close to the sea, or wade in above their knees. Further on one passes peculiar horseshoe coves, with contorted lines of sandstone on one side and slaty blue rocks on the other, and necks of transparent sea of wonderful blueness between them.

I walked up this morning along the slope from the east to the top of Sybil Head, where one comes out suddenly on the brow of a cliff with a straight fall of many hundred feet into the sea. It is a place of indescribable grandeur, where one can see Carrantuohill and the Skelligs and Loop Head and the full sweep of the Atlantic, and, over all, the wonderfully tender and searching light that is seen only in Kerry. Looking down the drop of five or six hundred feet, the height is so great that the gannets flying close over the sea look like white butterflies, and the choughs like flies fluttering behind them. One wonders in these places why anyone is left in Dublin, or London, or Paris, when it would be better, one would think, to live in a tent or hut with this magnificent sea and sky, and to breathe this wonderful air, which is like wine in one's teeth.

Here and there on this headland there are little villages of ten or twenty houses, closely packed together without any order or roadway. Usually there are one or two curious beehive-like structures in these villages, used here, it is said, as pig-sties or storehouses. On my way down from Sybil Head I was joined by a tall young man, who told me he had been in the navy, but had bought himself out before his time was over.

'Twelve of us joined from this place,' he said, 'and I was the last of them that stayed in it, for it is a life that no one could put up with. It's not the work that would trouble you, but it's that they can't leave you alone, and that you must be ever and always fooling over something.'

He had been in South Africa during the war, and in Japan, and all over the world; but he was now dressed in homespuns, and had settled down here, he told me, for the rest of his life. Before we reached the village we met Maurice, the fisherman I have spoken of, and we sat down under a hedge to shelter from a shower. We began to talk of fevers and sicknesses and doctors—these little villages are often infested with typhus—and Maurice spoke about the traditional cures.

'There is a plant,' he said, 'which is the richest that is growing out of ground, and in the old times the women used to be giving it to their children till they'd be growing up seven feet maybe in height. Then the priests and doctors began taking everything to themselves and destroyed the old knowledge, and that is a poor thing; for you know well it was the Holy Mother of God who cured her own Son with plants the like of that, and said after that no mother should be without a plant for ever to cure her child. Then she threw out the seeds of it over the whole world, so that it's growing every place from that day to this.'

I came out to-day, a holiday, to the Great Blasket Island with a schoolmaster and two young men from the village, who were coming for the afternoon only. The day was admirably clear, with a blue sea and sky, and the voyage in the long canoe—I had not been in one for two or three years—gave me indescribable enjoyment. We passed Dunmore Head, and then stood out nearly due west towards the Great Blasket itself, the height of the mountains round the bay and the sharpness of the rocks making the place singularly different from the sounds about Aran, where I had last travelled in a curagh. As usual, three men were rowing—the man I have come to stay with, his son, and a tall neighbour, all dressed in blue jerseys, homespun trousers and shirts, and talking in Irish only, though my host could speak good English when he chose to. As we came nearer the island, which seemed to rise like a mountain straight out of the sea, we could make out a crowd of people in their holiday clothes standing or sitting along the brow of the cliff watching our approach, and just beyond them a patch of cottages with roofs of tarred felt. A little later we doubled into a cove among the rocks, where I landed at a boat slip, and then scrambled up a steep zig-zag pathway to the head of the cliff, where the people crowded round us and shook hands with the men who had come with me.

This cottage where I am to stay is one of the highest of the group, and as we passed up to it through little paths among the cottages many white, wolfish-looking dogs came out and barked furiously. My host had gone on in front with my bag, and when I reached his threshold he came forward and shook hands with me again, with a finished speech of welcome. His eldest daughter, a young married woman of about twenty, who manages the house, shook hands with me also, and then, without asking if we were hungry, began making us tea in a metal tea-pot and frying rashers of bacon. She is a small, beautifully-formed woman, with brown hair and eyes —instead of the black hair and blue eyes that are usually found with this type in Ireland—and delicate feet and ankles that are not common in these parts, where the woman's work is so hard. Her sister, who lives in the house also, is a bonny girl of about eighteen, full of humour and spirits.

The schoolmaster made many jokes in English and Irish while the little hostess served our tea; and then the kitchen filled up with young men and women—the men dressed like ordinary fishermen, the women wearing print bodices and coloured skirts, that had none of the distinction of the dress of Aran—and a polka was danced, with curious solemnity, in a whirl of dust. When it was over it was time for my companions to go back to the mainland. As soon as we came out and began to go down to the sea, a large crowd, made up of nearly all the men and women and children of the island, came down also, closely packed round us. At the edge of the cliff the young men and the schoolmaster bade me good-bye and went down the zig-zag path, leaving me alone with the islanders on the ledge of the rock, where I had seen the people as we came in. I sat for a long time watching the sail of the canoe moving away to Dunquin, and talking to a young man who had spent some years in Ballyferriter, and had good English. The evening was peculiarly fine, and after a while, when the crowd had scattered, I passed up through the cottages, and walked through a boreen towards the north-west, between a few plots of potatoes and little fields of weeds that seemed to have gone out of cultivation not long ago. Beyond these I turned up a sharp, green hill, and came out suddenly on the broken edge of a cliff. The effect was wonderful. The Atlantic was right underneath; then I could see the sharp rocks of several uninhabited islands, a mile or two off, the Tearaught further away, and, on my left, the whole northern edge of this island curving round towards the west, with a steep, heathery face, a thousand feet high. The whole sight of wild islands and sea was as clear and cold and brilliant as what one sees in a dream, and alive with the singularly severe glory that is in the character of this place.

As I was wandering about I saw many of the young islanders, not far off, jumping and putting the weight— a heavy stone—or running races on the grass. Then four girls, walking arm-in-arm, came up and talked to me in Irish. Before long they began to laugh loudly at some signs I made to eke out my meaning, and by degrees the men wandered up also, till there was a crowd round us. The cold of the night was growing stronger, however, and we soon turned back to the village, and sat round the fire in the kitchen the rest of the evening.

At eleven o'clock the people got up as one man and went away, leaving me with the little hostess—the man of the house had gone to the mainland with the young men—her husband and sister. I told them I was sleepy, and ready to go to bed; so the little hostess lighted a candle, carried it into the room beyond the kitchen, and stuck it up on the end of the bed-post of one of the beds with a few drops of grease. Then she took off her apron, and fastened it up in the window as a blind, laid another apron on the wet earthen floor for me to stand on, and left me to myself. The room had two beds, running from wall to wall with a small space between them, a chair that the little hostess had brought in, an old hairbrush that was propping the window open, and no other article. When I had been in bed for some time, I heard the host's voice in the kitchen, and a moment or two later he came in with a candle in his hand, and made a long apology for having been away the whole of my first evening on the island, holding the candle while he talked very close to my face. I told him I had been well entertained by his family and neighbours, and had hardly missed him. He went away, and half an hour later opened the door again with the iron spoon which serves to lift the latch, and came in, in a suit of white home-spuns, and said he must ask me to let him stretch out in the other bed, as there was no place else for him to lie. I told him that he was welcome, and he got into the other bed and lit his pipe. Then we had a long talk about this place and America and the younger generations.

'There has been no one drowned on this island,' he said, 'for forty years, and that is a great wonder, for it is a dangerous life. There was a man—the brother of the man you were talking to when the girls were dancing—was married to a widow had a public-house away to the west of Ballydavid, and he was out fishing for mackerel, and he got a great haul of them; then he filled his canoe too full, so that she was down to the edge of the water, and a wave broke into her when they were near the shore, and she went down under them. Two men got ashore, but the man from this island was drowned, for his oilskins went down about his feet, and he sank where he was.'

Then we talked about the chances of the mackerel season. 'If the season is good,' he said, 'we get on well; but it is not certain at all. We do pay £4 for a net, and sometimes the dogfish will get into it the first day and tear it into pieces as if you'd cut it with a knife. Sometimes the mackerel will die in the net, and then ten men would be hard set to pull them up into the canoe, so that if the wind rises on us we must cut loose, and let down the net into the bottom of the sea. When we get fish here in the night we go to Dunquin and sell them to buyers in the morning; and, believe me, it is a dangerous thing to cross that sound when you have too great a load taken into your canoe. When it is too bad to cross over we do salt the fish ourselves—we must salt them cleanly and put them in clean barrels— and then the first day it is calm buyers will be out after them from the town of Dingle.'

Afterwards he spoke of the people who go away to America, and the younger generations that are growing up now in Ireland.

'The young people is no use,' he said. 'I am not as good a man as my father was, and my son is growing up worse than I am.' Then he put up his pipe on the end of the bed-post. 'You'll be tired now,' he went on, 'so it's time we were sleeping; and, I humbly beg your pardon, might I ask your name?' I told him.

'Well, good night so,' he said, 'and may you have a good sleep your first night in this island.'

Then he put out the candle and we settled to sleep. In a few minutes I could hear that he was in his dreams, and just as my own ideas were beginning to wander the house door opened, and the son of the place, a young man of about twenty, came in and walked into our room, close to my bed, with another candle in his hand. I lay with my eyes closed, and the young man did not seem pleased with my presence, though he looked at me with curiosity. When he was satisfied he went back to the kitchen, and took a drink of whiskey and said his prayers; then, after loitering about for some time and playing with a little mongrel greyhound that seemed to adore him, he took off his clothes, clambered over his father, and stretched out on the inner side of the bed.

I awoke the next morning about six o'clock, and not long afterwards the host awoke also, and asked how I did. Then he wanted to know if I ever drank whiskey; and when he heard that I did so, he began calling for one of his daughters at the top of his voice. In a few moments the younger girl came in, her eyes closing with sleep, and, at the host's bidding, got the whiskey bottle, some water, and a green wine-glass out of the kitchen. She came first to my bedside and gave me a dram, then she did the same for her father and brother, handed us our pipes and tobacco, and went back to the kitchen.

There were to be sports at noon in Ballyferriter, and when we had talked for a while I asked the host if he would think well of my going over to see them. 'I would not,' he said; 'you'd do better to stay quiet in this place where you are; the men will be all drunk coming back, fighting and kicking in the canoes, and a man the like of you, who aren't used to us, would be frightened. Then, if you went, the people would be taking you into one public-house, and then into another, till you'd maybe get drunk yourself, and that wouldn't be a nice thing for a gentleman. Stay where you are in this island and you'll be safest so.'

When the son got up later and began going in and out of the kitchen, some of the neighbours, who had already come in, stared at me with curiosity as I lay in my bed; then I got up myself and went into the kitchen. The little hostess set about getting my breakfast, but before it was ready she partly rinsed the dough out of a pan where she had been kneading bread, poured some water into it, and put it on a chair near the door. Then she hunted about the edges of the rafters till she found a piece of soap, which she put on the back of a chair with a towel, and told me I might wash my face. I did so as well as I was able, in the middle of the people, and dried myself with the towel, which was the one used by the whole family.

The morning looked as if it would turn to rain and

wind, so I took the advice I had been given and let the
canoes go off without me to the sports. After a turn on
the cliffs I came back to the house to write letters. The
little hostess was washing up the breakfast things when
I arrived with my papers and pens, but she made room
for me at the table, and spread out an old newspaper for
me to write on. A little later, when she had finished
her washing, she came over to her usual place in the
chimney corner, not far from where I was sitting, sat
down on the floor, and took out her hairpins and began
combing her hair. As I finished each letter I had to say
who it was to, and where the people lived; and then I
had to tell her if they were married or single, how many
children they had, and make a guess at how many
pounds they spent in a year, and at the number of their
servants. Just before I finished, the younger girl came
back with three or four other young women, who were
followed in a little while by a party of men.

I showed them some photographs of the Aran Islands
and Wicklow, which they looked at with eagerness.
The little hostess was especially taken with two or three
that had babies or children in their foreground; and as
she put her hands on my shoulders, and leaned over to
look at them, with the confidence that is so usual in these
places, I could see that she had her full share of the passion for children which is powerful in all women who
are permanently and profoundly attractive. While I
was telling her what I could about the children, I saw
one of the men looking with peculiar amazement at an
old photograph of myself that had been taken many
years ago in an alley of the Luxembourg Gardens,
where there were many statues in the background.
'Look at that,' he whispered in Irish to one of the girls,

pointing to the statues; 'in those countries they do have naked people standing about in their skins.'

I explained that the figures were of marble only, and then the little hostess and all the girls examined them also. 'Oh! dear me,' said the little hostess, 'Is deas an rud do bheith ag siubhal ins an domhain mor' ('It's a fine thing to be travelling in the big world').

In the afternoon I went up and walked along the narrow central ridge of the island, till I came to the highest point, which is nearly three miles west of the village. The weather was gloomy and wild, and there was something nearly appalling in the loneliness of the place. I could look down on either side into a foggy edge of grey moving sea, and then further off I could see many distant mountains, or look out across the shadowy outline of Inishtooskert to the Tearaught rock. While I was sitting on the little mound which marks the summit of the island—a mound stripped and riddled by rabbits—a heavy bank of fog began to work up from the south, behind Valentia, on the other jaw of Dingle Bay. As soon as I saw it I hurried down from the pinnacle where I was, so that I might get away from the more dangerous locality before the cloud overtook me. In spite of my haste I had not gone half a mile when an edge of fog whisked and circled round me, and in a moment I could see nothing but a grey shroud of mist and a few yards of steep, slippery grass. Everything was distorted and magnified to an extraordinary degree; but I could hear the moan of the sea under me, and I knew my direction, so I worked along towards the village without trouble. In some places the island, on this southern side, is bitten into by sharp, narrow coves, and when the fog opened a little I could see across them, where gulls and choughs were picking about on the grass, look-

ing as big as Kerry cattle or black mountain sheep. Before I reached the house the cloud had turned to a sharp
shower of rain, and as I went in the water was dripping
from my hat. 'Oh! dear me,' said the little hostess, when
she saw me, 'Ta tu an-rhluc anois' ('You are very wet
now'). She was alone in the house, breathing audibly,
with a sort of simple self-importance, as she washed her
jugs and teacups. While I was drinking my tea, a little
later, some women came in with three or four little
girls—the most beautiful children I have ever seen—
who live in one of the nearest cottages. They tried to
get the little girls to dance a reel together, but the smallest of them went and hid her head in the skirts of the
little hostess. In the end two of the little girls danced
with two of those who were grown up, to the lilting of
one of them. The little hostess sat at the fire while they
danced, plucking and drawing a cormorant for the
men's dinner, and calling out to the girls when they lost
the step of the dance.

In the evenings of Sundays and holidays the young
men and girls go out to a rocky headland on the north-
west, where there is a long, grassy slope, to dance and
amuse themselves; and this evening I wandered out
there with two men, telling them ghost stories in Irish
as we went. When we turned over the edge of the hill
we came on a number of young men lying on the short
grass playing cards. We sat down near them, and before long a party of girls and young women came up
also and sat down, twenty paces off, on the brink of the
cliff, some of them wearing the fawn-coloured shawls
that are so attractive and so much thought of in the
south. It was just after sunset, and Inishtooskert was
standing out with a smoky blue outline against the red-

ness of the sky. At the foot of the cliff a wonderful silvery light was shining on the sea, which already, before the beginning of autumn, was eager and wintry and cold. The little group of blue-coated men lying on the grass, and the group of girls further off, had a singular effect in this solitude of rocks and sea; and in spite of their high spirits it gave me a sort of grief to feel the utter loneliness and desolation of the place that has given these people their finest qualities.

One of the young men had been thrown from a cart a few days before on his way home from Dingle, and his face was still raw and bleeding and horrible to look at; but the young girls seemed to find romance in his condition, and several of them went over and sat in a group round him, stroking his arms and face. When the card-playing was over I showed the young men a few tricks and feats, which they worked at themselves, to the great amusement of the girls, till they had accomplished them all. On our way back to the village the young girls ran wild in the twilight, flying and shrieking over the grass, or rushing up behind the young men and throwing them over, if they were able, by a sudden jerk or trip. The men in return caught them by one hand, and spun them round and round four or five times, and then let them go, when they whirled down the grassy slope for many yards, spinning like peg-tops, and only keeping their feet by the greatest efforts or good luck.

When we got to the village the people scattered for supper, and in our cottage the little hostess swept the floor and sprinkled it with some sand she had brought home in her apron. Then she filled a crock with drinking water, lit the lamp and sat down by the fire to comb her hair. Some time afterwards, when a number of young men had come in, as was usual, to spend the evening, some one said a niavogue was on its way home from the sports. We went out to the door, but it was too dark to see anything except the lights of a little steamer that was passing up the sound, almost beneath us, on its way to Limerick or Tralee. When it had gone by we could hear a furious drunken uproar coming up from a canoe that was somewhere out in the bay. It sounded as if the men were strangling or murdering each other, and it seemed almost miraculous that they should be able to manage their canoe. The people seemed to think they were in no special danger, and we went in again to the fire and talked about porter and whiskey (I have never heard the men here talk for half an hour of anything without some allusion to drink), discussing how much a man could drink with comfort in a day, whether it is better to drink when a man is thirsty or at ordinary times, and what food gives the best liking for porter. Then they asked me how much porter I could drink myself, and I told them I could drink whiskey, but that I had no taste for porter, and would only take a pint or two at odd times, when I was thirsty.

'The girls are laughing to hear you say that,' said an old man; 'but whiskey is a lighter drink, and I'd sooner have it myself, and any old man would say the same.' A little later some young men came in, in their Sunday clothes, and told us the news of the sports.

This morning it was raining heavily, and the host got out some nets and set to work with his son and son-in-law, mending many holes that had been cut by dog-fish, as the mackerel season is soon to begin. While they were at work the kitchen emptied and filled continually with islanders passing in and out, and discussing the weather and the season. Then they started cutting each other's hair, the man who was being cut sitting with an oilskin round him on a little stool by the door, and some other men came in to sharpen their razors on the host's razor-strop, which seems to be the only one on the island. I had not shaved since I arrived, so the little hostess asked me after a while if I would like to shave myself before dinner. I told her I would, so she got me some water in the potato-dish and put it on a chair; then her sister got me a little piece of broken looking-glass and put it on a nail near the door, where there was some light. I set to work, and as I stood with my back to the people I could catch a score of eyes in the glass, watching me intently. 'That is a great improvement to you now,' said the host, when I had done; 'and whenever you want a beard, God bless you, you'll have a thick one surely.'

When I was coming down in the evening from the ridge of the island where I spent much of my time looking at the richness of the Atlantic on one side and the sad or shining greys of Dingle Bay on the other, I was joined by two young women and we walked back together. Just outside the village we met an old woman who stopped and laughed at us. 'Well, aren't you in good fortune this night, stranger,' she said, 'to be walking up and down in the company of women?'

'I am surely,' I answered; 'isn't that the best thing to be doing in the whole world?'

At our own door I saw the little hostess sweeping the floor, so I went down for a moment to the gable of the cottage, and looked out over the roofs of the little village to the sound, where the tide was running with extraordinary force. In a few minutes the little hostess came and stood beside me—she thought I should not be left by myself when I had been driven away by the dust

—and I asked her many questions about the names and relationships of the people that I am beginning to know.

Afterwards, when many of the people had come together in the kitchen, the men told me about their lobster-pots that are brought from Southampton, and cost half-a-crown each. 'In good weather,' said the man who was talking to me, 'they will often last for a quarter; but if storms come up on them they will sometimes break up in a week or two. Still and all, it is a good trade; and we do sell lobsters and crayfish every week in the season to a boat from England or a boat from France that does come in here, as you'll maybe see before you go.'

I told them I had often been in France, and one of the boys began counting up the numerals in French to show what he had learnt from their buyers. A little later, when the talk was beginning to flag, I turned to a young man near me—the best fiddler, I was told, on the island—and asked him to play us a dance. He made excuses, and would not get his fiddle; but two of the girls slipped off and brought it. The young man tuned it and offered it to me, but I insisted that he should take it first. Then he played one or two tunes, without tone, but with good intonation and rhythm. When it was my turn I played a few tunes also; but the pitch was so low I could not do what I wanted, and I had not much success with the people, though the fiddler himself watched me with interest. 'That is great playing,' he said, when I had finished; 'and I never seen anyone the like of you for moving your hand and getting the sound out of it with the full drag of the bow.' Then he played a polka and our couples danced. The women, as usual, were in their naked feet, and whenever there was a figure for

women only there was a curious hush and patter of bare
feet, till the heavy pounding and shuffling of the men's
boots broke in again. The whirl of music and dancing in
this little kitchen stirred me with an extraordinary
effect. The kindliness and merry-making of these
islanders, who, one knows, are full of riot and severity
and daring, has a quality and attractiveness that is absent
altogether from the life of towns, and makes one think
of the life that is shown in the ballads of Scotland.

After the dance the host, who had come in, sang a
long English doggerel about a poor scholar who went to
Maynooth and had great success in his studies, so that he
was praised by the bishop. Then he went home for his
holiday, and a young woman who had great riches asked
him into her parlour and told him it was no fit life for a
fine young man to be a priest, always saying Mass for
poor people, and that he would have a right to give up
his Latin and get married to herself. He refused her
offers and went back to his college. When he was gone
she went to the justice in great anger, and swore an oath
against him that he had seduced her and left her with
child. He was brought back for his trial, and he was in
risk to be degraded and hanged, when a man rode up on
a horse and said it was himself was the lover of the lady,
and the father of her child.

Then they told me about an old man of eighty years,
who is going to spend the winter alone on Inishvickillaun, an island six miles from this village. His son is making canoes and doing other carpenter's jobs on this
island, and the other children have scattered also; but
the old man refuses to leave the island he has spent his
life on, so they have left him with a goat, and a bag of
flour and stack of turf.

I have just been to the weaver's, looking at his loom and appliances. The host took me down to his cottage over the brow of the village, where some young men were finishing the skeleton of a canoe; and we found his family crowded round a low table on green stools with rope seats, finshing their dinner of potatoes. A little later the old weaver, who looks pale and sickly compared with the other islanders, took me into a sort of outhouse with a damp feeling in the air, where his loom was set up. He showed me how it was worked, and then brought out pieces of stuff that he had woven. At first I was puzzled by the fine brown colour of some of the material; but they explained it was from selected wools of the black or mottled sheep that are common here, and are so variegated that many tints of grey or brown can be had from their fleeces. The wool for the flannel is sometimes spun on this island; sometimes it is given to women in Dunquin, who spin it cheaply for so much a pound. Then it is woven, and finally the stuff is sent to a mill in Dingle to be cleaned and dressed before it is given to a tailor in Dingle to be made up for their own use. Such cloth is not cheap, but is of wonderful quality and strength. When I came out of the weaver's, a little sailing smack was anchored in the sound, and someone on board her was blowing a horn. They told me she was the French boat, and as I went back to my cottage I could see many canoes hurrying out to her with their cargoes of lobsters and crabs.

I have left the island again. I walked round the cliffs in the morning, and then packed my bag in my room, several girls putting their heads into the little window while I did so, to say it was a great pity I was not staying

for another week or a fortnight. Then the men went
off with my bag in a heavy shower, and I waited a minute or two while the little hostess buttered some bread
for my lunch, and tied it up in a clean handkerchief of
her own. Then I bid them good-bye, and set off down
to the slip with three girls, who came with me to see that
I did not go astray among the innumerable paths. It was
still raining heavily, so I told them to put my cape,
which they were carrying, over their heads. They did
so with delight, and ran down the path before me, to the
great amusement of the islanders. At the head of the cliff
many people were standing about to bid me good-bye
and wish me a good voyage.

The wind was in our favour, so the men took in their
oars after rowing for about a quarter of a mile and lay
down in the bottom of the canoe, while one man ran
up the sail, and the host steered with an oar. At Dunquin
the host hired me a dray, without springs, kissed my
hand in farewell, and I was driven away.

I have made my way round the foot of Dingle Bay
and up the south coast to a cottage where I often lodge.
As I was resting in a ditch some time in the afternoon,
on a lonely mountain road, a little girl came along with
a shawl over her head. She stopped in front of me and
asked me where I was going, and then after a little talk:
'Well, man, let you come,' she said; 'I'm going your
road as well as you.' I got up and we started. When I
got tired of the hill I mounted, and she ran along beside
me for several miles, till we fell in with some people cutting turf, and she stopped to talk to them.

Then for a while my road ran round an immense
valley of magnificent rich turf bog, with mountains all

round, and bowls where hidden lakes were lying bitten
out of the cliffs.

As I was resting again on a bridge over the Behy
where Diarmuid caught salmon with Grania, a man
stopped to light his pipe and talk to me. 'There are three
lakes above,' he said, 'Coomacarra, Coomaglaslaw and
Coomasdhara; the whole of this place was in a great
state in the bad times. Twenty years ago they sent down
a 'mergency man to lodge above by the lake and serve
processes on the people, but the people were off before
him and lay abroad in the heather. Then, in the course
of a piece, a night came, with great rain out of the
heavens, and my man said: "I'll get them this night in
their own beds, surely." Then he let call the peelers—
they had peelers waiting to mind him—and down they
came to the big stepping-stones they have above for
crossing the first river coming out of the lakes. My man
going in front to cross over, and the water was high up
covering the stones. Then he gave two leps or three, and
the peelers heard him give a great shriek down in the
flood. They went home after—what could they do?—
and the 'mergency man was found in the sea stuck in a
net.'

I was singularly pleased when I turned up the boreen
at last to this cottage where I lodge, and looked down
through a narrow gully to Dingle Bay. The people bade
me welcome when I came in, the old woman kissing my
hand.

There is no village near this cottage, yet many farms
are scattered on the hills near it; and as the people are
in some ways a leading family, many men and women
look in to talk or tell stories, or to buy a few pennyworth
of sugar or starch. Although the main road passes a few
hundred yards to the west, this cottage is well known

also to the race of local tramps who move from one family to another in some special neighbourhood or barony. This evening, when I came in, a little old man in a tall hat and long brown coat was sitting up on the settle beside the fire, and intending to spend, one could see, a night or more in the place.

I had a great deal to tell the people at first of my travels in different parts of the country, to the Blasket Islands—which they can see from here—Corkaguiney and Tralee; and they had news to tell me also of people who have married or died since I was here before, or gone away, or come back from America. Then I was told that the old man, Dermot (or Darby, as he is called in English), was the finest story-teller in Iveragh; and after a while he told us a long story in Irish, but spoke so rapidly and indistinctly—he had no teeth—that I could understand but few passages. When he had finished I asked him where he had heard the story.

'I heard it in the city of Portsmouth,' he said. 'I worked there fifteen years, and four years in Plymouth, and a long while in the hills of Wales; twenty-five years in all I was working at the other side; and there were many Irish in it, who would be telling stories in the evening, the same as we are doing here. I heard many good stories, but what can I do with them now and I an old lisping fellow, the way I can't give them out like a ballad?'

When he had talked a little more about his travels, and a bridge over the Severn, that he thought the greatest wonder of the world, I asked him if he remembered the famine.

'I do,' he said. 'I was living near Kenmare, and many's the day I saw them burying the corpses in the ditch by the road. It was after that I went to England,

for this country was ruined and destroyed. I heard there
was work at that time in Plymouth; so I went to Dublin
and took a boat that was going to England; but it was
at a place called Liverpool they put me on shore, and
then I had to walk to Plymouth, asking my way on the
road. In that place I saw the soldiers after coming back
from the Crimea, and they all broken and maimed.'

A little later, when he went out for a moment, the
people told me that he beats up and down between Killorglin and Ballinskelligs and the Inny river, and that he
is a particular crabby kind of man, and will not take
anything from the people but coppers and eggs.

'And he's a wasteful old fellow with all,' said the
woman of the house, 'though he's eighty years old or
beyond it, for whatever money he'll get one day selling
his eggs to the coastguards, he'll spend it the next getting
a drink when he's thirsty, or keeping good boots on his
feet.'

From that they began talking of misers, and telling
stories about them.

'There was an old woman,' said one of the men,
'living beyond to the east, and she was thought to have
a great store of money. She had one daughter only,
and in the course of a piece a young lad got married to
her, thinking he'd have her fortune. The woman died
after—God be merciful to her!—and left the two of
them as poor as they were before. Well, one night a man
that knew them was passing to the fair of Puck, and he
came in and asked would they give him a lodging for
that night. They gave him what they had and welcome;
and after his tea, when they were sitting over the fire—
the way we are this night—the man asked them how
they were so poor-looking, and if the old woman had
left nothing behind her.

' "Not a farthing did she leave," said the daughter.

' "And did she give no word or warning or message in her last moments?" said the man.

' "She did not," said the daughter, "except only that I shouldn't comb out the hair of her poll and she dead."

' "And you heeded her?" said the man.

' "I did, surely," said the daughter.

' "Well," said the man, "to-morrow night when I'm gone let the two of you go down the Relic (the graveyard) and dig up her coffin and look in her hair and see what it is you'll find in it."

' "We'll do that," said the daughter, and with that they all stretched out for the night.

'The next evening they went down quietly with a shovel and they dug up the coffin, and combed through her hair, and there behind her poll they found her fortune, five hundred pounds, in good notes and gold.'

'There was an old fellow living on the little hill beyond the graveyard,' said Danny-boy, when the man had finished, 'and he had his fortune some place hid in his bed, and he was an old weak fellow, so that they were all watching him to see he wouldn't hide it away. One time there was no one in it but himself and a young girl, and the old fellow slipped out of his bed and went out of the door as far as a little bush and some stones. The young girl kept her eye on him, and she made sure he'd hidden something in the bush; so when he was back in his bed she called the people, and they all came and looked in the bushes, but not a thing could they find. The old man died after, and no one ever found his fortune to this day.'

'There were some young lads a while since,' said the old woman, 'and they went up of a Sunday and began searching through those bushes to see if they could find anything, but a kind of a turkey-cock came up out of the stones and drove them away.'

'There was another old woman,' said the man of the house, 'who tried to take down her fortune into her stomach. She was near death, and she was all day stretched in her bed at the corner of the fire. One day when the girl was tinkering about, the old woman rose up and got ready a little skillet that was near the hob and put something into it and put it down by the fire, and the girl watching her all the time under her oxter, not letting on she had seen her at all. When the old woman lay down again the girl went over to put on more sods on the fire, and she got a look into the skillet, and what did she see but sixty sovereigns. She knew well what the old woman was striving to do, so she went out to the dairy and got a lump of fresh butter and put it down into the skillet, when the woman didn't see her do it at all. After a bit the old woman rose up and looked into the skillet, and when she saw the froth of the butter she thought it was the gold that was melted. She got back into her bed—a dark place, maybe—and she began sipping and sipping the butter till she had the whole of it swallowed. Then the girl made some trick to entice the skillet away from her, and she found the sixty sovereigns in the bottom and she kept them for herself.'

By this time it was late, and the old woman brought over a mug of milk and a piece of bread to Darby at the settle, and the people gathered at the table for their supper; so I went into the little room at the end of the cottage where I am given a bed.

When I came into the kitchen in the morning, old Darby was still asleep on the settle, with his coat and trousers over him, a red night-cap on his head, and his half-bred terrier, Jess, chained with a chain he carries with him to the leg of the settle.

'That's a poor way to lie on the bare board,' said the woman of the house, when she saw me looking at him; 'but when I filled a sack with straw for him last night he wouldn't have it at all.'

While she was boiling some eggs for my breakfast, Darby roused up from his sleep, pulled on his trousers and coat, slipped his feet into his boots and started off, when he had eaten a few mouthfuls, for another house where he is known, some five miles away.

Afterwards I went out on the cnuceen, a little hill between this cottage and the sea, to watch the people gathering carragheen moss, a trade which is much followed in this district during the spring tides of summer. I lay down on the edge of the cliff, where the heathery hill comes to an end and the steep rocks begin. About a mile to the west there was a long headland, 'Feakle Callaigh' ('The Witch's Tooth'), covered with mists, that blew over me from time to time with a swish of rain, followed by sunshine again. The mountains on the other side of the bay were covered, so I could see nothing but the strip of brilliant sea below me, thronged with girls and men up to their waists in the water, with a hamper in one hand and a stick in the other, gathering the moss, and talking and laughing loudly as they worked. The long frill of dark golden rocks covered with seaweed, with the asses and children slipping about on it, and the bars of silvery light breaking through on the further inlets of the bay, had the singularly brilliant liveliness one meets everywhere in Kerry.

When the tide began to come in I went down one of the passes to the sea, and met many parties of girls and old men and women coming up with what they had gathered, most of them still wearing the clothes that had been in the sea, and were heavy and black with salt water. A little further on I met Danny-boy and we sat down to talk.

'Do you see that sandy head?' he said, pointing out to the east, 'that is called the Stooks of the Dead Women; for one time a boat came ashore there with twelve dead women on board her, big ladies with green dresses and gold rings, and fine jewelries, and a dead harper or fiddler along with them. Then there are graves again in the little hollow by the cnuceen, and what we call them is the Graves of the Sailors; for some sailors, Greeks or great strangers, were washed in there a hundred years ago, and it is there that they were buried.'

Then we began talking of the carragheen he had gathered and the spring-tides that would come again during the summer. I took out my diary to tell him the times of the moon, but he would hardly listen to me. When I stopped, he gave his ass a cut with his stick, 'Go on, now,' he said; 'I wouldn't believe those almanacks at all; they do not tell the truth about the moon.'

The greatest event in West Kerry is the horse-fair, known as Puck Fair, which is held in August. If one asks anyone, many miles east or west of Killorglin, when he reaped his oats or sold his pigs or heifers, he will tell you it was four or five weeks, or whatever it may be, before or after Puck. On the main roads, for many days past, I have been falling in with tramps and trick characters of all kinds, sometimes single and sometimes in parties of four or five, and as I am on the roads a great deal I have often met the same persons several days in succession—one day perhaps at Ballinskelligs, the next day at Feakle Callaigh, and the third in the outskirts of Killorglin.

Yesterday cavalcades of every sort were passing from the west with droves of horses, mares, jennets, foals and asses, with their owners going after them in flat or railed carts, or riding on ponies.

The men of this house—they are going to buy a horse —went to the fair last night, and I followed at an early hour in the morning. As I came near Killorglin the road was much blocked by the latest sellers pushing eagerly forward, and early purchasers who were anxiously leading off their young horses before the roads became dangerous from the crush of drunken drivers and riders.

Just outside the town, near the first public-house, blind beggars were kneeling on the pathway, praying with almost Oriental volubility for the souls of anyone who would throw them a coin.

'May the Holy Immaculate Mother of Jesus Christ,' said one of them, 'intercede for you in the hour of need. Relieve a poor blind creature, and may Jesus Christ relieve yourselves in the hour of death. May He have mercy, I'm saying, on your brothers and fathers and sisters for evermore.'

Further on stalls were set out with cheap cakes and refreshments, and one could see that many houses had been arranged to supply the crowds who had come in. Then I came to the principal road that goes round the fair-green, where there was a great concourse of horses, trotting and walking and galloping; most of them were of the cheaper class of animal, and were selling, apparently to the people's satisfaction, at prices that reminded one of the time when fresh meat was sold for three pence a pound. At the further end of the green there were one or two rough shooting galleries, and a number

of women—not very rigid, one could see—selling, or
appearing to sell, all kinds of trifles: a set that come in, I
am told, from towns not far away. At the end of the
green I turned past the chapel, where a little crowd
had just carried in a man who had been killed or badly
wounded by a fall from a horse, and went down to the
bridge of the river, and then back again into the main
slope of the town. Here there were a number of people
who had come in for amusement only, and were walking up and down, looking at each other—a crowd is as
exciting as champagne to these lonely people, who live
in long glens among the mountains—and meeting with
cousins and friends. Then, in the three-cornered space
in the middle of the town, I came upon Puck himself, a
magnificent he-goat (Irish puc), raised on a platform
twenty feet high, and held by a chain from each horn,
with his face down the road. He is kept in this position,
with a few cabbages to feed on, for three days, so that
he may preside over the pig-fair and the horse-fair and
the day of winding up.

At the foot of this platform, where the crowd was
thickest, a young ballad-singer was howling a ballad in
honour of Puck, making one think of the early Greek
festivals, since the time of which, it is possible, the goat
has been exalted yearly in Killorglin.

The song was printed on a green slip by itself. It
ran:—

A NEW SONG ON THE GREAT
PUCK FAIR

BY JOHN PURCELL.

All young lovers that are fond of sporting, pay attention
    for a while,

I will sing you the praises of Puck Fair, and I'm sure
   it will make you smile;
Where the lads and lassies coming gaily to Killorglin
   can be seen,
To view the Puck upon the stage, as our hero dressed
   in green.

CHORUS

And hurra for the gallant Puck so gay,
For he is a splendid one:
Wind and rain don't touch his tail,
For his hair is thirty inches long.

Now it is on the square he's erected with all colours
   grand and gay;
There's not a fair throughout Ireland, but Puck Fair
   it takes the sway,
Where you see the gamblers in rotation, trick-o-the-loop
   and other games,
The ballad-singers and the wheel-of-fortune, and the
   shooting-gallery for to take aim.

CHORUS

Where is the tyrant dare oppose it?
Our old customs we will hold up still,
And I think we will have another—
That is, Home Rule and Purchase Bill.

Now, all young men that are not married, next Shrove
   can take a wife,
For before next Puck Fair we will have Home Rule,
   and then you will be settled down in life.
Now the same advice I give young girls for to get married and have pluck.

Let the landlords see that you defy them when coming
to fair of Puck.

Céad Mlle Fáilte to the Fair of Puck.

When one makes the obvious elisions, the lines are
not so irregular as they look, and are always sung to a
measure; yet the whole, in spite of the assonance, rhymes,
and the 'colours grand and gay' seems pitifully remote
from any good spirit of ballad-making.

Across the square, a man and a woman, who had a
baby tied on her back, were singing another ballad on
the Russian and Japanese War, in the curious method
of antiphony that is still heard in the back streets of Dublin. These are some of the verses:—

MAN

Now provisions are rising, 'tis sad for to state,
The flour, tea and sugar, tobacco and meat;
But, God help us! poor Irish, how must we stand the
test

AMBO

If they only now stop the trade of commerce.

WOMAN

Now the Russians are powerful on sea and on land;
But the Japs they are active, they will them command,
Before this war is finished I have one word to say,

AMBO

There will be more shot and drowned than in the
Crimea.

MAN

Now the Japs are victorious up to this time,
And thousands of Russians I hear they are dying.
Etc., etc.

And so it went on with the same alternation of the voices through seven or eight verses; and it was curious to feel how much was gained by this simple variation of the voices.

When I passed back to the fair-green, I met the men I am staying with, and went off with them under an archway, and into a back yard to look at a little two-year-old filly that they had bought and left for the moment in a loose box with three or four young horses. She was prettily and daintily shaped, but looked too light, I thought, for the work she will be expected to do. As we came out into the road, an old man was singing an outspoken ballad on women in the middle of the usual crowd. Just as we passed it came to a scandalous conclusion; and the women scattered in every direction, shrieking with laughter and holding shawls over their mouths.

At the corner we turned into a public-house, where there were men we knew, who had done their business also; and we went into the little alcove to sit down quietly for a moment. 'What will you take, sir,' said the man I lodge with, 'a glass of wine?'

I took beer and the others took porter, but we were only served after some little time, as the house was thronged with people.

The men were too much taken up with their bargains and losses to talk much of other matters; and before long we came out again, and the son of the house started homewards, leading the new filly by a little halter of rope.

Not long afterwards I started also. Outside Killorglin rain was coming up over the hills of Glen Car, so that there was a strained hush in the air, and a rich, aromatic smell coming from the bog myrtle or boggy shrub, that grows thickly in this place. The strings of horses and jennets scattered over the road did not keep away a strange feeling of loneliness that seems to hang over this brown plain of bog that stretches from Carrantuohill to Cuchulain's House.

Before I reached the cottage dense torrents of rain were closing down through the glens, and driving in white sheets between the little hills that are on each side of the way.

One morning in autumn I started in a local train for the first stage of my journey to Dublin, seeing the last of Macgillicuddy's Reeks, that were touched with snow in places, Dingle Bay and the islands beyond it. At a little station where I changed trains, I got into a carriage where there was a woman with her daughter, a girl of about twenty, who seemed uneasy and distressed. Soon afterwards, when a collector was looking at our tickets, I called out that mine was for Dublin, and as soon as he got out the woman came over to me.

'Are you going to Dublin?' she said.

I told her I was.

'Well,' she went on, 'here is my daughter going there too; and maybe you'd look after her, for I'm getting down at the next station. She is going up to a hospital for some little complaint in her ear, and she has never travelled before, so that she's lonesome in her mind.'

I told her I would do what I could, and at the next

station I was left alone with my charge, and one other passenger, a returned American girl, who was on her way to Mallow, to get the train for Queenstown. When her mother was lost sight of the young girl broke out into tears, and the returned American and myself had trouble to quiet her.

'Look at me,' said the American. 'I'm going off for ten years to America, all by myself, and I don't care a rap.'

When the girl got quiet again, the returned American talked to me about scenery and politics and the arts —she had been seen off by her sisters in bare feet, with shawls over their heads—and the life of women in America.

At several stations girls and boys thronged in to get places for Queenstown, leaving parties of old men and women wailing with anguish on the platform. At one place an old woman was seized with such a passion of regret, when she saw her daughters moving away from her for ever, that she made a wild rush after the train; and when I looked out for a moment I could see her writhing and struggling on the platform, with her hair over her face, and two men holding her by the arms.

Two young men had got into our compartment for a few stations only, and they looked on with the greatest satisfaction.

'Ah,' said one of them, 'we do have great sport every Friday and Saturday, seeing the old women howling in the stations.'

When we reached Dublin I left my charge for a moment to see after my baggage, and when I came back I found her sitting on a luggage barrow, with her package in her hand, crying with despair because several cabmen had refused to let her into their cabs, on the pretext that they dreaded infection.

I could see they were looking out for some rich tourist with his trunks, as a more lucrative fare; so I sent for the head porter, who had charge of the platform. When the porter arrived we chose a cab, and I saw my charge driven off to the hospital, sitting on the front seat, with her handkerchief to her eyes.

For the last few days—I am staying in the Kerry cottage I have spoken of already—the people have been talking of horse-races that were to be held on the sand, not far off, and this morning I set out to see them with the man and woman of the house and two of their neighbours. Our way led through a steep boreen for a quarter of a mile to the edge of the sea, and then along a pathway between the cliffs and a straight grassy hill. When we had gone some distance the old man pointed out a slope in front of us, where, he said, Diarmuid had done his tricks of rolling the barrel and jumping over his spear, and had killed many of his enemies. He told me the whole story, slightly familiarised in detail, but not very different from the version everyone knows. A little further on he pointed across the sea to our left— just beyond the strand where the races were to be run— to a neck of sand where, he said, Oisin was called away to the Tir-na-nOg.

'The Tir-na-nOg itself,' he said, 'is below that sea, and a while since there were two men out in a boat in the night-time, and they got stuck outside some way or another. They went to sleep then, and when one of them wakened up he looked down into the sea, and he saw the Tir-na-nOg and people walking about, and side-cars driving in the squares.'

Then he began telling me stories of mermaids—a common subject in this neighbourhood.

'There was one time a man beyond of the name of Shee,' he said, 'and his master seen a mermaid on the sand beyond combing her hair, and he told Shee to get her. "I will," said Shee, "if you give me the best horse you have in your stable." "I'll do that," said the master. Then Shee got the horse, and when he saw the mermaid on the sand combing her hair, with her covering laid away from her, he galloped up, when she wasn't looking, and he picked up the covering and away he went with it. Then the waves rose up behind him and he galloped his best, and just as he was coming out at the top of the tide the ninth wave cut off his horse behind his back, and left himself and the half of his horse and the covering on the dry land. Then the mermaid came in after her covering, and the master got married to her, and she lived with him a long time, and had children— three or four of them. Well, in the wind-up, the master built a fine new house, and when he was moving into it, and clearing the things out, he brought down an old hamper out of the loft and put it in the yard. The woman was going about, and she looked into the hamper, and she saw her covering hidden away in the bottom of it. She took it out then and put it upon her and went back into the sea, and her children used to be on the shore crying after her. I'm told from that day there isn't one of the Shees can go out in a boat on that bay and not be drowned.'

We were now near the sandhills, where a crowd was beginning to come together, and booths were being put up for the sale of apples and porter and cakes. A train had come in a little before at a station a mile or so away, and a number of the usual trick-characters, with

their stock-in-trade, were hurrying down to the sea.
The roulette man passed us first, unfolding his table and
calling out at the top of his voice:

Come play me a game of timmun and tup,
The more you puts down the more you takes up.

'Take notice, gentlemen, I come here to spend a fortune, not to make one. Is there any sportsman in a hat or
a cap, or a wig or a waistcoat, will play a go with me
now? Take notice, gentlemen, the luck is on the green.'

The races had to be run between two tides while the
sand was dry, so there was not much time to be lost,
and before we reached the strand the horses had been
brought together, ridden by young men in many variations of jockey dress. For the first race there was one
genuine race-horse, very old and bony, and two or three
young horses belonging to farmers in the neighbourhood.
The start was made from the middle of the crowd at the
near end of the strand, and the course led out along the
edge of the sea to a post some distance away, back again
to the starting-point, round a post, and out and back
once more.

When the word was given the horses set off in a wild
helter-skelter along the edge of the sea, with crowds
cheering them on from the sandhills. As they got small
in the distance it was not easy to see which horse was
leading, but after a sort of check, as they turned the post,
they began nearing again a few yards from the waves,
with the old race-horse, heavily pressed, a good length
ahead. The stewards made a sort of effort to clear the
post that was to be circled, but without much success, as
the people were wild with excitement. A moment later
the old race-horse galloped into the crowd, twisted too

suddenly, something cracked and jolted, and it limped out on three legs, gasping with pain. The next horse could not be stopped, and galloped out at the wrong end of the crowd for some little way before it could be brought back, so the last horses set off in front for the final lap.

The lame race-horse was now mobbed by onlookers and advisers, talking incoherently.

'Was it the fault of the jock?' said one man.

'It was not,' said another, 'for Michael (the owner) didn't strike him, and if it had been his fault, wouldn't he have broken his bones?'

'He was striving to spare a young girl had run out in his way,' said another. 'It was for that he twisted him.'

'Little slut!' said a woman; 'what did she want beyond on the sand?'

Many remedies were suggested that did not sound reassuring, and in the end the horse was led off in a hopeless condition. A little later the race ended with an easy win for the wildest of the young horses. Afterwards I wandered up among the people, and looked at the sports. At one place a man, with his face heavily blackened, except one cheek and eye—an extraordinary effect—was standing shots of a wooden ball behind a board with a large hole in the middle, at three shots a penny. When I came past half an hour afterwards he had been hit in the mouth—by a girl some one told me —but seemed as cheerful as ever.

On the road, some little distance away, a party of girls and young men were dancing polkas to the music of a melodeon, in a cloud of dust. When I had looked on for a little while I met some girls I knew, and asked them how they were getting on.

'We're not getting on at all,' said one of them, 'for

we've been at the races for two hours, and we've found no beaux to go along with us.'

When the horses had all run, a jennet race was held, and greatly delighted the people, as the jennets—there were a number of them—got scared by the cheering and ran wild in every direction. In the end it was not easy to say which was the winner, and a dispute began which nearly ended in blows. It was decided at last to run the race over again the following Sunday after Mass, and everyone was satisfied.

The day was magnificently bright, and the ten miles from Dingle Bay were wonderfully brilliant behind the masses of people, and the canvas booths, and the scores of upturned shafts. Towards evening I got tired taking or refusing the porter my friends pressed on me continually, so I wandered off from the racecourse along the path where Diarmuid had tricked the Fenians.

Later in the evening news had been coming in of the doings in the sandhills, after the porter had begun to take effect and the darkness had come on.

'There was great sport after you left,' a man said to me in the cottage this evening. 'They were all beating and cutting each other on the shore of the sea. Four men fought together in one place till the tide came up on them, and was like to drown them; but the priest waded out up to his middle and drove them asunder. Another man was left for dead on the road outside the lodges, and some gentleman found him and had him carried into his house, and got the doctor to put plasters on his head. Then there was a red-headed fellow had his finger bitten through, and the postman was destroyed for ever.'

'He should be,' said the man of the house, 'for

Michael Patch broke the seat of his car into three halves on his head.'

'It was this was the cause of it all,' said Danny-boy: 'they brought in porter east and west from the two towns you know of, and the two porters didn't agree together, and it's for that the people went raging at the fall of night.'

I have been out to Bolus Head, one of the finest places I have met with. A little beyond Ballinskelligs the road turns up the side of a steep mountainy hill where one sees a brilliant stretch of sea, with many rocks and islands—Deenish, Scariff, the Hog's Head, and Dursey far away. As I was sitting on the edge of the road an old man came along and we began to talk. He had little English, but when I tried him in Irish we got on well, though he did not follow any Connaught forms I let slip by accident. We went on together, after a while, to an extraordinary straggling village along the edge of the hill. At one of the cottages he stopped and asked me to come in and take a drink and rest myself. I did not like to refuse him, we had got so friendly, so I followed him in, and sat down on a stool while his wife—a much younger woman—went into the bedroom and brought me a large mug of milk. As I was drinking it and talking to the couple, a sack that was beside the fire began to move slowly, and the head of a yellow, feverish-looking child came out from beneath it, and began looking at me with a heavy stare. I asked the woman what ailed it, and she told me it had sickened a night or two before with headache and pains all through it; but she had not had the doctor, and did not know what was the matter. I finished the milk without much enjoyment, and went on my way up Bolus Head and then back to this cottage, wondering all the time if I had the germs of typhus in my blood.

Last night when I got back to the cottage, I found that another 'travelling man' had arrived to stay for a day or two; but he was hard of hearing and a little simple in his head, so that we had not much talk. I went to bed soon after dark and slept till about two o'clock in the morning, when I was awakened by fearful screams in the kitchen. For a moment I did not know where I was; then I remembered the old man, and I jumped up and went to the door of my room. As I opened it I heard the door of the family room across the kitchen opening also, and the frightened whispers of the people. In a moment we could hear the old man, who was sleeping on the settle, pulling himself out of a nightmare, so we went back to our beds.

In the morning the woman told me his story:—

'He was living above on a little hillside,' she said, 'in a bit of a cabin, with his sister along with him. Then, after a while, she got ailing in her heart, and he got a bottle for her from the doctor, and he'd rise up every morning before the dawn to give her a sup of it. She got better then, till one night he got up and measured out the spoonful, or whatever it was, and went to give it to her, and he found her stretched out dead before him. Since that night he wakes up one time and another, and begins crying out for Maurya—that was his sister—and he half in his dreams. It was that you heard in the night, and indeed it would frighten any person to hear him screaming as if he was getting his death.'

When the little man came back after a while, they began asking him questions till he told his whole story, weeping pitiably. Then they got him to tell me about the other great event of his life also, in the rather child-ish Gaelic he uses.

He had once a little cur-dog, he said, and he knew nothing of the dog licence; then one day the peelers—the boys with the little caps—asked him into the bar-racks for a cup of tea. He went in cheerfully, and then they put him and his little dog into the lock-up till some one paid a shilling for him and got him out.

He has a stick he is proud of, bound with pieces of leather every few inches—like one I have seen with a beggar in Belmullet. Since the first night he has not had nightmare again, and he lies most of the evening sleep-ing on the settle, and in the morning he goes round among the houses, getting his share of meal and pota-toes.

I do not think a beggar is ever refused in Kerry. Sometimes, while we are talking or doing something in the kitchen, a man walks in without saying anything and stands just inside the door, with his bag on the floor beside him. In five or ten minutes, when the woman of the house has finished what she is doing, she goes up to him and asks: 'Is it meal or flour?' 'Flour,' says the man. She goes into the inner room, opens her sack, and comes back with two handfuls. He opens his bag and takes out a bundle carefully tied up in a cloth or handkerchief; he opens this again, and usually there is another cloth inside, into which the woman puts her flour. Then the cloths are carefully knotted together by the corners, put back in the bag, and the man mutters a 'God bless you,' and goes on his way.

The meal, flour and potatoes that are thus gathered up are always sold by the beggar, and the money is spent on porter or second-hand clothes, or very occasionally on food when he is in a neighbourhood that is not hospitable. The buyers are usually found among the coast-guards' wives, or in the little public-houses on the road-side.

'Some of these men,' said the woman of the house, when I asked her about them, 'will take their flour nicely and tastily and cleanly, and others will throw it in any way, and you'd be sorry to eat it afterwards.'

The talk of these people is almost bewildering. I have come to this cottage again and again, and I often think I have heard all they have to say, and then some one makes a remark that leads to a whole new bundle of folk-tales, or stories of wonderful events that have happened in the barony in the last hundred years. To-night the people were unusually silent although several neighbours had come in, and to make conversation I said something about the bull-fights in Spain that I had been reading of in the newspapers. Immediately they started off with stories of wicked or powerful bulls, and then they branched off to clever dogs and all the things they have done in West Kerry, and to mad dogs and mad cattle and pigs—one incident after another, but always detailed and picturesque and interesting.

I have come back to the north of Dingle, leaving Tralee late in the afternoon. At the station there was a more than usually great crowd, as there had been a fair in the town and many people had come in to make their Saturday purchases. A number of messenger boys with parcels from the shops in the town were shouting for the owners, using many familiar names. Justin Mac-Carthy, Hannah Lynch and the like. I managed to get a seat on a sack of flour beside the owner, who had other packages scattered under our feet. When the train had started and the women and girls—the carriage was filled with them—had settled down into their places, I could see I caused great curiosity, as it was too late in the year for even an odd tourist, and on this line everyone is known by sight.

Before long I got into talk with the old man next me, and as soon as I did so the women and girls stopped their talk and leaned out to hear what we were saying.

He asked first if I belonged to Dingle, and I told him I did not.

'Well,' he said, 'you speak like a Kerry man, and you're dressed like a Kerry man, so you belong to Kerry surely.'

I told him I was born and bred in Dublin, and that I had travelled in many places in Ireland and beyond it.

'That's easy said,' he answered, 'but I'd take an oath you were never beyond Kerry to this day.'

Then he asked sharply:—'What do you do?'

I answered something about my wanderings in Europe, and suddenly he sat up, as if a new thought had come to him.

'Maybe you're a wealthy man?' he said.

I smiled complacently.

'And about thirty-five?'

I nodded.

'And not married?'

'No.'

'Well then,' he said, 'you're a damn lucky fellow to be travelling the world with no one to impede you.'

Then he went on to discuss the expenses of travelling.

'You'll likely be paying twenty pounds for this trip,' he said, 'with getting your lodging and buying your tickets, till you're back in the city of Dublin?'

I told him my expenses were not so heavy.

'Maybe you don't drink so,' said his wife, who was

near us, 'and that way your living wouldn't be so costly at all.'

An interruption was made by a stop at a small station and the entrance of a ragged ballad-singer, who sang a long ballad about the sorrows of mothers who see all their children going away from them to America.

Further on, when the carriage was much emptier, a middle-aged man got in, and we began discussing the fishing season, Aran fishing, hookers, nobbies and mackerel. I could see, while we were talking, that he, in his turn, was examining me with curiosity. At last he seemed satisfied.

'Begob,' he said, 'I see what you are; you're a fish-dealer.'

It turned out that he was the skipper of a trawler, and we had a long talk, the two of us and a local man who was going to Dingle also.

'There was one time a Frenchman below,' said the skipper, 'who got married here and settled down and worked with the rest of us. One day we were outside in the trawler, and there was a French boat anchored a bit of a way off. "Come on," says Charley—that was his name—"and see can we get some brandy from that boat beyond." "How would we get brandy," says I, "when we've no fish, or meat, or cabbages or a thing at all to offer them?" He went down below then to see what he could get. At that time there were four men only working the trawler, and in the heavy season there were eight. Well, up he comes again and eight plates under his arm. "There are eight plates," says he, "and four will do us; so we'll take out the other four and make a swap with them for brandy." With that he set the eight plates on the deck and began walking up and down and looking on them.

' "The devil mend you," says I. "Will you take them up and come on, if you're coming?"

' "I will," says he, "surely. I'm choicing out the ones that have pictures on them, for it's that kind they do set store on." '

Afterwards we began talking of boats that had been upset during the winter, and lives that had been lost in the neighbourhood.

'A while since,' said the local man, 'there were three men out in a canoe, and the sea rose on them. They tried to come in under the cliff, but they couldn't come to land with the greatness of the waves that were breaking. There were two young men in the canoe, and another man was sixty, or near it. When the young men saw they couldn't bring in the canoe, they said they'd make a jump for the rocks and let her go without them, if she must go. Then they pulled in on the next wave, and when they were close in the two young men jumped on to a rock, but the old man was too stiff, and he was washed back again in the canoe. It came on dark after that, and all thought he was drowned, and they held his wake in Dunquin. At that time there used to be a steamer going in and out trading in Valentia and Dingle, and Cahirciveen, and when she came into Dingle two or three days after, there was my man on board her as hearty as a salmon. When he was washed back he got one of the oars, and kept her head to the wind; then the tide took him one bit and the wind took him another, and he wrought and he wrought till he was safe beyond in Valentia. Wasn't that a great wonder?' Then as he was ending his story we ran down into Dingle.

Often, when one comes back to a place that one's

memory and imagination have been busy with, there is a feeling of smallness and disappointment, and it is a day or two before one can renew all one's enjoyment. This morning, however, when I went up the gap between Croagh Martin and then back to Slea Head, and saw Innishtooskert and Inishvickillaun and the Great Blasket Island itself, they seemed ten times more grey and wild and magnificent than anything I had kept in my memory. The cold sea and surf, and the feeling of winter in the clouds, and the blackness of the rocks, and the red fern everywhere, were a continual surprise and excitement.

Here and there on my way I met old men with tail-coats of frieze, that are becoming so uncommon. When I spoke to them in English they shook their heads and muttered something I could not hear; but when I tried Irish they made me long speeches about the weather and the clearness of the day.

In the evening, as I was coming home, I got a glimpse that seemed to have the whole character of Corkaguiney—a little line of low cottages with yellow roofs, and an elder tree without leaves beside them, standing out against a high mountain that seemed far away, yet was near enough to be dense and rich and wonderful in its colour.

Then I wandered round the wonderful forts of Fahan. The blueness of the sea and the hills from Carrantuohill to the Skelligs, the singular loneliness of the hillside I was on, with a few choughs and gulls in sight only, had a splendour that was almost a grief in the mind.

I turned into a little public-house this evening, where Maurice—the fisherman I have spoken of before—and some of his friends often sit when it is too wild for fish-ing. While we were talking a man came in, and joined rather busily in what was being said, though I could see he was not belonging to the place. He moved his position several times till he was quite close to me, then he whis-pered: 'Will you stand me a medium, mister? I'm hard set for money this while past.' When he had got his medium he began to give me his history. He was a journeyman tailor who had been a year or more in the place, and was beginning to pick up a little Irish to get along with. When he had gone we had a long talk about the making of canoes and the difference between those used in Connaught and Munster.

'They have been in this country,' said Maurice, 'for twenty or twenty-five years only, and before that we had boats; a canoe will cost twelve pounds, or maybe thirteen pounds, and there is one old man beyond who charges fifteen pounds. If it is well done a canoe will stand for eight years, and you can get a new skin on it when the first one is gone.'

I told him I thought canoes had been in Connemara since the beginning of the world.

'That may well be,' he went on, 'for there was a certain man going out as a pilot, up and down into Clare, and it was he made them first in this place. It is a trade few can learn, for it is all done within the head; you will have to sit down and think it out, and then make up when it is all ready in your mind.'

I described the fixed thole-pins that are used in Con-naught—here they use two freely moving thole-pins, with the oar loose between them, and they jeered at the simplicity of the Connaught system. Then we got on the relative value of canoes and boats.

'They are not better than boats,' said Maurice, 'but

they are more useful. Before you get a heavy boat swimming you will be up to your waist, and then you will be sitting the whole night like that; but a canoe will swim in a handful of water, so that you can get in dry and be dry and warm the whole night. Then there will be seven men in a big boat and seven shares of the fish; but in a canoe there will be three men only and three shares of the fish, though the nets are the same in the two.'

After a while a man sang a song, and then we began talking of tunes and playing the fiddle, and I told them how hard it was to get any sound out of one in a cottage with a floor of earth and a thatched roof over you.

'I can believe that,' said one of the men. 'There was a man a while since went into Tralee to buy a fiddle; and when he went into the shop an old fiddler followed him into it, thinking maybe he'd get the price of a pint. Well, the man was within choicing the fiddles, maybe forty of them, and the old fiddler whispered to him to take them out in the air, "for there's many a fiddle would sound well in here wouldn't be worth a curse outside," says he; so he was bringing them out and bringing them out till he found a good one among them.'

This evening, after a day of teeming rain, it cleared for an hour, and I went out while the sun was setting to a little cove where a high sea was running. As I was coming back the darkness began to close in except in the west, where there was a red light under the clouds. Against this light I could see patches of open wall and little fields of stooks, and a bit of laneway with an old man driving white cows before him. These seem transfigured beyond any description.

Then I passed two men riding bare-backed towards

the west, who spoke to me in Irish, and a little further on I came to the only village on my way. The ground rose towards it, and as I came near there was a grey bar of smoke from every cottage going up to the low clouds overhead, and standing out strangely against the blackness of the mountain behind the village.

Beyond the patch of wet cottages I had another stretch of lonely roadway, and a heron kept flapping in front of me, rising and lighting again with many lonely cries that made me glad to reach the little public-house near Smerwick.

IN THE CONGESTED DISTRICTS

FROM GALWAY TO GORUMNA

SOME of the worst portions of the Irish congested districts—of which so much that is contradictory has been spoken and written—lie along the further north coast of Galway Bay, and about the whole seaboard from Spiddal to Clifden. Some distance inland there is a line of railway, and in the bay itself a steamer passes in and out to the Aran Islands; but this particular district can only be visited thoroughly by driving or riding over some thirty or forty miles of desolate roadway. If one takes this route from Galway one has to go a little way only to reach places and people that are fully typical of Connemara. On each side of the road one sees small square fields of oats, or potatoes, or pasture, divided by loose stone walls that are built up without mortar. Wherever there are a few cottages near the road one sees barefooted women hurrying backwards and forwards, with hampers of turf or grass slung over their backs, and generally a few children running after them, and if it is a market-day, as was the case on the day of which I am going to write, one overtakes long strings of country people driving home from Galway in low carts drawn by an ass or pony. As a rule one or two men sit in front of the cart driving and smoking, with a couple of women behind them stretched out at their ease among sacks of flour or young pigs, and nearly always talking continuously in Gaelic. These men are all dressed in homespuns of the grey natural wool, and the women in deep madder-dyed petticoats and bodices, with brown shawls over their heads. One's first feeling as one comes back among these people and takes a place, so to speak, in this noisy procession of fishermen, farmers, and women, where nearly everyone is interesting and attractive, is a dread of any reform that would tend to lessen their individuality rather than any very real hope of improving their well-being. One feels then, perhaps a little later, that it is a part of the misfortune of Ireland that nearly all the characteristics which give colour and attractiveness to Irish life are bound up with a social condition that is near to penury, while in countries like Brittany the best external features of the local life—the rich embroidered dresses, for instance, or the carved furniture —are connected with a decent and comfortable social condition.

About twelve miles from Galway one reaches Spiddal, a village which lies on the borderland between the fairly prosperous districts near Galway and the barren country further to the west. Like most places of its kind, it has a double row of houses—some of them with two storeys—several public-houses with a large police barracks among them, and a little to one side a coastguard station, ending up at either side of the village with a chapel and a church. It was evening when we drove into Spiddal, and a little after sunset we walked on to a rather exposed quay, where a few weather-beaten hookers were moored with many ropes. As we came down none of the crews was to be seen, but threads of turf-smoke rising from the open manhole of the forecastle showed that the men were probably on board. While we were looking down on them from the pier—the tide was far out—an old grey-haired man, with the inflamed eyes that are so common here from the continual itching of the turf-smoke, peered up through the manhole and watched us with vague curiosity. A few moments later a young man came down from a field of black earth, where he had been digging a drain, and asked the old man, in Gaelic, to throw him a spark for his pipe. The latter disappeared for a moment, then came up again with a smouldering end of a turf sod in his hand, and threw it up on the pier, where the young man caught it with a quick downward grab without burning himself, blew it into a blaze, lit his pipe with it, and went back to his work. These people are so poor that many of them do not spend any money on matches. The spark of lighting turf is kept alive day and night on the hearth, and when a man goes out fishing or to work in the fields he usually carries a lighted sod with him, and keeps it all day buried in ashes or any dry rubbish, so that he can use it when he needs it. On our way back to the village an old woman begged from us, speaking in English, as most of the people do to anyone who is not a native. We gave her a few halfpence, and as she was moving away with an ordinary 'God save you!' I said a blessing to her in Irish to show her that I knew her own language if she chose to use it. Immediately she turned back towards me and began her thanks again, this time with extraordinary profusion. 'That the blessing of God may be on you,' she said, 'on road and on ridgeway, on sea and on land, on flood and on mountain, in all the kingdoms of the world'—and so on, till I was too far off to hear what she was saying.

In a district like Spiddal one sees curious gradations of types, especially on Sundays and holidays, when everyone is dressed as their fancy leads them and as well as they can manage. As I watched the people coming from Mass the morning after we arrived this was curiously noticeable. The police and coastguards came first in their smartest uniforms; then the shopkeepers, dressed like the people of Dublin, but a little more grotesquely; then the more well-to-do country folk, dressed only in the local clothes I have spoken of, but the best and newest kind, while the wearers themselves looked well-fed and healthy, and a few of them, especially the girls, magnificently built; then, last of all, one saw the destitute in still the same clothes, but this time patched and threadbare and ragged, the women mostly barefooted, and both sexes pinched with hunger and the fear of it. The class that he would be most interested to see increase is that of the typical well-to-do people, but except in a few districts it is not numerous, and is always aspiring after the dress of the shop-people or tending to sink down again among the paupers.

Later in the day we drove on another long stage to the west. As before, the country we passed through was not depressing, though stony and barren as a quarry. At every crossroads we passed groups of young, healthy-looking boys and men amusing themselves with hurley or pitching, and further back on little heights, a small field's breadth from the road, there were many groups of girls sitting out by the hour, near enough to the road to see everything that was passing, yet far enough away to keep their shyness undisturbed. Their red dresses looked peculiarly beautiful among the fresh green of the grass and opening bracken, with a strip of sea behind them, and, far away, the grey cliffs of Clare. A little further on, some ten miles from Spiddal, inlets of the sea begin to run in towards the mountains, and the road turns north to avoid them across an expanse of desolate bog far more dreary than the rocks of the coast. Here one sees a few wretched sheep nibbling in places among the turf, and occasionally a few ragged people walking rapidly by the roadside. Before we stopped for the night we had reached another bay coast-line, and were among stones again. Later in the evening we walked out round another small quay, with the usual little band of shabby hookers, and then along a road that rose in some places a few hundred feet above the sea; and as one looked down into the little fields that lay below it, they looked so small and rocky that the very thought of tillage in them seemed like the freak of an eccentric. Yet in this particular place tiny cottages, some of them without windows, swarmed by the roadside and in the 'boreens,' or laneways, at either side, many of them built on a single sweep of stone with the naked living rock for their floor. A number of people were to be seen everywhere about them, the men loitering by the roadside and the women hurrying among the fields, feeding an odd calf or lamb, or driving in a few ducks before the night. In one place a few boys were playing pitch with trousers buttons, and a little farther on half-a-score of young men were making donkeys jump backwards and forwards over a low wall. As we came back we met two men, who came and talked to us, one of them, by his hat and dress, plainly a man who had been away from Connemara. In a little while he told us that he had been in Gloucester and Bristol working on public works, but had wearied of it and came back to his country.

'Bristol,' he said, 'is the greatest town, I think, in all England, but the work in it is hard.'

I asked him about the fishing in the neighbourhood we were in. 'Ah,' he said, 'there's little fishing in it at all, for we have no good boats. There is no one asking for boats for this place, for the shopkeepers would rather have the people idle, so that they can get them for a shilling a day to go out in their old hookers and sell turf in Aran and on the coast of Clare.' Then we talked of Aran, and he told me of people I knew there who had died or got married since I had been on the islands, and then they went on their way.

BETWEEN THE BAYS OF
CARRAROE

In RURAL Ireland very few parishes only are increasing in population, and those that are doing so are usually in districts of the greatest poverty. One of the most curious instances of this tendency is to be found in the parish of Carraroe, which is said to be, on the whole, the poorest parish in the country, although many worse cases of individual destitution can be found elsewhere. The most characteristic part of this district lies on a long promontory between Cashla Bay and Greatman's Bay. On both coast-lines one sees a good many small quays, with, perhaps, two hookers moored to them, and on the roads one passes an occasional flat space covered with small green fields of oats—with whole families on their knees weeding among them—or patches of potatoes; but for the rest one sees little but an endless series of low stony hills, with veins of grass. Here and there, however, one comes in sight of a fresh-water lake, with an island or two, covered with seagulls, and many cottages round the shore; some of them standing almost on the brink of the water, others a little higher up, fitted in among the rocks, and one or two standing out on the top of a ridge against the blue of the sky or of the Twelve Bens of Connaught.

At the edge of one of these lakes, near a school of lace or knitting—one of those that have been established by the Congested Districts Board—we met a man driving a mare and foal that had scrambled out of their enclosure, although the mare had her two off-legs chained together. As soon as he had got them back into one of the fields and built up the wall with loose stones, he came over to a stone beside us and began to talk about horses and the dying out of the ponies of Connemara. 'You will hardly get any real Connemara ponies now at all,' he said; 'and the kind of horses they send down to us to improve the breed are no use, for the horses we breed from them will not thrive or get their health on the little patches where we have to put them. This last while most of the people in this parish are giving up horses altogether. Those that have them sell their foals when they are about six months old for four pounds, or five maybe; but the better part of the people are working with an ass only, that can carry a few things on a straddle over her back.'

'If you've no horses,' I said, 'how do you get to Galway if you want to go to a fair or to market?'

'We go by the sea,' he said, 'in one of the hookers you've likely seen at the little quays while walking down by the road. You can sail to Galway if the wind is fair in four hours or less maybe; and the people here are all used to the sea, for no one can live in this place but by cutting turf in the mountains and sailing out to sell it in Clare or Aran, for you see yourselves there's no good in the land, that has little in it but bare rocks and stones. Two years ago there came a wet summer, and the people were worse off then than they are now maybe, with their bad potatoes and all; for they couldn't cut or dry a load of turf to sell across the bay, and there was many a woman hadn't a dry sod itself to put under her pot, and she shivering with cold and hunger.'

A little later, when we had talked of one or two other things, I asked him if many of the people who were living round in the scattered cottages we could see were often in real want of food. 'There are a few, maybe, have enough at all times,' he said, 'but the most are in want one time or another, when the potatoes are bad or few, and their whole store is eaten; and there are some who are near starving all times, like a widow woman beyond who has seven children with hardly a shirt on their skins, and they with nothing to eat but the milk from one cow, and a handful of meal they will get from one neighbour or another.'

'You're getting an old man,' I said, 'and do you remember if the place was as bad as it is now when you were a young man growing up?'

'It wasn't as bad, or a half as bad,' he said, 'for there were fewer people in it and more land to each, and the land itself was better at the time, for now it is drying up or something, and not giving its fruits and increase as it did.'

I asked him if they bought manures.

'We get a hundredweight for eight shillings now and again, but I think there's little good in it, for it's only a poor kind they send out to the like of us. Then there was another thing they had in the old times,' he continued, 'and that was the making of poteen (illicit whiskey), for it was a great trade at that time, and you'd see the police down on their knees blowing the fire with their own breath to make a drink for themselves, and then going off with the butt of an old barrel, and that was one seizure, and an old bag with a handful of malt, and that was another seizure, and would satisfy the law; but now they must have the worm and the still and a prisoner, and there is little of it made in the country. At that time a man would get ten shillings for a gallon, and it was a good trade for poor people.'

As we were talking a woman passed driving two young pigs, and we began to speak of them.

'We buy the young pigs and rear them up,' he said, 'but this year they are scarce and dear. And indeed what good are they in bad years, for how can we go feeding a pig when we haven't enough, maybe, for ourselves? In good years, when you have potatoes and plenty, you can rear up two or three pigs and make a good bit on them; but other times, maybe, a poor man will give a pound for a young pig that won't thrive after, and then his pound will be gone, and he'll have no money for his rent.'

The old man himself was cheerful and seemingly fairly well-to-do; but in the end he seemed to be getting dejected as he spoke of one difficulty after another, so I asked him, to change the subject, if there was much dancing in the country. 'No,' he said, 'this while back you'll never see a piper coming this way at all, though in the old times it's many a piper would be moving around through those houses for a whole quarter together, playing his pipes and drinking poteen and the people dancing round him; but now there is no dancing or singing in this place at all, and most of the young people is growing up and going to America.'

I pointed to the lace-school near us, and asked him how the girls got on with the lace, and if they earned much money. 'I've heard tell,' he said, 'that in the four schools round about this place there is near six hundred pounds paid out in wages every year, and that is a good sum; but there isn't a young girl going to them that isn't saving up, and saving up till she'll have enough gathered to take her to America, and then away she will go, and why wouldn't she?'

Often the worst moments in the lives of these people are caused by the still frequent outbreaks of typhus fever, and before we parted I asked him if there was much fever in the particular district where we were.

'Just here,' he said, 'there isn't much of it at all, but

there are places round about where you'll sometimes hear of a score and more stretched out waiting for their death; but I suppose it is the will of God. Then there is a sickness they call consumption that some will die of; but I suppose there is no place where people aren't getting their death one way or other, and the most in this place are enjoying good health, glory be to God! for it is a healthy place and there is a clean air blowing.'

Then, with a few of the usual blessings, he got up and left us, and we walked on through more of similar or still poorer country. It is remarkable that from Spiddal onward—that is, in the whole of the most poverty-stricken district in Ireland—no one begs, even in a roundabout way. It is the fashion, with many of the officials who are connected with relief works and such things, to compare the people of this district rather unfavourably with the people of the poor districts of Donegal; but in this respect at least Donegal is not the more admirable.

AMONG THE RELIEF WORKS

BEYOND Carraroe, the last promontory on the north coast of Galway Bay, one reaches a group of islands which form the lower angle of Connemara. These islands are little more than a long peninsula broken through by a number of small straits, over which, some twelve years ago, causeways and swing-bridges were constructed, so that one can now drive straight on through Annaghvaan, Lettermore, Gorumna, Lettermullan, and one or two smaller islands. When one approaches this district from the east a long detour is made to get round the inner point of Greatman's Bay, and then the road turns to the south-west till one reaches Annaghvaan, the first of the islands. This road is a remarkable one. Nearly every foot of it, as it now stands, has been built up in different years of famine by the people of the neighbourhood working on Government relief works, which are now once more in full swing; making improvements in some places, turning primitive tracts into roadways in others, and here and there building a new route to some desolate village.

We drove many miles, with Costello and Carraroe behind us, along a bog-road of curious formation built up on a turf embankment, with broad grassy sods at either side—perhaps to make a possible way for the barefooted people—then two spaces of rough broken stones where the wheel-ruts are usually worn, and in the centre a track of gritty earth for the horses. Then, at a turn of the road, we came in sight of a dozen or more men and women working hurriedly and doggedly improving a further portion of this road, with a ganger swaggering among them and directing their work. Some of the people were cutting out sods from grassy patches near the road, others were carrying down bags of earth in a slow, inert procession, a few were breaking stones, and three or four women were scraping out a sort of sandpit at a little distance. As we drove quickly by we could see that every man and woman was working with a sort of hang-dog dejection that would be enough to make any casual passer mistake them for a band of convicts. The wages given on these works are usually a shilling a day, and, as a rule, one person only, generally the head of the family, is taken from each house. Sometimes the best worker in a family is thus forced away from his ordinary work of farming, or fishing, or kelp-making for this wretched remuneration at a time when his private industry is most needed. If this system of relief has some things in its favour, it is far from satisfactory in other ways, and is not always economical. I have been told of a district not very far from here where there is a ganger, an overseer, an inspector, a paymaster, and an engineer superintending the work of two paupers only. This is possibly an exaggerated account of what is really taking place, yet it probably shows, not too inexactly, a state of things that is not rare in Ireland.

A mile or two further on we passed a similar band of workers, and then the road rose for a few feet and turned sharply on to a long causeway, with a swing-bridge in the centre, that led to the island of Annagh-vaan. Just as we reached the bridge our driver jumped down and took his mare by the head. A moment later she began to take fright at the hollow noise of her own hoofs on the boards of the bridge and the blue rush of the tide which she could see through them, but the man coaxed her forward, and got her over without much difficulty. For the next mile or two there was a continual series of small islands and causeways and bridges that the mare grew accustomed to, and trotted gaily over, till we reached Lettermore, and drove for some distance through the usual small hills of stone. Then we came to the largest causeway of all, between Lettermore and Gorumna, where the proportion of the opening of the bridge to the length of the embankment is so small that the tide runs through with extraordinary force. On the outer side the water was banked up nearly a yard high against the buttress of the bridge, and on the other side there was a rushing, eddying torrent that recalled some mountain salmon-stream in flood, except that here, instead of the brown river-water, one saw the white and blue foam of the sea.

The remainder of our road to the lower western end of Gorumna led through hilly districts that became more and more white with stone, though one saw here and there a few brown masses of bog or an oblong lake with many islands and rocks. In most places, if one looked round the hills a little distance from the road, one could see the yellow roofs and white gables of cottages scattered everywhere through this waste of rock; and on the ridge of every hill one could see the red dresses of women who were gathering turf or looking for their sheep or calves. Near the village where we stopped things are somewhat better, and a few fields of grass and potatoes were to be seen, and a certain number of small cattle grazing among the rocks. Here also one is close to the sea, and fishing and kelp-making are again possible. In the village there is a small private quay in connection with a shop where everything is sold, and not long after we arrived a hooker sailed in with a cargo of supplies from Galway. A number of women were standing about expecting her arrival, and soon afterwards several of

them set off for different parts of the island with a bag
of flour slung over an ass. One of these, a young girl of
seventeen or eighteen, drove on with her load far into
Lettermullan, the next island, on a road that we were
walking also; and then sent the ass back to Gorumna in
charge of a small boy, and took up the sack of flour,
which weighed at least sixteen stone, on her back, and
carried it more than a mile, through a narrow track, to
her own home. This practice of allowing young girls to
carry great weights frequently injures them severely,
and is the cause of much danger and suffering in their
after lives. They do not seem, however, to know anything of the risks they run, and their loads are borne
gaily.

A little further on we came on another stretch of
the relief works, where there were many elderly men
and young girls working with the same curious aspect
of shame and dejection. The work was just closing for
the evening, and as we walked back to Gorumna an old
man who had been working walked with us, and com-
plained of his great poverty and the small wages he was
given. 'A shilling a day,' he said, 'would hardly keep a
man in tea and sugar and tobacco and a bit of bread to
eat, and what good is it all when there is a family of
five or six maybe, and often more?' Just as we reached
the swing-bridge that led back to Gorumna another
hooker sailed carefully in through the narrow rocky
channel, with a crowd of men and women sitting along
the gunwale. They edged in close to a flat rock near the
bridge, and made her fast for a moment while the wom-
en jumped on shore; some of them carrying bottles,
others with little children, and all dressed out in new
red petticoats and shawls. They looked as they crowded
up on the road as fine a body of peasant women as one

could see anywhere, and were all talking and laughing eagerly among themselves. The old man told me in Irish that they had been at a pattern—a sort of semi-religious festival like the well-known festivals of Brittany—that had just been held some distance to the east on the Galway coast. It was reassuring to see that some, at least, of these island people are, in their own way, prosperous and happy. When the women were all landed the swing-bridge was pushed open, and the hooker was poled through to the bay on the north side of the islands. Then the men moored her and came up to a little public-house, where they spent the rest of the evening talking and drinking and telling stories in Irish.

THE FERRYMAN OF DINISH
ISLAND

WHEN wandering among lonely islands in the west of Ireland, like those of the Gorumna group, one seldom fails to meet with some old sailor or pilot who has seen something of the world, and it is often from a man of this kind that one learns most about the island or hill that he has come back to, in middle age or towards the end of his life. An old seafaring man who ferries chance comers to and from Dinish Island is a good example of this class. The island is separated from Furnace—the last of the group that is linked together by causeways and bridges—by a deep channel between two chains of rock. As we went to this channel across a strip of sand-hill a wild-looking old man appeared at the other side, and began making signs to us and pushing off a heavy boat from the shore. Before he was half-way across we could hear him calling out to us in a state of almost incoherent excitement, and directing us to a ledge of rock where he could take us off. A moment later we scrambled into his boat upon a mass of seaweed that he had been collecting for kelp, and he poled us across, talking at random about how he had seen His Royal Highness the Duke of Edinburgh, and gone to America as interpreter for the emigrants in a bad season twenty-one years ago. As soon as we landed we walked across a bay of sand to a tiny schoolhouse close to the sea, and the old man turned back across the channel with a travelling tea merchant and a young girl who had come down to the shore. All the time they were going across we could hear him talking and vociferating at the top of his voice, and then, after a moment's silence, he came in sight again, on our side, running towards us over the sand. After he had been a little while with us, and got over the excitement caused by the sudden arrival of two strangers—we could judge how great it was by a line of children's heads who were peeping over the rocks and watching us with amazement—he began to talk clearly and simply. After a few of the remarks one hears from everyone about the loneliness of the place, he spoke about the school behind us.

'Isn't it a poor thing,' he said, 'to see a school lying closed up the like of that, and twenty or thirty scholars, maybe, running wild along the sea? I am very lonesome since that school was closed, for there was a school-mistress used to come for a long while from Lettermullan, and I used to ferry her over the water, and maybe ten little children along with her. And then there was a school-mistress living here for a long while, and I used to ferry the children only; but now she has found herself a better place, and this three months there's no school in it at all.'

One could see when he was quiet that he differed a good deal, both in face and in his way of speaking, from the people of the islands, and when he paused I asked him if he had spent all his life among them, excepting the one voyage to America.

'I have not,' he said; 'but I've been many places, though I and my fathers have rented the sixth of this island for near two hundred years. My own father was a sailorman who came in here by chance and married a woman, and lived, a snug, decent man, with five cows or six, till he died at a hundred and three. And my mother's father, who had the place before him, died at a hundred and eight, and he wouldn't have died then, I'm thinking, only he fell down and broke his hip. They were strong, decent people at that time, and I was

going to school—travelling out over the islands with
my father ferrying me—till I was twenty years of age;
and then I went to America and got to be a sailorman,
and was in New York, and Baltimore, and New
Orleans, and after that I was coasting till I knew every
port and town of this country and Scotland and Wales.'

One of us asked him if he had stayed at sea until he
came back to this island.

'I did not,' he said, 'for I went ashore once in South
Wales, and I'm telling you Wales is a long country, for
I travelled all a whole summer's day from that place
till I reached Birkenhead at nine o'clock. And then I
went to Manchester and to Newcastle-on-Tyne, and I
worked there for two years. That's a rich country, dear
gentlemen, and when a payman would come into the
works on a Saturday you'd see the bit of board he had
over his shoulder bending down with the weight of
sovereigns he had for the men. And isn't it a queer thing
to be sitting here now thinking on those times, and I
after being near twenty years back on this bit of a rock
that a dog wouldn't look at, where the pigs die and the
spuds die, and even the judges and quality do come out
and do lower our rents when they see the wild Atlantic
driving in across the cursed stones.'

'And what is it brought you back,' I said, 'if you
were doing well beyond in the world?'

'My two brothers went to America,' he said, 'and I
had to come back because I was the eldest son, and I got
married then, and I after holding out till I was forty.
I have a young family now growing up, for I was snug
for a while; and then bad times came, and I lost my
wife, and the potatoes went bad, and three cows I had
were taken in the night with some disease of the brain,
and they swam out and were drowned in the sea. I got

back their bodies in the morning, and took them down to a gentleman beyond who understands the diseases of animals, but he gave me nothing for them at all. So there I am now with no pigs, and no cows, and a young family running round with no mother to mind them; and what can you do with children that know nothing at all, and will often put down as much in the pot one day as would do three days, and do be wasting the meal, though you can't say a word against them, for it's young and ignorant they are? If it wasn't for them I'd be off this evening, and I'd earn my living easy on the sea, for I'm only fifty-seven years of age, and I have good health; but how can I leave my young children? And I don't know what way I'm going to go on living in this place that the Lord created last, I'm thinking, in the end of time; and it's often when I sit down and look around on it I do begin cursing and damning, and asking myself how poor people can go on executing their religion at all.'

For a while he said nothing, and we could see tears in his eyes; then I asked him how he was living now from one day to another.

'They're letting me out advanced meal and flour from the shop,' he said, 'and I'm to pay it back when I burn a ton of kelp in the summer. For two months I was working on the relief works at a shilling a day, but what good is that for a family? So I've stopped now to rake up weed for a ton, or maybe two tons, of kelp. When I left the works I got my boy put on in my place, but the ganger put him back; and then I got him on again, and the ganger put him back. Then I bought a bottle of ink and a pen and a bit of paper to write a letter and make my complaint, but I never wrote it to this day, for what good is it harming him more than another? Then I've a daughter in America has only been there nine months, and she's sent me three pounds already. I have another daughter, living above with her married sister, will be ready to go in autumn, and another little one will go when she's big enough. There is a man above has four daughters in America, and gets a pound a quarter from each one of them, and that is a great thing for a poor man. It's to America we'll all be going, and isn't it a fearful thing to think I'll be kept here another ten years, maybe, tending the children and striving to keep them alive, when I might be abroad in America living in decency and earning my bread?'

Afterwards he took us up to the highest point of the island, and showed us a fine view of the whole group and of the Atlantic beyond them, with a few fishing-boats in the distance, and many large boats nearer the rocks rowing heavily with loads of weed. When we got into the ferry again the channel had become too deep to pole, and the old man rowed with a couple of long sweeps from the bow.

'I go out alone in this boat,' he said, as he was rowing, 'across the bay to the northern land. There is no other man in the place would do it, but I'm a licenced pilot these twenty years, and a seafaring man.'

Then as we finally left him he called after us:

'It has been a great consolation to me, dear gentlemen, to be talking with your like, for one sees few people in this place, and so may God bless and reward you and see you safely to your homes.'

SOME of those who have undertaken to reform the congested districts have shown an unfortunate tendency to give great attention to a few canonised industries, such as horse-breeding and fishing, or even bee-keeping, while they neglect local industries that have been practised with success for a great number of years. Thus in the large volume issued a couple of years ago by the Department of Agriculture and Technical Instruction for Ireland, which claims to give a comprehensive account of the economic resources of the country, hardly a word has been said of the kelp industry, which is a matter of the greatest importance to the inhabitants of a very large district. The Congested Districts Board seems to have left it on one side also, and in the Galway neighbourhood, at least, no steps appear to have been taken to ensure the people a fair market for the kelp they produce, or to revise the present unsatisfactory system by which it is tested and paid for. In some places the whole buying trade falls into the hands of one man, who can then control the prices at his pleasure, while one hears on all sides of arbitrary decisions by which good kelp is rejected, and what the people consider an inferior article is paid for at a high figure. When the buying is thus carried on no appeal can be made from the decision of one individual, and I have sometimes seen a party of old men sitting nearly in tears on a ton of rejected kelp that had cost them weeks of hard work, while, for all one knew, it had very possibly been refused on account of some grudge or caprice of the buyer.

The village of Trawbaun, which lies on the coast opposite the Aran Islands, is a good instance of a kelp-making neighbourhood. We reached it through a nar-

row road, now in the hands of the relief workers, where
we hurried past the usual melancholy line of old men
breaking stones and younger men carrying bags of earth
and sods. Soon afterwards the road fell away quickly
towards the sea, through a village of many cottages
huddled together, with bare walls of stone that had
never been whitewashed, as often happens in places that
are peculiarly poor. Passing through these, we came out
on three or four acres of sandhill that brought us to a
line of rocks with a narrow sandy cove between them
just filling with the tide. All along the coast, a little
above high-water mark, we could see a number of tall,
reddish stacks of dried seaweed, some of which had probably been standing for weeks, while others were in various unfinished stages, or had only just been begun. A
number of men and women and boys were hard at
work in every direction, gathering fresh weed and
spreading it out to dry on the rocks. In some places the
weed is mostly gathered from the foreshore; but in this
neighbourhood, at least in the early summer, it is pulled
up from rocks under the sea at low water, by men working from a boat or curagh with a long pole furnished
with a short crossbar nailed to the top, which they en-
tangle in the weeds. Just as we came down, a curagh,
lightly loaded by two boys, was coming in over a low
bar into the cove I have spoken of, and both of them
were slipping over the side every moment or two to push
their canoe from behind. Several bare-legged girls,
crooning merry songs in Gaelic, were passing backwards and forwards over the sand, carrying heavy loads
of weed on their backs. Further out many other curaghs,
more heavily laden, were coming slowly in, waiting for
the tide; and some old men on the shore were calling
out directions to their crews in the high-pitched tone

that is so remarkable in this Connaught Irish. The whole scene, with the fresh smell of the sea and the blueness of the shallow waves, made a curious contrast with the dismal spectacle of the relief workers we had just passed, for here the people seemed as light-hearted as a party of schoolboys.

Further on we came to a rocky headland where some men were burning down their weed into kelp, a process that in this place is given nearly twelve hours. As we came up dense volumes of rich, creamy-coloured smoke were rising from a long pile of weed, in the centre of which we could see here and there a molten mass burning at an intense heat. Two men and a number of boys were attending to the fire, laying on fresh weed wherever the covering grew thin enough to receive it. A little to one side a baby, rolled up in a man's coat, was asleep beside a hamper, as on occasions like this the house is usually shut up and the whole family scatters for work of various kinds. The amount of weed needed to make a ton of kelp varies, I have been told, from three tons to five. The men of a family working busily on a favourable day can take a ton of the raw weed, and the kelp is sold at from three pounds fifteen shillings or a little less to five pounds a ton, so it is easy to see the importance of this trade. When all the weed intended for one furnace has been used the whole is covered up and left three or four days to cool; then it is broken up and taken off in boats or curaghs to a buyer. He takes a handful, tests it with certain chemicals, and fixes the price accordingly; but the people themselves have no means of knowing whether they are getting fair play, and although many buyers may be careful and conscientious, there is a very general feeling of dissatisfaction among the people with the way they are forced to carry on the trade.

When the kelp has been finally disposed of it is shipped in schooners and sent away—for the most part, I believe, to Scotland, where it is used for the manufacture of iodine.

Complaints are often heard about the idleness of the natives of Connemara; yet at the present time one sees numbers of the people drying and arranging their weed until nightfall, and the bays where the weed is found are filled with boats at four or five o'clock in the morning, when the tide is favourable. The chances of a good kelp season depend, to some extent, on suitable weather for drying and burning the weed; yet on the whole this trade is probably less precarious than the fishing industry or any other source of income now open to the people of a large portion of these congested districts. In the present year the weather has been excellent, and there is every hope that a good quantity of kelp may be obtained. The matter is of peculiar importance this year, as for the last few months the shopkeepers have been practically keeping the people alive by giving out meal and flour on the security of the kelp harvest—one house alone, I am told, distributed fourteen tons during the last ten days—so that if the kelp should not turn out well, or the prices should be less than what is expected, whole districts will be placed in the greatest difficulty.

It is a remarkable feature of the domestic finance of this district that, although the people are so poor, they are used to dealing with fairly large sums of money. Thus four or five tons of kelp well sold may bring a family between twenty and thirty pounds, and their bills for flour (which is bought in bags of two hundredweight at a good deal over a pound a bag) must also be considerable. It is the same with their pig-farming, fishing, and other industries, and probably this familiarity with considerable sums causes a part, at least, of the sense of shame that is shown by those who are reduced to working on the roadside for the miserable pittance of a shilling a day.

THE BOAT BUILDERS

WE LEFT Gorumna in a hooker managed by two men, and sailed north to another district of the Galway coast. Soon after we started the wind fell, and we lay almost becalmed in a curious bay so filled with islands that one could hardly distinguish the channel that led to the open sea. For some time we drifted slowly between Dinish Island and Illaunearach, a stony mound inhabited by three families only. Then our pace became so slow that the boatmen got out a couple of long sweeps and began rowing heavily, with sweat streaming from them. The air was heavy with thunder, and on every side one saw the same smoky blue sea and sky, with grey islands and mountains beyond them, and in one place a ridge of yellow rocks touched by a single ray of sunlight. Two or three pookawns—lateen-rigged boats, said to be of Spanish origin—could be seen about a mile ahead of us sailing easily across our bows, where some opening in the islands made a draught from the east. In half an hour our own sails filled, and the boatmen stopped rowing and began to talk to us. One of them gave us many particulars about the prices of hookers and their nets, and the system adopted by the local boat-builders who work for the poorer fishermen of the neighbourhood.

'When a man wants a boat,' he said, 'he buys the timber from a man in Galway and gets it brought up here in a hooker. Then he gets a carpenter to come to his house and build it in some place convenient to the sea. The whole time the carpenter will be working at it the other man must support him, and give him whiskey every day. Then he must stand around while he is working, holding boards and handing nails, and if he doesn't do it smart enough you'll hear the carpenter scolding him and making a row. A carpenter like that will be six weeks or two months, maybe, building a boat, and he will get two pounds for his work when he is done. The wood and everything you need for a fifteen-foot boat will cost four pounds, or beyond it, so a boat like that is a dear thing for a poor man.'

We asked him about the boats that had been made by the local boatwrights for the Congested Districts Board.

'There were some made in Lettermullan,' he said, 'and beyond in an island west of where you're going to-day there is an old man has been building boats for thirty years, and he could tell you all about them.'

Meanwhile we had been sailing quickly, and were near the north shore of the bay. The tide had gone so far out while we were becalmed that it was not possible to get in alongside the pier, so the men steered for a ledge of rock further out, where it was possible to land. As we were going in an anchor was dropped, and then when we were close to the rocks the men checked the boat by straining on the rope, and brought us in to the shore with a great deal of nicety.

Not long afterwards we made our way to see the old carpenter the boatmen had told us of, and found him busy with two or three other men caulking the bottom of a boat that was propped up on one side. As we came towards them along the low island shore the scene reminded one curiously of some old picture of Noah building the Ark. The old man himself was rather remarkable in appearance, with strongly formed features, and an extraordinarily hairy chest showing through the open neck of his shirt. He told us that he had made several nobbies for the Board, and showed us an arrangement that had been supplied for steaming the heavy timber needed for boats of this class.

'At the present time,' he said, 'I am making our own boats again, and the fifteen-foot boats the people do use here have light timber, and we don't need to trouble steaming them at all. I get eight pounds for a boat when I buy the timber myself, and fit her all out ready for the sea. But I am working for poor men, and it is often three years before I will be paid the full price of a boat I'm after making.'

From where we stood we could see another island across a narrow sound, studded with the new cottages that are built in this neighbourhood by the Congested Districts Board.

'That island, like another you're after passing, has been bought by the Board,' said the old man, who saw us looking at them; 'and it is a great thing for the poor people to have their holdings arranged for them in one strip instead of the little scattered plots the people have in all this neighbourhood, where a man will often have to pass through the ground of maybe three men to get to a plot of his own.'

This rearrangement of the holdings that is being carried out in most places where estates have been bought up by the Board, and resold to the tenants, is a matter of great importance that is fully appreciated by the people. Mere tenant purchase in districts like this may do some good for the moment by lowering rents and interesting the people in their land; yet in the end it is likely to prove disastrous, as it tends to perpetuate holdings that are not large enough to support their owners and are too scattered to be worked effectively. In the relatively few estates bought by the Board—up to March, 1904, their area amounted to two or three hundred thousand acres

out of the three and a half million that are included in
the congested districts—this is being set right, yet some
of the improvements made at the same time are perhaps
a less certain gain, and give the neighbourhoods where
they have been made an uncomfortable look that is, I
think, felt by the people. For instance, there is no pressing need to substitute iron roofs—in many ways open
to objection—for the thatch that has been used for centuries, and is part of the constructive tradition of the
people. In many districts the thatching is done in some
idle season by the men of a household themselves, with
the help of their friends, who are proud of their skill;
and it is looked on as a sort of a festival where there is
great talk and discussion, the loss of which is hardly made
up for by the patch of ground which was needed to grow
the straw, and is now free for other uses. In the same
way, the improvements in the houses built by the Board
are perhaps a little too sudden. It is far better, wherever
possible, to improve the ordinary prosperity of the people till they begin to improve their houses themselves on
their own lines, than to do too much in the way of building houses that have no interest for the people and dis-
figure the country. I remember one evening in another
congested district—on the west coast of Kerry—listening to some peasants who discussed for hours the propor-
tions of a new cottage that was to be built by one of
them. They had never, of course, heard of proportion;
but they had rules and opinions, in which they were
deeply interested, as to how high a house should be if it
was a certain length, with so many rafters, in order that
it might look well. Traditions of this kind are destroyed
for ever when too sweeping improvements are made in
a district, and the loss is a great one. If any real improvement is to be made in many of these congested dis-

tricts the rearrangement and sale of the holdings to the tenants, somewhat on the lines adopted by the Board, must be carried out on a large scale; but in doing so care should be taken to disorganise as little as possible the life and methods of the people. A little attention to the wells, and, where necessary, greater assistance in putting up sheds for the cattle and pigs that now live in the houses, would do a great deal to get rid of the epidemics of typhus and typhoid, and then the people should be left as free as possible to arrange their houses and way of life as it pleases them.

THE HOMES OF THE
HARVESTMEN

THE general appearance of the North Mayo country round Belmullet—another district of the greatest poverty—differs curiously from that of Connemara. In Mayo a waste of turf and bog takes the place of the waste of stones that is the chief feature of the coast of Galway. Consequently sods of turf are used for all sorts of work—building walls and ditches, and even the gables of cottages—instead of the loose pieces of granite or limestone that are ready to one's hand in the district we have left. Between every field one sees a thin bank of turf, worn away in some places by the weather, and covered in others with loose grass and royal flowering ferns. The rainfall of Belmullet is a heavy one, and in wet weather this absence of stone gives one an almost intolerable feeling of dampness and discomfort.

The last forty miles of our journey to Belmullet was made on the long car which leaves Ballina at four o'clock in the morning. It was raining heavily as we set out, and the whole town was asleep; but during the first hour we met many harvestmen with scythe-handles and little bundles tied in red handkerchiefs, walking quickly into Ballina to embark for Liverpool or Glasgow. Then we passed Crossmolina, and were soon out on the bogs, where one drives for mile after mile, seeing an odd house only, scattered in a few places with long distances between them. We had been travelling all night from Connemara, and again and again we dozed off into a sort of dream, only to wake up with a start when the car gave a dangerous lurch, and see the same dreary waste with a few wet cattle straggling about the road, or the corner of a lake just seen beyond them through a

break in the clouds. When we had driven about fifteen
miles we changed horses at a village of three houses,
where an old man without teeth brought out the new
horses and harnessed them slowly, as if he was half in
his sleep. Then we drove on again, stopping from time
to time at some sort of post-office, where a woman or
boy usually came out to take the bag of letters. At
Bangor Erris four more passengers got up, and as the
roads were heavy with the rain we settled into a slow
jog-trot that made us almost despair of arriving at our
destination. The people were now at work weeding potatoes in their few patches of tillage, and cutting turf in
the bogs, and their draggled, colourless clothes—so un-
like the homespun of Connemara—added indescribably
to the feeling of wretchedness one gets from the sight of
these miserable cottages, many of them with an old
hamper or the end of a barrel stuck in the roof for a
chimney, and the desolation of the bogs.

Belmullet itself is curiously placed on an isthmus—
recently pierced by a canal—that divides Broad Haven
from Blacksod Bay. Beyond the isthmus there is a long
peninsula some fourteen miles in length, running north
and south, and separating these two bays from the Atlantic. As we were wandering through this headland in
the late afternoon the rain began again, and we stopped
to shelter under the gable of a cottage. After a moment
or two a girl came out and brought us in out of the
rain. At first we could hardly see anything with the
darkness of the rain outside and the small window and
door of the cottage, but after a moment or two we grew
accustomed to it, and the light seemed adequate enough.
The woman of the house was sitting opposite us at the
corner of the fire, with two children near her, and just
behind them a large wooden bed with a sort of red

covering, and red curtains above it. Then there was the
door, and a spinning-wheel, and at the end opposite the
fire a couple of stalls for cattle and a place for a pig with
an old brood sow in it, and one young one a few weeks
old. At the edge of the fireplace a small door opened into
an inner room, but in many of the cottages of this kind
there is one apartment only. We talked, as usual, of the
hardships of the people, which are worst in places like
this, at some distance from the sea, where no help can
be got from fishing or making kelp.

'All this land about here,' said the woman, who was
sitting by the fire, 'is stripped bog'—that is, bog from
which the turf has been cut—'and it is no use at all without all kinds of stuff and manure mixed through it. If
you went down a little behind the house you'd see that
there is nothing but stones left at the bottom, and you'd
want great quantities of sand and seaweed and dung to
make it soft and kind enough to grow a thing in it at
all. The big farmers have all the good land snapped up,
and there is nothing left but stones and bog for poor
people like ourselves.'

The sow was snorting in the corner, and I said, after
a moment, that it was probably with the pigs that they
made the most of their money.

'In bad years,' she said, 'like the year we've had, when
the potatoes are rotten and few, there is no use in our
pigs, for we have nothing to give them. Last year we
had a litter of pigs from that sow, and they were little
good to us, for the people were afraid to buy at any price
for fear they'd die upon their hands.'

One of us said something of the relief work we had
seen in Connemara.

'We have the same thing here,' she said, 'and I have
a young lad who is out working on them now, and he

has a little horse beast along with him, so that he gets a week's pay for three days or four, and has a little moment over for our own work on the farm.'

I asked her if she had many head of cattle.

'I have not, indeed,' she said, 'nor any place to feed. There is some small people do put a couple of yearlings out on the grass you see below you running out to the sands; but where would I get money to buy one, or to pay the one pound eight, or near it, you do pay for every yearling you have upon the grass? A while since,' she went on, 'we weren't so bad as we are at this time, for we had a young lad who used to go to Scotland for the harvest, and be sending us back a pound or two pounds maybe in the month, and bringing five or six or beyond it when he'd come home at the end of autumn; but he got a hurt and never overed it, so we have no one at this time can go from us at all.'

One of the girls had been carding wool for the spinning-wheel, so I asked her about the spinning and weaving.

'Most women spin their wool in this place,' she said, 'and the weaver weaves it afterwards for threepence a yard if it is a single weaving, and for sixpence a yard if it is double woven, as we do have it for the men. The women in this place have little time to be spinning, but the women back on the mountains do be mixing colours through their wool till you'd never ask to take your eyes from it. They do be throwing in a bit of stone colour, and a bit of red madder, and a bit of crimson, and a bit of stone colour again, and, believe me, it is nice stuffs they do make that you'd never ask to take your eyes from.'

The shower had now blown off, so we went out again and made our way down to a cove of the sea where a seal was diving at some distance from the shore, putting up its head every few minutes to look at us with a curiously human expression. Afterwards we went on to a jetty north of the town, where the Sligo boat had just come in. One of the men told us that they were taking over a hundred harvestmen to Sligo the next morning, where they would take a boat for Glasgow, and that many more would be going during the week. This migratory labour has many unsatisfactory features; yet in the present state of the country it may tend to check the longing for America that comes over those that spend the whole year on one miserable farm.

THE SMALLER PEASANT
PROPRIETORS

THE car-drivers that take one round to isolated places
in Ireland seem to be the cause of many of the mislead-
ing views that chance visitors take up about the country
and the real temperament of the people. These men
spend a great deal of their time driving a host of inspec-
tors and officials connected with various Government
Boards, who, although they often do excellent work,
belong for the most part to classes that have a traditional
misconception of the country people. It follows naturally enough that the carmen pick up the views of their
patrons, and when they have done so they soon find apt
instances from their own local knowledge that give a
native popular air to opinions that are essentially foreign. That is not all. The car-driver is usually the only
countryman with whom the official is kept in close personal contact; so that, while the stranger is bewildered,
many distinguished authorities have been pleased and
instructed by this version of their own convictions. It is
fair to add that the carman is usually a small-town's
man, so that he has a not unnatural grudge against the
mountain squatter, for whom so much has apparently
been done, while the towns are neglected, and also that
the carman may be generally relied on when he is
merely stating facts to anyone who is not a total stranger
to the country.

We drove out recently with a man of this class, and
as we left Belmullet he began to talk of an estate that has
been sold to the tenants by the Congested Districts
Board.

'Those people pay one or two pounds in the year,' he
said, 'and for that they have a house, and a stripe of

tilled land, and a stripe of rough land, and an outlet
on the mountain for grazing cattle, and the rights of
turbary, and yet they aren't satisfied; while I do pay
five pounds for a little house with hardly enough land
to grow two score of cabbages.'

He was an elderly man, and as we drove on through
many gangs of relief workers he told us about the building of the Belmullet Workhouse in 1857, and I asked
him what he remembered or had heard of the great
famine ten years earlier.

'I have heard my father say,' he said, 'that he often
seen the people dragging themselves along to the workhouse in Binghamstown, and some of them falling down
and dying on the edge of the road. There were other
places where he'd seen four or five corpses piled up on
each other against a bit of a bank or the butt of a bridge,
and when I began driving I was in great dread in the
evenings when I'd be passing those places on the roads.'

It was a dark, windy day, and we went on through
endless wastes of brown mountain and bog, meeting no
one but an occasional woman driving an ass with meal
or flour, or a few people drying turf and building it up
into ricks on the roadside or near it. In the distance one
could see white roads—often relief roads—twisting
among the hills, with no one on them but a man here
and there riding in with the mails from some forlorn
village. In places we could see the white walls and gables
of one of these villages against the face of a hill, and
fairly frequently we passed a few tumbled-down cottages with plots of potatoes about them. After a while
the carman stopped at a door to get a drink for his horse,
and we went in for a moment or two to shelter from
the wind. It was the poorest cottage we had seen. There
was no chimney, and the smoke rose by the wall to a

hole in the roof at the top of the gable. A boy of ten was sitting near the fire minding three babies, and at the other end of the room there was a cow with two calves and a few sickly-looking hens. The air was so filled with turf-smoke that we went out again in a moment into the open air. As we were standing about we heard the carman ask the boy why he was not at school.

'I'm spreading turf this day,' he said, 'and my brother is at school. To-morrow he'll stay at home, and it will be my turn to go.'

Then an old man came up and spoke of the harm the new potato crop is getting from the high wind, as indeed we had seen ourselves in several fields that we had passed, where whole lines of the tops were broken and withered.

'There was a storm like this three weeks ago,' he said, 'and I could hardly keep my old bonnet on me going round through the hills. This storm is as bad, or near it, and wherever there are loops and eddies in the wind you can see the tops all fluttered and destroyed, so that I'm thinking another windy day will leave us as badly off as we were last year.'

It seems that about here the damage of the sea-winds, where there is no shelter, does as much or more harm than the blight itself. Still the blight is always a danger, and for several years past the people have been spraying their crops, with sufficiently good results to make them all anxious to try it. Even an old woman who could not afford to get one of the machines used for this purpose was seen out in her field a season or two ago with a bucketful of the solution, spraying her potatoes with an old broom——an instance which shows how eager the people are to adopt any improved methods that can be shown to be of real value. This took place in the neigh-

bourhood of Aghoos—the place we were driving to—
where an estate has been bought by the Congested Districts Board and resold to the tenants. The holdings are
so small that the rents are usually about three pounds a
year, though in some cases they are much less, and it is
easily seen that the people must remain for a while at
least as poor, or nearly as poor as they have been in the
past. In barren places of this kind the enlarging of the
holdings is a matter of the greatest difficulty, as good
land is not to be had in the neighbourhood; and it is hard
to induce even a few families to migrate to another place
where holdings could be provided for them, while their
absence would liberate part of the land in a district that
is overcrowded. At present most of the holdings have,
besides their tilled land, a stripe of bog-land, which is to
be gradually reclaimed; but even when this is done the
holdings will remain poor and small, and if a bad season comes the people may be again in need of relief.
Still no one can deny the good that is done by making
the tenants masters of their own ground and consolidat-
ing their holdings, and when the old fear of improvements, caused by the landlord system, is thoroughly forgotten, something may be done.

A great deal has been said of the curse of the absentee
landlord; but in reality the small landlord, who lived on
his property, and knew how much money every tenant
possessed, was a far greater evil. The judicial rent system was not a great deal better, as when the term came
to an end the careless tenant had his rent lowered, while
the man who had improved his holding remained as he
was—a fact which, of course, meant much more than
the absolute value of the money lost. For one reason or
another, the reduction of rents has come to be, in the
tenants' view, the all-important matter; so that this sys-

tem kept down the level of comfort, as every tenant was anxious to appear as poor as possible for fear of giving the landlord an advantage. These matters are well known; but at the present time the state of suspended land-purchase is tending to reproduce the same fear in a new form, and any tenants who have not bought out are naturally afraid to increase the price they may have to pay by improving their land. In this district, however, there is no fear of this kind, and a good many small grants have been given by the Board for rebuilding cottages and other improvements. A new cottage can be built by the occupier himself for a sum of about thirty pounds, of which the Board pays only a small part, while the cottages built by the Board on their own plan, with slated roofs on them, cost double, or more than double, as much. We went into one of the reslated cottages with concrete floors, and it was curious to see that, however awkward the building looked from the outside, in the kitchen itself the stain of the turf-smoke and the old pot-ovens and stools made the place seem natural and local. That at least was reassuring.

ERRIS

IN THE poorest districts of Connemara the people live, as I have already pointed out, by various industries, such as fishing, turf-cutting, and kelp-making, which are independent of their farms, and are so precarious that many families are only kept from pauperism by the money that is sent home to them by daughters or sisters who are now servant-girls in New York. Here in the congested districts of Mayo the land is still utterly insufficient—held at least in small plots, as it is now—as a means of life, and the people get the more considerable part of their funds by their work on the English or Scotch harvest, to which I have alluded before. A few days ago a special steamer went from Achill Island to Glasgow with five hundred of these labourers, most of them girls and young boys. From Glasgow they spread through the country in small bands and work together under a ganger, picking potatoes or weeding turnips, and sleeping for the most part in barns and outhouses. Their wages vary from a shilling a day to perhaps double as much in places where there is more demand for their work. The men go more often to the north of England, and usually work together, where it is possible, on small contracts for piecework arranged by one of themselves until the hay harvest begins, when they work by the day. In both cases they get fairly good wages, so that if they are careful and stay for some months they can bring back eight or nine pounds with them.

This morning people were passing through the town square of Belmullet—where our windows look out—towards the steamer, from two o'clock, in small bands of boys and girls, many of them carrying their boots under their arms and walking in bare feet, a fashion to which they are more used. Last night also, on our way back from a village that is largely inhabited by harvest people, we saw many similar bands hurrying in towards the town, as the steamer was to sail soon after dawn. This part of the coast is cut into by a great number of shallow tidal estuaries which are dry at low tide, while at full tide one sees many small roads that seem to run down aimlessly into the sea, till one notices, perhaps half a mile away, a similar road running down on the opposite headland. On our way, as the tide was out, we passed one of these sandy fords where there were a number of girls gathering cockles, and drove into Geesala, where we left our car and walked on to the villages of Dooyork, which lie on a sort of headland cut off on the south by another long estuary. It is places like this, where there is no thoroughfare in any direction to bring strangers to the country, that one meets with the most individual local life. There are two villages of Dooyork, an upper and lower, and as soon as we got into the first every doorway was filled with women and children looking after us with astonishment. All the houses were quite untouched by improvements, and a few of them were broken-down hovels of the worst kind. On the road there were several women bringing in turf or seaweed on horses with large panniers slung over a straw straddle, on which usually a baby of two or three years old was riding with delight. At the end of the village we talked to a man who had been in America, and before that had often gone to England as a harvestman.

'Some of the men get a nice bit of money,' he said, 'but it is hard work. They begin at three in the morning, and they work on till ten at night. A man will sometimes get twelve shillings an acre for hoeing turnips, and a skilful man will do an acre or the better part of it in one day; but I'm telling you it is hard work, and before the day is done a man will be hard set to know if it's the soil or the turnips he's striking down on.'

I asked him where and how they lodged.

'Ah,' he said, 'don't ask me to speak to you of that, for the lodging is poor, surely.'

We went on then to the next village, a still more primitive and curious one. The houses were built close together, with passages between them, and low, square yards marked round with stones. At one corner we came on a group of dark brown asses with panniers, and women standing among them in red dresses, with white or coloured handkerchiefs over their heads; and the whole scene had a strangely foreign, almost Eastern, look, though in its own way it was peculiarly characteristic of Ireland. Afterwards we went back to Geesala, along the edge of the sea. This district has, unexpectedly enough, a strong branch of the Gaelic League, and small Irish plays are acted frequently in the winter, while there is also an Agricultural Co-operative Bank, which has done excellent work. These banks, on the Raiffeisen system, have been promoted in Ireland for the last nine or ten years by the Irish Agricultural Society, with aid from the Congested Districts Board, and in a small way they have done much good, and shown —to those who wished to question it—the business intelligence of the smallest tenant-farmers. The interest made by these local associations tends to check emigration, but in this district the distress of last year has had a bad effect. In the last few months a certain number of men have sold out the tenant-right of their holdings— usually to the local shopkeeper, to whom they are always in debt—and shipped themselves and their whole families to America with what remained of the money.

This is probably the worst kind of emigration, and one fears the suffering of these families, who are suddenly moved to such different surroundings, must be great.

This district of the Erris Union, which we have now been through, is the poorest in the whole of Ireland, and during the last few months six or seven hundred people have been engaged on the relief works. Still, putting aside exceptionally bad years, there is certainly a tendency towards improvement. The steamer from Sligo, which has only been running for a few years, has done much good by bringing in flour and meal much more cheaply than could be done formerly. Typhus is less frequent than it used to be, probably because the houses and holdings are improving gradually, and we have heard it said that the work done in Aghoos by the fund raised by the *Manchester Guardian* some years ago was the beginning of this better state of things. The relief system, as it is now carried on, is an utterly degrading one, and many things will have to be done before the district is in anything like a satisfactory state. Yet the impression one gets of the whole life is not a gloomy one. Last night was St. John's Eve, and bonfires—a relic of Druidical rites—were lighted all over the country, the largest of all being placed in the town square of Belmullet, where a crowd of small boys shrieked and cheered and threw up firebrands for hours together. To-day, again, there was a large market in the square, where a number of country people, with their horses and donkeys, stood about bargaining for young pigs, heather brooms, homespun flannels, second-hand clothing, blacking-brushes, tinkers' goods and many other articles. Once when I looked out, the blacking-brush man and the card-trick man were getting up a fight in the corner of the square. A little later there was another stir, and I saw a Chinaman wandering about, followed by a wondering crowd. The sea in Erris, as in Connemara, and the continual arrival of islanders and boatmen from various directions, tend to keep up an interest and movement that is felt even far away in the villages among the hills.

THE INNER LANDS OF MAYO

THE VILLAGE SHOP

THERE is a curious change in the appearance of the country when one moves inland from the coast districts of Mayo to the congested portion of the inner edge of the country. In this place there are no longer the Erris tracts of bog or the tracts of stone of Connemara; but one sees everywhere low hills and small farms of poor land that is half turf-bog, already much cut away, and half narrow plots of grass or tillage. Here and there one meets with little villages, built on the old system, with cottages closely grouped together and filled with primitive people, the women mostly in bare feet, with white handkerchiefs over their heads. On the whole, however, one soon feels that this neighbourhood is far less destitute than those we have been in hitherto. Turning out of Swinford, soon after our arrival, we were met almost at once by a country funeral coming towards the town, with a large crowd, mostly of women, walking after it. The coffin was tied on one side of an outside car, and two old women, probably the chief mourners, were sitting on the other side. In the crowd itself we could see a few men leading horses or bicycles, and several young women who seemed by their dress to be returned Americans. When the funeral was out of sight we walked on for a few miles, and then turned into one of the wayside public-houses, at the same time general shop and bar, which are a peculiar feature of most of the country parts of Ireland. An old one-eyed man, with a sky-blue handkerchief round his neck, was standing at the counter making up his bill with the publican, and disputing loudly over it. Here, as in most of the congested districts, the shops are run on a vague system of credit that is not satisfactory, though one does not see at once what other method could be found to take its place. After the sale of whatever the summer season has produced—pigs, cattle, kelp, etc.—the bills are paid off, more or less fully, and all the ready money of a family is thus run away with. Then about Christmas time a new bill is begun, which runs on till the following autumn—or later in the harvesting districts—and quite small shopkeepers often put out relatively large sums in this way. The people keep no passbooks, so they have no check on the traders, and although direct fraud is probably rare it is likely that the prices charged are often exorbitant. What is worse, the shopkeeper in out-of-the-way places is usually the only buyer to be had for a number of home products, such as eggs, chickens, carragheen moss, and sometimes even kelp; so that he can control the prices both of what he buys and what he sells, while as a creditor he has an authority that makes bargaining impossible: another of the many complicated causes that keep the people near to pauperism! Meanwhile the old man's bill was made out, and the publican came to serve us. While he did so the old man spoke to us about the funeral, and I asked him about the returned Americans we had seen going after it.

'All the girls in this place,' he said, 'are going out to America when they are about seventeen years old. Then they work there for six years or more, till they do grow weary of that fixed kind of life, with the early rising and the working late, and then they do come home with a little stocking of fortune with them, and they do be tempting the boys with their chains and their rings, till they get a husband and settle down in this place. Such a lot of them is coming now there is hardly a marriage made in the place that the woman hasn't been in America.'

I asked a woman who had come in for a moment if she thought the girls kept their health in America.

'Many of them don't,' she said, 'working in factories with dirty air; and then you have likely seen that the girls in this place is big, stout people, and when they get over beyond they think they should be in the fashions, and they begin squeezing themselves in till you hear them gasping for breath, and that's no healthy way to be living.'

When we offered the old man a drink a moment later, he asked for twopenny ale.

'This is the only place in Ireland,' he said, 'where you'll see people drinking ale, for it is from this place that the greatest multitudes go harvesting to England —it's the only way they can live—and they bring the taste for ale back home with them. You'll see a power of them that come home at Michaelmas or Martinmas itself that will never do a hand's turn the rest of the year; but they will be sitting around in each other's houses playing cards through the night, and a barrel of ale set up among them.'

I asked him if he could tell about how many went from Swinford and the country round in each year.

'Well,' he said, 'you'd never reckon them, but I've heard people to say that there are six thousand or near it. Trains full of them do be running every week to the city of Dublin for the Liverpool boat, and I'm telling you it's many are hard set to get a seat in them at all. Then if the weather is too good beyond and the hay is near saved of itself, there is some that get little to do; but if the Lord God sends showers and rain there is work and plenty, and a power of money to be made.'

While he was talking some men who were driving cattle from a fair came in and sat about in the shop, drinking neat glasses of whiskey. They called for their drinks so rapidly that the publican called in a little barefooted girl in a green dress, who stood on a box beside a porter barrel rinsing glasses while he served the men. They all appeared to know the old man with one eye, and they talked to him about some job he had been doing on the relief works in this district. Then they made him tell a story for us of a morning when he had killed three wild ducks 'With one skelp of a little gun he had,' and the man who was sitting on a barrel at my side told me that the old man had been the best shot in the place till he got too fond of porter, and had had his gun and licence taken from him because he was shooting wild over the roads. Afterwards they began to make fun of him because his wife had run away from him and gone over the water, and he began to lose his temper. On our way back an old man who was driving an ass with heavy panniers of turf told us that all the turf of this district will be cut away in the next twenty years, and the people will be left without fuel. This is taking place in many parts of Ireland, and unless the Department of Agriculture, or the Congested Districts Board, can take steps to provide plantations for these districts there may be considerable suffering, as it is not likely that the people even then will be able to buy coal. Something has to be done and a great deal has been said on the subject of growing timber in Ireland, but so far there has been little result. An attempt was made to establish an extensive plantation near Carna, in Connemara, first by the Irish Government in 1890, and then by the Congested Districts Board since 1902; but the work has been a complete failure. Efforts have been made on a smaller scale to encourage planting among the people, but I have not seen much good come from them. Some turf tracts in Ireland are still of great extent, but they are not inexhaustible, and even if turf has to be brought from them, in a few years, to cottagers great distances away, the cost of it will be serious and additional hardship for the people of many poor localities.

THE SMALL TOWN

MANY of the smaller towns of the west and south of Ireland—the towns chiefly that are in or near the congested districts—have a peculiar character. If one goes into Swinford or Charlestown, for instance, one sees a large dirty street strewn in every direction with loose stones, paper, and straw, and edged on both sides by a long line of deserted-looking shops, with a few asses with panniers of turf standing about in front of them. These buildings are mostly two or three storeys high, with smooth slate roofs, and they show little trace of the older sort of construction that was common in Ireland, although there are often a few tiny and miserable cottages at the ends of the town that have been left standing from an older period. Nearly all towns of this class are merely trading centres kept up by the country people that live round them, and they usually stand where several main roads come together from large, out-of-the-way districts. In Swinford, which may be taken as a good example of these market towns, there are seven roads leading into the country, and it is likely that a fair was started here at first, and that the town as it is now grew up afterwards. Although there is at present a population of something over 1,300 people, and a considerable trade, the place is still too small to have much genuine life, and the streets look empty and miserable till a market-day arrives. Then, early in the morning, old men and women, with a few younger women of about thirty who have been in America, crowd into the town and range themselves with their asses and carts at both sides of the road, among the piles of goods which the shopkeepers spread out before their doors.

The life and peculiarities of the neighbourhood—the

harvesting and the potato blight, for instance—are made curiously apparent by the selection of these articles. Over nearly every shop door we could see, as we wandered through the town, two scythe-blades fixed at right angles over the doorways, with the points and edges uppermost, and in the street below them there were numbers of hay-rakes standing in barrels, scythe-handles, scythe-blades bound in straw rope, reaping-hooks, scythe-stones, and other things of the kind. In a smith's forge at the end of the town we found a smith fixing blades and hand-grips to scythe-blades for a crowd of men who stood round him with the blades and handles, which they had bought elsewhere, ready in their hands. In front of many shops also one could see old farmers bargaining eagerly for second-hand spraying machines, or buying supplies of the blue sulphate of copper that was displayed in open sacks all down the street. In other places large packing-cases were set up, with small trunks on top of them, and pasted over with advertisements of various Atlantic lines that are used by emigrants, and large pictures of the *Oceanic* and other vessels. Inside many of the shops and in the windows one could see an extraordinary collection of objects— saddles, fiddles, rosaries, rat-traps, the Shorter Catechism, castor-oil, rings, razors, rhyme-books, fashion plates, nit-killer, and fine-tooth combs. Other houses had the more usual articles of farm and household use, but nearly all of them, even drapers' establishments, with stays and ribbons in the windows, had a licenced bar at the end, where one could see a few old men or women drinking whiskey or beer. In the streets themselves there was a pig-market going on at the upper end of the town near the court-house, and in another place a sale of barrels and churns, made apparently by a local

cooper, and also of many-sided wooden bowls, pig-
troughs, and the wooden bars and pegs that are used on
donkeys' saddles to carry the panniers. Further down
there were a number of new panniers set out, with long
bundles of willow boughs set up beside them, and
offered for sale by old women and children. As the day
went on six or seven old-clothes brokers did a noisy trade
from three large booths set up in the street. A few of the
things sold were new, but most of them were more or
less worn out, and the sale was carried on as a sort of
auction, an old man holding up each article in turn and
asking first, perhaps, two shillings for a greasy blouse,
then cutting away the price to sixpence or even four-
pence-halfpenny. Near the booth a number of strolling
singers and acrobats were lounging about, and starting
off now and then to sing or do contortions in some part
of the town. A couple of these men began to give a performance near a booth where we were listening to the
bargaining and the fantastic talk of the brokers. First
one of them, in a yellow and green jersey, stood on his
hands and did a few feats; then he went round with his
hat and sold ballads, while the other man sang a song to
a banjo about a girl:

> . . . whose name it was, I don't know,
> And she passed her life in a barber's shop
> Making wigs out of sawdust and snow.

Not far away another man set up a stall, with tremen-
dous shouting, to sell some little packets, and we could
hear him calling out, 'There's envelopes, notepaper, a
pair of boot-laces, and corn-cure for one penny. Take
notice, gentlemen.'

All the time the braying of the asses that were standing about the town was incessant and extraordinarily noisy, as sometimes four or five of them took it up at the same time. Many of these asses were of a long-legged, gawky type, quite usual in the country, and due, we were told, to a Spanish ass sent here by the Congested Districts Board to improve the breed. It is unfortunate that most attempts to improve the live stock of Ireland have been made by some off-hand introduction of a foreign type which often turns out little suited to the new conditions it is brought to, instead of by the slower and less exciting method of improving the different types by selection from the local breeds. We have heard a great deal in passing through Connemara of the harm that has been done by injudicious 'improving' of the ponies and horses, and while it is probable that some of the objections made to the new types may be due to local prejudice, it should not be forgotten that the small farmer is not a fool, and that he knows perfectly well when he has an animal that is suited to his needs.

Towards evening, when the market was beginning to break up, an outside car drove through the town, laden on one side with an immense American trunk belonging to a woman who had just come home after the usual period of six years that she had spent making her fortune. A man at a shop door who saw it passing began to talk about his own time in New York, and told us how often he had had to go down to Coney Island at night to 'recoup' himself after the heat of the day. It is not too much to say that one can hardly spend an hour in one of these Mayo crowds without being reminded in some way of the drain of people that has been and is still running from Ireland. It is, however, satisfactory to note that in this neighbourhood and west of it, on the

Dillon estate, which has been bought out and sold to the tenants by the Congested Districts Board, there is a current of returning people that may do much good. A day or two ago we happened to ask for tea in a cottage which was occupied by a woman in a new American blouse, who had unmistakably come home recently from the States. Her cottage was perfectly clean and yet had lost none of the peculiar local character of these cottages. Almost the only difference that one could point to was a large photograph of the head of the Sistine Madonna, hanging over the fire in the little room where we sat, instead of the hideous German oleographs on religious subjects that are brought round by pedlars, and bought by most of the simpler Irish women for the sake of the subjects they represent.

POSSIBLE REMEDIES

IT IS not easy to improve the state of the people in the congested districts by any particular remedy or set of remedies. As we have seen, these people are dependent for their livelihood on various industries, such as fishing, kelp-making, turf-cutting, or harvesting in England; and yet the failure of a few small plots of potatoes brings them literally to a state of famine. Near Belmullet, during a day of storm, we saw the crop for next year in danger of utter ruin, and if the weather had not changed, by good luck, before much harm was done, the whole demoralizing and wretched business of the relief works would have had to be taken up again in a few months. It is obvious that the earnings of the people should be large enough to make them more or less independent of one particular crop, and yet, in reality, it is not easy to bring about such a state of things; for the moment a man earns a few extra pounds in a year he finds many good and bad ways of spending them, so that when a quarter of his income is cut away unexpectedly once in seven or eight years he is as badly off as before. To make the matter worse, the pig trade—which is often relied on to bring in the rent-money—is, as I have shown, dependent on the potatoes, so that a bad potato season means a dearth of food, as well as a business difficulty which may have many consequences. It is possible that by giving more attention to the supply of new seed potatoes and good manure—something in this direction is being done by the co-operative societies—the failure of the crop may be made less frequent. Yet there is little prospect of getting rid of the danger altogether, and as long as it continues the people will have many hardships.

The most one can do for the moment is to improve their condition and solvency in other ways, and for this purpose extended purchase on the lines adopted by the Congested Districts Board seems absolutely necessary. This will need more funds than the Board has now at its disposal, and probably some quicker mode of work. Perhaps in places where relief has to be given some force may have to be brought to bear on landlords who refuse to sell at fair terms. No amount of purchase in the poorer places will make the people prosperous—even if the holdings are considerably enlarged—yet there is no sort of doubt that in all the estates which the Board has arranged and sold to the tenants there has been a steady tendency towards improvement. A good deal may be done also by improved communications, either by railroad or by sea, to make life easier for the people. For instance, before the steamer was put on a few years ago between Sligo and Belmullet, the cost of bringing a ton of meal or flour by road from Ballina to Belmullet was one pound, and one can easily estimate the consequent dearness of food. That is perhaps an extreme case, yet there are still a good many places where things are almost as bad, and in these places the people suffer doubly, as they are usually in the hands of one or two small shopkeepers, who can dictate the price of eggs and other small articles which they bring in to sell. At present a steamer running between Westport and Belmullet, in addition to the Sligo boat, is badly needed, and would probably do a great deal of good more cheaply than the same service could be done by a line of railway. If the communications to the poorest districts could be once made fairly satisfactory it would be much easier for the Congested Districts Board, or some similar body, to encourage the local industries of the people and to enable them to get the full market value for what they produce.

The cottage industries that have been introduced or encouraged by the Board—lace-making, knitting, and the like—have done something; yet at best they are a small affair. In a few places the fishing industry has been most successfully developed, but in others it has practically failed, and led to a good deal of disappointment and wasted energy. In all these works it needs care and tact to induce the people to undertake new methods of work; but the talk sometimes heard of sloth and ignorance has not much foundation. The people have traditional views and instincts about agriculture and live stock, and they have a perfectly natural slowness to adopt the advice of an official expert who knows nothing of the peculiar conditions of their native place. The advice is often excellent, but there have been a sufficient number of failures in the work done by the Congested Districts Board, such as the attempt at forestry in Carna and the bad results got on certain of their example plots laid out to demonstrate the best methods of farming, to make the conservatism of the people a sign of, perhaps, valuable prudence. The Board and the Department of Agriculture and Technical Education have done much excellent work, and it is not to be expected that improvements of this kind, which must be largely experimental, can be carried on without failures; yet one does not always pardon a sort of contempt for the local views of the people which seems rooted in nearly all the official workers one meets with through the country.

One of the chief problems that one has to deal with in Ireland is, of course, the emigration that I have mentioned so often. It is probably the most complicated of all Irish affairs, and in dealing with it it is important to remember that the whole moral and economic condition of Ireland has been brought into a diseased state by prolonged misgovernment and many misfortunes, so that at the present time normal remedies produce abnormal results. For instance, if it is observed in some neighbourhood that some girls are going to America because they have no work at home, and a lace school is started to help them, it too often happens that the girls merely use it as a means of earning money enough to pay for their passage and outfit, and the evil is apparently increased. Further, it should not be forgotten that emigrants are going out at the present time for quite opposite reasons. In the poorest districts of all they go reluctantly, because they are unable to keep themselves at home; but in places where there has been much improvement the younger and brighter men and girls get ambitions which they cannot satisfy in this country, and so they go also. Again, where there is no local life or amusements they go because they are dull, and when amusements and races are introduced they get the taste for amusements and go because they cannot get enough of them. They go as much from districts where the political life has been allowed to stagnate as from districts where there has been an excess of agitation that has ended only in disappointment. For the present the Gaelic League is probably doing more than any other movement to check this terrible evil, and yet one fears that when the people realise in five, or perhaps in ten, years that this hope of restoring a lost language is a vain one the last result will be a new kind of hopelessness and many crowded ships leaving Queenstown and Galway. Happily in some places there is a counter-current of people returning from America. Yet they are not very numerous, and one feels that the only real remedy for emigration is the restoration of some national life to the people. It is this conviction that makes most Irish politicians scorn all merely economic or agricultural reforms, for if Home Rule would not of itself make a national life it would do more to make such a life possible than half a million creameries. With renewed life in the country many changes of the methods of government, and the holding of property, would inevitably take place, which would all tend to make life less difficult even in bad years and in the worst districts of Mayo and Connemara.

UNDER ETHER

UNDER ETHER

THE operation was fixed for Saturday; so at ten o'clock on Friday evening I found myself at the door of the private hospital where I was to lodge. I was received in the office by Nurse Smith. . . . Nurse Smith gave me her parting directions—I was to be in bed before midnight, when a night nurse would come round to bandage my neck—and went off to other duties. The door closed behind her and I was alone. For a while I roved through my room, peering into cupboards and presses, half dreading to uncarth the débris of mutilated victims. Then I sank into a chair, and drew out the last volume I had been studying. It was Spinoza's ethics, and I found my excited thoughts refused the lead of the great pantheist, and I abandoned myself again to incoherent reverie till eleven and a half struck heavily on the clock before my door. Then I unpacked the few necessaries I had brought with me and arranged them in drawers with which the room abounded, and went to bed in a few moments.

Next morning I found the operation was not to take place till mid-day, so I had long to wait.

At half-past eleven I slipped down to get a look at the preparations in my own room. They were worth seeing. In the window stood a long stretcher, some four feet high and two wide, rigged out as a bed but looking ghastly enough. Every available table was covered with enamelled hardware, showing many fantastic shapes whose use I was yet to learn. Strange bottles stood in groups beside articles I had never seen, even in the windows of surgical outfitters. My room looked south, and the low winter sun threw in an almost dazzling illumination at the large panes from which all blinds had been removed. While I was taking an inventory of what was to be seen a nurse came in, and was horrified to find me on the scene of action. Patients, as I afterwards learned, are banished till the last moment to avoid needless anxiety.

The doctors were now announced, and I was hurried upstairs to give them a moment to make ready their own instruments. In a few minutes Nurse Smith came and brought me down. Three doctors were awaiting me, and I was followed by Nurse Smith and two younger nurses. I was irritated by the solemnity of the whole party. When I tried jokes on my own account they met them with sickly smiles, as an attempt to cloak a timidity I did not feel. In a moment the surgeon directed me to mount the scaffold. At other times one would feel an embarrassment in divesting oneself to a single smock in the presence of three young women, but it seemed as natural in the circumstances as walking bareheaded in a church. I mounted the operating table, warning them as I did so that they would have no slight task to retain me on my plank bed. The moment my head touched the pillow one of the doctors bent over me to test my heart. An instant later he placed something over my mouth and nose directing me to breathe with usual regularity. He was standing behind my head, so I saw only his face stooping above me. I clasped my hands over my breast, and decided to allow my fingers some motion to let off the inevitable excitement. The only anxiety I remember to have felt was lest I should become unruly as the ether gained on me, and disgrace my stoic resolution.

For what seemed an eternity no change came. Suddenly the light grew brighter, and a rigidity tingled through my limbs. It was not pleasant, and I felt my fingers flying in a rhythm of fearful velocity. Even this was not enough; my toes—always agile as a monkey's —joined in the dance. I wondered how long I could retain self-control in presence of such awful discomfort. A change passed across me, and my fingers locked with sudden stiffness. Speech was gone. Volition was gone. I was a dead weight; a subject on a board; toy of other wills. It was agony. My eyes rolled swiftly from one side to the other, seeing now with phantasmal and horrible distortion. A break came, and I forgot one moment where I was. I passed again into sense; my mouth was uncovered; no one seemed at hand. Horrible noises were in my ears. The ceiling, which now shone with terrible distinctness, seemed bending over the nurses; and the nurses, some without heads, some with two, were floating in the air. Voices were behind me. Fifty suggestions flashed through my brain; had the ether apparatus broken? Did they think me insensible? Would I have to lie feeling all with treble intensity, unable to speak or move? I raised myself on my elbows and asked with sudden effort:

'What has happened?'

Two doctors were at my side in an instant. They assured me that I was doing excellently, and begged me to lie still for my further dose of ether.

Now I was told to draw long breaths, and I drew eagerly and angrily, resolved to put myself, at any cost, out of pain.

I felt what seemed currents of blue vapour curling to my utmost extremities. Suddenly I was in a chaos of excitement, talking loudly and incoherently. Clouds of luminous mist were swirling round me, through which heads broke only at intervals. I felt I was talking of a lady I had known years before, and sudden terror seized me that I should spread forth all the secrets of my life. I could not be silent. The name was on my lips. With wild horror I screamed:

'Oh, no, I won't!'

'No, I won't!'

'No, I won't!'

'Oh, no, I won't!'

'No, I won't!'

'No, I won't!'

Using the sullen rhythm that forms in one's head during a railway journey. This did not suffice; I changed to a shrieking imprecation. Another blast of ether rolled through my veins. My hands broke from my control and waved in the luminous clouds. I saw them, and in an instant one hand went out before the other, my fingers spread and one thumb approached my nose after the manner of a street arab. At the same moment the clouds rolled aside, and I saw the doctor bending over me. He called to the surgeon:

'Batby, look!'

The words reached me, and I echoed:

'Batby, look, amn't I funny?'

They laughed aloud.

'Now you're laughing,' I cried: 'Ha, ha, ha!' Mimicking with a frantic crescendo. Then their mirth infuriated me.

'I'm an initiated mystic,' I yelled with fury; 'I could rend the groundwork of your souls.'

Not wishing to exasperate me they grew serious. 'Ha, ha, ha!' I roared in ironical triumph, 'now you're serious. Now you know what you have to deal with.'

The clouds rolled over me again, now heavy, now

opaque. Something thrilled in my neck. Were they beginning? The memory of control was obliterated; I yelled, I writhed with appalling agony. Another paroxysm of frenzy, and my life seemed to go out in one spiral yell to the unknown.

The next period I remember but vaguely. I seemed to traverse whole epochs of desolation and bliss. All secrets were open before me, and simple as the universe to its God. Now and then something recalled my physical life, and I smiled at what seemed a moment of sickly infancy. At other times I felt I might return to earth, and laughed aloud to think what a god I should be among men. For there could be no more terror in my life. I was a light, a joy.

These earthly recollections were few and faint, for the rest I was in raptures I have no power to translate. At last clouds came over me again. My joy seemed slipping from my grasp, and at times I touched the memory of the operation as one gropes for a forgotten dream. I heard noises and grew conscious of weight. The weight took shape; it was my body lying motionless in a bed. The clouds broke, and I saw a gaselier over my head. I realized with intense horror that my visions were fleeing away, leaving scarcely a trace. I groaned in misery.

'Oh, if I could only remember! If I could only remember—remember.'

I was sick, and people were attending me.

I groaned still: 'Oh, if I could only remember.'

The clouds rolled further away; I recognised one of the nurses, and called out to her with sudden incongruity:

'By Jove, there's Nurse Smith!'

She heard me, and bending over me she said: 'Are

you coming to? It was very satisfactory.' 'What was satisfactory?' I asked, still dwelling on my dreams.

'The operation,' she replied.

'D—— the operation,' I groaned. 'If I could only remember, I'd write books upon books; I'd teach all earth of delight.'

Every moment the recollection of my dreams was going off from me, being replaced by drunken exhilaration.

I was still suffering a good deal from nausea, but was so impressed with my wit that my drunken vanity left no room for low spirits. At this stage I began to regain power over my body; I remember moving each limb in succession, calling out in delight as I did so:

'There goes one leg. There's the other. There's one hand. There's the other.'

Then I tried to raise my head but failed, and apostrophised it in language too racy to repeat.

Presently the nurses left me for their dinner, putting a hand-bell in easy reach.

The nausea returned and I rang lustily. My hand was still weak, and the bell slipped from my hold, tumbling nearly into my mouth. When the nurses ran in I cried out in mock anger:

'Why the devil do you leave a fellow alone like that, I've been sick into the bell!'

This was my last joke, and for the rest of the afternoon and evening I lay quiet enough.

The next day I felt unenterprising enough but in no pain or uneasiness. My weakness made it most natural and agreeable of all things to lie still and be talked to. The room I occupied opened from a hall, so a pleasant stir outside kept me gently alert. The doctors looked in during the forenoon, and now that the ordeal was over, threw aside their gravity, and were as jovial as one could desire.

When they left me I looked vaguely through some books that were brought to me, and here became aware of my own collapse, for all allusion to sadness or affairs of the heart sent up a dew into my eyes. That afternoon my friends were admitted to see me, and my weakness came still more to the front. From five o'clock deep drowsiness came over me, and I lay as in lethargy with the lights carefully lowered. A faint jingle of tram-bells sounded far away, and the voices of Sunday travellers sometimes broke into my room. I took notice of every familiar occurrence as if it were something I had come back to from a distant country. The impression was very strong on me that I had died the preceding day and come to life again, and this impression has never changed.